ALSO BY PETER RAND

Gold from Heaven
The Private Rich
The Time of the Emergency
Firestorm

China hands

The Adventures and Ordeals
of the American Journalists
Who Joined Forces with
the Great Chinese Revolution

PETER RAND

SIMON & SCHUSTER
New York • London • Toronto
Sydney • Tokyo • Singapore

SIMON & SCHUSTER
Rockefeller Center
1230 Avenue of the Americas
New York, NY 10020

10 9 8 7 6 5 4 3 2 1

Library of Congress Cataloging-in-Publication Data

Rand, Peter.
    China hands : the adventures and ordeals of the
American journalists who joined forces with the
great Chinese revolution / Peter Rand.
        p.   cm.
    Includes bibliographical references and index.
    1. Foreign correspondents—United States.
2. Foreign correspondents—China.   3. China—
History—Republic, 1912–1949.
4. Communism—China—History.   I. Title.
PN4871.R36 1995
070.4'332'09227—dc20   95-20929   CIP
ISBN 0-684-80844-7

Contents

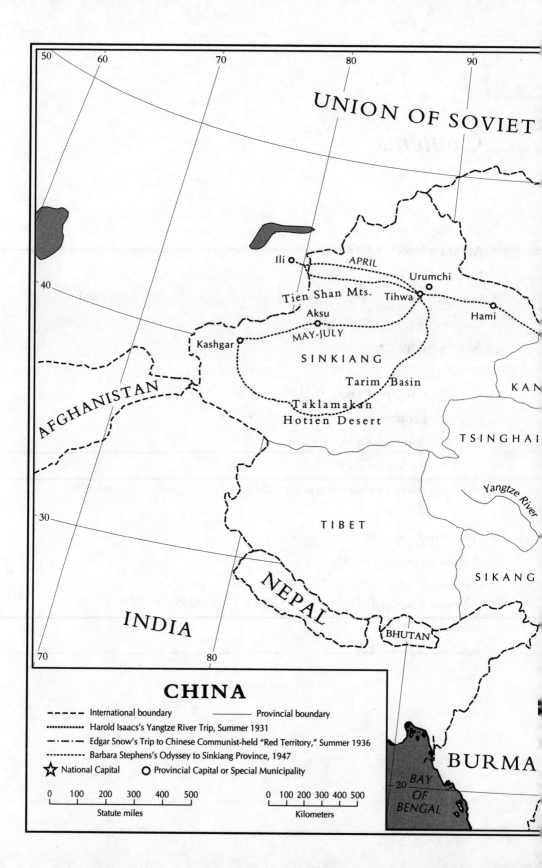

UNION OF SOVIET

50 60 70 80 90

Ili ○

APRIL

Urumchi ○

Tien Shan Mts. Tihwa ○

40

Aksu ○ Hami ○

Kashgar ○ MAY-JULY

SINKIANG

AFGHANISTAN

Tarim Basin

KAN

Taklamakan
Hotien Desert

TSINGHAI

Yangtze River

30

TIBET

NEPAL

SIKANG

INDIA

BHUTAN

70 80

CHINA

- - - - International boundary　————— Provincial boundary
•••••••••••• Harold Isaacs's Yangtze River Trip, Summer 1931
—·—·— Edgar Snow's Trip to Chinese Communist-held "Red Territory," Summer 1936
------------ Barbara Stephens's Odyssey to Sinkiang Province, 1947
☆ National Capital　○ Provincial Capital or Special Municipality

0 100 200 300 400 500
Statute miles

0 100 200 300 400 500
Kilometers

BURMA

20 BAY
OF
BENGAL

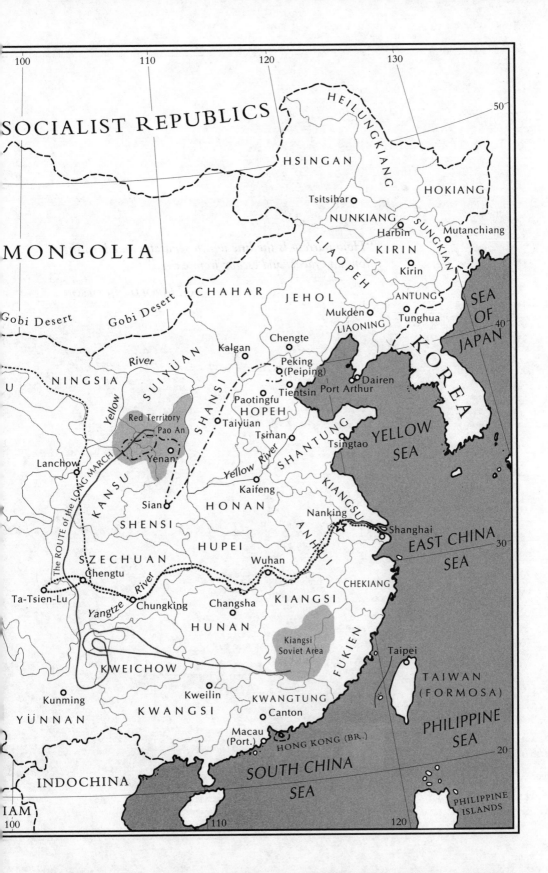

"How narrow is the line which separates an adventure from an ordeal, and escape from exile."

—HAROLD NICOLSON

Author's Note

In this book I have used the Wade-Giles method of spelling Chinese words. This system has been replaced in modern times with pinyin, but I have stuck with the old system because it was the spelling used in the era about which I have written, and it is the one that I think somehow conveys the feeling of those times.

Preface

THIS IS A BOOK about American dreamers and misfits who went to China to seek escape and adventure during the first half of this century. Some came back, others did not, but they all achieved a moment of fame and glory, however fleeting, as China Hands who wrote about the Chinese people and publicized their struggle.

I never would have embarked on a book of this kind, about misfits and dreamers in China, if my father had stayed home, or gone to Europe, during World War Two. He is the inspiration for this book. His name was Christopher Rand, and he made a reputation for himself as a reporter in China, where he had gone in 1943 with the United States Office of War Information. After the war, as a China correspondent for the *New York Herald Tribune,* he covered the collapse of Chiang Kai-shek's government and the civil war, between 1946 and 1949, when the Communists, led by Mao Tse-tung, came to power. Later, my father went on to achieve greater recognition as a reporter-at-large for *The New Yorker,* but he first made a name for himself in China, where he was known to other correspondents as a man of unusual insights and habits. Dad belonged to a tradition of distinguished American eccentrics among China Hands, but when I started to research this book I was unaware of that.

I began this book as a tribute to my father's experience in China, as a process of excavation of that time in his life, which had always been something of a mystery to me, and I was motivated to write it at all because long after his self-inflicted death in 1968, I came across his China files, papers, letters and diaries, all neatly and compactly stored away in a warehouse in Salisbury, Connecticut, his town of origin, where his brother Jake still lived. I realized, however, once I took up a serious study of China Hands, that others before him had fallen in thrall to China. So what began as the story of my father in China expanded into the present chronicle of larger-than-life American romantics who found themselves in China, in every sense of that phrase.

The will to a solitary destiny begins early. My father began life as the product of an unusual union. He was the eldest son of a portrait painter named Ellen Emmet Rand, a warmhearted woman, once described by my own mother as "an open fire," who in the 1920s and 1930s established herself as one of the most sought-after portrait artists in America. Dad's father, William Blanchard Rand, known as W.B., was a striking, darkly handsome equestrian from Long Island, a polo player and fox hunter of private means more than ten years younger than his wife (he was twenty-five, she was thirty-six). W.B. may have experienced his marriage as a kind of captivity. For the rest of his life he drank copiously and rode furiously while Ellen Emmet Rand made a small fortune supporting her family as a painter of eminent Yankees, which she did in her studio on Washington Square, in New York City. It became W.B.'s lot to live almost exclusively in the Berkshire foothills with his three sons while his wife commuted to work in the city during the week by train.

My father was always a loner. Partly, this was a reaction to his father, with whom he never saw eye-to-eye, a euphemism for a somewhat darker condition of enmity. W.B., in stark contrast to his bohemian, highly amusing wife, a woman utterly indifferent to matters of detail, was a punctilious martinet who used to throw stones at his sons to make them sit up straight in the saddle. My father happened to be by temperament more like his mother. He was not exactly indifferent to details or appearances, as she was, but he disdained above all things convention for the sake of appearances. As a young boy Dad gave up riding and took to wandering alone through the rural Connecticut countryside of his youth in Litchfield County, which he later likened to the Shropshire of *Tom Jones*.

The family spent the summers on a farm called Hamlet Hill where Dad and his brothers baled hay and otherwise helped with the farmwork. (In the winter they moved to a rented house in the village of Salisbury.) Much of Dad's boyhood, however, was spent among the mountain men, hunters and fishermen known as "Raggies," descendants of a tribe of people who in the nineteenth century used to burn charcoal in pits on nearby Mount Riga for use in the local steel mills. "The Raggies belonged in part to what Oscar Lewis calls the culture of poverty," my father later recalled, "but their version of it was infinitely more vivid and dramatic than the life of any urban poor. When I was a boy they kept coon dogs and used them at night. They kept ferrets and put them down rabbit holes. They had square dances where they variously called and played the music. They were full of tales, and I would listen open-mouthed." From these mountain men Dad learned his life-long love of roaming free in the countryside, his love of nature, and birdsong, and the native wisdom he found in other mountain people elsewhere in the world. In some ways he came to model himself on these men, who, if not altogether hostile to women, nevertheless went up into the mountains to escape the claims of domesticity in order to drink moonshine and carouse to the music of nature with their fellow Raggies. Later in life, he even developed a theory that in most ways mountain men were possessed of a wisdom and originality of spirit far superior to men of the valley.

Dad was wrenched from this idyllic boyhood scene at the age of twelve when he was sent without much ceremony in the middle of winter to Groton, an Episcopalian boy's boarding school in northeastern Massachusetts where, in exchange for tuition, his mother painted portraits of the Rector, Endicott Peabody, Peabody's wife and members of the faculty. Groton was a school for the children of rich, socially prominent people from New York and Boston. It's true that Dad was related to boys at Groton; he was, moreover, a member of the social class to which they belonged; but his rural childhood had not in any way prepared him for the companionship of these boys, who mostly belonged to a well-heeled suburban culture of tennis and golf and country club dances, all things from which my father shrank. He wasn't any good at football, either, or baseball, the two muscularly Christian sports to which the school was devoted, along with God and the classics. Nothing in my father's background prepared him for a Groton education, either. For despite his mother's brilliant family background—her friendship with her cousin Henry James, her artistic training in the Paris atelier of Frederick MacMonnies, her brilliant gift for conversation— she was all but illiterate, and so was W.B., his father. "I never saw anybody open a book around their house," my mother once said.

The education my father received at Groton equipped him superbly to get his thoughts out and to express them on paper as a writer. That was the Groton paradox: children of often undistinguished intellectual background received at the hands of brilliant and eccentric masters a superb classical education. My father emerged from Groton with the dash of British influence that later informed his rugged individualism, along with a solid grounding in Latin and Greek.

Dad left Groton with a grudging respect for the place that later in life blossomed into genuine affection, as often happens. His first choice for college had been Harvard, but his father, who had never gone to college himself, retained the last word on where his sons went to college, and, as a good Connecticut Yankee, he insisted that they attend Yale, where he could keep an eye on them. My father thought Yale was somehow fraudulent, its traditions and academic pretensions hollow. He thought Groton, for all its Britishness, was fundamentally the true thing, while Yale he found to be a cold, sterile institution, a processing plant where the sons of Midwestern industrialists were initiated into the

Eastern Establishment. In his four years there my father made few friends.

Mainly, at Yale, he drank. He also drank at home. Although his earliest drinking bouts took place in his childhood among the Raggies, he probably learned much more about drinking from his father, who—this being the time of Prohibition—stored cider brandy, distilled in neighboring counties and procured for him by the Raggies, in a row of ten five-gallon kegs upstairs in the attic at Hamlet Hill. The warm air up there aged it quickly. W.B. used to siphon the brandy into decanters through a rubber tube, and then drink the stuff in great quantity over a prolonged cocktail hour that lasted through Prohibition. My father, home on vacations from Groton, used to steal upstairs to the attic during family parties and siphon the cider brandy through the rubber tube directly into his mouth. He was always someone who, if necessary, could dispense with the finer points of drinking. He was positively explosive with mirth afterward, so much so that he quite shocked and delighted his family and friends when he reappeared from the attic. For the most part he was considered an "odd Dick"—a family reference to his mother's eccentric cousin, Dick Emmet. My father was withdrawn and somewhat forbiddingly cerebral. In his teenage years, he used to test his physical endurance by walking shirtless across the countryside in the wintertime in subzero weather. His hilarity more than made up for all that, however. He was a furious Puritan inhabited by a Dionysian soul.

"Any ambitious project led to getting drunk," my father once wrote. It got him through Yale. It also got him through his courtship of my mother. He met my mother foxhunting at a place called Old Chatham, in upstate New York, where his father throughout the 1930s was Master-of-Fox-Hounds, in a rather glamorous setting of country squires, many of whom W.B. had known on Long Island in his polo-playing youth. My father had succumbed to this irresistibly attractive pastime, along with his brothers and his mother, nicknamed Bay, who loved horses and used to ride sidesaddle to the hunt "though she looked neither deft nor safe while doing so," as my father once observed. My father liked the drinking that surrounded the hunt. He was a whipper-in, and as such his role in the hunt was to keep the hounds in order at the head of the hunting party, which enabled him to evade the more social aspects of riding, and to dress in clothes considerably more eccentric than the pink foxhunting habit worn by others in the party. This my mother found attractive. Indeed, when they first met, he was wearing what she called "a crumpled green outfit," and he won her heart when he offered to share with her a piece of stale chocolate he happened to dig out of his pocket.

Though not someone you would ever describe as a misfit, my mother was sufficiently original and bright to appreciate my father. She was especially impressed by his mind, which she felt went generally unappreciated in his own family. She was a smart and attractive Vassar girl majoring in French who happened, like my father, to find the social conventions of their upper-class world fairly crippling. She was a skilled horsewoman, and passionate about the hunt, which she enjoyed partly for the sense of physical danger it supplied, a thrill that my father also relished. Mom came out of a Victorian background of considerable culture and social prestige. Her father, Richard Aldrich, was for many years the *New York Times* music critic. Her mother was one of the "Astor orphans," ten great-grandchildren of William B. Astor, whose parents died while they were still children and who were raised on their family estate by a maidenly cousin from South Carolina and an English tutor. It was an overbearing and anachronistic family milieu, and one that my mother found particularly stifling, given her mother's strength of will and tendency to dominate all who came within her orbit. As a young adult, my grandmother had visited China during the Boxer Rebellion, and in later life she was often referred to by a family wit as "the last of the Manchus," a reference to the Empress Dowager, Tzu Hsi. As a China Hand, my father surely did not miss the humor of this observation. He called her "Belle-Mère" and donned earphones during her visits, so he could listen to the radio while she talked.

My parents escaped from the East Coast and their extensive, interconnected families. It was perhaps the best thing they ever did for each other. In the San Francisco Bay area, where they went to live, they could flourish among new friends in an environment fresh to them both. My father, moreover, was able to write full-time as a founding member of a group of people he had known at Yale who launched *The Coast,* a weekly magazine modeled on *The New Yorker* and *Vanity Fair*. Though the magazine only lasted a short while (three years), it published memorable fiction by William Saroyan and John Steinbeck, among others, and articles and profiles of interest to people on the West Coast written with distinction and flair, often accompanied by photographs that vividly capture the time and the place. My father never could have flourished this way in the East, and the feature writing he did for *The Coast* enabled him to develop a writing style that served him well later on, in China. After *The Coast* folded, he went to work, in 1939, for the *San Francisco Chronicle,* where he was employed as a reporter until he went to China in 1943.

By that time he had fathered four children. This was undoubtedly constricting. He also found the local Marin County social scene not altogether to his liking. But I think domestic and suburban life in any form was finally more than Dad could stand, and in those years leading up to China his behavior showed some of the signs he exhibited in later life on a grand scale. He took to long, solitary walks on the slopes of Mount Tamalpais, and roamed the streets of San Francisco at night. He also worked at night at the *Chronicle*. He came home at dawn, and repaired to the roof, which was his resting place of choice (although I've never quite been able to figure out why he didn't fall off it). He'd stopped drinking during these early years of marriage, and that made him more tense. So by the time he was recruited for civilian wartime service by the Office of War Information he was ready to make a move. He wrote his cousin Robert Sherwood, an OWI chieftain who helped to secure his wartime assignment, that he was ready to swim to Chungking if he had to.

Such was the early formation of one offbeat China Hand, propelled to put all known ways of life behind him, to lose himself in some new adventure. It was as though my father once and for all wanted to burst out of his own history in order to expand into a much greater life.

Introduction

*I*T SHOULD NOT SEEM all that strange if China from the earliest years of this century attracted Americans who, if they were not actually misfits, could nevertheless be called loners and dreamers. Nor does it seem very unusual that many of these notable oddballs and loners were journalists, since the profession of journalism has always attracted nonconformists. These people somehow or other did not belong, and the urge to which they responded was that of escape. That is one reason why we should not be so surprised to find them, in this book, in China.

The China Hand relied on the loner's peculiar ability to set out solo for parts unknown and the instinct to get as far away as possible from convention to the most interesting of all possible places. Intelligence is one notable characteristic of the lone wolf. None of the ones in this book were short on intellectual curiosity. Once they got to China they were still loners. They carried their problems with them to that distant land. Yet, once there, they found problems that were different and at least as vast as those personal bedevilments they brought with them. They found people more troubled than they were whom they could truly find it in their hearts to love and in some way or other to assist. It was the empathy of the troubled for the afflicted. For these China Hands, although some came to China as journalists and others became journalists once they got there, were not reporters in the ordinary sense of the word. They were individualists and writers who were lost and found in China.

There were plenty of American reporters in China during the three decades covered by this book: the 1920s, the 1930s and the 1940s. Not very many of them qualify as China Hands in the way that those who populate this chronicle do. Few distinguished themselves by the passionate if tormented obsession for China that evinced itself in the books the China Hands eventually wrote.

"That's a Shanghai journalist," remarks a character in *The General Died at Dawn,* the old warlord melodrama starring Gary Cooper and Madeleine Carroll. "You could buy him for a bag of salt." You would not say such a thing of Rayna Prohme or Edgar Snow or Harold Isaacs or Theodore H. White. These people derived their reward from their passionate commitment to the Chinese, and the strange happiness, not undiluted with suffering, they experienced being in China, where, at last, they were, however fleetingly, in harmony with their surroundings. By this I do not by any means wish to suggest that all oddball China Hands were unavailable for payoffs. Indeed, the payoff was part of the honorable tradition of American journalism in China almost from the very beginning of this century, with the arrival on the scene of Thomas F. F. Millard, the patriarch of China Hand journalists.

Millard was the misfit par excellence, who established the rules of the game. He was a bantam-sized man and all else may have stemmed from that fact. Millard was from Missouri and possessed a large and easily wounded ego. He began his career as a journalist on the *New York Herald,* where he was a drama critic in the 1890s. As such, he was formed, professionally, in the employ of James Gordon Bennett, the lordly publishing magnate who lived in expatriate splendor on the Champs-Elysées, in Paris.

Millard flourished as a war correspondent. Trained as a critic of the New York theater, he seems to have moved effortlessly to the theater of battle. As Millard's theater enlarged, so did his vanity. Although he was without any private income whatever of his own, Millard nevertheless appears to have adopted James Gordon Bennett as the model for his subsequent comportment, which suited his new endeavor. Bennett was a grandee, who traveled the seven seas on his yacht, the tellingly named Lysistrata, and sported with kings. In an echo of this grandeur, Millard began to appear at military encampments accompanied by walk-in wardrobe trunks. He passed the morning hours in his tent attired in a silk dressing gown, and went forth later in the day to the scene of battle dressed in the impeccably pressed khaki uniform of a military correspondent.

In later years, Millard was famous in Shanghai for his sartorial splendor and his superb ballroom dancing. He was a darling of the Shanghai matrons in the International Settlement. He was famous, also, for the extreme violence of his temper. This, too, was a feature of his outsized vanity and an arrogance he may well have adapted from his early master, who, like Millard, was not only fastidious but a lifelong bachelor, one who concealed in drink his own enormous wounds.

In the department of sexual grief we know more of Bennett's wounds than we do about Millard's. Bennett expatriated himself after committing some unspeakably abominable act by the standards of late Victorian New York in the presence of his fiancée. He may have urinated in the piano. Whatever the atrocity was, he left town soon thereafter. Similarly, whatever Millard's problems may have been, he chose to endure them mostly abroad, although he spent his life restlessly crisscrossing the Pacific Ocean on the luxury liners of his day.

Millard made his name as a war correspondent, and earned a disfiguring facial scar in the process. His writings on the subject of the Afrikaner guerrilla in the Boer War are inspired. He quite brilliantly grasped the temperament of the South African Dutch, whose side he favored in their epic struggle against the British. That war determined once and for all his hatred of the British and his hatred of empire. The British commander, Lord Kitchener, ultimately expelled Millard from South Africa altogether.

Millard's hatred of empire was only aggravated by Kitchener's behavior, and he found further expression for his finely honed fury when in Manchuria after the Boxer Siege he witnessed the Japanese ambitions and depradations that led directly to the Russo-Japanese War of 1904–1905, which he also covered for Bennett's papers in New York and Paris. It was this experience that turned Millard into a China Hand. He was no great partisan of Russian imperial designs in the Far East (and later he came to fear and detest the Bolsheviks). But what got to Millard was the way the Japanese treated the Chinese in Manchuria, how they uprooted them, plundered their food stocks, usurped their land and taxed them into servitude. He decided that the Japanese empire posed a dangerous threat to all of China, and also to American commercial interests in China. This became his cause.

Millard did not regard the American expansion in the Far East, beginning with the annexation of the Philippines in 1899, as an exercise in imperial adventure. He was a chauvinist. He was also a Missourian. He believed in Manifest Destiny. He believed in the American right to exploit a free market, and he argued, as did John Hay and Teddy Roosevelt, that the American military presence in the far Pacific was there to insure that the Great Powers—France, Germany, Japan and Great Britain—did not carve up for themselves the Middle Kingdom, as China, situated as it was between heaven and earth, had come to be called. This was the Open Door argument, formulated by John Hay when he was Roosevelt's secretary of state to gain entry for the United States into the China market. Essentially, James Gordon Bennett aside, Millard was the quintessential little guy. He identified with the underdog. As a little guy himself, he had an emotional investment in the Chinese cause. He hated bullies, the big bullies in the playground who beat up defenseless smaller boys, and in Great Britain and Japan he had found his bullies and his cause. This matters to us here precisely because these were the values that became encoded in the work of China Hands to come. This was the lasting contribution that Millard made to China journalism and we see it expressed in the attitudes of all the misfits and dreamers who like Millard made a name for themselves in China.

After the Russo-Japanese War, Millard stayed on in China. There were no more wars for him to cover. He decided to make China his career. In American journalism this was something new. There were few, if any, specialists in foreign residence outside the Mediterranean. Readers of American newspapers were not by and large very interested in news, or news analysis, from places like China. Most of the globe at that time was dominated by the British, and what Far Eastern news was deemed of sufficient interest came by prearrangement between two news forces, the Associated Press and Reuters, via London.

Only one American newspaper competed with the British press for an English-speaking readership and that was James Gordon Bennett's *Paris Herald,* which was popular with British and American readers on both sides of the English Channel. Bennett was furious that Dr. Morrison of the London *Times* had scooped his papers on the Boxer Siege. He beefed up his China coverage after that, and launched Millard as the patriarch of China Hands.

Still, it was not enough to keep Millard afloat just to pay him a stipend in China, even though in the waning days of the Manchus and on into the Republic, established in 1912, a man alone in China could live like a prince on very little. Millard's ambitions were kingly, not princely. He wanted to influence American policy. All China Hands since then have entertained this desire, but Millard is among the few who actually laid claim to a presidential ear.

Teddy Roosevelt was a fan of Millard's war reporting. On the occasion of a visit paid by Millard to the president at Oyster Bay, Roosevelt encouraged Millard in his endeavors to arouse the American public to the opportunities that China presented and to the danger that Japan posed to these opportunities. The century was yet young. In 1906, Roosevelt still had reason to believe that China was a potential market for American industrial glut. By that time he may have perceived how misinformed he had been, because not only could the Chinese not afford most of the material goods being shipped to their shores, they had no basic desire for them or even any way of getting them, since travel in and around China was still at best rudimentary. But Roosevelt urged Millard to educate the American people through his articles and books. This added fuel to Millard's ambitions and he went back to China full of purpose, although even then American business was having second thoughts about China.

Japan was the real up-and-coming market for American investment in Asia. Roosevelt knew this. Whether or not he expressed his fascination for Japanese whizzbang industrial and military might to Millard we do not know. He had, we do know, through Hay, and the Open Door policy, encouraged China to believe that a special relationship existed between them and the government of the United States. In that sense Roosevelt was committed to a special protective role in China. But the relationship he really wanted was the one with Japan. The United States in this respect was like someone who has married in good faith the wrong person, and proceeds to entertain a more exciting affair with the enemy of the new spouse. A very Edwardian situation.

Millard went back to China and from then on tilted at windmills. The effort was always noble. No matter that he went on the payroll of the Republican government of China. No matter that he became a lobbyist and a paid propagandist for the Chinese in the United States. It was all in a noble cause. Encoded thus in the work of the future China Hand was Millard's paradox: the romantic advocate, the journalist committed to the cause of the Chinese, a cause so noble that it justifies a stipend from the host country. So that although you would not say of Rayna Prohme or Edgar Snow or Harold Isaacs or Theodore H. White that "you could buy them for a bag of salt," you could say of them all at one time or another that they worked for the Chinese.[1]

It was a noble paradox, and you had to be offbeat to pull it off. You had to be something of a dreamer. There was inherent danger in the paradox. Edgar Snow, also from Missouri, and one of many who came in Millard's wake to practice journalism in China, considered himself a direct heir to Millard's China Hand values. To this day Snow is accused by some of operating as Mao's public relations man. Rayna Prohme made no bones about it: she, and Bill, her significant other, were revolutionary propagandists in China. But it was not for money that these people gave their lives to China.

Modern Chinese history begins in 1911, when the Ch'ing Dynasty, the Manchurian imperial line that had ruled China for almost three centuries, was brought down by a military uprising that started in the Wuchang garrison, in the city of Wuhan, and spread swiftly through the empire. The so-called father of modern China was a political visionary named Sun Yat-sen, a trained physician who abandoned a career in medicine in the late nineteenth century to pursue the cause of a China free from foreign exploitation, sufficient unto itself under democratic rule. Dr. Sun wanted to bring China into the twentieth century as a peer of Western nations, even as he made use of Western resources, with its Chinese soul intact. Dr. Sun in many ways was an impractical dreamer, but he was inspired by his dreams to overthrow China's decadent Manchu overlords, and this is what he repeatedly sought to do over the years, even when it seemed like utter folly. Although Dr. Sun was in the United States on one of his many fund-raising expeditions to drum up support for the Revolution when the Manchu edifice came crashing down, the 1911 insurgency was conducted under the banner of his leadership.

Dr. Sun soon returned to China, but he lacked the military power to outmaneuver his rival in north China, a political infighter and one-time Manchu insider named Yuan Shih-k'ai, who wrested control of the infant Republic and turned it into his personal satrapy. China was a republic in name only until Yuan Shih-k'ai passed from the scene in 1916, after an unsuccessful attempt to declare himself emperor and reactivate the Dragon Throne left vacant by his former masters.

China was up for grabs after that. Provincial warlords throughout China fought each other for territorial supremacy. In north China, powerful generals battled over Peking, seat of the so-called Central Government. During this warlord phase, Dr. Sun returned from Japan, where he had fled in 1913, following an unsuccessful coup attempt against Yuan. But his political party, the Kuomintang, or Nationalist Party, had become moribund. Many of his early followers had taken advantage of the Great War in Europe, when Western imperial exploitation was at a low ebb in China, to make their fortunes. They had grown somewhat reactionary. History seemed to have passed Sun Yat-sen by. Dr. Sun had never lost his own youthful fire, however, or his vision of a unified, democratic China.

The end of World War One brought about a revival of Dr. Sun's political fortunes. This happened after May 4, 1919, when students in Peking rose up in protest against the regime of the day. May 4 lives on as the pivotal event among many great moments in the history of twentieth-century China, and it is celebrated annually as the birthday of the student movement in China. The Allied European powers had signed a secret treaty with Japan that would have allowed it to annex Shantung Province after the war. China was not consulted in this matter. Shantung was a territory that Germany had colonized at the end of the nineteenth century, and it had been occupied by Japan once the Germans had departed after war broke out in Europe in 1914. In Versailles, at the postwar treaty conference, Chinese representatives of the Peking regime, which was heavily indebted to Japan, were prepared to sign away this precious chunk of coastal China when student protesters toppled the government. In so doing they saved the integrity of China. After the May 4 protests, they became a great new force in China's destiny, and established a tradition of student protest that has often played an important role in Chinese politics ever since (most recently in 1989, in the events leading up to the Tiananmen Square massacre).

Chinese workers rallied behind the students. So did the more than one hundred thousand Chinese who had served as laborers in the Allied war effort in France, and were sailing back to China with a new political consciousness.

The student movement turned for leadership to Dr. Sun. This reinvigorated the Kuomintang. It gave his party an infusion of new, radical members, to whom Dr. Sun assigned positions of leadership, so that the Kuomintang was now a party of broad and often conflicting membership. Greatly assisted by Soviet advisers and military support, Dr. Sun established a Kuomintang government in Canton, which became the base of operations for his political aspirations. He raised a Nationalist army down there, and staffed it with officers trained under his protégé, Chiang Kai-shek, at the Whampoa Military Academy, founded in 1924 with Soviet help.

Dr. Sun never lived to see his dream of a unified China realized. He died on March 12, 1925, in Peking, where he had gone to explore the possibility of making common cause with the warlords who ruled north China. However, China was on the verge of a new revolutionary phase. On May 30, 1925, all hell broke loose when British police opened fire on unarmed demonstrators in Shanghai who were protesting the killing of a striking Chinese laborer in a Japanese-owned textile mill outside Shanghai. This time the fury was directed at the British, whose colonial presence along the China coast had long been a sore subject among Chinese. The strikes and boycotts sparked by this event spread like wildfire up and down coastal China, and to inland trading ports along the Yangtze River as far west as Wuhan, a thousand miles upriver from Shanghai. A year later, Dr. Sun's self-appointed heir, Chiang Kai-shek, launched the Northern Expedition, to unify China. In early August 1926, the Nationalist armies of Chiang Kai-shek swarmed out of the uncharted hinterland of south China into the Yangtze River Valley. This took nearly everyone by surprise, including most of the foreign journalists in China, who were sitting around in bars in Shanghai or Hong Kong, unaware that Chiang Kai-shek had been plotting a northern campaign.

By order of the Soviet military commander, General Galen, who accompanied Chiang Kai-shek on the Northern Expedition, no journalists were permitted among the ranks of the combined Nationalist forces as they advanced northward through the countryside. Few observers could get close enough to the scene to report accurately on the sudden developments in the Yangtze Valley. Everyone had to rely on conflicting military dispatches from the front.

The battle for central China was joined in Wuhan, known as the Chicago of China, a cluster of three cities, Wuchang, Hanyang and

Hankow, situated on the Yangtze. Hanyang was the site of China's greatest arsenal, which dominated an eminence overlooking the surrounding countryside. Whoever held the arsenal would command the Yangtze and, of course, Wuhan, the industrial center of China.

Wu P'ei-fu, the warlord whose troops at that time held Wuhan, was caught napping by the Nationalist campaign in the northern military base of Paotingfu. By the time he got to Wuhan, the Nationalist armies had already seized the arsenal. What followed was one of the bloodiest battles in the history of warfare up to that time.

Wu P'ei-fu threw more than a hundred thousand men into his siege of the arsenal. He forced his men to mount the walls by rope and ladder in a classic medieval assault, while Nationalist riflemen fired on them from above. For days the outcome of this stupendous assault was uncertain as the battle raged on. By the tenth of September, however, the air had cleared sufficiently for all to see that the Nationalist forces of the Kuomintang had prevailed. The battlefield was strewn with dead bodies numbering in the tens of thousands. Wu, who was known as the "scholar general" because he was a student of Buddhism and a man of intellectual refinement, had retreated northward with his surviving troops into the province of Honan, abandoning a trove of personal treasures, including a custom-built, bulletproof, twelve-cylinder French convertible touring car upholstered with brown leather cushions. The Nationalists had conquered the Yangtze River Valley. Peking appeared to be their next objective.

Here begins the story of *China Hands*.

The heroes of this book are the adventurous dreamers who set out for China on their own in a spirit of fervor and romance as a dark night of terror and war descended on the Chinese people. They discovered the story of the Chinese people and brought the world's attention to bear on the plight of a land in chaos. They took up the cause of the Chinese people and in so doing, more often than not they sided with the forces of revolution. It's hard to imagine that such people still exist in this day and age. They lived in a simpler, more heroic time, when it was possible to see the world in terms of good and evil. They were to their time in China what John Reed was to the Russian Revolution: they were young and impassioned, romantic and inspired, and, like Reed, they were brave, sometimes to the point of recklessness, as dreamers will be.

Chronology

1900	Boxer rebels hold foreign legations under siege in Peking
1904–1905	Russo-Japanese War
October 10, 1911	Wuchang Rebellion leads to overthrow of Ch'ing Dynasty and founding of Republic of China in 1912
July 28, 1914	World War One begins
June 6, 1916	Death of Yuan Shih-k'ai; Warlord Era begins
November 11, 1918	World War One armistice
May 4, 1919	Student protests bring down Peking government over Versailles treaty terms
July 1921	Chinese Communist Party founded in Shanghai
January 1923	Sun Yat-sen sets up Nationalist government in Canton
October 6, 1923	Borodin, Soviet adviser, arrives in Canton
January 21, 1924	Lenin dies
March 12, 1925	Sun Yat-sen dies in Peking
May 30, 1925	Shanghai Incident sparks strikes and boycotts against the British in China
Fall 1925	Rayna Prohme arrives in Peking
March 20, 1926	Chiang Kai-shek stages coup in Canton and takes over Kuomintang
April 1926	Chang Tso-lin takes over Peking government
July 1, 1926	Chiang launches the Northern Expedition to the Yangtze Valley
December 1926	Nationalist capital established in Wuhan under Left Kuomintang leadership
February 1927	Rayna Prohme arrives in Wuhan
April 12, 1927	Chiang Kai-shek stages massacre in Shanghai

July 1927	Fall of Wuhan Revolutionary Center
August 1927	Rayna Prohme flees China for Moscow with Madame Sun and Eugene Chen
November 1927	Rayna Prohme dies in Moscow
January 1928	Trotsky goes into exile
Winter 1928	Agnes Smedley arrives in China
June 4, 1928	Chang Tso-lin is killed in train explosion in Manchuria after departing Peking
June 1928	Edgar Snow arrives in Shanghai
March 20, 1930	Harold Isaacs leaves New York for China
June–September 1931	Harold Isaacs travels up the Yangtze with Frank Glass
September 18, 1931	Mukden Incident triggers Japanese invasion of Manchuria
January 1932	*The China Forum* is launched; Japanese invade Shanghai
January 1934	Last issue of *China Forum* goes to press
October 16, 1934	Long March begins in Kiangsi
October 20, 1935	Long March ends in northern Shensi
December 9, 1935	Students in Peiping protest Chiang Kai-shek's appeasement of the Japanese
Summer 1936	Edgar Snow visits Red territory
December 12, 1936	Sian Incident: Chiang Kai-shek is kidnapped
Summer 1937	Helen Foster Snow visits Red territory
July 7, 1937	Lukouch'iao Incident near Peiping triggers Japanese invasion of China
December 1937	Chiang Kai-shek flees to Wuhan; Rape of Nanking
Winter 1939	Teddy White arrives in China
Winter 1939	Chiang Kai-shek retreats with Free China to Chungking in Szechuan Province
January 4–15, 1941	New Fourth Army Incident
December 7, 1941	Japanese bomb Pearl Harbor
May 30, 1943	Christopher Rand arrives in Chungking
October 1944	Stilwell crisis
October 23, 1944	Battle of Leyte Gulf
August 6, 1945	U.S. drops A-bomb on Hiroshima
August 9, 1945	U.S. drops A-bomb on Nagasaki
August 14, 1945	Hostilities between U.S. and Japan cease
September 1945	Teddy White leaves China
December 1945	General Marshall arrives in China

Spring 1946	Christopher Rand becomes China correspondent for the *New York Herald Tribune*
Fall 1946	Barbara Stephens leaves for Sinkiang
July 12, 1946	Civil war resumes in China
January 22, 1947	Peiping falls to the Communists
May 27, 1949	Shanghai falls to the Communists
October 1, 1949	People's Republic of China is formally established in Peiping

Abbreviations

AVG	American Volunteer Group
CAT	China Air Transport
CBI	China-Burma-India theater
CIC	China Industrial Cooperatives
CID	Criminal Investigative Department
CNAC	China National Aviation Corporation
ECCI	Comintern
IPR	Institute of Pacific Relations
KUTV	Communist University for Toilers of the East
MOI	Ministry of Information
OWI	Office of War Information
SMP	Shanghai Municipal Police
UCR	United China Relief

Crown of Fire

RAYNA PROHME was instantly notable wherever she went because of her fiery hair. Her hair, it is believed, was a characteristic of Rayna's Sephardic ancestry. On her mother's side of the family she was descended from Sephardic Jews. On the side of her father, a tyrannical Chicago grain merchant named Joseph Simons, Rayna was descended from a tribe of Jewish tinkers, or Gypsies, who had emigrated to the Midwest from England in the nineteenth century.

Rayna's hair was an attribute that people never forgot. One memoirist recalls for instance that Rayna's hair actually stopped the traffic once on Throckmorton Avenue, in Mill Valley, California, when she was living there in her early twenties.[1]

Dorothy Day, founder of the *Catholic Worker,* recalled that Rayna "stood out like a flame with her red hair, brown eyes and vivid face."[2] Day was deeply affected by Rayna's angelic nature, her instinct for giving help to people in need.[3] Indeed, to many who knew her, Rayna's hair was a symbol of inner radiance, while to others it became a sign of her transcendent revolutionary spirit.

To diplomats in the American legation in Peking, Rayna signified danger. For both Rayna and her mate, William Prohme, a stolid German-American newspaper editor from San Francisco, worked as propagandists for the Chinese Revolution. To these people Rayna came to represent the flaming red fire of the Bolshevik Revolution, which seemed now to have spread to China, although Rayna, personally, knew nothing of Marx, or Engels, or Lenin, except that which she heard from William, who was what used to be called an armchair revolutionary.[4] He was a self-taught and voracious student of nineteenth- and twentieth-century revolutionary movements who expounded at great length and very emphatically his views on the subject to whoever would listen.

Rayna took on this revolutionary role with dignity and a not unselfconscious sense of higher purpose. It was just this sense of higher purpose that so impressed all who met her. She embraced her cause with the fervor of an angel of mercy.

Rayna never seems to have stopped moving. She was always dashing here and there, so that a flash of bright hair, the color of a blood orange, and the whiteness of her visage are what people remember, although in brief repose she could be seen to possess a thin, bright smile and merry eyes. This quick, fleeting transitory figure seems to have sped across whole continents and oceans unencumbered by anything at all except the men she sometimes took with her.

There were two of these. One of them, Samson Raphaelson, she actually married. He was her first love, a Chicago stray whom she discovered when they were teenagers. Rayna and Raphaelson became high school sweethearts. They went to the University of Illinois together. Rayna married him, and together they went west to San Francisco after college. Raphaelson soon went his own way with Rayna's blessing and became one of the most successful screenwriters in the history of Hollywood, and author of *The Jazz Singer,* the first talking motion picture.[5]

The other man in Rayna's life was Prohme, another lost soul, the divorced father of an only son, an editor at the *San Francisco Examiner,* seven years older than Rayna, who fell in love with her almost at once, when he met her in the company of Raphaelson. Exactly what Rayna made of Prohme is a mystery. When her marriage to Raphaelson broke up, Rayna almost immediately left for China, where she planned to stay for at least five years. "I want to see for myself what happens to a people when their friendly familiar world suddenly becomes strange and bewildering," Rayna had written. "I want to see what happens to them—and help, if I can, in keeping the new forces under control, of preventing the changes from coming too fast."[6] None of Rayna's plans seem to have included the husky Prohme, who liked to sign his letters "Yours Solid."

Prohme fled Brooklyn in his teens to evade a career in the church that his father, a Lutheran pastor, had staked out for him. He had learned the newspaper trade on various papers out west. He worked as a journeyman editor and reporter in Denver and then in Sacramento before he finally landed a job as an editorial writer on the *Examiner.* He was a man who had never attended college, but who had worked hard to educate himself in the ways of the world and in the finer things of life. To him, the highly intelligent, refined Rayna, who moved in the intellectual circle at Berkeley of the great cultural anthropologist A. L. Kroeber, was the epitome of all that was desirable in life.

Prohme saw Rayna off to China when she sailed away aboard the *Tenyo Maru,* a Japanese liner. Although on that occasion he was in tears, he seems only to have moved Rayna to mercy later on, when she was living in Peking, pursuing her destiny.[7] There, word reached Rayna that

Prohme had disappeared. Her friends feared the worst. Despondent, tubercular, he'd abandoned his job at the *Examiner* and vanished without leaving any forwarding address.

Rayna returned to San Francisco and tracked Prohme down in Texas, where he was expiring from a tubercular hemorrhage in an El Paso flophouse.[8] Rayna got Prohme to a doctor he knew in Santa Monica, California, named Max Pinner, who wrapped him in wet sheets to bring down his fever, a treatment Prohme detested, but one that seems to have worked. Rayna then took flight, with Prohme, for China, via Hawaii and Japan.[9]

After that, although there is no reason to believe that she actually married Prohme, Rayna took his last name. She was probably not even divorced from Raphaelson at the time. It was the last thing that mattered to Rayna. She hated all her last names, anyway. The name Simons she abhorred because it was the name of her father, the original oppressor in her life. She also disliked the name Prohme. Last names were of no interest to her, she wrote in a letter to her close friend, Helen Freeland. Her only meaningful identity was Rayna, which is the word Sephardis use for queen.[10]

Hawaii made Rayna very impatient. She and Prohme stayed there for half a year. Prohme had taken a job on the *Honolulu Advertiser,* and found that the climate was marvelous for his health, but although Rayna loved the beauty of it, she was critical of the Never-Never Land hedonism, the drinking, the deviled-ham sandwiches on the hot white virgin beaches of this island paradise, the endless stretch of blue Pacific, beyond which beckoned the starving people of China. She had things to do.[11]

She and Prohme moved on. Prohme was in great demand as a floater, as tramp journalists in the Far East were called, because, older than most, he was also more experienced as an editor. In Tokyo, Prohme worked for a few months on the *Japan Times* before he and Rayna made their way to Peking in 1925, where Prohme was offered the job as editor-in-chief of an English-language daily called the *Peking Leader.*

Rayna was clearly the guiding spirit. She was the redheaded angel of destiny with an as yet undefined trajectory, and Prohme, madly in love, followed along. Rayna's father had by now disowned her,[12] and Rayna relied on Prohme to support them on the salary he earned as an itinerant newsman. He was not, however, quite the solid, dependable fellow he wanted so badly to be for Rayna, due to the fragile state of his health.

In Peking, he suffered yet another tubercular collapse. Rayna put him in a hospital, and took over running the paper herself, so that she was perfectly positioned when destiny, in the guise of one Eugene Chen, minister of information and foreign minister of the Kuomintang, came, at the invitation of Rayna, to tea, after she read in an article that he had just been released from a jail in the nearby port city of Tientsin.[13]

Chen was a smooth-talking barrister from Trinidad, half-Chinese and half-Afro-Caribbean, who spoke no Chinese but commanded the King's English. Chen needed people to run his combined operation, an English-language propaganda sheet, the *Peking People's Tribune,* and news service. Chen himself had to get out of town. He was on the run from the Manchurian warlord Chang Tso-lin, who was heading their way. Chen pulled Rayna into the Revolution. Prohme, still convalescing in their courtyard, followed.

The Prohmes seemed perfectly suited to his needs. They were professionals, and they were Westerners. They could operate safely outside the reach of Chinese jurisprudence, if such it could be called. Chen himself was not safe from Chinese justice. He was a chronic gadfly, much hated by the northern warlords who haggled among themselves over north China. Chen had never ceased to bait them in the inflammatory pages of his various journals in the years since he had first come to China from London in 1911 with Dr. Sun.

Dr. Sun's revolution, which had gone underground in 1913 and resurfaced again in 1919 with the student protests of May 4, waxed and waned. Dr. Sun himself had died of stomach cancer in Peking that March. But his revolution was alive and kicking down in Canton, where with the help of Soviet advisers, Dr. Sun had set up a revolutionary government. Chen was headed that way when, over tea, he hired the Prohmes.

Chen installed Rayna in the offices of his combined newspaper and news service, which included a Chinese section. He paid her several visits there before he departed for Canton. "The Kuomintang never forgets its friends," he told Rayna, with a dramatic intensity.[14] Then he left. The Prohmes were now on the other side of the Looking Glass, which was where Rayna had been headed all along.

Here at last was Rayna's purpose in life, the opportunity to save not just a few lives but the lives of millions, and she took it on without missing a beat, slightly giddy as she always was and tripping along at her customary clip. Prohme, as usual, was the bedrock. He took upon himself the editorial burden of running both the news service and the paper, which he was now well enough to do. Rayna helped him write the copy. Presumably, the Prohmes were educated to the needs of the Revolution, and the history of the Revolution, by Li Ta-chao, a founder

of the Chinese Communist Party, who directed the editorial policy of
the Prohmes's paper. Li would have been able to fill the Prohmes in on
how agents from the Soviet Union, and the Communist International,
also known as the Comintern, an organization formed by Lenin to
spread the Russian Revolution abroad, had so swiftly and quietly filtered down into China after the Russian Revolution, how Comintern
agents had fingered Dr. Sun's Kuomintang for support, and simultaneously set up Marxist study groups in various Chinese cities. This had
led, in July 1921, to the founding of the Chinese Communist Party in
Shanghai.

Dr. Sun was not himself a Marxist, but he had turned to Lenin for
support when the Great Powers, the United States included, refused to
heed his calls for help to unify China. Dr. Sun had been reluctant to
form a United Front with the Communists, but once he formed a
government in Canton, he joined forces with them. Assisted by Mikhail
Borodin, his high adviser, he restructured the Kuomintang in the image
of the Communist Party of the Soviet Union. He permitted the Russians to train the officers at the new Whampoa Military Academy,
where Chou En-lai was deputy director of the political department.[15]
Russian freighters began dropping anchor in the Pearl River to deliver
arms and ammunition to the Kuomintang.[16]

All this Li Ta-chao would have explained to the Prohmes. He
would have informed Rayna that Leo Karakhan, the Soviet ambassador
in Peking, had bankrolled student and worker protests in Shanghai in
1925 that led to massive boycotts and shipping strikes. These had virtually shut down Hong Kong the previous spring, only months after the
death of Dr. Sun, who had traveled to Peking by boat from Canton
with Eugene Chen, among others, to parley with the warlords who
dominated the scene in north China. Leo Karakhan had left Peking in
April 1926, when Chang Tso-lin came to town. He knew that Chang
Tso-lin was trouble.

Chang Tso-lin was a former Manchurian bandit leader promoted
to military power and preeminence by the Japanese. Chang had helped
the Japanese beat back the Russians in 1905, during the Russo-Japanese
War, which took place mostly in Manchuria, either on water or on
land. The Japanese wanted to extend their rapidly burgeoning power in
Manchuria into north China. Now their man was running the show in
Peking.[17]

Neither Chang nor the Japanese wanted to see Russia supporting
revolution in China. They didn't want the Russians running a revolution out of the Soviet embassy. Chang Tso-lin's chief goal, when he
took Peking, was to root out the Communists, Russian, Chinese or any

other kind. That's why Karakhan had decided to take a leave of absence. Right off, Chang's soldiers started marching suspected Chinese Communists outside the Peking wall in groups and executing them.

Li Ta-chao and other Communists on Chang's most-wanted list took refuge in the Soviet embassy in the Legation Quarter, where the foreign ministries were housed on a street of Western-style mansions, each of which had been built in the manner of the country to which it belonged.

In the spring of 1926, Rayna used to hurry over to the Legation Quarter on a daily basis to confer with Li, who gave her editorial directions. According to the international rules of diplomacy, the ministries, including the Soviet embassy, were supposed to be off-limits to the host country police. So was Rayna's house. According to another set of rules, those of extraterritoriality, established between the Manchu court and Western trading powers in the nineteenth century, the citizens of countries signatory to extrality, as it was called, could operate outside the reach of Chinese law in certain designated areas defined as foreign concessions. This treaty by unwritten agreement was believed to apply to Westerners no matter where they happened to be in China, which is one reason Eugene Chen had hired the Prohmes to run his outfit.

But Chang Tso-lin was not someone who paid attention to treaties cooked up between the long-gone Manchus and Western barbarians. He was a cocky, Napoleonic little man who wore sweeping black mustachios to conceal a crudely sutured harelip. His favorite instrument of execution was the garrote, and he showed no reluctance to use it. Nobody was safe from this man in Peking in 1926, and certainly not Li Ta-chao. It was only a matter of time before Chang's gendarmes, with the unspoken agreement of the Great Powers, raided the Soviet embassy and dragged Li Ta-chao and his Chinese Communist colleagues off to the garrote.

But that was later. In the meantime, his gendarmes began to harass the offices of the *Peking People's Tribune*. One day they burst into the premises and took away one of the Chinese editors, whom they promptly killed. They came back a few weeks later for another one. In the summer of 1926, they looted the offices and sealed them up. For a time, it looked as though the Prohmes were out of work. The police reopened the English-language operation, but left the Chinese one sealed.[18]

The Prohmes became a little uneasy. They moved their editorial offices into their house, where they were supposed to be safe from the Manchurian warlord's brutal police. One day, when Miles Vaughn, a UP correspondent who happened to be in Peking at the time, relayed to Rayna the rumor that Chang Tso-lin was going to abduct her and Prohme, she just laughed.

Rayna thought it would be wonderful, she told Vaughn, if the legation marines had to come to their rescue. "Rayna despised the Legation," Vaughn wrote. But the legation also despised Rayna. To Minister J. V. A. MacMurray, she and Prohme were no better than traitors. The American government was on the side of Chang Tso-lin, in keeping with the British and their Japanese ally. Minister MacMurray was perfectly prepared to sacrifice the Prohmes to Chang.

Prohme seemed to grasp the gravity of their situation. He was ready to go. Rayna balked. To Vaughn, she was "merely a stubborn American girl filled with half-digested revolutionary ideas and almost totally lacking in common sense." Only that morning he had watched some Chinese spies being garroted. They were forced to kneel down, he told the Prohmes, in front of a post. Their wrists were tied behind them. A soldier placed a braided leather belt around each victim's throat and ran both ends through holes in the post and fastened them to a wheel "which was so arranged that when it was turned the noose was tightened" until the victim's eyes protruded and his face turned purple.[19]

Vaughn took some time to describe how this was done. He explained to the Prohmes how "the noose was loosened and the prisoner revived" repeatedly until he was ready to sign a confession. Vaughn took particular pains to describe the dry gasps the victim made in his agonized effort to get oxygen into his lungs when the noose was loosened. Once the prisoner signed a confession he was then strangled to death, Vaughn told the Prohmes.[20]

Finally, this got to Rayna. She was ready to go. She and Prohme telegraphed Milly Bennett, a journalist they knew, who had recently arrived in Shanghai from Honolulu. They summoned her to Peking. They quickly told her all she had to know about running a news service, and left her in charge. By early October, they were headed south, to see the Revolution firsthand.

If Diego Rivera, the great Mexican artist who was a member of the world socialist movement, had painted a series of murals of China's Great Revolution covering the important years of 1925 through 1927, he would have devoted one panel to Wuhan, which for half a year, in 1927, was the capital of liberated China. He might have depicted the Revolutionary Center as a teeming crowd of Chinese workers on the Bund, along the muddy chocolate-colored expanse of the Yangtze, a river scene broken in the middle distance by a cluster of foreign gunboats riding at anchor, interspersed with Chinese junks in full sail; big chimneys would be blasting fire from factories on the far bank, and then, in the distant perspective, rendered as a somewhat surreal and far-flung landscape, the green countryside, with armed peasants in revolt. The background would be various shades of green, surmounted by a deep blue sky, but the crowded foreground, the Hankow Bund, would have to be depicted in dark colors, browns and blacks and dark grays, a dense mass of black-haired strikers, rickshaw boys, student organizers, Communist cadres and revolutionary troops of the southern Chinese Fourth Route Army in gray coolie uniforms and straw coolie hats.

Some of these Chinese would be recognizable to the Western visitor as the youthful Mao Tse-tung, and Chou En-lai and Ch'en Tu-hsiu, co-founder and secretary general of the Chinese Communist Party. You would also be able to pick out Borodin, the Revolution's high adviser, with his black walrus mustache. Down in the lower-right-hand corner the great artist might have painted Rayna Prohme's bright orange plumage and her starkly white face beneath it and in this particular panel— other panels might depict revolutionary Canton, the worker's insurrection in Shanghai, scenes of the Northern Expedition—that's where the eye would first be drawn, to that vivid splash of brightness, like a fiery solar orb at sunset, in a scene of somber colors.

You might spot elsewhere in the crowd the youthful Randall Gould, of UP, and Vincent Sheean, even Anna Louise Strong, and possibly Bill Prohme, slightly understated. Then after some perusal you might pick out Madame Sun Yat-sen, unexpectedly small and slight, not yet the benign and somewhat roundish matriarch she in later life became, and Eugene Chen, brown-skinned, with African features, "brilliantined," as Harold Isaacs called him in *The Tragedy of the Chinese Revolution*.

That would be the Wuhan story of 1927. Manabendra Nath Roy, a towering Bengali Comintern representative with his carven oak features and black Indian skin, would also be mingling in the crowd, along with other Comintern colleagues, Earl Browder of Kansas, and Jacques Doriot, and the bantam English labor leader Tom Mann. They all have their place in the Wuhan story. Rayna stands for something more than revolutionary thrill and that's why today she continues to arrest the eye. She stands for pure revolutionary spirit, naive as it always has to be. Rayna was the crown princess of Hankow.

She became chief assistant to Borodin, who in a sense had borrowed her from Prohme to help him run the Revolutionary Center.

Eugene Chen had a way of splitting the Prohmes up. He'd sent Prohme downriver in early April on a long assignment to Nanking and Shanghai, and he had taken Prohme away from Rayna in Canton, where they'd gone after Peking to join the Revolution. At that time, in early

December, he'd taken Prohme to Wuhan with the Left Kuomintang government, leaving Rayna in Canton to overhaul his *Canton Gazette,* although she soon tired of that and made her way to Wuhan via Shanghai, with a German shepherd she'd acquired along the way by the name of Dan.

Chen was something of a manipulator and may have wanted the Prohmes apart to control them better, but this tactic also suited Borodin, who for a time had Rayna all to himself.

If I were asked to point out Borodin in the mural, he would be the somewhat masked gentleman, in a not altogether conspicuous part of the painting, sitting in the brown leather back seat of Wu P'ei-fu's bulletproof car almost concealed by the crowd. He has large, hooded, dark eyes, a thick mustache and deep creases around his mouth. His black hair is parted near the middle and falls slightly across his forehead. In this mural the face is lean, and Borodin, looking somewhat small in the great car, is peering nervously from the automobile at the anarchy around him, in the suspicious manner of the *agent provocateur.*

People at the time thought of Borodin as grand, and bearlike, but he was only five foot ten. They thought of him as a kind of Lone Ranger of the Chinese Revolution, who single-handedly held the Revolution together, but he was really Stalin's man in China. He was a professional revolutionary who had been dispatched to China to advise Dr. Sun in October 1923, as an agent of the Politburo of the Central Committee of the Russian Communist Party, which Stalin by that time controlled.[21]

In China, Borodin was so far removed from Stalin that he made most decisions on his own, but he could be called to account, as he was in Peking, for instance, in the late winter of 1926, when a commission of high-ranking members of the Central Committee sent by Stalin to plot the future of Russia's involvement in the Revolution interrogated Borodin on the way he'd handled matters in Canton. On that occasion he defended himself brilliantly before an essentially friendly delegation. He was actually out of touch with Canton, however, where, in his absence, Chiang Kai-shek, who was at that time the commandant of the Whampoa Military Academy, staged a coup d'etat against Wang Ching-wei, chairman of the National Government of Canton. Chiang held the Soviet military advisers under house arrest and put Canton under martial law, patrolled by troops who were loyal to him. Borodin returned to Canton posthaste, but after that he no longer called the shots, as he had been doing ever since the death of Dr. Sun, because Chiang Kai-shek was now in charge.[22]

Chiang Kai-shek had the support of the old conservative branch of the Kuomintang, merchants and bankers in Shanghai opposed to the revolutionary policies of the USSR and the Chinese Communist Party.

This was his true constituency. But he still needed Russian help to mount his Northern Expedition. He needed his military strategist, General Galen, and he needed Russian arms, and so he released the Russian advisers and maintained the United Front. It was a complicated situation for Borodin. He was under Stalin's orders to support the military ambitions of Chiang Kai-shek over those of the Chinese Communist Party, which the Russians had helped to organize. This policy was an extension of Stalin's power struggle with Trotsky in the Kremlin, which had begun even before the death of Lenin in January 1924 of complications from a stroke.

Trotsky had been second only to Lenin in the leadership of the new revolutionary state. Under Lenin, he had served as Commissar for Foreign Affairs and Commissar of War, and he had organized the Red Army. Trotsky passionately argued Lenin's position that the Soviet Union had to export revolution, and support social revolution in other countries, in order to keep the Russian Revolution alive. He insisted that the Communists had to make a break with the Kuomintang before the military-bourgeois faction in the national revolution turned and crushed the Communist revolutionaries. Stalin ran the party apparatus in the Kremlin, however. He silenced Trotsky, whom he kept from publishing his views and even from being heard outside of committee meetings.

Stalin was pushing a doctrine he called Socialism in One State. Instead of world revolution, this policy advanced the idea that Russia should use its resources to develop internally, and give support to strong nationalist movements that could be expected to act in Russia's interests against the forces of imperialism. In China, that meant opposing the influence of Great Britain and Japan. Stalin deemed Chiang Kai-shek, who appeared to be pro–Communist, a stronger force in China than the Chinese Communists. He announced in a speech to three thousand functionaries in the Hall of Columns in Moscow on April 5, in response to Trotsky's criticisms, that the Revolution would use Chiang Kai-shek and his supporters among the rich merchants and other Chinese reactionaries and then throw them away, "squeezed out like a lemon."[23]

Borodin carried out his mandate by refusing to allow the Chinese Communists to break with Chiang Kai-shek after his impudent coup d'etat. Instead, he ordered them to do "coolie service" for the Kuomintang. Borodin knew Chiang Kai-shek. He knew that it was just a matter of time before Chiang turned on the Communists, as Trotsky knew he would, but Borodin's hands were tied.

Chiang broke decisively with the Left Kuomintang and the Chinese Communists and his Russian advisers once he reached the Yangtze River Valley. In December 1926, Borodin and the Left Kuomintang

government from Canton set up their capital in Wuhan, on the understanding that the Nationalist armies would proceed to north China, to
complete the process of unification. Chiang repudiated this course of
action, which was favored by General Galen. Instead, early in 1927 he
turned east, and headed downriver in the direction of Shanghai, where
workers organized by the Chinese Communist Party awaited his arrival
as the Messiah of liberation.[24]

On April 12, when Prohme was in Shanghai and Rayna was up in
Wuhan with Borodin, Chiang Kai-shek, with the help of gangsters,
crushed the striking workers in Shanghai's Chinese city who had staged
a successful insurrection on his behalf. He thereby saved Shanghai for
the Chinese bankers and merchants who feared the Revolution, and
held them hostage to his personal ambitions. It was a terrible, bloody
betrayal of the workers, who at Stalin's insistence had been ordered to
put away their arms. When thugs in the pay of a gruesome former
dockworker named Tu Yueh-sheng slipped through the high iron gates
of the International Settlement in Shanghai with the foreknowledge of
the Western leaders and, disguised as workers, gunned them down, the
strikers were helpless.[25]

This high-handed *coup de main* won for Chiang Kai-shek the money
he needed to set up a government of his own several hours upriver in
Nanking. He had already turned against Wuhan. He had already called
upon the Russian advisers to leave China. Now his right-wing terrorist
reaction went into high gear in river towns under his control up and
down the Yangtze.

A thousand miles west, in Wuhan, the myth of revolution per-
sisted. Borodin was still the high adviser. That nothing really revolutionary was happening in Hankow or Wuhan did not prevent Rayna
and other visiting Westerners from expecting something to happen. It
was a mood, euphoric and expectant, kept alive by Rayna and the
coterie of Westerners led by Rayna and fed by Borodin, in whom everyone invested such hope. Borodin's very presence conveyed a slightly
world-weary authority. He was ponderous in manner, and somehow
this made him seem very weighty and large. He had such fluent English
at his command and knew so much and had done so many things in his
life that he inspired his visitors with awe. He was also at least a decade
older than most of the journalists and other observers who flocked to
the Revolution, one of whom, Nordahl Grieg, was a Norwegian composer and playwright who later wrote a play called *Barrabas* which he
dedicated to Borodin.

Borodin held forth late at night from a deep leather armchair in his
living room, attired for the evening hours in an embroidered Russian
blouse of the sort that Tolstoy favored, worn loosely over his sharply

creased trousers, and discoursed at great length and with considerable knowledge about all kinds of things: Shakespeare's plays, and Lindbergh's transatlantic flight, and the intricacies of the Chinese Revolution. All the while a white-robed manservant glided silently around the room like a ghost among the rapt listeners, bearing a tray of little liqueur glasses filled with some sweet, sticky *digestif* that Borodin was not, himself, observed to drink.[26]

Borodin, born Mikhail Grusenberg, was a Latvian Jew from Vitebsk who had known Stalin at the barricades in St. Petersburg in 1905. He was arrested after the 1905 Revolution, and in the amnesty that followed made his way to Valparaiso University, in Indiana, where under the name of Mike Berg he met and married another Russian, Fanny Arbuk, with whom he opened a night school in Chicago for émigrés and their children. In 1917, he and Fanny were back in Petrograd, as St. Petersburg was now called. In the years that followed, he was an active presence at various revolutionary hotspots around the world, including Mexico and Turkey. In England, in 1922, under the nom de guerre of George Brown, he oversaw the reorganization of the Communist Party of Great Britain, sought members for the Communist International's trade union, Profintern, among coal miners, and traveled throughout England attending to party activities until he was arrested by Scotland Yard and sent to Glasgow, where he served out a six-month term in Barlinnie Prison. There, he worked in the laundry and made a study of the King James version of the Bible. He was a great music lover, according to Milly Bennett, who came upriver soon after Chiang's Shanghai coup to join Rayna. He liked Tchaikovsky and Meyerbeer. He told Milly that he'd taken the name Borodin in honor of A. P. Borodin, the Russian composer and physician.[27]

He was also, according to Milly, a great actor. He played the role of high adviser with consummate skill. He may have been better at performing the role of revolutionary professional than he was at actually being one. If the art of dissembling is a skill of the revolutionist, however, then Borodin was a pro. He ran things the way Stalin told him to, and pretended that he was making up the rules as he went, according to circumstances as they arose. He appeared to be nursing the Revolution along, while all the time he was putting the brakes on the Chinese Revolution, and nobody knew it.

Borodin appropriated Rayna to be his spokesperson to the Western world and as such she was the director of public relations in Wuhan. She was the chief editorial writer of the *Peking People's Tribune,* the daily newspaper established by Eugene Chen and Borodin with the help of Bill and Rayna Prohme in March 1927, to broadcast word of the Wuhan

Revolutionary Center to everyone in the world socialist movement. This was an important service, because it was the first socialist government to put down roots outside the Soviet Union since the October Revolution, and there was passionate interest all around the world in its daily news.

Borodin told Rayna what to write in her think pieces for the newspaper, supervised her editorials, and instructed her on what to tell the visiting members of the press, whom she met at the boat when they disembarked in Wuhan. Rayna met with reporters throughout the day in her office at the *People's Tribune* and gave them Borodin's view of the Revolution. She also escorted correspondents to interviews with other leaders of the collective government: Eugene Chen, Sun Fo, only son of Sun Yat-sen, Madame Sun Yat-sen and Wang Ching-wei, the former head of the Canton government, who had recently returned from France, where he had fled after Chiang Kai-shek's Canton coup d'etat.

Rayna was a fortunate find for Borodin, because she fell deeply under his spell, and became a true believer. As such, she dramatizes the delusion China Hands often used to entertain that only Westerners could really run things in China, that whatever happened in China was due to the beneficent influence of foreigners. Borodin reinforced this attitude among his admirers when he justified his own failures by intoning, "China is trying to catch up, to make up for lost time. The diehards call it 'communism.' Let them! When the people in China have something to eat, a shirt on their backs, and free schools, when China is in a position comparable to the rest of the world, then it will be time to talk politics. Politics is a luxury," he said, "enjoyed alone by the rich, Western countries today."[28] Like other China Hands to come, Rayna believed that she knew much more about what was going on than she really did in a country where she couldn't read or speak the language.

She was also an asset to Borodin because of her star quality, which made her a great public relations organizer for the Revolutionary Center. The visiting firemen, the journalists, the Western observers, the Comintern delegates were dazzled by her. "Men were drawn to Rayna, men found her tantalizing," Milly wrote. "Her remarkable hair would stop them. Once stopped, they loitered. Her quickness of spirit, her delight in merry things, her absorption in the cause of China, even her withdrawal at times when she was not available to anybody; all of this added up to a baffling and fabulous woman." In fact, inaccessibility was part of Rayna's allure. "Rayna accepted none, Rayna rejected none," Milly wrote. "Hers was a chaste spirit, hers the soul of a female Galahad."[29]

The visitors came to Rayna's office even when she wasn't there and waited for her to return. Often at night, if they weren't upstairs in

Borodin's private quarters above the *People's Tribune,* they congregated in Rayna's flat in the Lutheran Mission Building. "By day," Randall Gould of UP later recalled, "we interviewed government leaders or inspected propaganda factories or dropped in at the offices of the daily *People's Tribune.* By night we gathered in Rayna's apartment to listen to classical records on her phonograph or join with an ex-I.W.W. [Industrial Workers of the World] (whom I had seen sentenced to prison by Judge Landis in Chicago years before) in singing 'There'll Be Pie In The Sky When I Die!' "[30]

So many of them—Rayna, Gould, Borodin, Vincent Sheean, Anna Louise Strong—had lived in Chicago, and now here they were in the Chicago of China, a drab, flat torrid town of low modern buildings beside the wide, brown Yangtze. The heat was barely tolerable. The British call such weather "filthy." "The days were fiery and scorching," Milly wrote. "The setting of the sun brought no relief. The brown twilight closed in, and as if it were a wet, wadding comforter the sky pressed down on the helpless town. No breeze stirred among us down below, no breath of air moved in the sealed, sweltering hollow in the Yangtze."[31] Rayna thrived in this atmosphere. She loved the thrilling sense of risk that a state of siege can induce, when there seems to be no time to spare, and yet all time is suspended. She could also relate to the hostile countryside that was in revolt all around her, because she herself was in revolt.

Furthermore, Prohme was out of the picture for the time being. He was the one who killed the fun by insisting on orderly mealtimes and things like that. He was firmly rooted to the ground, and she hated the ground, she confided to a friend in a letter. Their flat in the Lutheran Mission Building seemed to bring out Prohme's long-buried Lutheran gloom, from which he'd fled so many years before only to find it summoned forth out of the grave in Wuhan, over dinner, by the lugubrious strains of hymns drifting upward from below. Now Prohme was gone, on assignment for Chen in Shanghai.

Milly had moved in with Rayna. They were the only two Western women left in Wuhan. All the others had been evacuated during the Hankow Incident, in January, when Chinese workers took over the British Concession. "To my way of thinking you two women are the best story in Hankow," one British reporter told Rayna. "How do a couple of American girls happen to be mixed up in this? Adventure? Fun? Do you take all this fol-de-rol seriously?"[32]

Rayna stopped eating almost entirely. She indulged in madcap races through the flat with Dan, the German shepherd. She and Milly Bennett wrapped themselves in wet sheets, à la Dr. Max Pinner, to keep cool, and took to putting on kimonos, which Prohme wouldn't allow Rayna to wear in his presence because he considered this garment "sluttish." They were an odd couple: the wisecracking city reporter who could belt them down with the boys, and the rarified redhead, who despite her revolutionary fervor was also a bluestocking, a Ph.D. candidate at the University of Chicago in comparative civilizations. They went everywhere together. They were down at the station when the revolutionary Fourth Route Ironsides troops set out by train northward to do battle with the troops of Chang Tso-lin, the Manchurian warlord ruler of north China. It was a last desperate gamble to beat Chiang Kai-shek to Peking and save the Revolution. The troops were preceded by a shiny, freshly painted twelve-car train full of high-spirited young girls in blue uniforms. These were the propaganda cadres, who were setting out ahead of the troops as they had in the Northern Expedition to pacify the countryside.

Rayna and Milly were together also at the May 1 rally on International Labor Day to celebrate the Revolution. "A milling, churning mass of human beings," Milly wrote. The speakers "were howling themselves hoarse through cardboard megaphones," and when they shouted out revolutionary slogans "the people picked up the catch phrases and roared like boiling thunder."[33]

But most of all, the two women worked furiously. Milly was "reading out a revolution across a copy desk," as she put it, "slugging it out with poorly translated manifestoes, fierce proclamations and tormented programs of reform."[34] She was a foil and a source of practical advice for Rayna, who needed some kind of anchor, although she exhibited her own aura of irreproachable command, informed by the conviction that she was delivering the Chinese people from capitalist imperialist enslavement. "Rayna was possessed, absolutely possessed," Milly wrote, "by a single idea: China. An enlightened, democratic, Republican China."[35]

Every so often Rayna was stricken, suddenly, with killer headaches so excruciatingly painful that they drove her to bed, sometimes for days at a time. Then she bounced back, though, and more than made up for her absence. She was once again dashing up the back stairs of the *People's Tribune* to Borodin's quarters, working out with him the wording of the latest communiqué, or some other public relations matter. "Borodin was forever demanding her personal presence," Milly observed.[36]

"Rayna ran, ran, ran. There was no end to it," Milly wrote. "Oh, the speeding, winged Rayna."[37]

Vincent Sheean was one of the few reporters Rayna did not meet on arrival in Wuhan. He was at the time writing for the North American Newspaper Alliance. He was twenty-seven. He belonged to a new species of foreign correspondent known as the Young Falcons, reporters who made their own adventures a part of the news stories they filed, in the tradition of Richard Harding Davis, who won fame as a reporter for William Randolph Hearst during the Spanish-American War.[38] Vincent Sheean had taken off in 1924 to test his falcon wings as an intrepid reporter in the Moroccan Rif, where, on two separate occasions, he had made his way to the rebel redoubt of a revolutionary sultan named Sheikh Abd el-Krim. Sheean's dispatches included the account of a lone German adventurer, El-Hadj Aleman, who had deserted from the French Foreign Legion and subsequently hired himself out as a mercenary to the Moroccans, an account that inspired Sigmund Romberg to write the enormously popular operetta, *Desert Song*.

Sheean had long since ceased to be a Young Falcon by the time he turned up in Hankow. He had managed to create for himself the persona of a worldly and sophisticated interpreter of global happenings who could hobnob with British aristocracy at the League of Nations in Geneva, cover the rise of Fascism in Italy, drink Pernod in Left Bank cafés in Paris with expatriate writers and next be found in, say, Persia, or Moscow. Sheean's latest employers were not at all sure that his particular qualifications suited the China story, which, he later wrote, was regarded by them as "too large, too complicated, and in a general way too unexciting"[39] to justify sending a swashbuckler to cover. News organizations dispatched correspondents to China only when American lives were endangered by the sudden violent seizures to which the Middle Kingdom was every so often prey. In February, however, when it looked as though the Nationalists would soon seize Shanghai, the outpost of American capitalism, Sheean got the all-clear signal.

His timing was exquisite. Sheean's trans-Pacific liner dropped anchor off the Shanghai Bund on April 13, one day after Chiang Kai-shek's bloody Shanghai massacre. Missing one of the signal stories of the century troubled Sheean not at all. He soon set off upriver for Hankow, where he engaged a room in the Hotel des Wagons-Lits in the French Concession.

Of the Chinese he met, Sheean found hardly any who compelled his admiration. Wang Ching-wei he thought was picturesque. Eugene Chen was "all of a piece, a small, clever, venomous, faintly reptilian man, adroit and slippery in the movements of his mind, combative in temper, with a kind of lethal elegance in appearance, voice and gesture."[40]

Madame Sun, however, enchanted Sheean. It awed the young cosmopolite that "this exquisite apparition, so fragile and timorous," could actually be the "most celebrated woman revolutionary in the world."

Her dignity was "so natural and certain that it deserved the name of stateliness." She really was, he wrote, "China's Joan of Arc."[41]

Sheean was utterly taken by Borodin. No leader since Sheikh Abd el-Krim had so impressed him. They both had the "special quality of being in, but above, the battle," he later wrote.[42] He described Borodin as a "large, calm man with the natural dignity of a lion or a panther."[43] The high adviser refused to be hurried or to get excited. "He seemed to take 'the long view' by nature," Sheean wrote, "by an almost physical superiority of vision."[44] To Sheean, Borodin represented an idealized mentor. "I found an older, better disciplined, better trained and more experienced intelligence than my own: it had already traversed regions that still lay before me."[45]

But the person who transfixed Vincent Sheean was Rayna Prohme. He was knocked into a cocked hat the moment he set eyes on her one evening outside the *People's Tribune* building.

Henry Misselwitz, the young *New York Times* correspondent, introduced them. "She was on her way home to dinner," Sheean later wrote, "and it was neither the time nor the place for any kind of serious conversation. She was slight, not very tall, with short red-gold hair and a frivolous turned up nose." Her eyes, Sheean wrote, could change color with her changes of mood. "Her voice, fresh, cool and American, sounded as if it had secret rivulets of laughter running underneath it all the time, ready to come to the surface without warning. All in all, she was most unlike my idea of a 'wild Bolshevik,' and I told her so. She laughed. I had never heard anybody laugh as she did—it was the gayest, most unself-conscious sound in the world. You might have thought that it did not come from a person at all, but from some impulse of gaiety in the air."[46]

Sheean fell deeply in thrall to Rayna. Ultimately, she became his China story. He later professed that his attraction to Rayna was not erotic. "I shall not attempt to explain the mystery of an all-pervading, all-controlling emotion that had no physical basis," he wrote in *Personal History,* the memoir of his youthful exploits in which Rayna played a starring role, "but it existed."[47] Like others, Sheean was haunted by Rayna's elusive spirit, which was not something that could be possessed physically. "Star-struck" is the term that Israel Epstein uses in his biography of Madame Sun to describe Sheean's reaction to Rayna.[48]

Rayna had no interest herself in Vincent Sheean. She was not quite as cutting about him as Milly Bennett was. Milly called him "tall, tweedy, well-favored, reckless, intense Sheean," and "a roving reporter deluxe," and added that "disillusion, cynicism, boredom and recklessness were his pose."[49] Rayna, though kinder than Milly, found Sheean tiresome. He was not the sort of person to whom she was drawn. For one thing, he wore white silk suits. He also drank heavily—Scotch, mostly—a habit Rayna particularly disliked in men, or so she told Milly. Sheean was not deterred by Rayna's aversions. He understood perfectly well why she was put off by him. "In the beginning of our acquaintance it was inevitable," he wrote, "for she could see at a glance . . . the American bourgeois as modified by Paris and London, with a goodish but lazy mind."[50] She knew him too well. "She could easily, perhaps too easily, consign me to the pigeonhole where many of her own friends and relations belonged. She was from Chicago, had been educated at the University of Illinois, and must have known hundreds of our contemporaries of the same general social, economic and intellectual stamp as myself."[51] He decided that they were like a brother and sister who had gone off in different directions. "She had, in a sort of way, 'known me all her life'; not only that, but I was an American newspaper man from Paris (i.e, the worst kind), and she could not take me seriously."[52]

Indeed, Sheean had certain reservations about Rayna. "Exactly the same thing was true, of course, on my side of the argument," he wrote. "She was the kind of girl I had known all my life, but she had, by the direction she had taken, acquired a purpose and point of view that did not seem to belong to her."[53] This bore some looking into. He decided that "there was a basis of perfect misunderstanding, with a superstructure of familiarity (sameness of culture, social and economic identity, Illinois, Illinois!)."[54] As a result of the misunderstanding, he wrote, he himself underestimated Rayna, just as she underrated him, which explained why in the weeks that followed their meeting they treated each other with such flippancy. "The most important conversation I have ever had—began, and for months continued, as a kind of joke,"[55] Vincent Sheean wrote some years later, when he was thirty-four, of his relationship—with Rayna.

As de facto propaganda minister for the Wuhan government, Rayna had to meet with Sheean, but sometimes the intensity of his obsession was more than she could handle, according to Milly. "Jimmy Sheean is thoroughly spoiled, he's a child," she told Milly. "I wish he'd sober up and get out of town . . . he makes me tired around the eyes."[56] Rayna would dash up the back stairs to Borodin's office when she heard Sheean's footsteps in the hallway and leave Milly to take the brunt of his frustration. In Milly's account, "the door would still be on a quiver when the flushed, inquiring face of Jimmy Sheean would be looming over my typewriter." Milly then had to wrestle Sheean's disappointment. " 'Yeah Jimmy, Rayna was here. No Jimmy, I don't know when she'll be back. She just took off, she didn't say where. You might try

calling the house tonight, say around midnight.' " Milly seems to have
drawn a certain sadistic pleasure from all of this. She taunted Sheean by
mentioning Prohme. "Bill'll be back from Shanghai any day now," she
told him. "It'll be a lot less frantic around here then." She added, "Oh
that baffled, that crestfallen Sheean face."[57] Sheean, however, refused
to let Milly get between him and Rayna. "Rayna's assistant was an
American woman journalist who regarded every moment I spent in the
office of the *People's Tribune* as a calamity," he wrote. "Under these
circumstances a more sensitive subject might have stayed away, but I
didn't. The daily conversations with Rayna Prohme had become such a
necessity that when a day passed without my seeing her at all (as happened twice when she was ill) it left an extraordinary sense of blankness
and malaise."[58]

These are the sentiments of a lovelorn man. Was it true love, or the
romantic delusion of a young journalist, naive in matters of the heart,
sophisticated globetrotter though he was? Sheean was captivated by
the spirit of Hankow. It supplied an "electrical thrill"[59] that had been
unimaginable to him in postwar Europe, especially among the somewhat jaded young literary lights with whom he had recently played in
Paris. He was in romantic awe of Madame Sun and Borodin, who
became his heroes, and Rayna was the very embodiment of that revolutionary spirit. He refused to buy the daily dose of propaganda that he
says she dished out in her office. He refused, in fact, to believe that her
propaganda came from Borodin, with his "high respect for the truth."[60]
Eugene Chen was the villain. "Consequently," Sheean wrote, "for propaganda purposes, Rayna Prohme was often obliged to write and say
things her own candour resented." She was, he wrote, "a very bad liar
indeed"; after a while she gave up trying to feed him "official versions";[61] she told him the truth, as she knew it personally, or else said
nothing. He was grateful to her when she told him the truth. He could
finally begin to perceive that the situation in Wuhan was bleak. Meanwhile, as things went from bad to worse, Sheean was impressed by the
spirit of sacrifice the Chinese demonstrated on the streets of Hankow.
It was not at all "a suicidal, neurotic yearning for Nirvana," as it might
have been in Japan or India, he wrote, but a "colder and purer conviction," sacrifice in the service of an idea.[62] It was this refreshing conviction he craved in Rayna, in her laughter, in her gaiety.

Wuhan entered what Milly Bennett called "a dizzy spell."[63] Every-
where now the Chinese were turning on the Russians. "Send the
Russians back to Russia! But for them we'd still be with Chiang
Kai-shek!"[64] That, or something like it, was the cry on everyone's lips.
Chiang Kai-shek had successfully cut off the money supply in Wuhan.

Furthermore, he had imposed an embargo on goods going up and down the Yangtze between Shanghai and Wuhan. Economic panic was setting in. There was no more small change. People rushed to the Central Bank to convert bank notes into silver, but the doors were bolted. "The area around the Central Bank got to looking like a mob scene from 'Ben Hur,' " Milly Bennett wrote. "Day after day, the hungry and the poor collected there. They howled for silver and copper, they shrieked and threw their bodies against the bronze doors."[65] Upstairs, Madame Sun Yat-sen peered down at them from behind her silk curtains, her ears stuffed with cotton batting to block out the cries of rage that came to her from down below.

Rayna wrote in the *People's Tribune* of watching frightened people drawing carts laden with household goods past her windows. She could hear whispers of woe in the air. "Open carriages, jewels of black laquer and crammed with people of fashion, went clattering over the cobblestones in the general direction of the French Concession," Milly Bennett wrote. "The French would as usual give refuge to the rich Chinese, at a price."[66]

Not only was Hankow threatened, Borodin's options were also limited by the hostile foreign gunboats that sat at anchor on the Yangtze River off the Hankow Bund. The imperialists had threatened action against the revolutionaries as soon as the foreign concessions had begun to appear imperiled by the Northern Expedition. The power structure in Wuhan also lived in constant fear of General T'ang Sheng-chih, a big Hunan landlord who was also the military protector of Hankow. His forces had helped to conquer Wuhan for the Nationalists, but his tendency was to side more and more against the Revolution and with the big landowners in the countryside. Borodin laughed when Anna Louise Strong, the American correspondent who, like Sheean, had arrived belatedly to report on the Revolution, suggested that if the civil power stood firm, the military would have to yield. "Did you ever see a rabbit before an anaconda," Borodin asked her, "trembling, knowing it is going to be devoured, yet fascinated? That's the civic power before the military in Wuhan, staring at the military and trembling."[67]

The mood of dread and panic lifted, briefly, when word reached Wuhan that the Fourth Route Army Ironsides soldiers of General Chang Fa-k'uei, armed with rifles and machine guns, had hurled back the mercenaries of Chang Tso-lin led by his son, Chang Hsueh-liang, the Young Marshal, in Honan. It was a great victory. The northerners had come to battle equipped with trench mortars and bombs supplied by the Japanese, who controlled Chang Tso-lin and through him hoped to wrest control over China's three northern provinces. Now these slipshod troops under the Young Marshal had fallen back. Wuhan could entertain the possibility of somehow going farther, and grasping the distant prize of Peking. But the price of victory had been devastating. Two thousand bodies lay scattered across the dun-colored hills and valleys of Honan. Chang Fa-k'uei's army was decimated. Madame Sun Yat-sen began to set up emergency hospital stations to receive the wounded and crippled survivors as they came on stretchers back to the Revolutionary Center aboard the very trains that had taken them to the battlefield.

William Prohme was the messenger of doom. He finally came back from Shanghai. He told Rayna and Milly that nothing this side of a miracle would save Wuhan now. Chiang Kai-shek, he explained, had lined up rich and influential Shanghailanders on his side, and was now making arrangements for a fashionable Methodist wedding to Soong Mei-ling, the younger sister of Madame Sun Yat-sen, in the fall. Prohme told them what it was like to lie in the dark, alone, on his mattress at the Hotel Plaza, while the workers were being gunned down in the Chinese city. "It was like listening to the sounds of my own funeral," he said. He couldn't free himself of Shanghai. "Machine gunning makes a special kind of talk," he said. "Once you have heard it you can't get it out of your head."[68]

Prohme resumed his role as boss, at work and at home. In the Lutheran Mission Building, Prohme played Beethoven's Fifth Symphony incessantly. "Rayna and I became accustomed to having the 'Fifth' shout us out of sleep each morning," Milly wrote, "to having it roar us to our hot little beds at night. We began by loving it, but as time went on it became painful, tormenting."[69] Prohme also worked obsessively. At the *People's Tribune* he sat in a cubicle near the entrance, and received the heavy traffic of visitors—"newspapermen of every nationality," Milly wrote, "politicians, adventurers and book writers, preachers, snoopers, spies and agents of many causes"[70]—all of whom made their way to the *People's Tribune*.

Prohme and Vincent Sheean met. Sheean wrote, "We did not hit it off as well as might be expected. His violent revolutionary enthusiasm resented my bourgeois lethargy, my innumerable changes of white silk clothes, my Scotch whiskey and Egyptian cigarettes. In turn I disliked his excitability, his refusal to argue a subject through in a clear and logical manner; I suspected that his revolutionary convictions were not grounded in economic and social science—that he was an emotional Red, if a Red at all; and that his presence in China in his present role was due to the accident of his marriage to Rayna Prohme."[71]

The great fear, always, was that Prohme's tuberculosis would recur. "If he starts hemmorhaging, we're sunk!" Rayna told Milly.[72]

Gone, then, were the happy-go-lucky days of March and April and early May. No more idle late-night parties, no more kimonos, no more wrapping up in wet sheets at night to keep cool, because it reminded Bill of the treatment Dr. Pinner had forced on him back in Santa Monica. No more races with the German shepherd, either. Dan was exiled to the pantry. "The house," Prohme declared, "is no place for a dog."[73] Now, they ate regular meals, on schedule. "White man eat when whistle blow, Eskimo eat when hungry," Milly told Prohme one day when she was late for lunch.[74] He was not amused. "Bill's never been able to laugh at his own foibles," Milly observed. "It's that stuffy Brooklyn-Prussian blood of his."[75]

Laughter all but vanished from the house of Prohme. Conversation circled around whether Borodin, and the Russians, could have saved the Revolution, and whether Borodin still could. The Prohmes, it seemed to Milly, at times believed that Borodin *was* the Revolution. He was a great man, in their unreconstructed opinion. A genius. Like Vincent Sheean and so many others, they had fallen under Borodin's spell. Yet everyone was a little confused about what he was doing. "Bee's a great guy, a remarkable human being," Milly argued, "but where was he when Chiang Kai-shek took the jump into Shanghai?"[76] Milly was skeptical of Borodin's powers. "Borodin, Galen, both of them, caught with their pants down! Galen at Nanking,★ Borodin marooned with the bickering politicians at Hankow! Now we hear that Borodin and Galen knew all along that Chiang was not to be trusted, knew that he was getting ready to jump their good advice and counseling. Still, right up to the point when Chiang Kai-shek walked into Shanghai, machine-gunned the unions and told the Russians to get the hell out of China,

★ This is a reference to the so-called Nanking Incident of March 24, 1927, when Nationalist soldiers, who had routed the northern troops who had held the city, "systematically looted the British, American and Japanese consulates, wounded the British consul, attacked and robbed foreign nationals throughout the city, killed two Englishmen, an American, a French and an Italian priest, and a Japanese marine." (John K. Fairbank, ed., *The Cambridge History of China*, Vol. 12, *Republican China, 1912–1949*. Part 1 (Cambridge: Cambridge University Press, 1983), pp. 617–18.) This shocking "outrage" as it became known among the foreign community in China turned many foreigners against Chiang Kai-shek, who later tried to blame the Communists for planning the violence. Chiang wanted no interference from the foreign warships and troops that were being rushed to Shanghai to make a show of force on behalf of the international community, and he launched a campaign to distance himself from the Nanking Incident, which some believed at the time he had actually launched in order to discredit the Communists, including his Russian advisers, General Galen chief among them.

Borodin was supplying him with guns, ammunition and do-re-mi; he'd been palavering, making concessions, arranging compromises. . . ."[77]

This was too close to the bone. "Maybe that was his job, too," Rayna shot back. "Maybe he's taking orders, too."[78] It was very close to an admission that Borodin was not a free agent, as he had always claimed to be, but under orders from Moscow. Milly wondered out loud why Borodin hadn't persuaded the Wuhan government to arm the people, the factory workers and the farmers, using the Hanyang arsenal. "Why doesn't he? The working people at Shanghai were unarmed, remember? That's where Chiang Kai-shek got a break! That's a pretty touchy subject around here, I know."[79] Rayna reminded Milly that moderates dominated the Wuhan cabinet, that it was Borodin's job to go along with the cabinet. "Yes, Rayna, I do, savvy that . . . I do believe that Borodin is caught on the horns of the ugliest dilemma this side of hell."[80] Prohme was sitting in his leather Morris chair, appearing to sleep. He blurted out, "You hang around the Soviet Consulate and pick up idle gossip and loose talk from the crowd of disgruntled Russians and to you it's all fact!"[81] He knew, better in all probability than Milly, just what the horns of Borodin's dilemma were. Anna Louise Strong in her own way had picked up some inkling of this dilemma: once, when she happened to find herself in the company of Borodin and the general secretary of the Chinese Communist Party, Ch'en Tu-hsiu, Miss Strong remarked, as she liked to do, that because she had been too late for the Revolution in Russia, she had come to China earlier, "in order to be on time." As she related it in *China's Millions,* "Borodin turned with a smile and said: 'Miss Strong is unfortunate in her dates. She came too late for Russia and now she has come very much too early for China.' "[82]

Miss Strong was yet another admirer of Borodin, whom she'd first met in Seattle, in 1908, when he was going by the name of Michael Grusenberg. Then she'd met him again in Chicago, when he and his wife, Fanny, were running their night school for Russian Jewish émigré workers, adults and children, on the near North Side.[83] In Moscow she had come to know them both even better, and then on an earlier visit to China she had visited them in Canton, where she had also made the acquaintance of Madame Sun Yat-sen.[84] She showed up in Hankow as a reporter for the Federated Press, an American labor news outfit. She had made her mark, originally, as a social reform advocate in Seattle. Disenchanted with America's efforts at social reform, she found her spiritual home in the USSR of Lenin and Trotsky. The huge, earnest and rigid determination of the Bolsheviks to impose their social program on Russia through the imposition of planned reform entirely suited the huge, earnest and rigid Miss Strong. "Anna Louise had no patience with individuals," Ilona Ralf Sues wrote of another time, over a decade later, when Miss Strong was yet again a visitor in Hankow, in the home of the "Red" Bishop, Logan Roots. "When she shook her white mane lion-fashion and barked, or when she paced angrily up and down in her room overhead and made the candelabra tinkle in the parlor," Sues wrote, "we all trembled, even the Bishop."[85] Milly Bennett described her as "a dragon the way she consumed people, sights, sounds, experiences." She was "a tremendous woman in height and girth, about five feet, ten inches tall, with the hips of a giantess. Bobbed, silvery, spunglass hair framed a face of clear-cut, if rather commonplace features."[86]

Miss Strong was accustomed to having a place like Hankow all to herself. She had no use for other female American journalists on the scene. From the day of her arrival in Hankow, she presented yet another challenge to Rayna's spirited good nature, which was being assailed by the demands of her job, by those of Borodin, of her husband, of the besotted Vincent Sheean and the pounding headaches, all in the degenerating political carnival, in one-hundred-degree torpor. Now came Miss Strong to muscle in on her relationship with Borodin on the strength of a past friendship. This she managed to do, circumventing the Prohmes whenever she wanted a private séance with Borodin. When she did not get what she wanted, she was capable of throwing a shameless tantrum, complete with tears, which had the effect of terrifying the guilt-ridden spectator into submission.[87]

She found a sympathetic ear in Sheean, who tried to plead her case with the Prohmes. Rayna was outraged. "Rayna gave him book, chapter and verse," Milly wrote. "Anna Louise was a meddler, she was a troublemaker, she had set up an underground of her own in Hankow. She wasn't running guns. She was running gripes, grievances and complaints to Borodin, over Rayna's head. She had been getting away with it, too."[88] Such bickering was a strain on Borodin, who was already suffering from a malarial relapse, and sweating out the defections of Wuhan's supporters to Chiang Kai-shek. He was later heard to declare that China's Revolution had turned into a ladies' tea party.

The fall of Hankow was swift. Wang Ching-wei, head of the Wuhan regime, turned against the workers. The pickets were disarmed. Arrests and executions became daily happenings, and workers, especially Communist Party members, went into hiding. The Chinese Communist Party was now in utter disarray. The Communist International withdrew its support from the leaders of the Chinese party. Stalin already had consigned the CCP to oblivion with a telegram he had sent on the thirty-first of May, in which he'd ordered the Communists to confiscate land in the countryside without touching that of the military officers, to check the overzealous farmers and destroy "the present unreliable generals" and to "organize a revolutionary court with a well-known member of the Kuomintang as its chairman to try the reactionary officers."[89]

When the Central Committee members of the Chinese Communist Party assembled to hear the contents of this directive, according to one official, they didn't know whether to laugh or to cry. Ch'en Tu-hsiu, general secretary of the Chinese Communist Party, later wrote that to follow Stalin's orders would have been like "taking a bath in a toilet."[90] Borodin knew what the boss was up to. He had given the CCP an impossible set of instructions so that when it failed to carry them out he could blame the failure of Russia's China policy on CCP leaders, Ch'en Tu-hsiu in particular, as he soon did.

The Kuomintang Political Council in Wuhan ordered all Communist members of the Kuomintang to resign, and a few days later the Military Council ordered a purge of Communists within the army. "Punishment without leniency" was in store for those who refused to obey the order.[91] Ch'en Tu-hsiu resigned as general secretary of the CCP. "The International," he wrote, "wishes us to carry out our own policy on the one hand and does not allow us to withdraw from the Kuomintang on the other. There is really no way out and I cannot continue with my work."[92]

Borodin's Russian assistants began to slip away from Wuhan at the end of June. Borodin stayed on through July. His wife, Fanny Arbuk, "a bellicose little fat woman" as Milly describes her,[93] had been seized earlier in the year aboard a Russian ship, the *Pamyat Lenina,* in Nanking, by northern troops who had turned her over to Chang Tso-lin, the Manchurian warlord in Peking. Chang had put her in jail, where she'd been keeping herself fit on a vegetarian diet and a regimen of exercise.[94] Borodin could not leave leave for Russia until Fanny was released.

Vincent Sheean noted in his daybook on July 2, "The government here is doomed. It will fall very soon. God knows what will happen to Rayna."[95] He stayed long enough to celebrate the Fourth of July with the Prohmes. They were all in danger. Madame Sun Yat-sen tried to frighten Rayna with stories of the garrote, as Miles Vaughn had done in Peking. She was genuinely afraid for Rayna's safety, and she urged Rayna to seek asylum, with Prohme, at the U.S. consulate. This idea was repugnant to Rayna; earlier, she had protested to the consul, Frank Lockhart, because he had not invited her to seek asylum at the consulate, and Lockhart had replied that he'd assumed she would have rejected such an offer from him. Lockhart had told her, in a voice icy with sarcasm, that next time he'd send her an engraved invitation.[96]

He did not, however, send her one to the Fourth of July lawn party he held at the consulate. Undaunted, Rayna festooned her dining room at the Lutheran Mission Building with red, white and blue crepe paper and held a party of her own. Sheean had borrowed an American flag from Lockhart, and it was Prohme's idea that she should wrap herself in it and play the role of Miss Liberty. She mounted a pedestal on the dining room table under a blazing chandelier. At a signal from Milly Bennett, folding doors between the dining room and the living room were flung open by Huang, the Prohmes's houseboy, and the assembled gathering beheld Rayna, her graceful flag-enveloped figure and her brilliant red hair illuminated by the chandelier, as she broke into "The Star-Spangled Banner," augmented by Milly's contralto.[97]

Sheean departed the next day for Peking, via Shansi Province. He'd received a cablegram from his editors instructing him to "have personal adventures." He wrote, "Even in the desperate anxiety and tension of Hankow that lovely phrase 'have personal adventures' made an instant success. Borodin laughed out loud when I told him about it, and Rayna Prohme—even though she realized what a predicament it put me in —thought the wonderful cablegram should be framed and kept as a monument to American journalism."[98] Rayna saw him off with a smile and a wave as his train pulled out of the station.

Rayna and Prohme, and Milly Bennett, stayed a few weeks longer, to be at the side of Madame Sun Yat-sen. She and Rayna composed a statement repudiating Chiang Kai-shek as the legitimate heir to her late husband's dreams for China. It was at this juncture that Madame Sun declared herself the implacable opponent of her soon-to-be brother-in-law. By marrying into the Soong family, Chiang undoubtedly hoped to add legitimacy to his claim as heir to Dr. Sun. For the Soong family, the most powerful family in Republican China, was inextricably related to Dr. Sun and his cause. Charlie Soong, a Bible salesman who became a millionaire, was a close early supporter of Dr. Sun. Soong, like Dr. Sun, had ties to the U.S., and his children all went to college there and spoke excellent English. This gave them an inside track on Western influence. Not only had Soong's middle daughter, Ching-ling, married Dr. Sun (much to Charlie Soong's displeasure), but his oldest daughter married H. H. K'ung, scion of an important Shantung family. Said to be a descendant of Confucius, Dr. K'ung was educated at Oberlin and was at various times Chiang's finance minister, and front man for his wife's wheeling and dealing. T. V. Soong, Charlie Soong's son, was a graduate of the Harvard Business School who helped Dr. Sun set up the Central Bank of China. Though always envious of Chiang, and often at odds with him, Soong was so useful to Chiang in years to come that he was all but indispensable. Chiang regularly replaced K'ung with Soong in the finance ministry, and vice-versa. Soong was also foreign minister under Chiang, and over time proved to have valuable entrée to Washington circles. Chiang, in June, had sent T. V. Soong to Hankow to beg his sister to join the Nanking regime. Following the Northern Expedition, Soong had flip-flopped between the Hankow regime and Chiang Kai-shek, and finally had opted for Nanking over the Left Kuomintang. But Madame Sun alone had the power to bestow upon Chiang Kai-shek and his Kuomintang the legitimacy of her husband's revolution. She refused to bend an ear to the importunings her younger brother made on behalf of Chiang Kai-shek. She declared that the Kuomintang had become a "tool in the hands of this or that militarist." Her statement was composed in equal parts of hope and despair. "Today the lot of the Chinese peasant is ever more wretched than in those days when Dr. Sun was driven by his great sense of human wrongs into a life of revolution," she wrote. Dr. Sun, she asserted, was a true revolutionary, a leader who gave a voice to agrarian revolution in China. "All these years his purpose was clear. But today we talk of recent foreign influence. Was Sun Yat-sen—the leader who was voicing the agrarian revolution for China when Russia was still under the heel of the Czar— a tool of foreign scheming?"

Dr. Sun's policies were clear, Madame Sun wrote. "If certain leaders of the party do not carry them out consistently then they are not truly Dr. Sun's true followers, and the party is no longer a revolutionary party," she wrote. "Revolution in China is inevitable," she concluded. "There is no despair in my heart for the revolution. My disheartenment is only for the path into which some of those who had been leading the revolution have strayed."[99] Madame Sun dated her statement to coincide with Bastille Day—July 14—to show her solidarity with the ideals of the French Revolution, but it was not released until July 18, the day after she slipped out of town on a steamer bound for Shanghai. Her statement was printed across the entire front page of the last issue of the *People's Tribune* to be published by the Prohmes, who had been forced to resign. The July 18 issue of the *People's Tribune* never saw the light of day. It was confiscated by the government of Wang Ching-wei. Madame Sun Yat-sen's statement would have been altogether lost to history if William Prohme had not managed to telegraph it in its entirety to New York, where it appeared in papers the next day.

Borodin's wife was sprung from jail by a sympathetic judge, and Borodin departed from Hankow on the twenty-seventh of July with an entourage that included Anna Louise Strong and the two sons of Eugene Chen. They made a ceremonious getaway on a train that also transported, on flatcars, the automobiles, trucks and a huge supply of gasoline they needed to get them across the Gobi Desert overland into the Soviet Union.[100] Rayna left Hankow before Borodin. She was followed in early August by Milly Bennett, and finally by Prohme, accompanied by Eugene Chen, who was disguised as his servant.[101]

In Shanghai, Rayna stayed with Madame Sun in her house in the French Concession, on the Rue Molière, which was under heavy surveillance by the Shanghai Municipal Police, the police department of the international settlement, controlled by the British, and agents of Chiang Kai-shek. Prohme checked into a hotel, and made furtive visits to Rayna. "The next two weeks were taken up with comic opera stuff," Rayna noted in her short-lived diary, "Chen coming back and forth under a Japanese name, I going to see him, by circuitous routes, Bill coming down but not being allowed to see me."[102]

The plan was that the Prohmes would together accompany Chen and Madame Sun to Moscow. They were excited about this, and spent their last week together in Shanghai buying warm clothes. Two days before their scheduled departure, however, Chen announced that Prohme would have to stay behind, as a rearguard information dispatcher for the Chen party, to send them reports from China, and to broadcast telegrams Rayna would send, speeches and statements and information about the delegation's progress in the Soviet Union.[103]

This was a crushing blow. Prohme accepted the assignment—and the salary Chen promised to pay him—on the understanding that in two months he would rejoin Rayna in Moscow.

In Peking, Sheean, in characteristic style, took up residence in an aristocratic retreat in the Western Hills. "I lived in a temple in the Hunting Park," he writes, "a temple that had turned into a hotel. My part of the temple was a separate little house in the silver birch trees, isolated from the sights and sounds of the main buildings. There it was possible to spend days without seeing anybody but the silent Chinese who brought my food, and without hearing a sound but the slither of a scorpion across the terrace, or a chatter of a bird in the silver trees."[104]

Once a week Sheean barreled down to Peking in a hired Packard to drink whiskey or champagne in the hot summer night with what he calls "the gay world"[105] of the foreign legations and the Fourth Estate. Randall Gould, the gregarious UP correspondent, introduced Sheean to the skeleton crew of the recently raided Soviet embassy. Sheean particularly enjoyed conversational give-and-take with the Bolsheviks.[106]

During this time, Sheean was out of touch with his friends in Hankow. The collapse of Hankow was reported in the Peking press, but nobody was clear about what had become of Madame Sun, the Prohmes, Borodin and the others. Rumors of a spurious sort appeared in the *North China Daily News* that Rayna and Borodin had run off to the mountain resort of Kuling, where they were seen drinking champagne. Throughout China it was whispered that Madame Sun was on the verge of marrying Eugene Chen, an absurd and even somewhat obscene notion to anyone who knew them both, although a not altogether unimaginable one, since Chen was a widower, with children, who had devoted his life to the cause of Madame Sun's late husband.

Sheean stayed on in Peking through August, drinking with the foreigners, and writing in his rustic retreat in the Western Hills. Vaguely, he expected to meet up with his story again in Moscow. This was the hope with which Rayna had seen him off at the station in Hankow. As his train had pulled away, her last words, as he recalls them, were, "We'll probably meet in Moscow."[107]

Rayna was shocked and excited and despondent. With Milly Bennett, who came to see Rayna in her upstairs room at Madame Sun's house, she was manic. "Rayna was leaping around the room," Milly wrote. "The green silk dressing gown was a pale cloud flying through the air, the brown silk dress was going over her head. She was reaching for a comb."[108] Rayna implored Milly not to write about Hankow and what had happened there until she gave Milly the all-clear signal. She was in turmoil about leaving her companion behind while traveling on to Moscow, but it was an adventure, one with something about it of the forbidden, and she chanted a verse from James Elroy Flecker's "Hassan": "We travel not for trafficking alone/ By hotter winds our fiery hearts are fanned/ For lust of knowing what should not be known/ We take the golden road to Samarkand."[109]

She was just as confused as ever about marriage, and about the man she had dragged across the Pacific Ocean to participate in this Chinese catastrophe, whom she was now abandoning, on the orders of Eugene Chen, to an uncertain future, as she set forth, at 3:30 on the morning of August 22, through unfamiliar parts of Shanghai in a speeding automobile, then out across the black, oily Whangpoo River by sampan to a Russian freighter, bound for Vladivostok.[110]

Rayna missed Prohme, at once. She might not have missed him quite so much so soon if she had not been treated coldly by her Chinese and Russian fellow passengers. She wrote Prohme about how the Russians tried to consign her to a "vile hole," as she put it, between the engine room and the galley, in a section of the ship used by the crew, which she was supposed to share with "another woman."[111] It was the first signal of her true place in the hierarchy of the traveling party. Chen

became seasick at once and from that time forth ceased to be friendly to
Rayna. One member of the traveling party was a Russian Comintern
official who went by the code name of Fang. Fang was especially jealous
of her relationship to Madame Sun, to whom he appeared to be slavishly
devoted. He was, Rayna wrote Prohme, "insultingly rude to me."[112]
Rayna's only ally was Madame Sun, who invited Rayna to sleep on the
couch in her stateroom. This proximity was a mixed blessing. On closer
scrutiny Rayna began to perceive Madame Sun with a critical eye. "I
think she is more confused than anything else," she later confided to
Prohme. "I haven't yet been able to determine what the revolution
really means to her, if it is blind loyalty to her husband, or some active
driving force in herself. If the latter, there will be much to overcome,
an instinctive withdrawal from contacts, an almost pathological distaste
for anything that is not scrupulously clean, both in things and people,
and an impulse to be surrounded always by nice things."[113]

In Vladivostok, the Chen party, which included ten returning Russian advisers, boarded the trans-Siberian Railway Express for the long
journey across Russia. Rayna's sense of disillusion and despair gathered
momentum as the railroad train roared across the wasteland of the
steppes. Two days out of Vladivostok, she wrote in a letter to Prohme,
"Personally, as you can surmise, I am interested but not altogether
happy. I miss terribly the frankness of genuine contacts. God I wish you
were here."[114]

Rayna had no idea what her immediate future would be, although
she continued to entertain hopes for the Revolution. Like everyone else,
she placed a great deal of confidence in the resourcefulness of Borodin,
who at that point was somewhere in Mongolia. There was mention also
by Chen of a conference in Europe, but this was in the vaguest stages
of planning. Rayna wasn't even very clear about her role in the small
band of exiled revolutionaries. Her official title was "correspondent."[115]
She had hoped to bear the more imposing title of "foreign secretary,"
but the Chinese denied her this privilege because it gave too much rank
to a foreigner. It was, she wrote Prohme, one clue to their present
"unhappy situation."[116] On the train, Rayna performed the chores of a
press secretary. She wrote a statement for the delegation to issue on
arrival in Moscow, and composed answers, also, to a long list of questions submitted by *Pravda* correspondents on board.

Once in Moscow, Rayna was excited, but anguished. "Beanie,
darling, darling—I'm in Moscow and under the most amazing conditions," she wrote, "but although the Kremlin spires, which are outside
my windows, are magnificent beyond words, and although the whole
situation is a rare combination of high drama, historical significance and
comic opera as anyone could imagine, I'm aware keenly of only one big

emotion, homesickness for you."[117] She had not expected to feel this way, she told him. She was all one ache inside. "I think I know the main why of it," she wrote, "it's because this is a real experience—and I've grown to feel that the big experiences we should have together."[118]

It was a big experience, but it was also a confusing one. When the train arrived in Moscow on the morning of the sixth of September, the Chinese revolutionaries were met by a herd of cameramen and dignitaries and a reception committee of students from Sun Yat-sen University in Moscow lined up under banners that read DOWN WITH WANG CHING-WEI and COOPERATION BETWEEN THE KUOMINTANG AND THE CP. Karakhan, the ambassador to Peking, who had left China before the embassy was raided by Chang Tso-lin's gendarmerie, was now in Moscow. Karakhan and Maksim Litvinov, the foreign minister of the USSR, were among those who crowded into the railway car to greet Eugene Chen and Madame Sun. When they left in a group, Rayna wrote, "we all oozed through the mass on the platform with cameramen taking pictures from the tops of cars, from fences, the fenders of automobiles and whatnot."[119] Rayna was whisked off to the Hotel Metropole, where the Chens were housed, and which would serve as Chinese Left Kuomintang headquarters in Moscow, but she was writing to Prohme from her room in the Sugar Palace, a rococco mansion built by a nineteenth-century sugar baron, which was now a residence for Foreign Office dignitaries, including both Karakhan and Litvinov. Madame Sun was also lodged in the Sugar Palace. Eugene Chen had sent Rayna over there to keep Madame Sun company (and possibly to get her out of his own rooms).

The Sugar Palace provided Rayna with her one brief moment of luxury. She wrote Prohme of "a movie hallway with a staircase built for kings, doors many inches thick, everything panelled, high magnificent ceilings, mosaic wooden floors, furniture built specially of curly maple, mirrors that reach to the ceiling, many expensive lamps, candlesticks, etc.—of the funny 18th century patterns that are all marble and cupids and gold vines with little cupolas and crowns on top."[120] After the arduous overland journey by train, Rayna was ecstatic about the bathing facilities in her apartment. "*And* the bath! Beanie! It is roman [sic]," she wrote, "no less. You enter it by a panelled door, fit for a ballroom, and find yourself in short panelled hallway, leading to a small luxurious sitting room, deep carpeted with an enormous plate glass window looking out on the Kremlin. *That's* the place where supposedly you lounge after the bath. The bath itself is to the right, curtained off. The tub is marbelled [sic], with shower, built in, the walls are blue and white tile, the washstand is of wood—the same fine-grained, highly polished curly maple with a polished top. It's a bath for loitering. Oh beanie!"[121]

She clung to the expectation of his coming, she wrote Prohme. "Beanie, please start studying immediately. Get a teacher. You know I've got one date on my calendar—marked. The 6th of October which is the day I discuss with Chen about your coming. I put it at that because of the time for letters (altho' it'll probably be done by wires). Oh, beanie, beanie, it'll be different when you're here. I miss you so. I feel so damned little, alone and lost. I suppose we're making history—but I find it rather casual. I'm more thrilled by the thought that the city will be beautiful when you're here than by the rather pompous, rather bored maneuverings that are going on." [122]

They were in with a slippery crew. The Chinese, it turned out, had cut their losses in Shanghai. Chen had no intention of paying overdue Left Kuomintang news service bills in Shanghai. Prohme was left holding the bag. Chen had no intention, either, of keeping the Prohmes on salary. This became starkly clear long before the sixth of October. Chen was himself dependent financially on Russian support. There wasn't much he could do once Fang, Borodin's stand-in, told him to cut the superfluous Americans out of the budget. There was nothing Madame Sun could do, either. She was helpless. In Shanghai, William Prohme's best hope was that TASS might hire him as a roving correspondent. There was inconclusive talk about this that gave Rayna hope. [123] Meanwhile, there was also Borodin. Where *was* Borodin? "The fact of Bee's non-arrival," Rayna wrote, "—they seem not to know when he will come and the earlier word received on the train seems cock-eyed— makes things still more uncertain." [124]

Now that the Chinese were in Moscow, they began to feel the Moscow chill. Plans failed to progress as expected. Madame Sun was unhappy, and yet when Rayna tried to find out what was wrong, she, and Chen, were evasive. "They are seeing important people," Rayna wrote, "but not under the smooth circumstances they expected, I gather." The Chinese, in Shanghai, had fully expected the Russians to finance a government in exile. "And it becomes apparent—very much so—that the fund question is not so simple a one as Shanghai gestures would have led one to believe. What it will mean for us I do not know," Rayna wrote, "but am prepared for the worst." [125]

Moscow became a disturbing dream for Rayna. She now had just enough money to stay afloat through Christmas on a frugal budget. But she could no longer stay at the Sugar Palace. Madame Sun and the Russians had made it clear, in broad hints, that they wanted her to find lodging elsewhere. She was no longer employed by the Chinese, and besides, Madame Sun was about to depart with Eugene Chen on a trip to the Caucasus. Rayna wrote Prohme that she was glad, finally, when she left what she called the grand palace. "The strain of it was pretty awful," she wrote. "I was never accepted there as a legitimate member of the group from China, but as a sort of supermenial, something that the cat dragged in."[126] She hated that feeling, and could not remember ever having been quite so miserable as she was when she was living there, she wrote Prohme.

Her subsequent descent into homelessness was swift, the landing rough. It was almost impossible to find a decent place to live in Moscow in the fall of 1927. Luckily, Vincent Sheean had shown up in Moscow. Sheean had passed the hot summer nights in Peking with a Russian official named Kantorovich at the Soviet embassy. He now introduced Rayna to Mrs. Kantorovich, who invited her to share the single room where she was living with her baby and the baby's nurse. This was a stopgap solution to Rayna's problem. It was not really possible for Rayna to rent a hotel room without using up at least half of her savings. "I think with longing of quiet places and purposeless lives," she wrote Prohme.[127] Rayna soon left Mrs. Kantorovich, only to find herself sharing another single room with yet another mother, baby and nurse. "The room problem is simply terrible," Rayna wrote Prohme in early October. "They are the most awful, foul holes anyway—and there are almost none."[128] She had moved yet again, this time to the room occupied by the Veprentzevs, a couple she had known in Hankow. Veprentzev went to stay temporarily with his sister so that Rayna could move in with his wife.

Sheean came and went, introducing a note of surreal gaiety to the nightmare. While Rayna was feeling "lost, little, miserable, helpless,"[129] Sheean had turned up at the Hotel Metropole looking for Eugene Chen.[130] Calling Chen on the house phone, he got Rayna on the line instead. Rayna descended to the lobby to find him quite well lubricated with alcohol. She wrote Prohme, "He insisted upon taking me over to the opera where he fell asleep promptly and we stayed only fifteen minutes. If he had been awake, he would have joined the chorus; I was glad to get out."[131]

This was a week Sheean made famous in *Personal History,* in which he writes of his "continuous conversation with Rayna Prohme,"[132] but it was a week during which, Rayna wrote Prohme, "I've fought depression in the most idiotic way, by going on bats with Jimmie Sheean."[133] She couldn't actually remember very clearly how she and Sheean had spent their time together. "What we have done, I could scarcely relate," she wrote. "I don't drink, of course, except in my usual manner, but there seems to have been a bewildering succession of people and taxicabs and one thing and another, so jumbled that I might well have been drunk."[134] She liked Sheean, but he was totally disorganizing. "In Hankow it was all right. There was the rigidity of the job," she wrote Prohme. "Here, where things *can* be put off, they *are* put off, when Jimmie is around. He is positively contagious, of course. The past few days have been panoramic."[135]

Sheean, in *Personal History,* betrays no awareness of Rayna's true state. He seems to have had no idea that she was fighting a black depression, was trying to find some way to hang on in Moscow. Perhaps this was the effect of his own self-involvement. "Jimmie is a blithe companion, but not really concerned about you (his companion); only interested, gay, having a good time," Rayna wrote Prohme.[136] She was deeply concerned, also, about Prohme. They were both "high and dry" as she put it.[137] She hoped that either TASS or the Comintern would come up with a job for Prohme. Meanwhile, she was contemplating a trip to Berlin, so that her friend from Berkeley, Helen Freeland, could visit her there. "I feel the need of talking it all out with someone," she wrote Prohme, "and the only familiar face in town is Jimmie's with whom, of course, one doesn't talk very much."[138] Then Sheean was gone, off to Europe and London to find an assignment that would send him back to Moscow, and to Rayna.

Rayna was apprehensive about the coming of cold weather. Sheean had promised to buy her some woolens in Europe, and she had advanced him money on loan, on the understanding that he would send her what she needed. It got colder even sooner than she'd been led to expect. Sheean had agreed to send her the warm garments via the first person he met who was headed for Moscow—but forgot. "A thoroughly irresponsible person, thoughtless," she wrote Prohme. Still, she told Prohme not to worry. "I have bought a new coat, by the way very ugly—for 110 roubles and am going to buy big Russian felt boots. . . . The coat is made out of material that is as rough as an army blanket, and the same colour—I think it is an army banket, really."[139] The new coat was all very well—it was thickly padded with fake seal collar and cuffs—but what Rayna yearned for were hot baths, which were all but unavailable, and never private; a hot fireplace; and natural, honest conversation. Instead, she was shunted from one cramped room to another—by mid-October she was sharing a room with a voluble young Russian woman with whom she communicated in German—and meeting occasionally with Borodin.

Borodin finally arrived, by train, accompanied by Jack Chen. Others in his caravan, including Anna Louise Strong, were soon to follow. Rayna now referred to Borodin as "the Chief." He brought some hope of work. Rayna wrote Prohme, "If the Chief can fix it up, I can't think of anything that would argue against staying, except the beastly separation, and although it is pleasant to be adrift together, it is more expensive."[140]

The Chief had given her the task of writing a report on the 1925–1927 Revolution—a writing project that expanded to cover Borodin's four years in China, and then grew to include a history of the entire movement in China back to the nineteenth century, about which Rayna knew nothing, although she gamely took on the assignment. By day, she worked on her project, or waited to see Borodin, who kept putting her off. "Postponement follows postponement," she wrote Prohme.[141] And now, in Moscow, she had to contend with the "intrusive Anna Louise," who once again muscled in on her meetings with Borodin. "She ferrets out tasks for herself and is amazingly successful at browbeating people, even the Chief, into giving her stuff."[142] Anna Louise, she wrote, "is constantly hovering about trying to get a corner on all work connected with China. Somehow or other," Rayna wrote, "she makes all contacts with B. or anyone else seem a cheap affair, because she fawns and maneuvers so for them."[143]

Rayna had begun to notice in September that her mind sometimes didn't function very well. She attributed her state to the "deep hurt" inflicted by Eugene Chen. "I feel adrift," she wrote Prohme at the time. "A strange dullness has taken hold of me; I can't rouse myself to anything; my mind wanders about; I think I'm not quite cerebrating at times."[144] She suffered a "confusion of mind," as she put it in a letter to Prohme, during Sheean's whirlwind week, when she was still living in the Sugar Palace. "Since then, this sort of thing has happened every once in a while," she wrote Prohme. "I think my mind, all by its cute little self, puts itself in a vacuum," she wrote,[145] in order to escape the disappointments and uncertainties she had suffered. Violent headaches took up the attack toward the end of October. On October 26 she wrote Prohme: "Beanie Darling: For days now I've been nearly crazy with the same sort of neuralgic headache that laid me low in Hankow. It came on me Monday—this is Thursday—and I've been almost mad since. Incessant pound, pound, pound."[146] Finally, Rayna got her hands on a painkiller through Borodin, who sent her to a doctor he knew.

Madame Sun and Eugene Chen returned, separately, and several days apart, from the Caucasus. Rayna saw Chen at the Metropole, the day she wrote Prohme the account of her headache. "C nodded vaguely as if I were someone in his acquaintance and that was about all. And to tell the truth, I'm too cynical about it now to mind very much," she wrote Prohme. "I remember one evening vividly in Peking, just before he left for the South. I was getting out the paper in that first office—the house Ray Marshall used to live in (did you ever see it, I wonder). EC had come in and we had chatted, about my probably joining him later, etc., etc. There was sort of a comradeship, glow about which warmed me greatly. And as he left the room, he turned around in quiet but dramatic manner and said, 'The Kuomintang never forgets.' I remembered that little bit of acting today when I met him in the hotel corridor in Moscow, where he has brought me and washed his hands of me."[147]

Four days later, the headache was almost all gone. She wrote Prohme from 7 Bolchia Dmetrovka that she was "simply played out," so groggy from her headache and the dope she took to relieve it, and so exhausted by her five sleepless nights, that she'd passed out in the anteroom of Borodin's box during a production of Bizet's *Carmen,* and had gone home after the second act.[148]

Moscow had begun to prepare for the huge Tenth Anniversary celebration of the Bolshevik Revolution. Besides the friends and acquaintances who had already arrived in Moscow for the celebration, Louis Fischer, William Henry Chamberlin, Scott Nearing, Kenneth Durant and Walter Duranty, to name but some, others were on the way— thanks in part to Vincent Sheean, who, Rayna wrote Prohme, "seems to be touring Europe, inviting people at every booze party he attends— and he seems to have an international genius for finding them—and being successfully persuasive."[149] Walter Duranty, the Moscow correspondent of the *New York Times,* showed Rayna a letter Sheean had written to him, describing his efforts. "He is trying to get Sinclair Lewis to come; it seems to depend upon a passport visa for one Dorothy Thompson, for whom Jimmy writes in his usual gossipy manner, there will be a speedy divorce in the Lewis household."[150] Rayna wrote Prohme that her mood was a combination of doggedness and despair. She was not, she wrote, inclined to join the celebration. "I'm going to detach myself from the whirl, even if I'm invited in, which is not at all sure."[151] She was thinking about spending the next six months studying, and in the meantime she was trying to help Prohme from afar, with suggestions of how to build on their experiences in China by writing a book on "movements" elsewhere—in Mexico or South America—so that they would not have to start life all over again. For, as she wrote Prohme, "It is the scrapping of the only activity I've ever really been interested in that appals [sic] me."[152]

Rayna made a great story for Vincent Sheean. His relationship with Rayna, beginning in China, and concluding in Russia, was the centerpiece of *Personal History,* which, when it was published in 1934, was a great popular success, the kind of book that made college students like the young Harrison Salisbury, who at the time it was published was an undergraduate at the University of Minnesota, want to become professional foreign correspondents.[153] Sheean's portrait of Rayna gave a glamorous face to the concept of idealism on behalf of the downtrodden of the world at a time when Americans were plunged in a dark time of depression. Sheean immortalized Rayna as the conscience of revolution. His account of their passionate friendship reads like myth.[154]

And it is myth. The Rayna he rediscovers in the lobby of the Hotel Metropole is not the distraught, confused, lost person she reveals herself to be in her letters to Prohme, but a burning revolutionary who has reached her own personal "revolutionary center." According to Sheean, he was all set to rejoin Rayna as a revolutionary when he left her in Moscow to rush off to England to scrape up some money to get him through the long Russian winter. In England, however, he claims to have been brought back to his senses in the course of conversations with various friends and acquaintances, Vita Sackville-West and her cousin Eddie, scion of Knole House, in Kent, among them.[155] When he pulled into Moscow station on the seventh of November, the opening day of the great celebration, he had come back determined to save Rayna from her fate, "to get her away from her own essential centre—to recall her, by whatever means, to the half world in which I wanted to keep on living."[156] (For Sheean, to exalt Rayna involved debasing his own, bourgeois, inclinations.)

Rayna met him at the station—"Rayna's fiery hair was the first thing I saw on the platform"[157]—and took him to their digs. He relates that he took up residence at 7 Bolchia Dmetrovka in his bedroom-cum-sitting room next door to Rayna's "microscopic" room. From that day forth, Sheean writes, he "fought tooth and nail" to keep Rayna from joining the Comintern. "For six days and nights the struggle continued with hardly a respite," he writes. "Her room was on the other side of my sitting room, in the adjoining apartment, and when either of us thought of a new argument we kicked on the wall; in two minutes— the time required to take down the innumerable barricades of iron, wood and steel put up by my timorous landlady—we had met and started all over again."[158] Neither of them, Sheean writes, got much sleep. Sometimes they talked until four or five o'clock in the morning. He takes note of her fragility. "She had been having severe headaches for months, and they had lately grown more frequent; aspirin and phenecetin [sic] did not help them; sometimes in the midst of the argument a dazed stare would come into her eyes and she would say: 'Wait a minute. I must be quiet for a minute; it's the headache again.' "[159] Sheean wondered how, with such limited resources, she proposed to endure the rigors of the revolutionary life. "This argument had no effect. She would laugh and say: 'In or out of a revolution, I've got to die sometime, and what does it matter?' "[160]

According to Sheean, Rayna had decided to enter the Lenin Institute to be trained as a revolutionary, so that she could thenceforth serve in the Comintern. "No decision in life could be more final," Sheean writes. "The vows of a nun, the oaths of matrimony, the resolutions of a soldier giving battle, had not the irrevocable character of this decision. Rayna was not taking it lightly; she had had four years of intimate acquaintance with revolutionary work and knew what she was doing. Nothing I could bring up about the nature of the work or its effects made the slightest difference to her, for I found that she had considered it all before."[161]

God knows what to make of all this. It was a dark time. It was the last furious blaze of the Bolshevik bonfire in the cold nightfall of Stalin's terror. Rayna, Sheean and the Chinese fugitives had fled the death of one revolution at the hands of Stalin to witness the demise of the great one. Trotsky was rumored to have been arrested; Rayna had seen him try to address a crowd from a window near Theater Square the day of Sheean's arrival, and watched as he had been shouted down. Rumors flew through the pandemonium of the celebrating city: Kamenev exiled, Trotsky arrested, Dr. Adolph Joffe dead of self-inflicted gunshot wounds (true), the Comintern reorganized, the Soviet Congress suspended. Sheean confesses in *Personal History* submitting to the prevailing mood of madness. "In the frame of mind thus set up, dark with apprehension, gloomy with fear, shaken unbearably by the desire to save a human life of the first importance, my imagination seized upon all the sinister rumours afloat in Moscow and worked them into the growing horror with which I regarded the central problem."[162] Sheean also confesses to a certain abandon. "As the week wore on I took refuge more and more in vodka, for it seemed to me," he writes, "only a question of days before a violent crash of some kind must bring this tension to an end, and whatever the end might be, it could not be contemplated clearly and steadily."[163] The end Sheean foresaw, or so he says, "was the definitive entrance of Rayna into the Communist Party and the Lenin Institute, and to this event—which all of my struggles could not seem to postpone—I gave the name, during those days, of 'the end of Rayna Prohme.' "[164]

Whether or not Rayna really planned to enter the Lenin Institute and join the Communist Party is impossible to verify. We have only Sheean's account, which is not altogether trustworthy. Rayna never mentioned anything of the sort in her letters to Prohme. She wrote her last long letter to him on the ninth of November. "My mind is queer, Beanie, sometimes I think not actually quite right," she wrote. "Do you suppose I could be getting dimentia precox [sic] or some other mental disease? Else why should I have these maddening lapses of memory?"[165] She wrote, also, that she was reading up on the Taiping Rebellion, for Borodin. "I wonder about you just about a third of the day," she wrote. "What are you doing in Manila? If I don't hear in a day or two, I shall wire again. I find it hard to go on this way, uncertain, not knowing, without plans or reason."[166] This, somehow, does not sound like the determined, if fragile, revolutionary of whom Sheean writes. If anything, Rayna was dispirited. Borodin had told her that she was "in desperate need of background," and, she wrote Prohme, "I must study, but seem very out of the rut of it." She felt old, on the downgrade. "You will think that foolish of me, but really, beanie, I am not as young as I once was, in looks, brain, spirit, anything."[167]

She planned to move, Rayna wrote Prohme, into a hotel. "I simply cannot stand rooming houses any longer. The problem of getting a bath, of food, of community rooms of every kind, of having a roommate around and whole rafts of people in the rooms next door rather staggers me. I'm worn out. I must have a room—and a quiet one—all alone. I can't stand it otherwise."[168] Surely this was not written by someone on the verge of entering the Lenin Institute, as Sheean insists she was. Rayna wrote, also, in her last letter to Prohme, about Sheean. He reminded her more and more of Raph—Samson Raphaelson—her first husband, now a Broadway playwright. "Sheean," she wrote, "canters about in typically Raph manner. I see him a lot, but never seriously. He is a philanderer, but not with me. He has been in London where he has had a heavy flirtation about which he does not hesitate to talk."[169] He was kind, she wrote, but, unlike Raph, he was also hard. "He knows what he wants and is very sure he will get it." She found it difficult, she wrote, not to think of the two men together. "They are so much alike in so many ways. I can't decide which has the better mind. Sheean's is ever so much better furnished, but it hasn't the capacity for depths of feeling—which is Jewish, I suppose. He is sophisticated beyond words. I can't imagine him weeping at anything."[170] But this was silly talk, she wrote. She was writing lickety-split, she told Prohme, typing whatever came into her head. She was in a hurry because she was about to go out to dinner. She had not, after all, managed to detach herself from the whirl. "Duranty is having a party—only a few people, I understand," she wrote, "but I've put on the Paris suit and the top of the Japanese pyjamas we bought in Shanghai—it makes a stunning blouse—and my goldstone beads and have done interesting things with rouge. If you were here, you would certainly kiss me and I should have to stop writing. But if you were here, I wouldn't have to write my kisses on the typewriter, so there wouldn't be anything to interrupt."[171] She had an afterthought, about Jack Chen. Jack Chen was the younger of Eugene Chen's two sons, both of whom had known Rayna in Hankow. She had seen Jack in Moscow. She wanted to tell Prohme how fond she was of Jack. He was the nicest man in town, she wrote Prohme. "He has a graciousness I have seen in few human beings and it is possible to talk to him as to a very young person but without bending down to him. I say again—I wish he were my son. But he isn't. No one is." It was time to go. "Beanie, I have to quit and beat it," she wrote. "I send you a long row of kisses, to be taken before and after dinner. My love, Rayna."[172]

Nobody seems to have realized how very sick indeed Rayna Prohme was, least of all Vincent Sheean. Had he known, perhaps he would not have kept her awake all night, five nights in a row, with his ravings. On night number six, when he'd failed to swerve her from her revolutionary path, Sheean tells us that he persuaded Rayna to let him take her out to dinner at the Bolshaya Moscovskaya, for a final Saturday night fling. On the following Monday, he tells us, it was Rayna's intention to join the Lenin Institute. Sheean planned to leave Moscow within a few days. For their last outing, Rayna, he tells us, agreed to wear, at Sheean's request, a gold dress from China given to her by Madame Sun, and an amber necklace—the goldstone necklace—that was a gift from Prohme.[173]

That morning Rayna fainted in reporter Dorothy Thompson's room at the Grand Hotel.[174] This disturbing little episode was quickly dismissed by everyone present, including Rayna. "Silly of me to faint like that," she told Sheean, "but I do feel better now than I have for days."[175] She looked grand, Sheean writes. "She was merely a thin girl, with no particular stature or figure or conventional beauty, but her appearance was at all times lighted up by her expressive eyes and the glory of her hair. The red-brown gold of her short curls gave her the look of a lighted candle when she wore the gold dress from China."[176]

That night, Sheean got quite drunk. "The dinner, the gold dress, the certainty of the decision, the gloom of Moscow, the Napareuli wine and vodka, all together had operated to destroy my common sense that night," he writes. Dorothy Thompson came over to their table and Sheean announced to her, "It's the end of Rayna Prohme. No more Rayna. Finished. Revolutionary Instrument Number 257,849." Then he turned and started pounding Rayna's shoulders, he tells us, chanting, "The end of Rayna Prohme. The end of Rayna Prohme."[177]

After dinner Sheean and Rayna went to the Congress of Friends of the Soviet Union to watch the ceremonial decoration of foreign Bolsheviks in the old Hall of the Nobility. This immense marble palace thronged with Communists and Communist sympathizers from all over the world. Great red banners proclaimed in letters of gold, WORK-ERS OF THE WORLD, UNITE! From an upstairs gallery, Sheean and Rayna watched Kliment Voroshilov, head of the Red Army, pin a decoration on the Hungarian revolutionary Béla Kun. "As the roars of the crowd came up to us," Sheean writes, "crashing in successive, irregular waves like thunder, she looked up at me, and I could see that her eyes were brilliant with tears."[178] Sheean tells us he felt just then insanely jealous of the intensity of Rayna's emotions. It had been Rayna's idea to visit the congress. She was soon taken over by her Communist friends, Manabendra Nath Roy and the Chinese delegates to the celebration of the Tenth Anniversary. Sheean felt excluded. He returned alone to the Bolshaya Moscovskaya, where he drank "all the vodka I could contain," and then, at four o'clock in the morning, retired to his rooms.[179]

The next day, which was Sunday, the thirteenth of November, Rayna collapsed at the Hotel de l'Europe while visiting with members of the Chinese delegation. Sheean learned of this ominous development from a friend of Rayna's from Peking, Chang Ke, and Anna Louise Strong, when he encountered them on the steps of the Metropole. Together they went to the Hotel de l'Europe, where, in a small upstairs room, they found Rayna lying unconscious on a couch. Sheean carried Rayna out into the street and back to Miss Strong's room on the top floor of the Metropole.[180]

Rayna was now the captive of her nemesis. In Miss Strong's room, she was treated, ineptly, by a neighborhood doctor and his assistant. They gave her ether, which made her sick and delirious.[181] Sheean and Miss Strong both wanted to get Rayna to a hospital, but to do this they needed the help of Borodin and his wife, who could not be found.[182] Rayna rallied. The snow came in the night, and the next day was bitterly cold. Sheean, with the help of the young Bruce Hopper,[183] contacted a German physician attached to the German embassy, named Dr. Linck, who agreed to see Rayna. Dr. Linck was very grave, but Rayna cheered him up. She was now in a room of her own, where she received a stream of visitors, including Chang Ke, Louis Fischer, Scott Nearing and Madame Sun, from whom she had until recently been somewhat estranged, it seems, because Rayna had concealed from her a *New York Times* report concerning the rumor that Madame Sun had married Eugene Chen and that their trip to the Caucasus was a wedding present from the Soviet state.[184] Rayna had kept this story from Madame Sun at the urging of Eugene Chen. Borodin paid Rayna two visits, to discuss her report. "Dr. Linck had forbidden political discussion of any kind in Rayna's room," Sheean writes in his memoir, "and had made her promise that she would obey his orders."[185] This brought forth

Rayna's laughter, Sheean writes. " 'Will you tell me,' she said, poking at her pillows, 'what on earth anybody'd ever talk about in Moscow if political discussion was forbidden? What do you suppose we can talk about? I can't remember any other subjects!' "[186] The week passed almost gaily, Sheean tells us. They gossiped about Communist artists and intellectuals, chatted about Dreiser's latest novel, and Eisenstein's new film. Rayna repeated to Sheean Eugene Chen's parting words to her two years earlier in Peking—"The Kuomintang never forgets!"—and they both fell into helpless laughter.[187]

Then Rayna's spirits flickered. She lay in her darkened room, certain that she was losing her mind at last. Sheean spent most of that day —a Saturday—by her bedside. Strong was constantly in and out. "For God's sake get Anna Louise out and keep her out," Rayna implored Sheean. "I cannot bear having her in the room."[188] The next day, on Sunday, Sheean writes that he sat at Rayna's bedside "hour after hour in the dark, silent room, and blackness pressed down and in upon us."[189] She made Sheean promise not to tell anyone about her illness. Then she agreed that when she awoke, they would together compose a telegram to send to Samson Raphaelson in New York. "I never heard her speak again," Sheean writes.[190] In the evening, after his visit, Dr. Linck ordered a full-time nurse to attend Rayna. Her friends the Veprentzevs, Sonya and Vep, also maintained a vigil in her room. Veprentzev went to her side during the night. "I'm cold, Vep," Rayna told him. "I'm dying."[191]

Vincent Sheean was present, or nearby, throughout the ordeal. "I was dazed with horror and felt nothing," he writes. "I came and went; walked in the Red Square; went to the Bolshaya Moskovskaya and drank vodka; returned to the Metropol from time to time to speak to Sonya."[192] Nothing could be done. Rayna was dying of encephalitis.[193] She had been seriously ill for a long time. Sheean paid her a final visit, but she was unconscious by then, and at three or four in the morning he returned to the room he had taken at a nearby hotel. He was awakened at seven o'clock by the ringing of his telephone. It was Anna Louise Strong. "You'd better come," she said. "Rayna is dead."[194]

Sheean, Anna Louise Strong and Borodin's secretary, Voloshin, made the funeral arrangements. The funeral took place on Thanksgiving Day, Thursday, November 27, which happened also to be the birthday of Anna Louise Strong. None of those closest to Rayna's heart could be there. William Prohme, wild with grief, was stuck in Manila. Samson Raphaelson was in New York. Helen Freeland was in Zurich. Borodin did not attend. He explained to Sheean that he never went to funerals, on principle. In truth, he had been advised by the party to keep his distance from the Hankow refugees.[195]

The funeral procession was made up of about one hundred people, who went on foot from the University Clinic, where an autopsy had been performed, to the Moscow Crematorium. It was a distance of three or four miles, and the march lasted for two hours. Darkness fell as the mourners proceeded across the snow-covered city. The casket, draped with a red flag, was drawn on an open catafalque by six horses. A brass military band preceded the hearse playing, out of tune, alternately, the "Revolutionary Funeral March" and the "Funeral March of Chopin." The mourners followed behind.[196] "There were delegations of Chinese, Russian and American Communists, many of whom had never known Rayna," Sheean wrote.[197] Madame Sun Yat-sen chose to make the long walk through the cold and dreary winter streets on foot, although she was followed at a discreet distance by the car that the Soviet government had provided for her use in Moscow. She was bitterly cold, and shivered in her worn, cloth coat, but she was never one to pull rank. She had come to say farewell to Rayna, who had been the first of what would become a number of youthful American idealists to serve her public relations needs, and those of the United Front, in the years to come. Her devotion to Rayna was evident in the expression of grief she wore on her slender face, and in her solitude.

As the cortege drew near the crematorium beneath the towering walls of the Donskoia Monastery a carillon rang out for the five o'clock service. The crematorium itself, just outside the city, was a spare modern building, strictly without religious iconography. The main hall was brightly lit, and here, on a raised platform rising from the center of the floor, the bier was placed.[198] Upon it had been heaped masses of bright gold, red and brown flowers, to match all Rayna's own colors.[199]

There were four addresses. Anna Louise Strong declared that "we of America can well be glad that we still produce some pioneers who stand at the forefront of earth's battles; that, having given John Reed to the Russian Revolution, we gave Rayna Prohme to China."[200] Then Chang Ke, Rayna's friend from Peking, quoted Li Ta-chao, co-founder of the Chinese Communist Party, who had said of Rayna, "look at the good example of Rayna Prohme. See how devoted she is to our cause. She worked for us here for a considerable time, but never once did she express one word of complaint, even under all sorts of difficulties, which we had to face at that time."[201] A member of the American labor delegation named Harvey O'Connor, and Sung Fa, head of the Hupei Province Federation of Labor in the Wuhan government and a former waterfront laborer from Hankow, also spoke.

The speeches were delivered in Chinese, Russian and English. They were all speeches typical of any revolutionary gathering, impersonal and filled with rhetoric that in no way evoked the spirit of Rayna Prohme. When a signal was given, someone flicked a switch. The bier upon which Rayna's casket rested was slowly lowered into a bright red furnace, along with Rayna's brilliant tresses, the bright flowers and the red flag of the Bolshevik Revolution.[202]

Prophet
in a
Foreign Land

*W*HEN HAROLD ISAACS set off up the Yangtze River with an Englishman from South Africa named Frank Glass, he had no idea that one day soon he would be the man to unmask Stalin as the chief murderer of the Chinese Revolution. In June 1931, Isaacs was a young man of no decided political conviction. He was not without conviction. He was a great admirer of Norman Thomas, for instance. In 1929, at the age of nineteen, when he was fresh out of Columbia University, Isaacs had covered the New York mayoral campaign of Thomas for the *New York Times*.[1] At Columbia, Isaacs had made a study of imperialism in twentieth-century China. He had studied the writings of Parker Moon, Thomas Millard and Nathaniel Peffer, all of whom in their day were critics of colonial power and imperial aggression. These writers all had a profound effect on Isaacs,[2] a child of the Upper West Side of Manhattan, the son of an affluent real estate baron of Lithuanian Jewish descent.

Even at this early stage of Isaacs's life, one thing was clear: he was a born reporter. "When he was eleven he had an appendectomy and the next day he wrote an account of it on the inside of the top of a box of chocolates someone had given him as a get-well present," Viola, his wife of many years, once told me.[3] His Bar Mitzvah present was a three-bank portable Corona typewriter with two shifts, one for figures and one for caps, which served him as a high school journalist, an apprentice on the *New York Times* and out in the great world beyond as a freelance reporter.

Isaacs set sail for the Far East in 1930 with certain very strongly held attitudes.[4] He enjoyed the sun and the fresh air. He liked to drink Scotch. He was passionately in love with one Viola Robinson, also of the Upper West Side. Viola had attended Barnard College. Isaacs had courted her in his gentlemanly, if unorthodox, way. He had once arranged for someone else to escort her to a Columbia University dance, and had then made sure that he himself took her home. He did this in order to avoid making a formal arrangement with Viola. "The problem was dating,"[5] the future Mrs. Isaacs recalled many years later. They had become engaged to each other before his departure. He wrote letters of passionate intensity to his fiancée throughout their separation, and we know from these letters that Isaacs was a sensualist with a taste for adventure and excitement. "He was the kind of guy you kept by letting go," his fiancée later observed.[6]

He was not a hedonist, however. His *Wanderschaft* was a quest for meaning. He was not simply embarked on a journey to find *himself,* either. Isaacs was a man of unusual self-assurance for his age; he had few insecurities of a personal kind; he was not tormented by an identity crisis. He hoped to find in his travels more than an answer to some strictly personal dilemma. He was in search of an absolute moral task that would give meaning and purpose to his life. He was a moralist in search of an answer to the social and moral disillusion of the time.

Not surprisingly, when he got to Shanghai, Isaacs found a society deeply in need of the kind of direction he wanted somehow to signify himself. First, however, he had to find his feet in China. Work was no problem. He immediately found employment on a newpaper, the *Shanghai Post.* When that job proved to be unsatisfactory, he found another one. At the *China Press* he worked for Hollington Tong, a graduate of the Columbia University School of Journalism who later became, in Chungking, Chiang Kai-shek's Vice-Minister of Communications.[7] Isaacs was sick at heart in Shanghai, however. He was a loner. He made a few friends, but he felt isolated, in a dank city that was in the grip of Chiang Kai-shek's terror. He longed for Viola Robinson. In his letters home he indicated that he might leave China for the Philippines, look elsewhere for work, although he was, briefly, excited by his proximity to headline events at the *China Press,* where he was a writer and editor.[8]

The *China Press,* however, was owned by the Kuomintang. Hollington Tong showed no inclination to take on his masters, especially not Chiang Kai-shek, whom Isaacs and others liked to call "The Ningpo Napoleon."[9] Hollington Tong was "one of Chiang's most faithful, tense, timid, and voluble minions," as Isaacs later recalled.[10] He expressed his dissatisfaction with this servitude by writing stories that could only enrage the regime in Nanking, where Chiang had established his capital in 1927. Then, in swift succession, Isaacs met Ch'en Han-sheng, Agnes Smedley and Frank Glass; he quit his job, and he embarked on his Yangtze adventure.

Agnes Smedley saw them off. This was entirely appropriate. She had introduced Isaacs to Glass, and was the catalyst in their friendship. It was a role she took very seriously. Agnes Smedley was apt to become instantly and dramatically a part of the life of any person in whom she took an interest. Mao Tun, a Chinese novelist, wrote about Agnes Smedley, "knowing her was as if I had seen a comet shooting loftily and leisurely across the sky and then suddenly it disappeared."[11] She was a comet in the lives of many people in China and elsewhere, and when she disappeared, her vanishing was as dramatic as her original appearance.

Here it might be useful to divert the reader's attention with an introduction to the amazing Miss Smedley, whose head the author Emily Hahn has likened to that of a Roman Emperor. For Smedley, too, was a great American presence in the Chinese Revolution throughout the 1930s, and she intersected with Harold Isaacs at a time when she could, and did, influence the course of his life.

When Isaacs met Smedley, she had been in China for over three years. She was by then famous to American and European readers as the author of *Daughter of Earth,* an autobiographical novel in which she described her life as an impoverished alcoholic mineworker's daughter from Colorado who defied fate, got herself educated, fought male supremacy on all fronts, made her way to New York, became a journalist and joined the Indian Communist Independence Movement. Her route was ever embattled. She had written her book in Europe, in the course of psychoanalysis, following an ill-starred relationship with the eminent Indian scientist Virendranath Chattopadhyaya, who was the leading Indian Communist of his day, living in exile in Berlin.[12]

After the successful completion of *Daughter of Earth,* Smedley set out for China as a correspondent for the *Frankfurter Zeitung.* She made her way to Peking through Manchuria, and from Peking she went to Nanking, and Shanghai.[13] There, in Shanghai, Smedley found everything she needed to make her life worthwhile. If like Agnes Smedley you were a creature of torment in search of gratification you could have found no better place to be in 1930. In Shanghai, even someone as seditious as Smedley was believed to be could claim extraterritorial privilege, attracting the attentions of the Chinese police and British intelligence, not to mention the die-hard right-wing British press. Smedley was at home in Shanghai: illness-prone, paranoid, tempestuous and willfully radical, she could operate in that climate of sub-rosa intrigue with a certain robustiousness not elsewhere permissible.

There was a fragile branch of the Communist International in Shanghai in those days, for which the well-known social scientist Ch'en Han-sheng, author of *Landlord and Peasant in China,* was an operative.[14] Ch'en and Smedley became friends, and in the fall of 1929, Ch'en took Smedley on a tour for two weeks of the region around Wusih, so that she could study for herself the disparity of conditions that existed in a comparatively wealthy area of China between landlords and their destitute tenants.[15] Smedley was not, according to her biographers the MacKinnons, a Comintern agent herself. "She shared the anti-

imperialist goals of the Comintern and consciously cultivated friendships with leftists like the Eislers and the Ewarts [German Communists
in Shanghai], whom she undoubtedly knew were Comintern representatives, but a Comintern or Communist Party member she was not."[16]
Smedley was a spiritual Communist. "She sees the world in what I can
only describe as folklore terms—capitalist consuls, police and other
officials are all agents of the devil; Soviet generals, instead of being
militarists, are servants of the Kingdom of God." So wrote Owen Lattimore, who met Smedley on a trans-Pacific liner in 1934.[17] She was a
passionate student of the horrors of Shanghai capitalism. In 1929, Rewi
Alley, the New Zealander who at that time worked for the Shanghai
municipal government as a labor inspector of foreign-controlled factories, took Smedley on a tour of local sweatshops. "I can still see her great
eyes looking at me intently over the table as I told her some of the
suffering, some of the tragedy, some of the denial of life I moved
amongst in industrial Shanghai," Alley recalled, many years later.[18]
Smedley wrote about these injustices in articles for the *Frankfurter Zeitung.*

When Smedley went to southern China to inspect for herself labor
conditions in the silk industry, she came under the suspicion of the
Chinese police, who had been forewarned by the Criminal Investigative
Department of the British police. They took away her passport. "For
weeks I lived under house arrest, with armed gendarmes wandering in
and out of my apartment at will," Smedley later wrote. "If I went out,
they followed, with murmuring crowds trailing behind me, apparently
anticipating a Roman holiday. By the time Washington had verified my
citizenship, I had fallen ill."[19] While waiting for the verification, the
American consul general in Canton demanded that Smedley turn over
all the names of her Chinese friends. "When I replied that this was
journalistically unethical and that I also considered it unethical for a
consular official to act as an agent of the police, he was infuriated,"
Smedley recalled.[20] Smedley invited the suspicions of the CID, if only
by the company she kept. She was a dauntless friend of Chinese writers,
some of whom, like Ting Ling and Mao Tun, were avowed revolutionaries, while others, notably the great modernist Lu Hsun, were outspoken critics of Chiang Kai-shek and his accomplices. Smedley identified
with the cause of these writers. She worked with them, as a collaborator
on projects, and as the co-author of appeals they wrote for the press to
protest the Kuomintang reaction, which was aimed at Chinese intellectuals.

In 1931, on the night of February 21, twenty-four Chinese activists
were taken from the Lunghua Garrison, where they had been confined,
and in the bitter cold and snowy night were forced to dig their own

graves. Some were shot, others were buried alive. Among the twenty-four were five writers, two of whom were known to Agnes Smedley. With Smedley's help, Lu Hsun, who is generally acknowledged to be China's greatest literary figure in this century, and Mao Tun, the distinguished novelist, prepared a manifesto addressed to Western intellectuals concerning the execution of these writers and activists. The manifesto resulted in the first international recognition of Chiang Kai-shek's terror from the West. Over fifty American writers, including James Thurber, Sinclair Lewis and Langston Hughes, signed a protest —much to the surprise of the Kuomintang. Smedley also worked closely with Madame Sun Yat-sen, who campaigned from Shanghai to attract attention to the evils of Chiang Kai-shek's terrorist tactics.

Given her passionate attitudes, and her absolutely uncompromising nature, it is not surprising that Agnes Smedley antagonized not only the die-hards and the official American community in Shanghai, but others less morally indignant than she was among her colleagues. She steered clear of other journalists, with the notable exception of those who worked at the *China Weekly Review*. She liked J. B. Powell, the Missourian who was editor and owner of the *Review*. He published her articles and book reviews. He was a man of integrity. "Since he disliked the Communists and believed in the Kuomintang, we often disagreed," she wrote, "but he was one American democrat who always defended my right to think and write as I wished. We shared a fear and hatred of British and Japanese policies in the Far East, and after the Japanese invasion, which threw us together on a common front, he published everything I sent him."[21]

Smedley also befriended Edgar Snow, ten years her junior, who had arrived in China in 1928, and was employed as a writer and editor at the *Review* when Smedley met him. As time went on, they became friendly rivals, but in 1930, before Snow set out on his journey to India, Smedley wrote a warm letter on his behalf to Jawaharlal Nehru, the young leader of the Indian independence movement, whom she knew, which proved to be of great value to Snow. "For the rest," Smedley wrote, "there was a barrier between most foreigners and myself, and I rarely met men of my own profession."[22]

Yet Smedley was drawn to men more, perhaps, than she was to other women, although throughout her life she maintained complex relationships with members of both sexes. She was attracted to men physically and intellectually. In Shanghai for a time she was passionately involved with Richard Sorge, a Russo-German Communist, who was just the sort of handsome, rugged male she liked. Sorge was later convicted, during World War Two, of spying in Tokyo for the Soviet Union. As the member of an alleged spy ring, Sorge was accused of passing on to Moscow high-level communiqués between the governments of Germany and Japan. Smedley was later brushed with opprobrium for this association, but no evidence has ever surfaced that she was part of the Sorge espionage enterprise.[23]

Another German friend of Smedley's was a pilot named Hans Keister, who flew for the Eurasian Aviation Corporation. "He was a neurotic man, inclined to mysticism, and I remained in touch with him only because he was a valuable source of news," Smedley later recalled.[24] When he returned from his trips to inland cities, Keister brought Smedley news of what was happening, along with photographs he took with his own camera. "One afternoon," she wrote, "after a flight to Hankow, he entered my apartment and slumped into a chair. His face was pale and his lips were twitching."[25] Keister tossed a package to Smedley that contained photos of Communists being beheaded in front of the customs house in Hankow. "A few showed the bodies of beheaded workers lying in the streets. One was of a very chic Chinese Army officer with a pistol in his hand," Smedley wrote, "behind him towered the walls of a foreign factory, and at its base lay the bodies of a number of workers whom he had apparently shot."[26]

Keister introduced Frank Glass to Smedley. Glass was a founding member of the Communist Party of South Africa. He was running a small left-wing bookstore in Johannesburg when Keister paid a visit to his store one day in 1929. Glass had become disenchanted with the Stalinists in the Communist Party, and had been expelled by the South African Communist Party for his Trotskyist sympathies. He was prepared to leave South Africa, and was considering a visit to China when he met Keister. The pilot told Glass about Agnes Smedley, and when he turned up in Shanghai, they became friends.[27] At that time, Harold Isaacs was already in Shanghai, although he did not meet either Glass or Smedley until May 1931. By then, Isaacs was ready to cut loose from the China Press. He was in search of other options.

The defining motif of Isaacs's life just then was a besetting confusion. He had lost the "true North" of his destiny, and was swamped by a sense of purposelessness. He confided about this to Viola. When filled with a sense of purpose, his letters to Viola reflected a vigorous passion; when in the doldrums, his ever-lyrical missives are lovesick paeans to his fiancée, filled with angst and self-doubt. "Myself, a reasonably intelligent news paper man with a minimum of sticktoitiveness," he wrote Viola at this time on China Press stationery. "Sometimes I wish I could work up the emotional drive necessary for me to hurl myself into some cause . . . to lose myself in it . . . but i almost always find myself seeing too much that is incontrovertible on the other side—or else a distorted and unexpected sense of humor intrudes at the wrong moment." It seemed to Isaacs that Viola, about to embark on a transatlantic voyage to Dresden for the summer, was, of the two of them, the one who had found a sense of purpose—in teaching, in dance, in travel. "You are you, viola and that is the major reason in this narrow, crazy world why i love you. Your being you is in no way incompatible with our eventual attack on love's young dream. In all this mess, we will yet find the terms and the circumstances—I don't suspect they're awfully far off. Under your influence I may lead a useful life yet."[28]

Then one day he had tea with Ch'en Han-sheng, who went by the name of Geoffrey Chen, "A slight chap," he wrote Viola, "with a tiny bow tie ridiculous under a receding chin and a large mouth. Huge goggles over squinting eyes and a wide, altho retreating forehead."[29] Ch'en was impressed by Isaacs, who seemed to him to have a certain well-informed prescience. Ch'en and Isaacs hit it off, and Ch'en immediately set about trying to line up a job for Isaacs as a teacher at Tsinghua University, in Peking.

Smedley surfaced in Isaacs's life the next day. She invited him, by telephone, he informed Viola Robinson, to come for tiffin, but he got the invitation too late to take her up on it. "Agnes Smedley is one of the most famous woman Communists still loose," he wrote, "you've probably heard of her. We never did make any contact altho I expect to have tea with her sometime this week. Meanwhile," he wrote, "there was mysteriously delivered to me a long proclamation . . . a hot and heavy piece of red propaganda of the usual type with the attached note —'to be delivered to Mr. Isaacs.' No indication of sender, altho I suspect it was Smedley. What she expected me to do with it I hardly knew. But that interesting situation will probably develop."[30] It developed very quickly. On May 21, Isaacs was writing his beloved, "Agnes Smedley is the burning Communist you may have heard or read about. We've had tiffin together once or twice—"[31] And by the fifth of June, Isaacs and Smedley had connected in a meaningful way. "I am being exposed to newer influences which are stirring something in me which may develop. . . . Something of the dynamics that is Agnes Smedley has communicated itself to some part of my spirit not yet articulate."[32]

Something about Isaacs had also piqued the curiosity of Agnes Smedley, not to mention that of her sidekick, Frank Glass. Glass was along when Smedley met Isaacs for tea that first afternoon. Together, Smedley and Glass went to work on Isaacs at the Palace Hotel. "We had a long talk," Glass later recalled. "He was rather adventurous. He had a very sharp mind. Very quick to pick up ideas. A good reporter, good observer. But he didn't have any principles. Petit bourgeois intellectual college student. Rather callow but with great promise. [Smedley] asked

Isaacs, 'How do you consider yourself? What are your motivations? What do you aim to do? Where do you stand?' And so on. His response was, 'oh, I don't wear any label.' She said, 'I'm going to pin one on you.' She did. She called him a wishy washy liberal."[33] Two weeks later, Isaacs was on his way up the Yangtze River with Frank Glass.

The journey was an inspiration on the part of Isaacs. The day after he had resigned his newspaper job at the *China Press,* Isaacs had encountered Glass at a coffee shop. "I was thinking of going to Australia," Glass recalled years later. "He said, 'Well why don't you give up that plan. I'm going to take a trip up the Yangtze River, how about coming along with me?' I thought that was a radical move, going into the interior of China."[34] On the eve of their departure, they had a final brainstorming session with Smedley at the Palace Hotel. "T'other night Glass and Smedley and I talked long," Isaacs wrote Viola (who was now on the high Atlantic on board an ocean liner bound for Europe). "I stood apart from these two believers. When I pricked weak spots, they tore themselves open and showed weaker ones. They are not zealots . . . they were discussing . . . not speechifying. . . .I listened. Strange," he wrote, "but my reaction to these convinced individuals is one of timidity . . . detached academics seem so naive. The difference between punching a bag and punching a man. But all of this is quite shadowy . . . it will take form and I will write you of it."[35]

The skipper of the little Yangtze rapids cargo boat was a crusty white-haired salt named Baker. He was outraged to find that he had acquired two unexpected passengers. What are you guys doing here? he demanded to know. Glass explained that he and Isaacs had made an arrangement with Mr. Hoyt, the manager. Well he didn't tell me anything, Baker said. I'm not in any position to *entertain* passengers. Isaacs assured him that they weren't looking for entertainment. "We'd be very happy if we can get a few pancakes for breakfast." As it happened, there was a Chinese cook on board who knew how to make oatmeal pancakes. Baker growled and grumbled, but in the early morning he set out upriver with both men on board.[36] "Dawn had touched the river and the Bund had just emerged from the shadows in which it is so much more attractive to behold," Isaacs wrote in his running commentary to Viola. "I stood wrapped in a blanket and watched it move as we puttered slowly down the Whangpoo." So began the education of what the French call *l'homme engagé,* the twentieth-century intellectual man of action.[37]

Isaacs had already learned an immense amount in a very short time about how Chiang Kai-shek's China operated. He'd added this to the store of knowledge about China that he'd brought with him from his Columbia University undergraduate education. What he did not have much of was a firsthand grasp of conditions in rural China. He was also innocent of any very deep understanding of Marx and Lenin, and he was almost completely ignorant of the political infighting that characterized the split in the Soviet Union between Stalin and Trotsky, and the basic issues over which they had fought. Unquestionably, Isaacs set out on his upriver trip with the intention of seeing what the Chinese interior was like. It's not clear, however, that Isaacs had planned any kind of intellectual regimen for himself when he invited Glass to join him on the Yangtze River trip. Still, that's what he got. For days on end, as they made their way first to Hankow, and then to the Yangtze Gorges and on up into Szechuan to Chungking, conversation was unavoidable. It was their chief diversion. (They'd brought along a few bottles of whiskey to help the flow.) So it was the perfect setting for a tutorial of sorts, in which Glass, fifteen years older than Isaacs, discoursed, often passionately, on the social disorder of the world and the need for action.

When it rained for days at a stretch, they sat on their bunks in a tiny, dirty cabin with the whiskey bottles between them while Isaacs peppered Glass with questions about his past as a Communist revolutionary in South Africa. Glass, he found, was both instructive and pleasant to be with, he was not without a sense of humor, and was always skeptical, although he was also a great believer in the practical applications of theory. Glass taught Isaacs to question everything, never to follow dogma of any kind blindly. "What I owe to Frank Glass was the timely inoculation of better-informed skepticism and questioning reservations that I was able to bring to all that I began to learn about the history and nature of Communist policies," Isaacs said in later years.[38]

On the ten days between Shanghai and Hankow there was almost nothing to relieve the monotony of the trip, and nothing, beyond the mud huts on the riverbank, to see of Chinese life. Once they passed Nanking, which Isaacs described as "flat and ugly."[39] The countryside was "green and quiet."[40] When the rain stopped it grew intensely hot, and the two men, unshaven, wearing pajamas, took their conversation and bottles out on deck to cool off. In Hankow things changed. Isaacs began to get a sense of the guerrilla war that was tearing little holes in the guts of central China. This insurgency was only sketchily understood in Shanghai and elsewhere, but it was the chief internal obstacle to the efforts of Chiang Kai-shek to impose his rule on China. At the time of Isaacs's river trip little was known to foreigners or Chinese about the guerrillas because no observers had successfully penetrated the areas they controlled. What was known to journalists and others was that after the Shanghai coup of 1927 and the ensuing bloodbath, Communist survivors in China had either gone underground or fled to the countryside. Chiang Kai-shek had hoped to wipe out the Communists altogether, but although Communist Party membership had fallen from fifty-eight thousand in April 1927 to ten thousand by the end of that year, those who survived were ardent revolutionaries. They trickled into the mountains of Kiangsi to join a small band of warriors assembled from the local peasantry by Mao Tse-tung and Chu Teh, Mao's colleague, the great guerrilla warrior.

While the central Chinese Communist Party organization stayed behind in underground urban China, still under the direction of the Communist International and the Kremlin, the movement that began to take shape in Kiangsi, and which was to become the new revolutionary opposition to the Nanking reactionaries, was no longer a workers' party. The Red Army fashioned by Mao and Chu Teh was an agrarian force: the guerrilla bases they established in the wilds of central and southwest China, called soviets, drew their strength not from the cities but from the countryside. It was Mao's belief that the Revolution could survive in the midst of Chiang Kai-shek's White power by operating out of bases in the "no man's land of provincial border regions where the ambitions of warlords were in conflict," to quote O. Edmund Clubb, the China historian, who at the time of Isaacs's river trip was a young consular official in Hankow.[41] Mao took advantage of the military disarray of China to build up Red Army bases and conduct an expanding guerrilla war in the countryside, liberating overtaxed local citizens from the grip of their landlords, who were sometimes brutally punished, sometimes indoctrinated with Mao's ideas, and sometimes both. Chiang Kai-shek refused to admit, publicly, that he was dealing with a well-organized guerrilla insurrection. He called the guerrilla forces "bandits." Much as he may have wanted to minimalize them, however, he found himself in trouble as soon as he set about trying to liquidate the "bandits."

His first campaign, under Ho Ying-ch'in, "failed ingloriously"[42] within a month. In May 1931 Chiang launched a second Bandit Suppression Campaign, once again in the Yangtze region into which Isaacs and Glass were presently traveling on their westward journey. Chiang used the same strategy that had lost him the first campaign, only this time he threw more troops at the Reds. He might have been merely throwing teacups at the guerrillas, who again used the strategy they had employed successfully in the first campaign. Although the Reds were far less well equipped than their aggressor, they were strategically smart. They let Chiang's men move deep into their territory. Then they struck. Two weeks later, they had Chiang's men on the run.

The second Bandit Suppression Campaign was winding down as Isaacs and Glass reached Hankow. They arrived just in time to watch more than a thousand Nationalist troops, accompanied by hundreds of coolie bearers, trudge through Hankow. This was the first of many revelations that supplemented Isaacs's radical education on the Yangtze. These so-called troops were ragged and footsore. Many of them were boys, ten or twelve years old, staggering along under the burden of backpacks. They carried rifles slung over their shoulders that appeared to be twice as long as their carriers were high. Many went unshod; others wore sandals made of grass. "Not all had ammunition belts," Isaacs reported, "but many did, and rows of blunt steel noses protruded from them at several angles . . . there were dozens of thingmajigs which looked like ancient blunderbusses. One Youngster sagged along under the weight of a huge mauser pistol of the pre-war type. One carried a rifle that looked like a fat and elongated salt sellar. . . ."[43] The straggling ranks of troops were separated occasionally by "slim and bespectacled" officers astride "skittish and handsome" ponies. Three or four youths carrying bugles followed each officer, and behind these came one or two men bearing dirty Kuomintang banners. They were a weary bunch of conscripts, Isaacs wrote, who had not the vaguest idea of what the hell it was all about. "The picture of this particular unit standing up in a fight against any kind of a seasoned enemy is a ludicrous one," he wrote.[44]

He and Glass boarded a steamer, the *I'fung,* on a rainy Friday afternoon, to continue their upriver journey. Now they headed for Sha-shih, on their way to I-ch'ang, at the entrance to the Three Gorges. One day from Sha-shih, Isaacs sighted some live action. On a bend in the river, the *I'fung* passed four junks, each carrying a squad of Nationalist soldiers waving a little white pennant. Perhaps fifteen more soldiers were marooned on a towpath along the shore. Through a pair of binoculars Isaacs could see hundreds of men running across a broad field toward a cover of thickets on the long embankment behind the stranded soldiers. These were Reds. "The soldiers on the towpath stood uncertainly for the few minutes during which we passed," Isaacs noted, "while the men in the junks waved wildly at us and shouted in our general direction. By that time the first of the running reds, un-uniformed peasants, reached the embankment, settled in the bushes and started to putter away at the troops."[45] White puffs of smoke burst from the green, but nobody dropped. The soldiers ran, the junks moved out into the river, and farther up the bank Isaacs saw another small band of soldiers on the river's edge. These soldiers waved, hopefully at first, and then indignantly, as the *I'fung* steamed past. "One or two shots were fired somewhere," Isaacs wrote, "which only furthered the disorganization, apparently, among the little group of beleaguered defenders of the might of the right. We were past them by now—in the stern of the last junk a soldier arose, bugle in hand, and shattered the air with a series of indistinguishable blasts as we passed from earshot—but the glasses showed him there still blowing sounds of marshal [sic] import for the edification of the unhappy and ragged little group on the river's edge. Score one," he added, "Yangtze's guerillas—Communistico—bandits. . . ." [46]

Glass and Isaacs, talking and looking, walked for hours in the back streets of the river ports along the way. At Sha-shih Isaacs first noted the dreadful stench, the swelter and the filth of inland China. "Everyone and everything are filthy beyond description," he noted in the account he was keeping. "Refuse, vegetable and human, does for paving in most cases. Most of the human beings in Shasi are mangy, bitten and half-skinned." [47] The smells got to him more than anything else. The smells of Shasi, he wrote, "don't drift through the atmosphere—they impregnate it and are reconceived thru a thousand unions with as many other smells along any given fifty yards of broad-cobbled street." [48] It was futile, he found, to hold his nose to try to block the putrid odors of human excrement and decaying garbage. The sights and smells of Sha-shih, and of the other river towns they visited, provided living color for Frank Glass's arguments on behalf of Marx and Lenin. Glass was now conducting his tutorials in a landscape of misery where the forces of history and revolution were already joined.

From I-ch'ang, the voyagers plunged upward into the gorges. "Alternating hours of brilliant sunlight, shadows and an incomplete moon," Isaacs noted, "have been spent breasting a full current westward between walls of rock." [49] Negotiating the rapids upstream was a tricky, laborious process. Boulders and dammed-up mud blocked the downward current. Water swirling through the canyons struck these dams with tremendous impact, turned mad and roared through the narrows. Isaacs directed his attentions for this part of the journey on the process of navigating the rapids. Coolies, known as trackers, buck naked in the steam heat of summer, hauled sampans and junks upstream by rope along paths cut out of the cliffs. Narrow draft steamships like the I'fung, on the other hand, mounted the rapids full steam ahead with the help of cables, secured by coolies to rocks above the rapids to prevent them from slipping backward as the boats were steered sideways from one side of the river to the other. Isaacs's journey up through the gorges was eased by the dangerously high level of the river, which was fed by torrential streams of melting ice and snow from the mountains of Tibet. "With the river at or near the full flood of high water," Isaacs wrote, "there haven't been many trackers seen at work. Infrequently a baremasted junk would edge along the bank, lines straining to the shoulders of a dozen or more coolies making slow progress on shore." [50]

One night, a local warlord, General Wang Fung-chow, came on board the *I'fung* with eight members of his entourage. This was at Wanhsien, site of a Standard Oil installation. "Wang is a Japanese trained militarist of the smooth and ruthless type," Isaacs observed.[51] He wore dark glasses and a drooping mustache; his skin was brown and leathery, stretched tightly over what Isaacs called his "Mongoloid skull."[52] The captain of the *I'fung* gave General Wang a small feast, and much whiskey was consumed by all. Isaacs was taking notes for articles he had agreed to write for the *China Press,* but he had trouble obtaining a satisfactory interview with Wang. The warlord spoke no English but he had some questions of his own, which he addressed to Isaacs and Glass through an interpreter on his staff. "He wanted to know how much we, newspapermen, could hope to learn about Szechuan by just scraping along the river and looking at it from the outside," Isaacs wrote. "I told him we had to see the outside before we could penetrate further."[53]

Isaacs parted company with Frank Glass in Chungking and continued on alone to Chengtu, the provincial capital, three hundred and fifty miles away. It took him more than a week to reach Chengtu in a drenching nonstop rain. He hiked through knee-deep mud for days at a time. He sat for hours in sedan chairs. When he assayed a motorbus, it broke down. Mainly, he subsisted on rice and eggs and fruit. He went beyond Chengtu, to Tatsienlu, where the Himalayas rise into Tibet. It was soon after he began the return trek that he experienced something like a religious seizure. "I believe, Viola, that I have reached an end to my aimlessness," he wrote in a letter dated July 24. "What brought this about was a simple statement made by Glass—it was before we left Shanghai, I think. 'You cannot sit on the fence. You cannot remain merely a spectator, on the sidelines.' "[54]

Isaacs had reached a point, he wrote, where, in outlook and opinions, he was a highly reprehensible Red, because he was harmless and ineffectual. Then, suddenly, he comprehended the meaning of Glass's statement. "I am not sure yet," he went on to write, "how much this trip has had to do with my odyssey of mental progress. I don't know if the sudden sight of a degraded mass of human beings living needlessly like animals had a telescopic effect upon my mind. Some of the long conversations with Glass along the river certainly did."[55] So did the six days he spent by himself on the way to Chengtu "amid hundreds of thousands—never a foreign voice nor face nor bit of food—trudging thru rain and mud and along the fringes of endless rice paddies—up and down hills and finally out onto the plain—there was much to think about—much to chew over."[56] In Chengtu he began to see people.

"Ignoramuses mostly, among these missionaries, but one or two with a gleam of light which unfits them for their position, and in which they are extremely unhappy."[57] Isaacs, in conversations, amazed himself by talking about the social order, as he called it, with a new realization, and a passionate conviction. "It is very much I suppose like a religious conversion," he wrote Viola. "I am conscious of nearly all the reactions common to such a conversion. But it gives me a basis—just as a conversion does. I can no longer bat about—I do a lot of talking—I MUST TURN MY HAND TO IT."[58] Isaacs had committed himself, he had become a China Hand. He was no longer an onlooker. "I must in other words," he wrote, "TAKE SIDES. I must cease being a neutral, a parasite, at the very best a parlor Red."[59] And a few days later he wrote: "All this sounds so damnably religious—but it is. There has awakened in what seems now stunning force to me this emotional response I used to bemoan the lack of—I have an idea more and more it was my first shock of China in the Yangtze basin which started my going—for the first time in my young life—purpose and direction. It is a new and dizzy feeling."[60]

Isaacs urgently wanted to get back to Shanghai. He traveled downriver by junk on the rising waters of the Min River to Chungking. The floods had begun. For three days his craft was held up at a little town south of Kiating, tied on one end to a treetop and the other to a roof protruding from the flood, until the water level had dropped. In Chungking, once again, he boarded the I'fung for the return trip down the Yangtze. The river was at its highest in fifty years. The I'fung shot down the swollen river on one engine at twenty knots. Below the gorges, the river smashed through dikes and inundated rice fields in every direction. At Hankow, Isaacs rejoined Frank Glass. They stayed at the U.S. consulate as a guest of O. Edmund Clubb, whom Isaacs had first met at the Palace Hotel in Shanghai in the company of Glass, Smedley and Slepach, the TASS correspondent. Hankow, Isaacs reported to Viola, was "a flooded shambles . . . magnify the lurid newspaper reports ten times and you approach some idea of the horror of it. . . ."[61]

Then on to Shanghai. "I watched it roll into view there," Isaacs wrote Viola. ". . . the imposingly ugly bund . . . the smoky terraces . . . Shanghai—all of it I hate so heartily. . . ."[62] This was a week that began with ominous calm and stifling heat, and ended with a typhoon that flooded the countryside for hundreds of miles up the Yangtze River, and drove thousands of Chinese to seek refuge on the outskirts of Shanghai. It was an epic storm that seemed to usher in the next phase of China's turbulent twentieth-century journey. Only a few weeks later, on September 18, the Japanese invaded Manchuria. Harold Isaacs never mentioned the typhoon in his letters, however. It was of little conse-quence compared to the storm inside him, which was raging with a fury all its own.

As always, Isaacs drew Viola into his inner state. She was the mainstay of his life, even if he did not at that precise moment know exactly where she was. But his transformation was also a challenge to their relationship. "My activities henceforth shall be devoted to an uncompromising anticapitalistic, communistic program. . . . I don't know if my letters from upriver managed to convey to you the stunning force of this sudden realization . . . and I don't quite know how to put over to you the changes it has wrought . . . what has happened is something new in my experience. I have taken sides. I have accepted and adopted a set of convixtions [sic] which eliminates the academic waverings. I have reached the end of an unhalting set of subconscious processes which have been actuating me one way or another for three years. I have reached conclusions. I feel strong and cruel and ruthless sometimes . . . altho I am still a pitiable excuse for a revolutionary . . . what does viola think of this new hri—the hri who is contemplating making his way to moscow . . . to work, if necessary, in factories there if nothing else presents itself . . . who is contemplating a stay in Soviet Russia entirely dictated by circumstances, who if he returns to the States will join the forces of revolution there in an active fashion, who will have to fight tooth and nail . . . the flower along with the manure . . . what does the viola he remembers think of this hri . . . viola, viola . . . TELL ME!"[63]

Isaacs was not interested in the typhoon. He was not interested in Charles Lindbergh, either. Lindbergh and his wife, the writer Anne Morrow Lindbergh, had flown from the East Coast of the United States over the Arctic Circle in their single engine plane, the *Sirius,* and were supposed to land in Shanghai. Instead, they flew on to Nanking to view the flooded river. "The fair-haired bastard fooled everyone . . . landed in Lotus Lake instead of on the Yangtze," Isaacs wrote Viola.[64] He had rushed up to Nanking with the rest of the Shanghai press corps to greet the American hero and his wife. Isaacs was not interested in the Shang-hai press corps, either. He called them "a crumby [sic] bunch undistin-guished by any intelligence beyond what i have come to regard as the 'newspaper keeners.' "[65] He was not even all that interested in the inva-sion of Manchuria, which happened almost the moment the Lindberghs landed, and distracted the "newspaper keeners," most of whom then made their way to the northeast.

The Japanese had been building up an industrial presence in Man-churia ever since the Russo-Japanese War of 1904–1905, which was fought over Manchuria. It was a long-held desire of the Japanese military to occupy Manchuria, and drive out the Chinese, who had been asserting their rightful presence there. Manchuria was rich in raw materials needed for Japanese industrial production, and it also provided much needed agricultural produce for a rapidly growing Japan. The Japanese were waiting for an "incident" that would give them the excuse they wanted to send in their troops, and they finally cooked one up on the night of September 18, when soldiers in the Japanese Manchurian army stationed in Manchuria to guard a Japanese-owned railway in Mukden blew up a section of their own tracks and claimed Chinese sabotage. When a Japanese patrol opened fire on a local barracks, it provoked a response from Manchurian troops loyal to the Chinese, which gave the Japanese the excuse they needed to invade Manchuria and annex it.

Isaacs could have gone to Manchuria for the *Christian Science Monitor,* but he discoursed at length with Willis Abbot, the *Monitor*'s editor, who was traveling in Asia, on his fervent new commitment to Red activism. Abbot gave it some thought. He then told Isaacs, "we're frankly capitalist. In the event of developments up there if we had a man who was on the russian [sic] side of things he wouldn't last two days."[66] So much for Manchuria.

As a theoretical issue, Manchuria mattered to Isaacs, and the invasion of Manchuria by the Japanese was obviously nothing to sneer at. For one thing, it was a shocking slap in the face of the League of Nations, to which Japan belonged, and which had been formed to put an end to unilateral acts of territorial aggression after the Great War. It was the first test case of the effectiveness of the Swiss-based League of Nations, and one that the League failed. No country, very notably including the United States, lifted a finger to stop the Japanese aggression. The Japanese invasion of Manchuria was the opening act of World War Two, and the first step in Japan's plan to take over China. When members of the League of Nations reprimanded Japan, the Japanese delegation simply got up and walked out of the League. Isaacs was aware, as everyone else was, of the grave implications the invasion of Manchuria had for the future of China and the rest of Asia. If the Japanese had not made their move, he might have left Shanghai for Russia. So in terms of his personal destiny Manchuria was of considerable importance to Isaacs.

What mattered most to Isaacs, just then, however, was not the business of news gathering, but the overthrow of an entire system. The invasion of Manchuria, Frank Glass explained to him, was merely symptomatic of the imperialist, or ruling-class, oppression that characterized the economic and social condition of Chinese people generally.

Isaacs began living in the French Quarter with Frank Glass, who continued the tutelage that had been interrupted by their temporary separation in Chungking. They were both extremely busy. Together they were writing, or collaborating on the idea, anyway, of writing a series of pamphlets on aspects of China, such as Chiang Kai-shek's terrorism, the Communist movement, the workers in Shanghai and the invasion of Manchuria.

At this moment, it was enough for Isaacs to be a Marxist and a revolutionary. He made no effort to conceal the fervor of his new mission. He was proud of what he called in letters to Viola his "transformation." His first act as a committed radical was to write a letter to the *Shanghai Post,* one of the local English-language papers, rebutting an attack made on Agnes Smedley the previous spring by H. G. W. Woodhead, III, an arch-conservative British journalist. After his letter was published, Isaacs was followed by the police, his mail was opened, and he was advised by onlookers both friendly and hostile to watch his step. He did nothing of the sort. He reveled in his notoriety. "Local ostracism," he wrote Viola. "Former friends speak to me surreptitiously as tho I were an escaped criminal. If only I had done something to deserve all of it!!!" He added, "It's fun being 'Red' in Shanghai."[67]

This early, enflamed "Red" Isaacs presented a version of himself to Viola that might have frightened away a less steadfast fiancée. They both belonged, it was true, to a generation of social activists. They were children of the Upper West Side in the 1920s, liberated by their college education from the constraints of the nineteenth-century European and Orthodox Jewish traditions that still gripped their parents. They had staked a claim to secular enlightenment. But where Isaacs had crossed the line into hard-core Marxist-Leninist revolutionary activism, Viola, insofar as she was at all political, remained true to the pragmatic social programs of people like John Dewey and Norman Thomas. So, in their epistolary way, the distant lovers were bound to clash. Isaacs fired the first shot on September 8, when he wrote Viola: "In the first place, I feel you are consistently absorbed in things which at best are only mildly interesting to me. For example scenery. Or the burning question of whether or not your Dresden companions are right in thinking you a poseure. Or the fact that your trip has convinced you that I am a 'swell guy' . . . I love you, true . . . ineradicably true. But the statement as such bears no meaning. . . . And there is this which I must at any cost make quite clear: To that dedication there is no qualification, no making allowances for personal intrusions. In other words if joining you would interfere I would not join you but relegate you to a past already fast receding."[68] This must have come as a shock to Viola, who nevertheless replied with an equanimity that moved the burning Isaacs to ardent sermonizing. The issue was whether bloodshed was justified or not, in the name of revolution. Isaacs thought it was. He wrote: "If you could see the price of blood being paid at the altar of the oppressors—here in China—no amount of the blood of the oppressors could flow, and flowing, move you to reaction. It is the means of human development. Trying to sidestep it is sidestepping the entire issue."[69]

Viola thought education came first. She wrote, "I maintain nothing is possible without educated and informed people . . . certainly whether or not the cataclysm comes, the fundamental change is in institutions and attitudes, not the superficial change of a revolutionary regime. Without this groundwork, no revolution can stand. I don't care whether the groundwork precedes or succeeds violence. Here and now the job at hand is one of education." Viola stood her familiar ground. As a teacher, she was absolutely secure about what she thought. Isaacs took serious issue with her nevertheless. "I am neither livid nor desirous of rending you limb from limb because of some of your paragraphs," he wrote, "(which incidentally were damn well written, even if somewhat hazy as to content). But," he declared, "in quite the same spirit I am going to proceed with the dismemberment of your intellectual structure in order to show the baselessness of many of your claims, fears and declarations." Viola, he wrote, failed "completely to realize that the futility of 'educating' without clearly delineating the *means* to the end you postulate as desirable . . . you speak as tho it makes no difference whether such education comes *before* or *after* the cataclysm." Viola had written that she wanted to be a "constructive revolutionary, to destroy the evils of the existing social order not by dynamite and leaving in their place nothing but a big hole, but by building up something that will inevitably throttle it, by its very force of foundation on honest recognition of the facts of human nature and of society, it must kill the old, it must insinuate its growing roots into the cracking institutions and when the old walls crumble down, the new tree will be found growing." Not possible, replied Isaacs. "The working class is starving and jobless and at the tether end of its rope within the capitalist system. You don't have to start making 'educated and well-informed' people out of the workers. You can't. They're too hungry to be well-informed as to theory and parlor concepts. You have to whip them into competent and efficient organizations—and *show them the way*. After they've moved and struck and seized the power—then the time for reconstruction. Then the time for the building of a society in which it is possible for them all to become 'educated and well-informed.' "[70] The argument between them continued for a time, but was subsumed by the events that swiftly followed.

Perhaps Isaacs's last protest, his final exhortation along these lines came in December, when he wrote, "until you see the general scene, Viola, in terms of the class struggle, you will never understand and you will always be muddled—even as i was until disgustingly recently, and for that no halting essays by a new convert will suffice. The case is stated and stated by those best able to state it in the works of Marx and Engels and those who followed. Sock into them viola, and see what you get out of it. Start with the Manifesto which itself should help clear away a lot of cobwebs."[71]

Where was the true enemy of China to be found? Was it outside, or inside? Was it Japan, or was it Chiang Kai-shek and his secret police? The question thus posed is deceptively simple. It was not necessarily an either-or proposition. Furthermore, Japan had its adherents among foreign journalists and editorialists, especially in the United States and Great Britain, and Chiang Kai-shek also had his admirers. At the time of the Mukden Incident, many observers believed that Japan had a legitimate claim on Manchuria. Some believed, furthermore, that a Japanese-controlled Manchuria would present a stronger obstacle to Russian influence in the Far East than a Manchuria ruled by a government in Nanking beset by bickering, civil war and economic crisis. Chiang Kai-shek's camp thought the Generalissimo was wise not to pursue a costly war with Japan while he was still trying to unify China and eradicate the Reds. Meanwhile, whatever favored the business climate in treaty port China, those coastal and river cities occupied by foreign trading communities, the Great Powers were for. Thus, the Powers tended to agree with the strategy of appeasement and submission pursued by Chiang Kai-shek. American journalists by and large were on the side of American and British business interests in Shanghai, and had come to terms, if only latterly, with Chiang Kai-shek, and his regime. These business interests had to live with the Japanese, both in Shanghai, where the Japanese maintained a strong presence, and on the world scene.

Nobody *liked* the Japanese. Nobody liked their exhibition of military might. And J. B. Powell, Thomas Millard and the "newspaper keeners," like Chiang Kai-shek, were opposed to Communism in any form. That is why, when it came down to the business of writing the China story, mainstream China reporters from 1931 on tended to emphasize the threat to China from the Japanese rather than Chiang Kai-shek's brutal reaction, which was ongoing, and was known as the White Terror. This was the story that played in the treaty port press, and it was the story that played in the American papers, which for the most part ran spot news stories on China rather than news analysis. In the West, Chiang Kai-shek had not yet by any means earned the status he later achieved as the Lone Ranger of China, but in the eyes of friends like the pro-German Karl von Wiegand of the Hearst Press, he was a man to be reckoned with, the strongest leader China had been able to boast since Yuan Shih-K'ai, who had died in 1916, shortly after failing in his attempt to mount the Dragon Throne.

Chiang did have critics. These critics were not necessarily leftists, either. In 1931, the Communist underground movement was fragmented and in disarray, and a new generation of Chinese youth was awakening to the China nightmare. Those who survived Chiang Kai-shek's terror were increasingly driven to find a political alternative to Chiang that would be willing to actively resist the oppressive Japanese presence. There was as yet no immediate alternative however. The Red guerrilla movement in Kiangsi was a will-o'-the-wisp to those Chinese who even knew of its existence; Chiang Kai-shek's news censorship worked very effectively to block most people's awareness that there might actually be an alternative in the making. Most of Chiang Kai-shek's critics among the students of China were uninformed about the guerrillas, and with the assistance of his ruthless followers in the Blue Shirts, his personal fraternity of devoted followers, Chiang Kai-shek eventually silenced campus critics of the early 1930s who protested his appeasement of Japan. By 1934 he had virtually eliminated campus activism.[72]

To people like Lu Hsun, the great modern Chinese essayist and short story writer, or even Madame Sun Yat-sen, Chiang and his political machine were the immediate evil. They saw little difference between Chiang's ruthless regime and the Japanese: Chiang was the evil that had penetrated Chinese lives, but even to begin to deal with Chiang's choke hold required freeing the Chinese from the Japanese menace. This was a radical, and an anti-imperialist, way of seeing things, and one that was naturally out of favor with an international community that had business interests in China, and in Japan.

Marxist doctrine was unsuited to the free-thinking Lu Hsun, and even to the good-natured Madame Sun, who was not, by nature, given to doctrinaire positions. Still, their hatred of Chiang and his methods made them sympathetic to colleagues in the far left, the novelists Mao Tun and Ting Ling, for example, or Agnes Smedley. These anti–Chiang Kai-shek partisans of Madame Sun had begun to make themselves heard, both in Shanghai and the radical American press of the Depression, in publications like the *New Masses, The Nation* and *The New Republic.* Much of this new publicity was the product of the collaboration between Madame Sun and Agnes Smedley.

Madame Sun had learned much over the years about how to publicize China in such a way that it would attract the attention of concerned human rights activists and intellectuals. Her experience as a student at

Wesleyan College in Macon, Georgia, undoubtedly had given her some understanding of what the problems were when putting something across to the American public. She had also learned the arts of political publicity from the master himself, her husband, Dr. Sun, who had used publicity to make his cause world-famous. She had worked with Eugene Chen, another public relations wizard. She'd also been on the international scene, in Moscow and Berlin. In China, when she returned from European exile in 1929, her chief occupation was publicizing abroad the Kuomintang terror.

Madame Sun was an avowed revolutionist, who had chosen sides in 1927, who in 1928, while she was still in Moscow, had met with Stalin and ascertained that he would commit himself to a Shanghai branch of the Communist International, and whose contacts in Berlin had been primarily with members of the international Communist movement. She was very clear about her decision as a Left Kuomintang spokesperson to turn to the Communists. This came at the end of 1931, in response to Chiang Kai-shek's summary execution of her great friend and colleague, Teng Yen-ta, who had been director of the General Political Department of the National Revolutionary Army on the Northern Expedition. It can be said that from then on Madame Sun enlisted a small group of Shanghai journalists in the cause of legitimizing the Chinese Communists by promoting a United Front between Communists and Nationalists to oppose Japanese aggression. She was also engaged in a struggle against Fascism in China in the person of Chiang Kai-shek. And it may further be added that although not unaware of the brutal character of the Communists, who were not gentleman scholars like the original founders of the Chinese Communist Party, Ch'en Tu-hsiu and Li Ta-chao, it was a side of her chosen revolutionaries she rarely emphasized among Western journalists like Harold Isaacs. Through the agency of a few chosen journalists, Madame Sun placed her cause in the minds of Western readers, in China and internationally. As such, she came to personify the conscience of modern China.

Harold Isaacs was one of her earliest, and surely the most astonishing, of her recruits. Agnes Smedley introduced Isaacs to Madame Sun. Together, Smedley, Frank Glass, Madame Sun and Harold Isaacs cooked up a newspaper called *The China Forum,* to be edited and published in the French Concession by Isaacs. Did Madame Sun have any idea that Isaacs was such a machine of energy and enthusiasm? Probably. Madame Sun, who was not known to have had a very active love life owing, in part, to her status as Dr. Sun's widow, was still a young woman when Isaacs happened on the scene, and she was clearly attracted to him. He was passionate and virile and young. He was like a racehorse at the starting gate. He was coiled to spring, but not on her.

He was saving himself for Viola. Instead, he directed his passion toward the joint project, and met frequently at the house on the Rue Molière to plan it. He'd already been contemplating a Far Eastern news service for the Communist press, a companion to Inprecorr or the International Press Correspondence, the Comintern news service. Called Fenprecor, it was conceived by Isaacs as a source of Far Eastern news written from a Communist point of view. Isaacs dropped Fenprecor in favor of starting *The China Forum*. The new paper would not be avowedly Communist, since the Chinese authorities would never permit such a publication to see the light of day. In order to qualify his paper for extraterritorial legal status, Isaacs began the process of incorporating *The China Forum* in the United States.

Though Isaacs had become a hotheaded radical, he recognized the need to steer clear of a blatantly Communist editorial stance (". . . its editorial line will necessarily be muddled and unclear," he wrote Viola, ". . . but it will be muddleheadedness with a purpose . . . other material in it will be worth the shame of the rest . . ."[73]). The weekly newspaper was his baby, almost. He would be editor-in-chief, responsible for soliciting material and putting it out.

From its conception, funds for *The China Forum* were supplied by the Chinese Communist Party in Shanghai, supplemented by the salary Isaacs earned from his new part-time job as the Shanghai translator for Havas, the French news agency. Yet because the Communists were operating underground in Shanghai, and *The China Forum* was aboveground and couldn't reflect an openly Bolshevik-Stalinist viewpoint, Isaacs was basically free to pursue the things that mattered to him personally. Nobody tried to force him to parrot party doctrine, which would not have worked, because whenever anybody tried to tell Harold Isaacs what to write he got suspicious. So it was an almost ideal situation for this *homme engagé,* and it created, for the period of its brief but explosive life, an outlet for all the concerns, emotional and intellectual, that Isaacs was impatient to explore. For although he had been coached in Marxist thought by Frank Glass, he'd also been inoculated by Glass to look at doctrine with a skeptic's eye. Anyway, he was not doctrinaire, by inclination or training. He was strictly his own man. He rejected orthodoxy in politics just as he had rejected the orthodoxy of his father's religion, when, because the rabbi began hectoring his congregation for money, Isaacs in his late teens had walked out of the synagogue on the Upper West Side where his father worshipped.[74]

"*The China Forum* is primarily the organ of no party or group," Isaacs announced in a press release issued on January 3, 1932, "but will appear as the vehicle for the publication of news and views now suppressed, ignored or distorted in the imperialist, bourgeois and Kuomintang press of China."[75] He then went on to assert that news of youth and student movements in China, news of the Soviet districts in Kiangsi, Hupei and other provinces of central China, news of the White Terror and workers' correspondence would find an outlet in *The China Forum*. This was a bold menu. By the ninth of January he was all set to go. He'd rented an office on a three-month lease in the Mission Building in Frenchtown, as the French Concession was sometimes called, and he'd begun to advertise the *Forum* in public places by plastering posters all around town: "The *China Forum,* News and Views of the Chinese scene now ignored distorted or suppressed!!"[76]

Boldness was not only part of Isaacs's personality, it was essential to his strategy. No one would agree to sell his paper at newsstands, so to make its presence known he had to take an aggressive advertising approach. Besides, he wanted to provoke the authorities. He wanted to get under the skin of all kinds of people, including the Shanghai Municipal Police, the Kuomintang, the mayor of Shanghai and the Shanghai Municipal Council. That was what *The China Forum* was all about. He hated the way the SMP in collaboration with the Bureau of Public Safety, Chiang's Shanghai police, hunted down so-called subversive Chinese. They broke down doors and ransacked boarding house rooms for subversive evidence so they could arrest students and workers, often newly arrived in Shanghai, who lived in the International Settlement but never got the benefit of Western legal procedure. Instead, they were promptly turned over to the Chinese police. "A slip means death," Isaacs wrote Viola, "agonized, tortured death . . . sometimes I could go mad with rage at these slimey [sic] bastards . . . a young fellow . . . with keen black eyes and a smiling mouth . . . we knew him. He's gone and nobody can be sure where."[77]

The China Forum was born to expose the murky facts of Shanghai life and political concerns even further afield under the bright glare of publicity. Isaacs specialized in a kind of tough-guy tabloid prose that combined effectively with social issues; he had the sound of a left-wing New York labor organizer with a college education. Isaacs's tough-guy style put zing into his *Forum* editorials. Meanwhile he signed on Ch'en Han-sheng to write a political column under the byline "Observer." Ch'en's style was in noticeable contrast to that of Isaacs. Ch'en wrote with subtle Oxonian irony about the distasteful inner workings of Chinese politics. Ch'en alternated as "Observer" with Garfield Huang, a leading critic of Chiang Kai-shek's opium policy. Isaacs also relied on anonymous underground Communists or Communist sympathizers for news items. He made a point of including in his paper short stories, some of them the work of the five writers executed in Lunghua in January 1931. These were translated by George Kennedy, a talented scholar of Chinese language and culture. In his first issue, Isaacs ran photos of the deceased five: Feng K'eng, Hu Yeh-p'in, Jou Shih, Tsung Hui and Yin Fu, plus a sixth writer, Li Wei-sen, who had been executed earlier. The "Observer" column, the fiction—which included work by such living masters of the new fiction as Ting Ling, Mao Tun and Lu Hsun—and Isaacs's own prose all made *The China Forum* a lively professional journal, more than a mere hortatory broadsheet.

From the beginning, Isaacs had also taken on the cause of the Noulenses, a Russian couple who served as liaisons in Shanghai between the Communist International and the Chinese Communist Party, not to mention other Communist parties in the Far East. (Between August 1930 and May 1931 the Far Eastern Bureau of the Comintern, based in Shanghai, and for which the Noulenses worked, paid out an average of more than twenty-five thousand gold dollars to the Chinese Communist Party.) Noulens and his wife were a sensational catch. The Shanghai Municipal Police had been tipped off to their presence in Shanghai after British intelligence in Singapore arrested a French Communist Party member and Comintern courier named Jacques Ducroux, and found on him two sheets of paper, including the Noulenses' Shanghai post office address, P.O. Box 206, Shanghai. The Noulenses were citizens of the USSR whose real names were Yakov Rudnnik and Tatyana Moiseenko, and they had a son, Dmitri, called Jimmy, who was three years of age at the time of their arrest. The Noulenses' true identities, however, were artfully concealed under a baffling assortment of assumed names and false passports, none of them verifiable on close investigation. When the SMP arrested Noulens, they found in his possession two Belgian passports bearing the names Samuel Herssens and Fernand Vandercruyssen, and the Canadian passport of one Donat Boulanger. At first, Noulens claimed to be the Belgian Vandercruyssen, but when the Belgian authorities refused to acknowledge his claims of citizenship, he asserted that he was really the Swiss citizen G. X. A. Beuret. Scotland Yard and the Swiss police located the real Beuret, however, and Noulens next claimed to be one Paul Ruegg, also Swiss. Madame Noulens, meanwhile, had gone by the names Adele Ruck and Mme. Motte. She, too, was in possession of a pair of Belgian passports, which identified her as Sophie Louise Herbet (née Lorent), and Marie Vandercruyssen (née Duson). Finally, in consort with her "husband," she claimed Swiss citizenship, and called herself Gertrud Ruegg. The Swiss government, however, refused to validate the Rueggs. In another time, and a different place, this might have supplied catchy material for a musical comedy.

It was not, however, musical comedy time for the Noulenses. Unable to establish their country of origin, the Noulenses were ineligible for protection under the laws of extraterritoriality. After a ruling by the Chinese court in Shanghai, the Shanghai Municipal Police turned them over to Chinese military authorities, who imprisoned them in Nan-king.[78] The Noulenses were undoubtedly key figures in the Far Eastern Bureau of the Comintern: documents found in one of their flats attested to that. In the opinion of Isaacs, however, these documents provided insufficient evidence that the Noulenses were running the Comintern outfit in Shanghai. Whether or not the charges were correct or verifiable, however, was perhaps less of an issue to Isaacs than that the Noulenses were deprived of extraterritorial legal protection. Under the circumstances, the Shanghai Municipal Police probably had little choice in the matter of turning them over to the Chinese. The SMP were hardly in a position to defy their host government on such a serious matter, even if they had wanted to do so. To Isaacs, Smedley and Madame Sun, all of whom actively supported the Communist underground, it was nevertheless an outrage, given the severity of the Chinese penal system. They made the Noulens case a cause célèbre among American and European intellectuals by publicizing it abroad. Meanwhile, in the pages of *The China Forum,* Isaacs kept the Noulens case on the front burner.

Soon war came to Shanghai, and provided *The China Forum* with a whole new range of subject matter. Anti-Japanese feeling ran strong in Shanghai. Partly because of the situation in Manchuria, but also because Japanese in Shanghai conducted themselves with a certain swagger, they were regarded with fear and loathing by the Chinese. Demonstrations against Japan erupted constantly. After a crowd of Chinese demonstrators fell upon a group of Japanese priests as they strolled in the Chinese city, the Japanese navy sent a detachment of armed men ashore, and issued an ultimatum demanding a complete surrender of the city by the Kuomintang. The Japanese probably wanted to use the opportunity to seize Shanghai as a bargaining chip that would force the imperial powers to concede Japan's right to annex Manchuria. The Nationalist government, and the mayor of Shanghai, were prepared to accept Japan's ultimatum.

Chiang Kai-shek in fact had ordered the troops of Tsai T'ing-kai's Nineteenth Route Army to leave Shanghai. The presence in Shanghai of the Nineteenth Route Army had been a sore point with Chiang and the Japanese both. The Nineteenth Route Army was violently anti-Japanese, and that it was in Shanghai at all—it was a fighting force born in the days of fiery revolution before Chiang Kai-shek turned on the Communists—may have stimulated the Japanese to action. These were not troops loyal to Chiang Kai-shek. In 1931 Eugene Chen, Wang Ching-wei and other former leaders of the Left Kuomintang had reassembled in Canton to set up an autonomous government there in the hopes of eventually driving Chiang Kai-shek from power. When peace negotiations between Chiang Kai-shek and these renegades were proposed, the Canton leaders insisted on the right to install the Nineteenth Route Army in Shanghai as a so-called bodyguard force. Naturally, the Japanese didn't want a well-trained anti-Japanese force in Shanghai. They were alarmed from the moment Tsai and his forces arrived. As far as the senior Japanese naval commander, Admiral Shiozawa, was concerned, it was not enough for the Nineteenth Route Army simply to withdraw from Shanghai. On the night of the twenty-eighth of January 1932, he sent marines to hasten the retreat of General Tsai's troops. Much to everyone's surprise, when the Japanese opened fire on them, Tsai's men returned fire, dug in their heels and drove the Japanese back to their ship.

The Nineteenth was a "new" army, a product of the Nationalist Revolution, and it was one of the best fighting forces in China. Although Tsai and his men had responded to Chiang's command, and had begun to withdraw, the Japanese attack provoked a passionate response. General Tsai's resistance was immediately cheered by the Chinese people. The whole country rallied. Thousands of young men volunteered to help. The battle for Shanghai was fought block by block. The battle between the Japanese and the Nineteenth Route Army raged on for thirty-four days. It cost the Nineteenth Route Army half of its fighting force of forty-five thousand men. In order to prevail, the Japanese threw sixty-five thousand men against them, deployed naval bombers and engaged a large part of their fleet as well.[79]

Isaacs managed to put out three issues of *The China Forum* before the Japanese invaded Shanghai. The International Settlement immediately imposed a state of emergency and banned *The China Forum*. No printer in the foreign enclave could be found who was willing, under those conditions, to accept Isaacs as a client. Isaacs was hardly surprised by this development. He'd gotten off to a rash start. He'd courted trouble by appealing in his pages for strike funds on behalf of Chinese workers in Japanese mills, hardly a popular move among Shanghai colonials in general. Instantly, he'd provoked the ire of the French authorities in whose precincts he operated, as well as the British and the Americans. He'd also invited the animosity of Chinese authorities by running "Life, Livelihood, Defense in Kiangsi," a piece of writing on the Kiangsi soviets by a Communist informant that supplied the very kind of evidence you would have to suppress if you were intent on proving, as Chiang Kai-shek was, that the Red menace no longer existed. He'd even managed to anger his friend Ted Thackrey, editor of the *Shanghai Post,* by calling him a liar. He was pleased. He wrote his family that the *Forum* was "in a state of coma after three lively issues which aroused considerable of a storm in some Shanghai quarters. . . ."[80]

Six weeks later he was back in business, but the state of emergency was still on. Isaacs decided to drop the strike appeal and forgo articles on the Red armies. No more "such wild (but damn good) stunts as appealing for strike funds," he wrote.[81] He also dropped the motto "A Vehicle for the Publication of News Now Ignored, Distorted or Suppressed." He wanted to establish his paper on a sounder footing. The Japanese had provided Isaacs with a wealth of material to sift through. He'd sat out the interim period during February and March, building up a head of steam. He was frustrated on the sidelines, but he was also enraged by what he witnessed, especially by the behavior of local Japanese civilians, who "were responsible for most of the murders and barbarities which were perpetrated *within the Settlement and out,*" he told his family.[82] The Japanese had launched their invasion of Shanghai from the International Settlement, apparently with the tacit agreement of the Shanghai Municipal Council, which was dominated by Americans. This belied the claim of foreigners that the International Settlement was a bastion of neutrality. "Nobody," Isaacs wrote his family in February, ". . . the Americans or anyone else . . . gives a goddam what further atrocities the Japanese commit on the Chinese . . . but they are all up in arms over their precious Settlement here . . . the Japanese have occupied a good slice of it and are using the foreign, supposedly neutral area, as a base for their operations against the Chinese lines."[83] For a time, it looked as though full-scale war might break out between American and Japanese forces over what Isaacs wrote was the "bitter antagonism towards the Japs who were stupid enough to have gone too far in encroaching on *foreign* rights in their mad and insane drive on the city. . . ."[84] Not that the Americans minded especially what the Japanese were doing to the Chinese who were putting up a heroic resistance under General Tsai T'ing-kai. They were only raising a force in order to get the Japanese out of the settlement. Isaacs sat in the midst of the war zone listening to the windows rattle. As he later pointed out, he also watched the Japanese raze the area of Chapei in the Chinese city during the thirty-four days of battle, in the course of which they invented a new military strategy, carpet bombing. To Viola, he compared the experience to being in Manhattan and hearing sounds of battle coming from Brooklyn.[85] He was discouraged that there was no underground support of Tsai T'ing-kai's forces. He began to realize for the first time just how crippled the Shanghai workers' movement now was. ". . . and the masses?" he wrote Viola. "Crushed. Docile. Quiet . . . more so than ever we had dreamed . . . even knowing as we did the terrific cost of the repression of the last four years . . . but i, for one, did not realize that the movement here in Shanghai was so badly off as that . . . another manifestation of the Chinese revolutionary paradox . . . all its strength in the agrarian districts where the revolution is comparatively triumphant (central China) . . . but smashed in the cities . . . smashed in the very places where it should be pulsing with most life. . . ."[86]

Despite the lamentable fragmentation of the workers' movement, the invasion soon brought forth a massive student protest, which provided an impetus to the Chinese Communist Party underground and the Shanghai workers. The protest undoubtedly also gave new vigor to *The China Forum*. It was back on the stands on the fifteenth of March, tackling the subject of the Japanese invasion, slashing at the Hydra-headed monster with a front-page essay on Japanese imperialism. A review of the Shanghai invasion concentrated on the role played by the Kuomintang and incorporated a protest by the League of Left Wing Writers of China in response to Kuomintang capitulation to the Japanese. Boldly, Isaacs made the point that the invasion was the means by which Japan secured a bargaining chip to force the Powers to accept their invasion of Manchuria, since, when it was all over, Japan had become the dominant power in Shanghai. The Nanking government was forced to negotiate a peace settlement with Japan, and in successive issues of *The China Forum* Isaacs followed this process. He also depicted the plight of the wounded heroes of the Nineteenth Route Army, who never saw any of the pay that was owed to them. This money had been donated in the amount of three million dollars for that purpose, much of it by overseas Chinese, and turned over to the Shanghai bankers for safekeeping.

Meanwhile, Isaacs kept one eye on the shambling progress of the Lytton Commission, a group appointed by the League of Nations to investigate the question of who, in fact, had begun hostilities in Manchuria: the Japanese or the Chinese. The Lytton Commission was led by Lord Lytton of Great Britain and was composed of delegates from France, Germany, Italy and the United States. The commission was accompanied by a Japanese assessor. After a detour to Hankow, the Lytton Commission went on to Peiping, as Peking was now called, where it dallied for a time en route to Manchuria. In Peiping the members found themselves laden with ceremonial gifts bestowed by their northern hosts. Isaacs took no small delight in describing their apprehension that bandits would kidnap them and steal their loot if they proceeded to Manchuria overland, by rail or road. The commission members decided to split up into two groups, one that would travel by land and the other by sea. The group was divided up by the flip of a coin. (The American delegate, General McCoy, and Count Marascotti of Italy, were forced to brave the "iron road"; the others traveled to Manchuria aboard a Japanese destroyer.)[87]

Isaacs saw the Japanese invasion as a manifestation of the deeper Chinese malaise. A browse through the article headings of his paper gives some idea of the variety of subjects that concerned him in the spring of 1932: "Chiang Kai-shek, Wang Ching-wei Earn Bitter Hatred; Called Yellow"; "China Teachers Face Paralysis of Schools as All Funds Cease"; "Shanghai Workers Seek Aid"; "Gorki Says Words Can't Help China"; "Demands for Back Pay Bring Arrest, Death to Eleven"; "Commercial Usury Ruinous to Peasantry"; "Six Young Patriots Slaughtered at Qinsan"; "New Drive on Against S-E Kiangsi"; "Amnesty Is Talked as Thousands Die in Jails"; "Anhwei Poor Starve as Gentry, Whores Fatten."[88]

Much of the stuff of *Forum* articles was about Chinese jail conditions, political prisoners, kangaroo justice, mass slaughters and executions. This material provided the raison d'être for Isaacs's paper. It was supplied to him mainly through contacts in the Communist underground who would meet him in back alleys or on street corners, slip him information and disappear. (Articles by his informants appeared as "Special to *The China Forum*.") Isaacs never knew who any of these people were. He was completely cut off from the subterranean councils of the party. He did not even know the real name of the young Chinese assistant who lived and worked in his apartment, nor did he know that Ch'en Han-sheng, who co-wrote the "Observer" column, was a member of the Comintern. His informants contacted him through a succession of Comintern agents in Shanghai, Westerners whose real names were concealed from Isaacs. He was kept in the dark on purpose. "The conspiratorial rule was that what one did not know one could not tell," he recalled in later years.[89]

It also benefited Isaacs not to be involved in the intricacies and conspiracies of the Chinese Communist Party. Although the party subsidized the *Forum,* it did not support Isaacs, who earned his living translating for Havas, a French news service. This left him with his independence intact. He ran the *Forum* more or less the way he wanted to, but as a Communist sympathizer, he naturally took up causes of importance to the party, causes that mattered, also, to Madame Sun, Agnes Smedley and Frank Glass, all of whom continued to work their influence on Isaacs through meetings and dinners and casual social contact.

Although Isaacs was sympathetic to issues that mattered to the Communists, his paper wasn't dogmatic in style or content. Only the book reviews authored by Frank Glass and others toed the party line.

That was probably a concession on Isaacs's part to his doctrinaire friends. His specialty was the exposé, and the inside story, which the "Observer" was so adept at providing in the column headed "The Great Game of Chinese Politics" (subheaded "Without the Trimmings"). For example, the "Observer" nailed down why the regime of Sun Fo, who briefly replaced Chiang Kai-shek as the president of China, was unable to function. In December, Chiang Kai-shek had been forced to resign in favor of national unity by the Canton clique, those former members of the Left Kuomintang who had set up an opposition government in Canton in May 1931. They had come to the Nanking-Shanghai area with the Nineteenth Route Army after dissolving their separatist government in Canton. Sun Fo, Wang Ching-wei and Eugene Chen took over the government of China. A few months later, however, in January, Chiang Kai-shek was recalled from retirement. In the analysis of the "Observer," Chiang had used up most of the eight hundred million dollars loaned to him by the Shanghai bankers after the Shanghai massacre of 1927, when he turned on the workers and "saved" Shanghai for the businessmen and bankers. The funds, given to launch his government and generate a treasury, had been "secretly disposed of and mortgaged for other purposes," and now, with Chiang Kai-shek in retirement, Sun Fo couldn't redeem the bonds Chiang had issued to raise the money and which the banks now held. His government was bankrupt. Chiang Kai-shek was the only leader who knew how to access the funds.[90]

The "Observer" was also very good on subsidiary characters in Chinese politics, like the political boss of Anhui Province, Ch'en T'iao-yuan, who, foreseeing the day when he might be asked to step aside, adroitly rerouted the provincial tax flow away from the Provincial Finance Bureau into the purse of his own, personal army. That day arrived. Wang Ching-wei ("Observer" called him Chiang Kai-shek's "concubine"), back once again in Nanking, had decided that provincial power should no longer be held by military men, and got Chiang to agree to replace Ch'en in Anhui with a civilian. Ch'en graciously went along with this. He was an ally of Chiang Kai-shek. Chiang gave him a new job, that of chief pacification minister of the province. Since all the provincial revenue was paid out to his own army, Ch'en continued to run the province. Upon taking office, Ch'en's successor issued the following statement: "All jobseekers and friends—please forgive me— if you understood the difficult position we are in, you should not be disappointed in not getting my help. Nearly all of the officials of the province have not been paid for five months and the provincial treasury is washed clean!"[91]

Isaacs was twenty-one years old when he launched *The China Forum*. He was so young that people took a parental stance toward him, even when he told them he was twenty-four. His friend Alma Ekins, wife of Bud Ekins, the UP correspondent in Shanghai, told Isaacs he was "emotionally sterile." For one thing, he was sex-starved. As he wrote Viola, "celibacy is not my forte. Nor, unhappily, are casual affairs," he added. "Nor, happily, are prostitutes. I have written before of how ludicrous are my attempts to wax casually amorous. I haven't the technique and no matter how keen my desire I invariably laugh! Damn it all, its unfair."[92] Isaacs was also isolated, socially, from the American community and the club life of Shanghai. He seems not to have made good friends with many of the journalists in town. He saw his old *China Press* colleague, Till Durdin, infrequently. His political passions probably made it hard to converse with others. He found his relationships with the intense, neurotic Agnes Smedley and the political extremist Frank Glass. He drank copiously at times (throughout his life he was fond of saying: "one drink—scotch; one flavor—chocolate; one woman—Viola"),[93] sitting at his desk, fire in the fireplace, in the chill, damp winter nights when it often rained, obsessively, compulsively writing. Such was the life of the precocious and in some ways callow youth who launched *The China Forum* and rattled the windows of the Shanghai establishment with his own mortar blasts. He was an *homme engagé* as André Malraux never was, barely out of his teens though he was.

If he'd been older, he might never have embarked on such a quixotic career. For apart from the obvious excitement involved in putting out a tabloid that boldly confronted the evils of the day, it was a marginal, unremunerative exercise. At his age, Isaacs felt he had nothing to lose. The enterprise suited him perfectly. What seems remarkable, in retrospect, is the professionalism and self-confidence Isaacs brought to the task. He turned out a news sheet that a seasoned, cigar-chomping city editor in New York or Chicago might have grudgingly acknowledged. It was not an endeavor that he could have launched in a big American city. It was extremely easy, however, to put out a paper in Shanghai. In fact, there was a plethora of newssheets—gossip rags, which existed to embarrass local citizens, and extort blackmail, known as the "mosquito press," in addition to the treaty port papers and the journals published in Chinese. Due to his apprenticeship on two Shanghai papers, Isaacs had developed a familiarity not only with Chinese politics but the practical aspects of putting out a journal of his own.

In May, to commemorate the fifth anniversary of Chiang Kai-shek's bloody Shanghai coup, Isaacs published a single special edition combining three issues entitled "Five Years of Kuomintang Reaction."

The cover illustration of this special edition, a charcoal drawing by a contributing editor of the *New Masses* named Adolph Dehn, showed a Chinese officer's sinister, bony face partly concealed by the brim of a stylishly high-crowned officer's cap of the SS kind and, in the foreground, a flow of human skulls. It was a drawing that might have been inspired by the photograph Hans Keister brought back to Shanghai from Hankow to show to Agnes Smedley, though it was probably also a depiction of Chiang Kai-shek.

Isaacs devoted twenty-four pages to a close examination of all aspects of Chiang Kai-shek's terror and its effect on China, and included photographs. (The special edition was also published separately as a paperbound book, with photos, consisting of 136 pages.) The premise of this feature was that with the old agricultural structure of Chinese society in ruins and the population largely in a state of impoverishment, the rulers of China could prevail only through terror, and only with the assistance of the imperialists. Isaacs wrote Viola: "the subjects start out with the Background, range through the White Terror, the Peasantry, the Working Class, Foreign Relations, the Bankers, the Gangsters, the Intellectuals, the Anti-Red Campaigns, the Red Districts, and the Japanese invasion of China—all done with a common framework—namely in relation to the Kuomintang during the past half-decade—." He added, "It's going to be a sizzling bit of work." [94]

Written with the help of Agnes Smedley and Frank Glass, "Five Years of Kuomintang Reaction" begins, appropriately, with an overview of the Terror. Hundreds of thousands of men and women, Communists or Communist suspects, were systematically butchered in successive waves of terror in the years between 1927 and 1932. "Red can mean almost anyone," a *China Forum* correspondent wrote, and the killing was often indiscriminate. In 1930, in Szechuan, the army offered fifty dollars for every Communist killed. Policemen and soldiers, eager to collect rewards, tended not to examine the political convictions of suspects whom they killed, often in cold blood on city streets, often just because they "looked" like Communists. Whole towns and villages were victimized by soldiers licensed to slaughter at the height of the Terror in 1927 and early 1928. Locked within the walls of their towns, people had nowhere to flee as soldiers set about raping and beheading. Butchery was widespread in the countryside, but it was intermittent. In the cities, where many non-Communist intellectuals were critics of the Kuomintang, the White Terror was ongoing, as Chinese and foreign police worked side-by-side to root out opposition of any kind to the regime in power. "Five Years of Kuomintang Reaction" documents a variety of tortures employed by the Chinese police, often in the presence of Western police. One method of inducing discomfort of a nonlethal sort favored by the Bureau of Public Safety was to repeatedly force kerosene, feces and urine up the nostrils of political prisoners and thence into their stomachs, so that they would stink for days on end. The Chinese police also used electroshock on their victims, or drove slivers of bamboo between their fingers and fingernails. One popular form of torture among the police was the "tiger's bench," which involved pulling out the ligaments of a victim's knees. They crushed the testicles of male prisoners, and slashed the breasts of their female counterparts, according to "Five Years of Kuomintang Reaction."[95]

The special edition also documented, in detail, the varieties of oppression brought to bear upon Chinese peasants and workers by the once revolutionary Kuomintang, including burdens of excessive taxation, land confiscation, and the discarding of rent regulations once favored by the Kuomintang and imposed as law. A separate section was devoted to the especially appalling conditions among factory workers, who so recently had been the very backbone of Sun Yat-sen's movement. The review went on to detail the political character of the Nanking regime, and its relationship to the Shanghai gangsters, to the bankers and to the Powers, to show how these groups had fastened their tentacles on the Kuomintang. Isaacs rounded out his document with an account of the failed efforts of the Kuomintang to stamp out the soviets, a little reminder that may have conveyed a special sting of its own to the authorities in Nanking.

Isaacs knew what he was in for. Agents from the Criminal Investigative Department had already come to call on him a month before he published his indictment of the Kuomintang. He wrote Viola that he had begun to feel a hovering ax. ". . . have had two visits from C.I.D. men who snooped around . . . asked questions that went unanswered . . . meanwhile the old furtive watch and be watch[ed] program has been resumed. . . ."[96] In April he wrote Viola that he was planning the special, "which may be both mine and the paper's funeral . . ." He was excited. ". . . it gonna take a lotta fast work . . . since i only thought of the idea last night . . . it will be the only available bit of wrk on an adequate history of China since 1927 and will provide an outline for what I hope to make into a more extended book sometime later on . . . but i've gotta hop to it. . . ." He knew, as he wrote Viola, that it would be "hot, hot, hot." After it was distributed on May 14, he wrote, "if the Forum is not suppressed now it never will be. . . ."[97]

Isaacs got his response. The British were annoyed by Isaacs's revelation that they had helped Chiang Kai-shek suppress the Shanghai workers in 1927 and had thereby held on to their special privileges in China. The Shanghai Municipal Police tried to halt publication of the *Forum* by requesting the Shanghai municipal advocate to look at the special edition and decide whether Isaacs could be prosecuted. The advocate, however, concluded that under American law Isaacs was entitled to hold the views he expressed—and in China, under the laws of extraterritoriality, Isaacs was subject only to American law. They next went to the U.S. district attorney in Shanghai, who gave them the same answer. British diplomats in Nanking, meanwhile, put pressure on the SMP to strongarm the Century Press, Isaacs's printer, into dropping the *Forum* as a client.

These British efforts were minor, however, compared to the campaign launched by the U.S. consulate to eliminate the paper and deport Isaacs. The consul general wanted the State Department to reject the application Isaacs had filed to register the Searchlight Publishing Company, the parent company of *The China Forum*. The Department of State decided not to refuse the application, but Edwin Cunningham, the consul general, held it up anyway. He made Isaacs a personal issue. He was under pressure from Wu Teh-chu, the mayor of Shanghai, to force Isaacs out of circulation. Mayor Wu was one of the *Forum*'s favorite targets. Isaacs had depicted him as a coward who had yielded to the Japanese, and he'd run a front-page photograph of Mayor Wu and Consul General Murai of Japan, cocktails in hand, under the caption, "Drinking the Blood of China." Mayor Wu informed Consul Cunningham that the Kuomintang had instructed him to close down the *Forum*. He claimed to have evidence to prove that Isaacs was funded by the Communists. Isaacs was under attack on other fronts. He had been expelled from his editorial offices in the Missionary Building. "The Missionary Building was erected primarily to house organizations connected with a Christian enterprise in China, and not as a commercial venture," his landlord told Isaacs. "As a matter of simple propriety, we cannot continue to house those who are openly attacking that for which we stand."[98] In early July, on board a plane to Shanghai from Nanking, where he had been covering the Noulens trial, Isaacs dashed off a note to Viola: "Called back by bad news—my printer has baulked at long last—a friend wired and I'm literally flying back to see what I can do about it."[99] He could do nothing. Century Press canceled its contract. Isaacs hired a Chinese printer and shot back with an editorial headed "Gag *The China Forum!*" Isaacs let himself vent a little fury. The Kuomintang, he wrote, "has gagged those whose speech alone threatens the very core of the rotten, brutal and corrupt system set up and defended by the Chinese bourgeoisie and the imperialists. It is now trying to gag us."[100]

Meanwhile, during most of June and July, Isaacs pressed the consul general to let him know the status of his company; Cunningham was in feverish communication with the State Department over the matter. He told Isaacs that his paper would have to be "modified" to win approval for registration, but refrained from telling Isaacs how this would have to be done. At the same time Cunningham was urging the State Department to withdraw Isaacs's extraterritorial rights, so that he would be subject to Chinese law. Of course the State Department could not have withdrawn Isaacs's extraterritorial privileges without undermining the sanctity of the concept and it did not do that, but it nevertheless broke precedent in order to deal with Isaacs. The legal adviser made a study for the State Department, and the State Department, through Cunningham, let Isaacs know of its displeasure. He had abused the rights of extraterritoriality, Cunningham intoned, and the United States government would not protect his publication from suppression by Chinese authorities.

Isaacs detested the laws of extraterritoriality. In a *Forum* article entitled "State Department Threatens *Forum*," he attacked the concept as "an instrument which serves not only the imperialists in the retention of their vise-like grip on China, but which is utilized by the Kuomintang as well for its own protection when need be."[101] These laws were really a screen behind which foreigners could exploit the Chinese with impunity. Isaacs pointed out how the Powers manipulated these laws for their own ends. It was acceptable under those laws when George Bronson Rea, a pro-Japan American who published a treaty port journal called the *Far Eastern Review*, "aided and abetted the predatory advance of Japanese imperialism," but those same laws were inapplicable to "anyone who aligns himself on the other side of the battlefront."[102] In his article, Isaacs interpreted the State Department move as a rap on his knuckles for championing the Noulenses, who by their very presence in Shanghai had threatened the foreign sanctuary.[103]

Isaacs had baited the State Department, forced it to consider making an exception to the letter of the law. This was serious stuff. It was deemed sufficiently important by the *New York Times* to warrant a story, which ran on July 29, under the heading "American Warned of Trial by China." "For the first time in the history of Chino-American relations," the story began, "the United States government is threatening to withdraw the protection of extraterritorial rights from an American citizen, leaving him to trial in the Chinese courts on serious charges carrying the possibility of life imprisonment or even the death penalty."[104] Isaacs could not have asked for better publicity. In one stroke, he embarrassed the State Department, and drew international attention to *The China Forum* and to his colleagues, Madame Sun and Agnes Smedley, who, as the *Times* noted, was "one of the noted revolutionary workers who have headquarters in Shanghai."[105] His father also contributed to the publicity by taking the matter to New York Representative Fiorello H. La Guardia. Robert Isaacs was seriously concerned for his son's safety. Indeed, he hoped that Harold might be deported back to the United States. La Guardia demanded and received a clarification from the State Department about the standing of Harold Isaacs in China. The Department of State hastened to assure the congressman that "Mr. Isaacs's extraterritorial status and rights in China are not the slightest degree impaired by the department's instructions."[106] Only his right to diplomatic protection as a citizen was in possible jeopardy, a vaguely menacing suggestion that could have been interpreted to mean that his passport might be revoked. The point was made, however, to distinguish the protection of Isaacs himself under the laws of extrality from the protection of an enterprise "which is deemed prejudicial to American interests abroad."[107]

"The fact of the matter seems to be that I have successfully called the bluff of the American authorities." Isaacs wrote his parents on August 6. "Since the day I was formally notified of the threat to withdraw my extrality privileges there has been nothing but profound silence rising like an uneasy cloud over the Consulate General."[108] Once Isaacs had broken the story to the press, the consul general had refused to utter a word about the case. Meanwhile, he'd stirred up controversy in both the Chinese- and English-language press in Shanghai. H. G. W. Woodhead, III, perhaps the most conservative columnist in China, raged in the *North China Daily News* that revoking Isaacs's rights, something Woodhead might otherwise have relished, would undermine the whole valid structure of extrality. Publicity of this sort, Isaacs wrote his family, had boosted the *Forum*'s circulation. "The central organ of the Nanking government said the *Forum* is more eagerly read by Chinese than the Chinese press," he wrote, and he added that the book, *Five Years of Kuomintang Reaction,* reprinted from his special edition, had sold well. The net result of all this attention was that the *Forum* was now firmly established as a mouthpiece in the Chinese revolutionary struggle.[109]

This was not the most reassuring news he could have passed on to his parents who only wanted him to come home. That was not about to happen, however, and so it came as a relief to them when Viola Robinson decided to set out for China by steamer from Vancouver, British Columbia, to join their son in Shanghai. Since Viola and Isaacs had been college sweethearts, Isaacs had never for a moment allowed the flame even to flicker. It's true that they continued to entertain political differences. Isaacs was no less fervently radical than in the autumn when he and Viola had exchanged heated words on the subject. "Pink is white," Isaacs wrote Viola in the spring, "Only red is red." The intensity of his revolutionary conversion had swept away some of his early romanticism. For example, he no longer thought there was any virtue to virginity. "I think, for my part," he wrote in April, "that every girl should have her hymen removed at the age of puberty. If you still have yours, that's the product of considerable stupidity. I don't know why you still have. I guess I never will know . . . although it's really my fault. You should have lost it years ago. . . . I don't happen to be in a class with the bloated, pudgy faced chinese gentry who will pay upwards of a thousand dollars for the privilege of having first chance at a girl of perhaps fourteen." Indeed, the draw of their as yet unconsummated love sustained the faithfulness of both Isaacs and his beloved Viola under circumstances that would have strained the constancy of other lovers separated by such a distance. "I love you viola robinson," Isaacs wrote to her, "and may the non-existent god have mercy on my non-existent soul!"[110]

Isaacs's parents not only knew Viola and liked her, they had also come to know her parents, who lived near them on the Upper West Side of Manhattan. Isaacs's parents hoped that Isaacs would marry Viola in Shanghai, rather than some unknown female Chinese revolutionary, but they also gave Viola five hundred dollars just in case it didn't work out and she wanted to come home. Among other things, Viola carried across the Pacific a copy of the first volume of Leon Trotsky's *History of the Russian Revolution,* newly published and unavailable in China, where it was a contraband item. Isaacs was waiting for Viola on the Bund when her ship, the *Empress of Asia,* docked in Shanghai. She was interested to discover on arrival that Isaacs's shirts were missing their buttons. He had pulled the top of his undershorts through the bottom buttonhole of his shirt to suggest a certain respectability. Viola also discovered that Isaacs had taken an apartment in the brand-new Embankment Building on Soochow Creek, near the Bund. He had furnished the apartment himself and hired a cook named Ch'ing.

They wasted no time. The very next day Viola and Harold registered at the consulate general for a marriage license. Cunningham, the consul general, would have nothing to do with them, nor would Sellett, the district attorney. On September 14, a day after his twenty-second birthday, Harold Isaacs and Viola Robinson were married by Vice Consul George Allen, the mail clerk. "She's twenty-one, he's twenty-two and they're very nice," Allen is reported to have said afterward.[111] Isaacs had intentionally waited until he turned twenty-two to marry Viola. He had five hundred dollars riding on a bet with his father, who'd entertained doubts that Isaacs could make it through his twenty-first year without getting married. And so, with a clear conscience, Isaacs banked the money Robert Isaacs had loaned Viola for the trip home.

•

Once Isaacs had sorted out his difficulties with the Department of State, he resumed the publication of his paper on a regular basis. This coincided with the arrival in Shanghai of Viola Robinson, their immediate marriage and the resulting domestication of Harold Isaacs. There was some domestication, also, of the *Forum*. Gone were the more provocative attacks on colonial policy, and accounts of the Red soviets in Kiangsi were almost entirely absent. In editions that were published simultaneously in English and Chinese, Isaacs concentrated his efforts on reporting the Kuomintang's persecution, especially insofar as it concerned Shanghai intellectuals and writers. Isaacs also publicized the activities of the Blue Shirts, Chiang Kai-shek's terrorist brotherhood.

With marriage, Isaacs acquired a certain respectability. For instance, his shirts now sported buttons. But he continued to operate on the fringes of danger. He still ventured forth to meet his underground contacts, and sometimes they even came to the door of his new apartment in the Embankment Building.[112] Viola Isaacs has described herself at that time as extremely naive. She knew Madame Sun, Smedley, Glass and other associates of Isaacs, but rarely set eyes on any of his underground contacts, and tried to remain ignorant of his activities. Insofar as the Noulenses were concerned, however, Viola Isaacs was given a role to play. Once a month, she traveled up to Nanking by train from Shanghai with Jimmy Noulens and Frau Holst, the German woman in Shanghai who looked after Jimmy, so that he could visit his parents. In the cold, dark confines of the prison, the Noulenses turned their pent-up wrath on Viola, who they assumed was a member of the Communist underground. The Noulenses castigated Viola as a representative of the Comintern for not doing more in their defense. "I didn't know what they were talking about," Viola says, "because I was completely in the dark, as I had to be, in case for some reason I was arrested by the Kuomintang and tortured."[113] Eventually in 1937, at the time of the Japanese invasion of Nanking, the Noulenses got out of prison. Jimmy Noulens returned to Russia and years later, while Viola sat watching a newsreel in a movie theater in New York, a distinctly familiar face suddenly appeared on the film before her eyes. "That's Jimmy Noulens!" she cried out in the darkened theater.[114]

Isaacs now printed the *Forum* at home on a hand press with the help of an assistant, a member of the Chinese Communist underground who in all the time he lived with them—almost a year—never revealed to the Isaacses his true name or identity. Although it was less racy, *China Forum* (no longer *The*) nevertheless supplied valuable information to interested Chinese and foreigners in Shanghai. Had publication continued it could have attracted more attention to Chiang's White Terror and other Kuomintang infamies, but *China Forum* ceased publication due to arguments that at the time were raging within the Chinese Communist underground.

In Isaacs's published memoirs of his Chinese experiences, *Reencounters in China,* he recalls his efforts on behalf of Ho Chi Minh, a fugitive in Shanghai during this period. Ho was living at the Navy YMCA. The French had tried to have him extradited to France from Hong Kong, had asked the British to do so, but instead the British had merely expelled him, and he had made his way to Shanghai, where Isaacs became his contact, and his conduit for information. Isaacs mused later in life on this acquaintance. "He was a slight wiry man who always seemed to regard his condition of constant peril with a certain humorous detachment. After finishing a prison term in Hong Kong, he had barely escaped being handed over to the French who wanted him on heavy charges of their own. With the help of English friends, he was put on a British steamer for Shanghai where he contacted someone—I never knew who it was—who put him in touch with me, dangerously, I thought, for I feared that every time we met he was taking a much greater risk than was needful. The Party people in Shanghai were presumably minimizing the possible risk to themselves. This purpose, besides keeping him supplied with money for his modest keep, was to help him get out and on his way to Europe."[115]

When Isaacs approached Slepach, the TASS representative[116] and the only Russian he knew in Shanghai at that time, about smuggling Ho aboard a Soviet freighter out of Shanghai, he was coldly rebuffed; the Soviet Union had just reopened diplomatic relations with China and wouldn't dream of risking this new trade link. "An alternative was to try to get Ho a passport with which he could leave Shanghai in some more conventional fashion," Isaacs wrote. "At one point this involved having photos taken in which, by way of disguise, he appeared with his hair parted in the middle instead of on the side as before, an episode in which we shared some hilarious moments. Ho's escape from Shanghai took place after I left," Isaacs wrote, "having turned my reponsibilities for him back to others through the good offices, as I remember it, of Soong Ching-ling [Madame Sun]."[117]

In the years 1932 and 1933, Isaacs had not yet aligned himself ideologically with the Trotsky faction of the CCP, as he was soon to do. He was, however, deeply troubled by the relationship of the local Communists, and the world Communist movement, to Stalin. He was by nature suspicious of authority and in his education and apprenticeship had refined his skills as a skeptic vis-à-vis authorities. It had bothered Isaacs in Bible study class, for instance, when his teacher quoted the biblical passage, "And the Lord smote the Amalachites: man, woman and child and beast." Although he was only ten years old at the time, Isaacs stood up and declared: "I can understand why God ordered the Amalachites to smite the men, but why the women, children, and the animals? What kind of a God would do this?"[118] If the Old Testament was a literal interpretation of God's truth, then God had serious things to answer for in the view of young Isaacs, for whom the use of language was like a bond of trust between author and reader, speaker and listener.

Isaacs disliked the way the local Communists paid reflex obeisance to Stalin, who appeared to have mismanaged the socialist revolution in China (not to mention Europe). He refused to use the pages of *China Forum* to genuflect to Stalin. He held Stalin in low esteem, if not healthy loathing. At that time the Chinese Communist Party, which was still operating out of Shanghai (though it was soon to move to Kiangsi) had been taken over by Wang Ming and Po Ku. These were two students who had been handpicked in Moscow by Pavel Mif, Stalin's China Hand. (Borodin, though he was not purged by Stalin until 1949, had been removed from matters having to do with China.) Wang Ming and Po Ku had been brought back to China from Russia to replace the disgraced labor organizer and party general secretary, Li Li-san, who, with disastrous results, had tried to revive the workers' revolution. The Stalinists were calling the shots within the Chinese Communist Party. They took note that Isaacs was giving Stalin the cold shoulder in his journal.

On the sixteenth anniversary of the October Revolution, in the fall of 1933, Isaacs recognized the event without once making mention of Stalin. This failure on the part of Isaacs simply enraged the Chinese Communist underground. To them, it was an act of heresy. At a clandestine night meeting, attended by Chou En-lai, Isaacs was called to account. The confrontation was explosive. Isaacs was ordered to go to Moscow for "reeducation."[119] Two years earlier Isaacs had been trying to figure out how to work his way to Russia via the Black Sea as a stevedore for this very purpose. He now declined the opportunity. In fact, he would soon be taking a very long, hard look at Stalin's role in the Chinese Revolution of 1925–1927.

Isaacs's days as *l'homme engagé* in Shanghai were numbered. Financial contributions from the Communist underground, which had paid the operating costs of *China Forum,* dried up altogether once Isaacs had made his opposition to Stalin a matter of record. For Isaacs, this spelled potential disaster. Fortunately, as it happened, Robert and Sophie, Isaacs's parents, had come to spend a month in Shanghai in the winter of 1934 in the course of a trip around the world. Robert Isaacs and Sam, his brother, had inherited the family business from their father, who had come to America as a young man in the 1860s on one of the earliest

Russian-Jewish migratory waves and started a rewarding career in real estate by buying up slices of land on the Lower East Side of Manhattan. His sons, expanding to the Upper West Side, had multiplied the family holdings many times over. Despite his wealth, however, Robert Isaacs was a rough diamond with some decidedly reactionary opinions. Once, to the dismay of his son, Robert Isaacs declared that if only Adolf Hitler had not exterminated the Jews he would have been a great man. Sam Isaacs, a Columbia Law School graduate, was more educated than his brother, and probably influenced the course of his nephew's intellectual development. Harold Isaacs also attended Columbia and had considered going into the legal profession, although later he dismissed this possibility because, he argued, it led to sophistry and considerations of a material kind.

Robert Isaacs was horrified by the ideological turn his son had taken in Shanghai. He enjoyed taking tea with Madame Sun Yat-sen at the house on the Rue Molière. He also enjoyed joshing with Ch'ing, the cook in the Embankment Building apartment, who, at fifty-seven, was the same age as Isaacs's father. Robert Isaacs was also undoubtedly proud, even awestruck, by the power of his son's intellect. Nevertheless, he wrote Sam and Sam's wife, Gertie, from Shanghai, "it is a pity to see that brilliant mind be just a one track affair."[120] The elder Isaacs felt more comfortable in Shanghai with the outlook of his son's nemesis, Consul General Cunningham, upon whom he called "to let him know that we are law abiding citizens of our beloved country and do not share in the views of Harold . . . we spent a very pleasant half hour there." (Edwin Cunningham assured the elder Isaacs that he was quite aware of his views "by reason of certain statement[s] I made, and which were called to his attention.")[121] Robert and Sophie were looking forward to leaving Shanghai and getting on with their trip around the world. "If we succeed in forgetting, and throwing off all about Harold's and Viola's ideas—and lousy ideals," he wrote Sam and Gertie, he expected to enjoy the rest of the trip thoroughly. He and Sophie, he wrote, "are happy the Forum is no more, the reasons I will tell you when we get home—no Forum—no trouble."[122]

One of the reasons for the *Forum*'s demise, which the elder Isaacs was reluctant to confide by letter, was that all Communist underground funds had dried up. Thanks to his father's munificence, however, Harold and Viola now planned to depart for Peiping. Radical though he was, Isaacs was not in total rebellion against his father. Isaacs regarded his father as a good-natured, but embarrassing, presence in the scheme of his life, wherein he, Harold Isaacs, was the true patriarch. He had no qualms whatever about accepting a stipend of a hundred dollars a month from his father, who paid it out from his own private bank to Harold's account. Robert Isaacs would have preferred, he wrote Sam and Gertie, "to see him in Europe, or California, would like to have about 3000 miles between us, where we could see him every once in a while" in New York, where "in his present state of mind I think he would be fighting all the cops in Columbus Circle or Union Sq."[123] Sophie, however, was Harold Isaacs's number one admirer. She was of a more graceful, civilized temperament than her husband. It was Harold, not her husband, who brought her flowers on her birthday. Sophie persuaded Robert Isaacs to support his son and his son's bride while they pursued Harold's radical studies in Peiping and beyond in the years that followed.[124] This was fortunate because Isaacs was through in Shanghai. Not only did the *Forum*'s financial contributions dry up, so did the documents and other source material that had supplied Isaacs with information for his most controversial and urgent articles. His shadowy Communist patrons dropped Isaacs and so did Agnes Smedley.

Smedley was passionate about her friends and allies, who were almost always of the same ideological commitment as she was (one exception being J.B. Powell). "She was an all or nothing person," Viola Isaacs recalls. Her friendship with Isaacs was rooted in their common, revolutionary cause. In Shanghai, Isaacs was a privileged member in good standing of Smedley's small coterie of leftist, Western friends. They met often, and when Viola arrived on the scene, Smedley quickly befriended her. She even bestowed upon the Isaacses a set of dishes as a wedding present. When Isaacs parted company with the Stalinists, however, Smedley took violent offense, perhaps because he was also her protégé and she had done so much to set him up with the Communist underground in Shanghai. Her allegiance was to the Chinese Communists—and to the international Communist movement, even though she herself was not a member of the Communist Party, in China or anywhere else for that matter. As one acquaintance once said of Smedley,[125] "In her heart she was a Communist." Isaacs's first allegiance was to the truth. The same claim has never been made on behalf of Smedley. As Viola Isaacs has somewhat delicately put it, Smedley "embroidered the truth."[126] When Isaacs broke with the Communists, she expressed her fury in the accusation, printed in the pages of the *Daily Worker,* that Isaacs was a "Japanese imperialist agent."[127]

In reality, Isaacs was more like a principled muckraker who functioned at his peak of enthusiasm when he was driven by a sense of outrage. Deprived of his outlet in Shanghai, he turned his printing press over to the Trotskyist Frank Glass (an act that further outraged his former Stalinist friends, who expected him to donate it to them), said goodbye to "Hsu," his assistant (who on parting told Isaacs with tears streaming down his cheeks, "I'll never believe you're a counter revolutionary!"[128]) and headed with Viola for Peiping. The Isaacses took affectionate leave of Madame Sun. She told them to be careful.

"And I don't mean the Kuomintang," she told Isaacs.

"Do you mean the Communists?" Isaacs asked her.

"Yes. I do," replied Madame Sun. "Be careful. You don't really know these people. They are capable of anything."[129]

In Peiping Isaacs planned to dedicate himself to a study of the Kiangsi soviets. Isaacs brought with him trunks full of papers published by Eugene Chen and Wang Ching-wei in the Kiangsi soviets, which he had acquired on a visit he had made to Foochow, during a brief insurrection down there in 1932.[130] Isaacs got started on this project in the fall of 1934, after he and Viola finished work on their anthology of Chinese fiction, entitled *Straw Sandals*.

When he and Viola began to explore the Kiangsi materials Isaacs realized that he needed a translator, one, moreover, whom he could trust. Isaacs decided to turn for help to his old friend and mentor Frank Glass. Glass had been a committed proponent of the theories of Leon Trotsky at the time he left South Africa. In Shanghai, he eventually became a confederate of the Trotskyists, who knew him as Li Fu-jen.

The Trotsky faction within the Chinese Communist Party originated in Moscow among students at KUTV, Communist University for the Toilers of the East, a political school established to train cadres for revolutionary work in Asia, and the faction also took hold at Sun Yat-sen University, which had been established in Moscow exclusively for Chinese students in 1925. In 1927, the provost of Sun Yat-sen University, Karl Radek, took an openly Trotskyist stand on the subject of the Chinese Revolution and its demise. This was intolerable to Stalin, who ousted Radek and replaced him with Pavel Mif, who subsequently went to China and established his protégé, Wang Ming, in the leadership of the CCP. But Trotsky's speeches and monographs were in circulation in Moscow in those days. A number of Chinese students got hold of these and secretly sided with Trotsky on the issue of China, an essential element of the increasingly bitter struggle that ended in Trotsky's deportation. A small group of the Chinese Trotskyists, undetected by Stalin's henchmen, went back to China armed with Trotsky's position papers. One, Liu Jen-ching, who had been present at the creation of the Chinese Communist Party in Shanghai in July 1921, returned to China in 1929 via Europe and visited Trotsky on the island of Prinkipo, which is near Istanbul, the first stop outside Russia on Trotsky's long journey into exile. Liu returned to China loaded down with minutes and other secret Comintern documents that documented the course of acrimonious meetings throughout the Trotsky-Stalin *mano a mano*. Stalin had seen to it that documents which exposed the inconsistencies and failures of his China policies were never allowed out of committee chambers in the Kremlin, except, of course, those belonging to Trotsky, who, as a member of the Central Committee of the Communist Party, USSR, had the right to keep stenograms of speeches and policy statements crafted by Stalin and others. Consequently, many of the documents Trotsky gave to Liu provided damning evidence of Stalin's miscalculations that could be found nowhere else.

Ch'en Tu-hsiu, the disgraced former Chinese Communist Party general secretary, had been almost entirely ignorant of the content of the Stalin-Trotsky fight insofar as it concerned the 1927 Chinese Revolution or anything else for that matter. When he was presented with these documents detailing the Stalin-Trotsky debate, Ch'en realized for the first time how and why he had been betrayed by Stalin. It came to Ch'en as a great revelation when he discovered that positions he had been accused of taking by Stalin were those that Stalin himself had at one time advocated. He realized how Stalin had made him the scapegoat for the failure of his own policies. Ch'en moved rapidly toward Trotskyism. In 1929, he was expelled from the Chinese Communist Party, which followed a strict Stalinist line. A purge of Chinese Trotskyists within the CCP followed swiftly. Stalin was shocked by Ch'en's outspoken conversion to Trotskyism and by the number of oppositionists in the Shanghai underground. Soon Stalin began to root out oppositionists among the Chinese students still in Moscow. By the end of 1929, Trotskyists accounted for approximately half the Chinese student body. Stalin rounded them up, shut down Sun Yat-sen University, and sent the Trotskyists off to labor camps in Siberia. According to reports, they were subjected to treatment worse than their Soviet counterparts. Hardly more than a handful returned to China. A lucky few had gone undetected and managed to make their way back to China, where they joined the breakaway Trotsky movement of expelled CCP workers under Ch'en Tu-hsiu. They suffered persecution by both the CCP and the KMT, who were each out to exterminate them and on occasion worked together to that end. [131]

There is nothing to suggest that during his two-year stewardship of *The China Forum* Isaacs was very much under the sway of the Chinese Trotskyists, who were either in jail, or so fragmented that their influence was minor.

Neither Isaacs nor Frank Glass knew a great deal about the Stalin-Trotsky debate insofar as it concerned China until they were informed of the official Moscow line on Ch'en Tu-hsiu in 1932 when he reappeared, a ghostly figure from the past, as leader of the Trotskyist opposition in the Chinese underground. When the CCP issued a strongly worded condemnation of Ch'en, Isaacs refused to print it in the *Forum*.[132] The Chinese Communist maneuver to get Isaacs to publish defamatory material on the Trotskyists pushed Isaacs into the Trotskyist camp. Frank Glass assisted in this process by recommending Liu Jen-ching to Isaacs as a translator in 1934.

Liu Jen-ching had made the acquaintance of Harold Isaacs in Shanghai. Liu was fluent in English, he was also intimately familiar with the sinuosities of the Stalin-Trotsky imbroglio, and equipped with the materials to document his knowledge. When the Isaacses were settled in Peiping, Liu moved into their compound at 1 Ta Yang Yi Pin Hu-tung, along with his wife, two children and all the documents that had been given to him by Trotsky. In the course of translating the Kiangsi documents, Isaacs and Liu worked day and night with the assistance of an active group of Peiping students. It was painstaking work, and it was dangerous. Much of the material of the greatest value was brought to the compound by Communists under assumed names. One, Viola Isaacs recalled not long ago, went by the name of "Miss Wang." She brought an entire file of Chinese Communist Party materials that no one had seen in the years since the Revolution of 1927. They had been buried in various grave sites along with the deceased during funeral ceremonies in 1927, in the aftermath of the collapse of the Wuhan Revolutionary Center, at roughly the time that Rayna Prohme and Madame Sun were making their way to Russia in the company of Eugene Chen. This precious cache had been exhumed by Trotskyist associates of Liu Jen-ching in the environs of Peiping.[133]

Liu and Isaacs went through the entire file page by page. Liu would describe the contents of each page to Isaacs. When he came up with an item of interest, he would then translate it while Isaacs copied it down in English. This modus operandi resulted in more than a thousand single-spaced typed pages of material. It was the manner in which they were proceeding when, one quiet afternoon in late 1934, Isaacs and Liu came upon a piece of information that Isaacs had never imagined could possibly exist. He felt "suddenly rammed by the severe blow of truths I had not known were there," he wrote many years later.[134] "In the obscure internal Party documents, mimeographed on thin paper already shredding and yellowed,"[135] the truth was disclosed to Isaacs regarding the arrest, three years earlier, of the so-called "five writers and nineteen others" who had been executed on the Lunghua Garrison grounds, whose cause Isaacs had embraced in the first issue of *The China Forum*.

The accent had always been on the five writers. This was the cause that Agnes Smedley, Lu Hsun and Madame Sun had chosen to publicize abroad. No explanation was ever given concerning the "nineteen others." Who were they? Nobody ever asked, and nothing was ever said by the Chinese Communist Party, which had used the execution of the five writers to stir up outrage against the Kuomintang. The "nineteen others" remained anonymous. The twenty-four victims had been rounded up at the Eastern Hotel, but the League of Left Wing Writers never provided any information about what they were all doing there. The league provided no motive for the mass arrest, except to state that one sixty-year-old participant was executed "because he had not betrayed his son, who was a Communist, to the police."[136] At the time of the arrests, the story was entirely in the hands of the Communist underground, which supplied Isaacs with money and supporting material, and which also communicated with the outside world through the ardent Miss Smedley and the League of Left Wing Writers. Now, suddenly and unexpectedly, Isaacs discovered, as Liu read out loud to him in English from a Chinese Communist Party document, that the five writers and "nineteen others" had been meeting in the Eastern Hotel that night to discuss an alternative to the leadership of the Chinese Communist Party imposed by Stalin and his henchman Pavel Mif. Some of the nineteen anonymous others were Trotskyists. Most of them were workers who had participated in the underground Communist movement. Because they were longtime party activists and trade union representatives, these nineteen apostates represented a real threat to the new order. They were betrayed by one of their own colleagues in the Chinese Communist Party, who tipped off the settlement police as to the whereabouts of the meeting. Thus, knowingly, the CCP had arranged to stifle dissent through the subsequent raid by the Shanghai Municipal Police, who, as was their custom, turned the captives over to the Chinese authorities.

It was a moment of truth for Harold Isaacs in the afternoon quiet of his study in Peiping. He had broken with the Communists over what he considered to be their unreasonable, authoritarian demands. He had not, however, prepared himself for the brutality disclosed by this revelation. He had never suspected the Communists, Chinese or any other kind, up to and including Stalin, of using such ruthless methods to silence dissent in their own ranks. The discovery switched on a light for Isaacs. In the beam, he caught a vivid glimpse of Stalin's hand at work behind the scenes.

With the help of Liu Jen-ching, Isaacs went back to the origins of the Chinese Communist Party and its relationship to the Kuomintang. He had most of the documents he needed to explore the role of Stalin in the course of events, equipped as he was with the Kiangsi files and the Stalin-Trotsky papers. The Old Testament prophet in him, who had stood up to wonder what kind of God it was who had condemned to slaughter the women and children and animals of the Amalachites, now began to trace the collapse of the Chinese Revolution back to Stalin, which, under the circumstances, was not unlike confronting the God of the Old Testament. To do this, Isaacs employed investigative research to produce a classic of contemporary historical analysis that to this day is used in courses on twentieth-century Chinese history. The original version, published in London in 1938 by Secker and Warburg, reads like a thriller.[137] The story is complex and detailed; Isaacs took possession of the material and wrote his chronicle in a prose that gleams with outrage.

In March 1935, Liu, along with his wife and children, were arrested in the Peiping train station, where they had gone to board a train for the south. During a routine baggage search, police had found CCP pamphlets, which Liu had carelessly packed in his luggage. Through the agency of Ida Pruitt, an American administrator at the Peking Union Medical College, Liu's wife and children were soon released. Liu's fate remained a mystery until many years later, when Isaacs learned that his colleague had been released from prison in Nanking after the flight of Chiang Kai-shek's government to Wuhan, on the eve of the Japanese invasion, along with all the other prisoners held in Nanking, including the Noulenses.[138]

Isaacs was conscience-stricken when the Liu family was arrested. He was also feeling the strain of working with contraband material of such explosive content. He had come to identify his political beliefs quite passionately with those of Leon Trotsky. He and Viola decided that the time had come to leave China and return to the United States where a teaching job awaited Viola in the fall. In June 1935, accompanied by ten trunks of documents and the partly written manuscript of Isaacs's book, they sailed on board the Messagerie Maritime liner *Aramis* from Shanghai to Marseilles, where they disembarked for a European journey. In Paris, Isaacs visited Albert Treint, the French Comintern delegate, looked up various Trotskyists and spent some time doing research on the Chinese Revolution at the Bibliotheque Nationale.[139]

At the Bibliotheque Nationale Isaacs's main objective was to study past issues of *Inprecorr,* the international newsletter of the Comintern, so that he could corroborate the version of events he had stitched together from his China materials with what had been reported abroad. Almost immediately it came to his attention that one issue was missing, published around the time of the Shanghai coup. It contained excerpts from the speech that Stalin had delivered on April 5, 1927, at the Hall of Columns, in response to Trotsky's criticisms of Stalin's support of

Chiang Kai-shek. The speech was made before a meeting of three thousand party functionaries, and contained this particular passage:

"Chiang Kai-shek is submitting to discipline. The Kuomintang is a bloc, a sort of revolutionary parliament, with the Right, the Left, and the Communists. Why make a coup d'état? Why drive away the Right when we have the majority and the Right listens to us? The peasant needs a worn-out jade as long as she is necessary. He does not drive her away. So it is with us. When the Right is of no more use to us, we will drive it away. At present, we need the Right. It has capable people, who still direct the army and lead it against the imperialists. Chiang Kai-shek has perhaps no sympathy for the revolution but he is leading the army and cannot do otherwise than lead it against the imperialists. Besides this, the people of the Right have relations with the generals of Chang Tso-lin and understand very well how to demoralize them and to induce them to pass over to the side of the revolution, bag and baggage, without striking a blow. Also, they have connections with the rich merchants and can raise money from them. So they have to be utilized to the end, squeezed out like a lemon, and then flung away."[140]

This became a piece of evidence damning to Stalin when, on April 12, 1927, Chiang Kai-shek turned and crushed the workers in Shanghai and then launched his terror against the Chinese Communists, subsequently expelling all the Soviet advisers from China. Who, in the end, was "squeezed out like a lemon, and then flung away"? Certainly not Chiang Kai-shek. Stalin's assessment of the situation was clearly mistaken, as everyone who heard the speech knew. Theoretically, Chiang's Shanghai massacre was a vindication of Trotsky's position that the Chinese Communists should have turned on Chiang Kai-shek first, before he could turn on them. Trotsky had argued that with the help of Russian advisers, workers and peasants should have seized control of the Revolution, certainly once the Northern Expedition had reached the Yangtze Valley. The workers should have taken over the factories in Wuhan, he argued; the peasants should have been instructed to establish soviets in the countryside. Instead, Stalin had ordered the Chinese Communist leadership to suppress the peasant revolt and disarm the workers. Stalin's speech, made only a week before Chiang's betrayal, showed what a massive blunder his policy had been. It was a speech that should have badly embarrassed Stalin in the eyes of his colleagues, and even loosened his iron grip on the leadership of the USSR. But Stalin cleverly suppressed this speech, and it was never published. In May, at the Eighth Plenum of the ECCI (the Comintern), Stalin was challenged to explain his words by Vuyovitch, a Trotsky ally, who declared, upon producing his own shorthand notes of the speech: "Comrade Stalin will always

Rayna Prohme as a young girl in Chicago.

Rayna Prohme with a dog in China.
(Two photos: courtesy Carol Lew Simons)

Manchurian warlord Chang Tso-lin, ruler of northern China from 1925–1928.

Madame Sun Yat-sen in the 1920s.
(Two photos: H. B. Elliston Archives)

Agnes Smedley in Red Army uniform, Yenan, 1937. *(Photo by Owen Lattimore; Peabody Museum, Harvard University)*

Harold Isaacs on the 1931 Yangtze River journey that changed his life. *(Courtesy Alexander Buchman)*

Harold and Viola Isaacs on board the Messagerie-Maritime liner *Aramis* in 1935. *(Courtesy Viola Isaacs)*

Mao Tse-tung, Yenan, 1937. *(Photo by Owen Lattimore; Peabody Museum, Harvard University)*

A Peiping Party, 1936: the actress Anna May Wong, Sydney Cooper, the esthete Harold Acton, and C. M. MacDonald, the China correspondent for the London *Times*. *(Photo by Graham Peck; Boston University)*

Helen Foster Snow and Edgar Snow.

Helen Foster Snow on the beach at Peitaiho with James Bertram, the New Zealand author and journalist.

Helen Foster Snow with Gobi, her Kansu greyhound, a gift from the explorer Sven Hedin.

Edgar Snow in the garden outside his Peiping studio.

Edgar Snow in a sun helmet, symbol of the foreign devil, talking with a young Red Army officer in North Shensi.

(All photos: Edgar Snow Collections, University of Missouri, Kansas City)

Teddy White at the Chungking Press Hostel, April 1940.

Mel Jacoby and Teddy White on assignment in Chungking, 1940. *(Two photos: Harvard University Archives)*

General Joseph Stilwell and Major General Patrick Hurley break bread with Chinese military officers on the eve of General Stilwell's recall. *(U.S. Army photograph)*

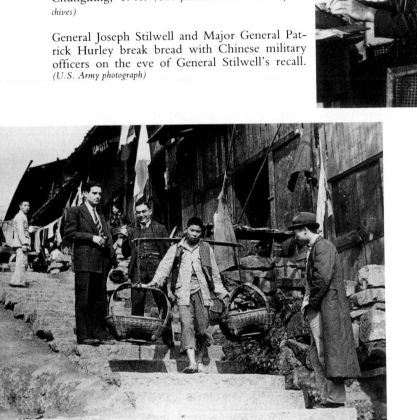

Barbara Stephens relaxing with a book in Peiping, 1946.

Pure discourse: Yeh Teh-chuang, Barbara Stephens, and Graham Peck in Peiping, 1946.

The memorial service in Nanking for Barbara
Stephens was attended by many of her friends
in the foreign press corps. *(Three photos: Boston University)*

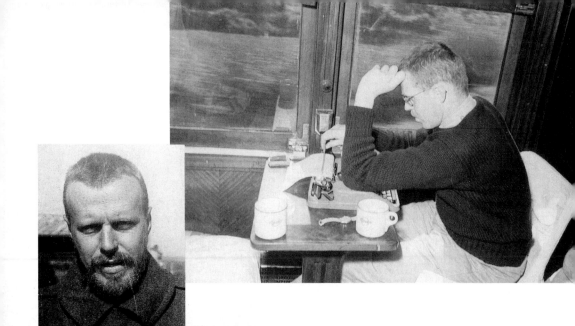

Christopher Rand on a train in China during World War II.

Christopher Rand, *New York Herald Tribune* correspondent in China from 1946–1948.

Maddie Rand at the Temple of Heaven, Peïping, 1947.

Chou En-lai with American reporters in Yenan, March 1947. Christopher Rand is on the far right. *(Four photos: Boston University)*

have the opportunity of rectifying unintentional inaccuracies by laying his stenogram before us."[141] Stalin evaded this trap, which was intended to force an admission from Stalin that he had badly misjudged Chiang Kai-shek. Apart from Vuyovitch's notes, there was no evidence that he had ever given the speech, because no stenogram existed. Trotsky pointed out at the same meeting, "a few days later the squeezed-out lemon seized power and the army. . . . As a member of the Central Committee I had the right to get the stenogram of this speech, but my pains and attempts were in vain."[142]

The missing passage was an important piece of evidence in the case that Isaacs was making against Stalin, which was that in the course of his struggle for power with Trotsky, Stalin had been instrumental in destroying China's social revolution. Isaacs knew that *Inprecorr* had reported the speech, and he was determined to get his hands on it, for it was a piece of evidence straight from Stalin's lips that he had pursued a ruinous China policy and then later covered his tracks. In London, where the Isaacses went next, at the British Museum, Isaacs once again found that the same issue was missing from the English-language copies of *Inprecorr* when these were brought before him.

The Isaacses sailed from Liverpool to Norway, to visit Leon Trotsky. Trotsky and his wife, Natalya, at the invitation of the Norwegian government, were living in the countryside two hours from Oslo, near the village of Honefoss, unencumbered, for a time, by the armed guards who were usually assigned to protect Trotsky at all times from Stalin's hit men. The Isaacses had caught them at a rare moment when, briefly, they were living outside the shadow of the fear of assassination. *"Nous avons faites la bombe!"* Trotsky cried to the Isaacses the day they met.[143] After this burst of exuberant French announcing that he and his wife had been celebrating, Trotsky explained that the night before he and Natalya had visited Oslo, where, for the first time in years, they had dined at a restaurant and gone to the theater, to attend a performance of an Ibsen play. The Isaacses stayed in a pension in Honefoss. Every day for a week, they pedaled over the countryside on bicycles to call on the Trotskys, and take their meals with them. One morning, as they pushed their bicycles up the hilly country road to the Trotskys' villa, small projectiles pinged off their bicycles and pelted them from some hidden place. "Standing behind a bush was Trotsky playfully throwing pebbles at us," Viola recalled.[144] By day, Isaacs interviewed Trotsky. At night, he translated an essay that Trotsky had written from French into English. The essay was entitled "The New French Revolution." It was about worker strikes currently taking place in Paris that Trotsky, who had only recently been refused permission to continue residing in France on the grounds that he was stirring the cauldron of worker discontent, wanted to publish in the United States.[145]

The two couples got on famously. The Isaacses were young, charming, full of life and enthusiasm, and this endeared them to the Trotskys. They conversed in three languages. Natalya understood no English but she spoke French and Russian. Trotsky and Isaacs communicated in French and English. Viola and Trotsky and Isaacs talked in English. Trotsky then translated, into Russian, for Natalya's benefit, every single item of conversation that was spoken in English. This impressed Viola. "He was very much of a feminist and made sure we were both a part of the conversation," Viola later recalled.[146] A bond of friendship was forged between Isaacs and Trotsky on the occasion of this visit that lasted for a number of years, strongly reinforced by the immense respect in which Isaacs held the older revolutionary, who wrote the introduction to Isaacs's book when it was finally completed. Indeed, although he withdrew Trotsky's introduction from later editions, Isaacs never altogether lost his feeling of deep admiration for Trotsky. He later rejected Trotsky's advocacy of revolutionary violence, but he never disavowed Trotsky's interpretation of the Chinese Revolution and its demise at the hands of Stalin, an interpretation that has withstood the test of time.

In New York, their ultimate destination, Isaacs and his bride settled down in an apartment on the Lower East Side of Manhattan, where the sinister charcoal drawing by Adolph Dehn of the Chinese officer and the heaped-up skulls adorned the wall of their bedroom. Isaacs once again was employed as a translator for the Havas News Agency. He went to the Havas office at five o'clock every morning and worked there until noon. This left him the rest of the day to work on his book.[147]

The *Daily Worker,* which subscribed to the Communist News Service, supplied Isaacs with all the copies of *Inprecorr* he asked for, except the elusive issue containing the report on Stalin's speech of April 5, 1927. He continued to hunt for it. One day, at the New York Public Library, he finally tracked it down. The article had been razored out. "This made the hairs on the back of Harold's neck stand up," Viola Isaacs recalled many years later.[148] Clearly it had been extracted on the orders of Stalin himself by some party operative in New York. It was palpable evidence of Stalin's ruthless thoroughness and total command over the party that not a single copy of the damning article could be found in a public archive anywhere in the world, as far as Isaacs could tell.

Isaacs finally obtained the purged material from Max Schachtman, a professional revolutionary who was head of the Trotskyist faction in New York and an associate of Isaacs. Schachtman kept voluminous files. He possessed every issue of the *Daily Worker* in print, including the one that Isaacs was looking for. Schachtman produced it at once, so that Isaacs was able to include the incriminating passage in his book, which, when he finished writing it, he called *The Tragedy of the Chinese Revolution*.[149]

Yin and Yang

SOME OF THE OTHER Westerners in Peiping found her abrasive. She was forward, ambitious. She was also tense. To many, she seemed driven by a compulsion to achieve success at any price. She seemed impatient for success. If anything, she was too impatient to settle easily into the never-never twilight of 1933 Peiping. Her plan had been to write a great book. She had fully intended to make her mark on the world as a China Hand and a foreign correspondent. Now here she was married to the man she'd come to China to eclipse.

She'd come to China with a slightly mad fixation. She had come to find Edgar Snow, to interview him, and to find out how he wrote those articles she so admired in the *New York Herald Tribune Magazine,* and then to write them herself. She was sure she could do it better. She had hardly any professional expertise, yet she had convictions and brains to back her up. Furthermore, the editor of the Herald Tribune magazine, Mrs. William Brown Mahoney, was a feminist. Surely she would prefer articles on China by a woman to those of a man.

She'd found Edgar Snow the very day her ship docked in Shanghai. It was a day of oppressive humidity and dreadful calm just before the worst typhoon of the century ripped through Shanghai and up the Yangtze Valley, the very week that Harold Isaacs returned from his journey to the interior. She'd interviewed Snow. "If I'd known you were going to interview me," he told her, "I would have done a better job." She'd even persuaded the infatuated Edgar Snow to get her press credentials, and accompany her on fact-finding trips. Even so, when all was said and done, her plans had been derailed. She had not, as planned, superceded Edgar Snow. She had married him. She was no longer Helen Foster. She was Helen Foster *Snow.*

She was extremely poised for someone so young. She was attractive as well. In September 1933 she wrote her father-in-law that she was considered beautiful by the Chinese because she had "a moon face, button nose, and slightly oblique eyes."[1] She pulled her light brown hair back tightly and wore it parted down the middle, in a knot at the back of her neck. This gave her the appearance of an older, sophisticated woman. She wore tight-fitting suits with short skirts that emphasized her chic, Parisian look and showed off her shapely legs. She wore high-heeled shoes.

In Peiping, the Snows soon found a quiet house on a quiet *hutung,* one of the many by-lanes that meander through the city, for fifteen dollars a month. Three servants—a number one boy, a cook and a coolie—all came to another fifteen. She neither drank nor smoked nor used coffee, and she forswore an abundant wardrobe and other luxuries, such as the Manchu jewelry available then in Peiping for a song. She suppressed her material yearnings in the higher service of ambition. She permitted Snow his Maxwell House coffee, his Gillette razors and his Camel cigarettes. For her part, she made do with the four formal evening dresses she'd brought along from the States.

Displacement, in any case, was one element in her theory of their marriage, which she compared to percussion. "Alone in an alien and cruel land, we were pressed in upon each other in a small vacuum," she later wrote. "We were under the pressure of poverty and cut off from the outside. Ed was the happy type and did not feel deprived. But I was well aware of what I had given up for this existence."[2] Instead of superseding or trying to eclipse her husband at this early stage of their life together, she made his success her objective. She buried her true ambition, reined it in, and set about the task of making Edgar Snow world-famous.

She called their relationship "this yin-yang atom."[3] The couple, as she saw it, had to be faithful and monogamous, so that the power line that held it together could be maintained in a state of high tension. To her, "the wife was the powerhouse that generated and regenerated the physical and spiritual energy that not only sustained the husband, but made all his higher achievements possible."[4] This was hardly a formula that by today's standards would be considered acceptable to women with Helen Snow's drive. "Such a wife," she wrote, "instinctively carried out a one-woman conspiracy, part of which was to keep her powers secret as a natural form of witchcraft, to build up the male ego."[5]

One hard and fast rule she established from the outset was a taboo on offspring. Career, fame, success, these were the object of their union, not children. Her passion was intellectual. She and her husband read the same books and talked intensely about what they read and thought. She was Edgar Snow's intellectual prod, and his disciplinarian. "Ed lived under a reign of terror," she later declared. "I trained him."[6] He was slow, or so she claimed. He was easygoing. Evans Carlson, marine adjutant of the legation guard, later a hero of World War Two, was a friend of theirs. "Don't ever give up criticizing Ed and pushing him," Carlson told her. "That's the making of him."[7]

Unquestionably, her convictions about self-deprivation and discipline were useful to Snow. Peiping was a drifter's paradise. In Peiping time slipped silently by. Someone as carefree as Edgar Snow, who always did whatever he felt inclined to do, "no matter," as his wife later wrote, "how inconvenient it might have been for me or others,"[8] could easily have become distracted by other pursuits. Beneath his casual veneer was a tough, serious soul, but "Lao Pei-ching," as the city was also called, was a play city of endless charms and temptations.

Now that Chiang Kai-shek had transferred the government from Peking to Nanking and renamed the former capital Peiping, "City of Northern Peace," the ancient imperial city was disencumbered of much purpose. It was a great walled city of the plain, a terminus for camel caravans from the Gobi Desert. "The autumn days were glorious in Peking," Helen Snow wrote.[9] In the winter, sometimes it snowed. Then, for a time, it glittered icy and brilliant white in the winter sun below a deep blue dome of sky. At night the city was still and silent under the vast and starry heavens. Sometimes, desert winds from the Gobi drove a dark and biting storm of dust and sand through the city. The fine ocher Gobi sand covered everything. It seeped into every little crevice, coated every surface. Peiping was also, Edgar Snow wrote, "A city of vivid springs."[10] In the summer, Peiping throbbed in heat.

It was a city enclosed by great earthen brick walls, thick enough, it was said, so that six horses could gallop abreast along the ramparts. Within the walls, situated behind the mulberry-colored private enclosure of the Forbidden City, where China's emperors had ruled for centuries under the Mandate of Heaven, lay preserved as they do today the artifacts of a sumptuous imagination, lakes, parks, palaces, rookeries and a man-made hill. In the lower, gray-walled compounds spread out through the rest of the city, and along the wide boulevards that traversed the precincts in a gigantic grid was to be found the charm of the city's life. "Peking," wrote Edgar Snow, "was a city of retired courtiers and soldiers of empire, of scholars and absentee landlords, of monks and artisan merchants and of ricksha coolies speaking a cultured tongue; a city nobly conceived and nobly made, a treasury of art, a place of gentle birth and of more knavery than down right wickedness," a city of "leisure and family love, of poverty and tragedy and indifference to dirt. . . ."[11]

What were the secrets of Peiping's enchantment for the Westerners who lived there? For one thing, it was very far from home. It was about as remote from the Western rat race as you could get in physical and spiritual terms and still feel that you were at the heart of civilization. "Isolated at the far end of the Orient," an observant young artist named Graham Peck wrote of the one thousand or so nonmissionary Westerners in Peiping, "their society made a concentrated and rather feverishly colored miniature of the western world with all its phobias, desires, ambitions and fallacies. Entertaining was cheap—vodka ten cents a bottle, flowers a penny a bush—and at endless lunches, dinners, picnics, and cocktail parties the Peking foreigners met to rub together their prejudices and peculiarities and exchange fantastic information about their neighbors."[12] For the diplomats, most of whom had simply ignored the removal of the government to Nanking and stayed where they were, in the Legation Quarter, it was possible to relax comfortably in the certainty that communication with the outside world was rarely an urgent matter. The diplomatic pouch traveled by sea.[13]

Peiping was also hermetic. Few in the foreign community paid much heed to what was happening in the rest of China. There were too many enchanting diversions in the environs of Peiping: tennis, polo, horse races at Paomachang, lunches and dinners and rooftop dancing at the Peking Hotel, weekend picnic jaunts to temples in the Western Hills. There was an intensely social side to life in Peiping for Westerners that had very little to do with China at all except insofar as China made it possible. Besides the usual diplomatic functions, dinner parties were held incessantly by the international socialites who had settled into Peiping to make use of the palaces once inhabited by the Manchu nobility for lavish entertainments. The guests available for soirees made an intoxicating mix: German and French and British sinophiles; aesthetes like the Anglo-American Oxford-educated "child of the sun," Harold Acton; archaeologists and explorers and scholars like Sven Hedin, or Roy Chapman Andrews, or Père Pierre Teilhard de Chardin; artists and vagabonds; and a steady trickle of celebrities from the West, among them J. P. Marquand, the Boston novelist, and the actress Anna May Wong.

"In the red-walled hothouse gloom of their elaborate homes in renovated temples or palaces," Peck wrote, "in the smoky European ballrooms and bars of the two big hotels, or, on hot evenings, at the favored picnic places in the imperial parks or the Western Hills, Peking gossip grew and flourished like some musky jungle flower." For all its intensity, however, the life led by Westerners was languid. "Eccentricity is demanding work," Peck wrote, "and the easy-going air of the city which had captured these folk soon made them feel that activity of any sort was not to be encouraged. As their time in Peking lengthened, they sat more continuously in their flower-decked courts behind the high gray walls, listening to the whistling doves and contemplating the wisdom of the old proverb: In leisure hours the nails grow best, and the hair grows luxuriant when the mind is at rest."[14]

The Snows entered into this life to some degree. For a time they owned one entire sleek Mongol racing pony and half of another. They went to the rooftop of the Peking Hotel. Helen Snow loved to waltz, and she made Snow accompany her to the dancing terrace even though she could never get him to dance. They gave dinner parties, and also attended them. Yet they kept their distance, perhaps because she was not, like her husband, a lover of all people. She looked down on the embassy wives. She took no solace from the conventional social life of the expatriate wives: tennis, bridge, ladies' luncheons and teas. She liked to have intense discussions about the spiritual side of mankind with Teilhard de Chardin, who became her friend. She and the Jesuit paleontologist took long walks together on the city battlements of the Tartar City.[15]

She became a student of anthropology. She took up the study of spoken Chinese. She took up the cause of the modern Chinese artist. She took great pride in the house, in her miniature rock garden, the profusion of plants, in her bamboo and wicker furniture that she herself designed, in her interior decoration. "Oh, how I loved yellow and sunlight!" she later exclaimed.[16] She ran the household, she explored the city, and occasionally she modeled clothes for a friend of hers named Helen Burton who owned a dress shop and put on fashion shows when the normally somnolent Peking Hotel was suddenly awash with tourists from one of the cruise ships that made scheduled stops at Tientsin, the nearby port city of north China. She cut a striking figure on the boulevards of Peiping. "Slim, casually elegant," the New Zealand China Hand, James Bertram, wrote of her, "always accompanied around the streets by her loping white Greyhound Gobi,"[17] half Kansu greyhound, half Borzoi, a gift of the Swedish explorer Sven Hedin. Most of all she guarded her husband, and protected his privacy behind the brilliant, hard surface of her personality so that he could work undisturbed at his writing. "I was willing to be only the power behind the throne," she wrote, "but I did not mean for that to be my only role in one lifetime."[18]

Edgar Snow had never actually planned to stay in China. He had set out on a youthful and lighthearted journey around the world that was inspired by the travels of a young Princeton graduate named Richard Halliburton, who had chronicled his offbeat adventures in a book called *The Royal Road to Romance*. Halliburton was encouraged by this early success to make a career out of exotic travel, and Edgar Snow vaguely thought that he might fashion a similar line of work for himself. He had like Halliburton a certain boyish glamour and a knack for publicity that he'd acquired working in the New York advertising world. He'd lined up a literary patron in the person of Charles Hanson Towne,

"Mr. New York" in editorial circles. With Towne's help he was almost immediately successful at writing copy from the Far East.

China snagged Snow by degrees. In Shanghai, which he quite disliked, he was hired on arrival by J. B. Powell, editor and publisher of the *China Weekly Review,* who presided over what has come to be known as the Missouri Mafia in Shanghai, newspapermen shipped out as apprentice foreign correspondents to English-language papers in the Far East by Dean Walter Williams of the University of Missouri School of Journalism. Powell himself had been sent to Shanghai in 1917 by Dean Williams at the urgent request of Thomas Millard, the original China Hand, who needed someone to run his new Shanghai weekly. Powell stayed on, took over Millard's journal, and eventually bought it. He became an avuncular Midwestern presence in the American Shanghai community, who took the side of Chiang Kai-shek in 1927, which earned him the allegiance ever after of the Kuomintang.

Snow arrived in the summer of 1928. He was the most successful of all Powell's young Missourians. Though Snow had impeccable all-American credentials—altar boy, Eagle Scout, Irish good looks—a journalism degree was not among them. In fact, his career in college had been sketchy and incomplete. But he came from a family of readers. His father was a printer, a freethinker who read constantly. Like many Midwesterners of that time, Snow had grown up with literary ambitions fed in part by the works of Mark Twain. Snow was gifted with an easy writing style, and he was soon embarked on a rail journey around China, an assignment conjured up by Sun Fo, son of the late Dr. Sun and director of the railroad system, who hired Snow to write pamphlets about China's tourist attractions. Snow's articles were also supposed to be printed in the *China Weekly Review,* as indeed they were, although their content was sometimes of a quality rather deeper and less inviting than Sun Fo might have wished. Snow spent a whole month in Manchuria, for instance, and wrote in some depth about the intense Japanese industrial buildup he witnessed there. Snow predicted that Japanese expansionism would become a threat to China's integrity and lead to armed conflict. He pointed out that the Japanese were even eager to provoke an incident, in order to find an excuse to invade Manchuria with their army. He also visited the scene of a terrible famine in north China. This was not on Sun Fo's agenda at all. In the course of his visit to Seretsai, Snow discovered that flesh from the corpses of people who had died in the famine was for sale in the local markets.

The revelation of human disaster on such a vast scale had a sobering effect on Snow, and made him more than ever eager to leave China. Powell made it difficult for him to do so, however. He gave Snow a raise, and left him in charge of the *Review* while he departed on a long trip to the Soviet Union. In Powell's absence, Snow also covered assignments for the *Chicago Daily Tribune,* for which Powell was the Shanghai correspondent. This experience convinced Snow that he never wanted to be tied down to daily journalism. Snow made use of Powell's extensive library to bone up on Chinese history and current events. He had already found that his views conformed to those of Millard and Powell, both of whom took offense at the open exploitation of China by imperialists. His studies in China deepened those views.

At last, Snow saw his chance to put China behind him. He plotted a slow, romantic *Wanderjahr* that would take him through Indochina, Burma, India and the Near East to Europe, and eventually back to the United States. In letters to his father, he found it hard to articulate what it was in himself that he yearned to satisfy. He wanted to "raise" his head above the crowd, he wrote before he left Shanghai, and somehow achieve recognition.

Snow's pursuit of the royal road to romance was arrested when he reached India, where for several months he immersed himself in the ferment of the freedom struggle launched by Mahatma Gandhi and Jawaharlal Nehru, who was to be India's first popularly elected prime minister. This was Snow's baptism in the business of serious political journalism, and during his Indian sojourn he began to grasp the issues that were driving the forces of national independence movements throughout the East.

Quite why Snow turned back in the summer of 1931 for Shanghai is unclear. His stated reason is that he was directed to do so by his editor. Yet he may also have been reluctant to go home. His mother had died a year earlier, and this had been a source of profound grief to him. He had derived much pleasure in his wanderings from her affectionate letters and the reactions she expressed to the news of his travel experiences. Snow may have been reluctant to face the pain of finding her gone when he got back to America. And then he might not have remained in Shanghai at all, for he was sick with a 104 degree malarial fever, depressed in the torpid, muggy heat of Shanghai in August, and he was in the doghouse with Powell and others in the American community in Shanghai for a somewhat derogatory piece he had written about them that had appeared in the *American Mercury*. At just that moment, however, destiny had stepped into his life in the person of the fetching Helen Foster, who had headed across the Pacific to find him after she had read his articles in the *New York Herald Tribune Magazine* and decided that she, too, wanted to write about China. She had been quite sure that she could do the job as well as he could, if not better, but she decided to track him down in order to find out how to do it, and to this end she had managed to obtain a job at the American consulate in

Shanghai. It had not been Snow's intention to stay in China, or to marry Helen Foster. But the Japanese made their grab for Manchuria, just as Snow had predicted they would, and so he headed up there to cover the story. When he returned to Shanghai to write a book about the invasion, Helen Foster was still there. He stayed, and so did she. He pursued her in a determined effort to conquer her resistance to his passionate desire. He gave her a pen name. He called her Nym Wales—Nym from Shakespeare, Wales from the home of her ancestors—and she led him a merry chase as they traveled together around central and south China.

By now Snow's understanding of China's crisis had advanced well leftward of his Missouri colleagues in Shanghai. Powell and Millard remained firmly in support of Chiang Kai-shek. They saw no appeal at that time in the United Front, or the Communist Party. In fact, both men were staunchly anti-Communist. To Snow, however, it was clear that Chiang Kai-shek was allied with the imperialists he had once talked of throwing out of China. In his zeal to destroy the Communists, he was even willing to appease China's aggressive neighbor, Japan. Snow's sympathies leaned toward China's underground revolutionary movement and the United Front, thanks in very great part to Madame Sun Yat-sen, whom he had gone to interview one day at the Chocolate Shop in the International Settlement. Out of this encounter a friendship had flowered that was not unlike the close relationship that Madame Sun had formed with Harold Isaacs. She was drawn to young men of enthusiasm and idealism. One of her gifts was the ability to size up correctly the talent that these men possessed to publicize the cause of the United Front. She drew Edgar Snow into a greater consciousness of China's situation, of Dr. Sun's vision, of the evils represented by Chiang Kai-shek. Madame Sun also gave her blessing to Edgar Snow's romance with Helen Foster. This was a significant signal, for Madame Sun was inclined to exclude from her inner councils the wives of her associates, according to Viola Isaacs, who recalled recently with some chagrin how Madame Sun had withheld from her an invitation to join a lunch party at her house for George Bernard Shaw, attended by Harold and others close to Madame Sun.[19] Snow married Helen Foster on Christmas Day 1932, in Tokyo. After their honeymoon trip to Bali, they returned to China, to stay. Quite exactly why was not yet clear.

His part of the marriage pact *was* clear. He was supposed to earn the money for their joint adventure. At first, when they set up house in Peiping after they got back to China from their idyll in the Indonesian archipelago, he had some trouble getting started. He still didn't know what exactly he wanted to do as a writer and journalist. The essential motive, the flame, was bright within him yet, however. He was— continued to be—animated by the poet's dream, the "eerie thing within one, that I foolishly dream of somehow making apparent on paper," which he'd described to his father as "an expiring memory of golden, island happiness, of that simple, idyllic existence which all men believe once was, and devout persons absurdly believe will be again."[20] He had made a brilliant marriage, without warning destiny had sent his way someone perfectly equipped to protect him so that in the quiet ease of the Peiping backwater he could nurture the dream, but how was he going to find a market for his writing until the dream, whatever it was, could reveal itself in the proper course of time? That was his conundrum, as 1933 drew to a close.[21]

He did not want to go back to work as a reporter. That would wreck his tranquil freedom altogether. Yet it began to look as though that was what he'd have to do. His old standby, the Consolidated Press, which had seen him through extensive travels and the year of Sino-Japanese warfare, went bankrupt in late 1933, a victim of the Great Depression. Then a job with the Associated Press for a spot news reporter opened up in Peiping. This was just the opportunity he didn't want. He'd done enough agency work in Shanghai to know what a mindless trap it was. Yet without the insurance of his Consolidated job he had no stake, and, as he observed in later years, "a free-lancer without capital is a slave adrift."[22]

The secret of Edgar Snow's seemingly flawless, entirely congenial passage in China—his youth, his early manhood, the salad days of his life—was a certain very private mysticism, well hidden perhaps from public scrutiny but certainly apparent in letters he wrote to his family and in his notes and diaries. The time to choose between the AP job and the void of unemployment was just when Edgar Snow put this inspired mysticism into play, took all his savings from the bank and set out for the racetrack, Paomachang, with his smart young wife at his side. He had decided to put all their money on the ponies.

At the "gentleman's racing club," he made a careful study of the racing form. He then divided his money. Half he put on the handicap, half on the sweepstakes. He mentioned nothing of this to his wife, who he suspected would not have approved of this gamble at all. Silently, he resolved that if he lost, he would sign on with the Associated Press. When the handicap race was run, he sat beside his wife with his eyes closed. "After the race I opened my eyes and looked at the tally," he later recalled. His pony had come in second. He'd trebled his money. He refrained, however, from telling his wife. Instead, he waited for the sweepstakes. This time he kept his eyes open. "It was an impossible storybook kind of thing, and it happened to me only this once," he wrote, "but there was my number." Altogether, his winnings amounted to a little more than a thousand Mexican dollars—silver Mexican dollars being the currency then in use in China—which was enough to support them in comfort, Peiping-style, for half a year, at least.[23]

Then, one day soon, another hunch paid off, this time in the form of a windowed envelope from the *Saturday Evening Post.* Snow thought it was an advertisement. When he examined the contents of the envelope, however, he found that it contained what appeared to be a bill for seven dollars and fifty cents. Frowning at his side, Helen studied the bill with him. Suddenly she shrieked, "that's no bill, it's a check! And it's not seven dollars and fifty cents, it's seven hundred and fifty dollars! For you!"[24] In Peiping, this sum amounted to about four thousand dollars. "We're rich!" Snow exclaimed to his wife.[25] A letter in the next mail from George Horace Lorimer cleared up the mystery. The editor of the *Saturday Evening Post* had bought Snow's article "The Decline of Western Prestige," which Snow had sent off to the *Post* months before, after the *Post* had returned an earlier piece by Snow, along with a letter criticizing the magazine for rejecting unread the work of an unknown young writer like himself. Lorimer—in his six-page reply—took exception to Snow's judgment of the magazine's editorial policy—Snow had also complained that *Post* writers were out of touch with Far Eastern developments—and he invited Snow to contribute more articles.[26]

The *Saturday Evening Post* was Snow's big break. Meanwhile, in addition to a column he was writing for the *New York Sun,* Snow was writing for the *London Daily Herald,* a socialist newspaper owned by Odhams, a decidedly capitalist publishing company in England. (In 1935, the *London Daily Herald* promoted Snow to the position of special correspondent, with a commensurate increase in pay.) These, plus his *Saturday Evening Post* articles, kept him at work and in funds.

In a time of magazine readers, the *Saturday Evening Post* commanded a vast American audience, second only to that of the *Reader's Digest.* Snow worked painstakingly to cultivate a relationship with his *Saturday Evening Post* readers. "Patiently he wrote and rewrote all his articles," Helen Snow recalled in her memoirs, "cut and edited them to make sure they would not be rejected and that they would not bore his reader."[27] In this effort, his wife played the role of his audience, as she had also done in Shanghai in the year leading up to their marriage, while Snow was writing his first book.[28] She was a canny judge, and a good editor. With her help, Snow crafted articles that were informative and easy to read. "He hated propaganda," Helen Snow wrote, "and part of his natural attractiveness was that he never intruded his ideas on anyone."[29] Snow also never took his readership for granted. He used his early success to expand his knowledge not just of the East, but of the political developments in Europe that were affecting the history of the

East, and China in particular. In this way, he soon became an interpreter of the East for a large audience on a regular basis.

In early 1934, a banker in Peiping named Jimmy Chuan, who was chairman of the board of directors of Yenching University, offered to rent the Snows a house he had recently built in the village of Hai-tien, northwest of Peiping, near Yenching. This was yet another stroke of luck. It was a dream house set in a historic spot near the Summer Palace. Chuan let the Snows have it for a song. "We have an acre of garden, laid out in fruit trees, vegetables, evergreens and a fine arbor of grapes," Snow wrote his sister. "There is a swimming pool on the grounds and we have our own water system, installed by the owner."[30] They also had electric lights and two baths. "I have a study in the corner wing and from my window I can look out upon the Summer Palace and the once forbidden playground of emperors. I can see the sunset over the Western Hills and by day trace the patterns of willow trees against a sky that, out here away from the city, is a blue of incredible purity. Indeed, it is difficult to work."[31]

Yet work he did. Every morning he went to his study, and did not emerge until it was time for lunch. He worked on articles, and translations of Chinese short stories for a collection he and Helen Snow were putting together for publication called *Living China*. Fortune smiled on Edgar Snow. He contributed to this impression. He was relaxed and good-natured. By contrast, his wife struck friends as severe and even aggressive. She corrected Snow in front of other people, finished his sentences for him and contradicted him.

Snow never seemed to mind any of this. A visitor to Hai-tien recalled in later years going out one afternoon to visit the Snows. In the middle of tea, Gobi, the hound, swept all the teacups off the table with his tail. The visitor recalled that Snow laughed it off in his easygoing way. His wife was the one who reacted with outrage and fury and chased the dog from the room. She was an intense, voluble conversationalist, others have recalled. People considered her shrill. "She went on too much," Arch Steele later said.[32] He admired Helen Snow. He had shipped out to China in early 1932, and stayed on to become a reporter, eventually, for the *New York Herald Tribune*. He knew the Snows well. He called Helen a "digger," because she was so determined to get to the bottom of things.[33]

Hai-tien was a refuge, far from the distractions of Peiping. Yenching provided the Snows with a place of learning, which was particularly useful to them both at that time.

Yenching was the most Western of universities in China. An aggregate of four mission institutions, it was founded between 1890 and 1904. Dr. John Leighton Stuart, who became its president in 1919, was a missionary and educator. His ambition was to foster a Christian Chinese university with academic standards that would—according to the Eurasian writer Han Suyin, who attended Yenching—"be as good as anywhere else in the world and which would rival the atheistic, left-wing, and brilliant focus of intellectuals represented by Peking University," birthplace of the May Fourth Movement in 1919, when Chinese students protested the signing of the Versailles Treaty, and brought down the government of China.[34] Dr. Stuart in 1926 moved Yenching out to Hai-tien, onto the grounds of the old Yuan Ming Yuan summer palace complex, which in the nineteenth century had been destroyed by Western troops. Here, in a landscape that had once been the playground of legation picnickers, of which the centerpiece was the lovely nameless lake, amid gardens and willow trees, Dr. Stuart had employed the American architect Henry Killam Murphy to construct a Western university of traditional Chinese design.[35]

Yenching was only a few years old when the Snows moved out to Hai-tien. Only five American students were enrolled in the university. The rest were Chinese, many of them Manchurians in exile from their homeland, which was now occupied by the Japanese. The Snows used Yenching in different ways. Helen took courses there. She studied economics with Harry Price, a Yale graduate from a China missionary family, who became a great friend of the Snows. She also studied Hegel, in a philosophy course taught in Chinese by a Chinese professor. Edgar Snow taught a course in journalism at Yenching. They both made use of the Yenching library. Snow read widely in basic Marxist texts; he also read the complete works of George Bernard Shaw. This is how he came to adopt a Fabian view of socialism, espoused by Shaw, as his own political point of view. The Hai-tien period was thus an interlude of calm study, which further contributed to the Snows' evolution as China Hands, and during which Edgar Snow also learned to read Chinese.[36]

The Snows also got to know Chinese students they never otherwise would have met. They divided the work of translation for *Living China* between them, and while Helen worked on the contemporary stories of Yenching writers Hsiao Chi'en and Yang Ping, who later became prominent journalists, Snow translated the stories of Lu Hsun with the help of a Chinese assistant. The Snows discovered much about contemporary Chinese thought as they worked on these stories. "It was not often rewarding as literature," Snow later wrote, "but it was a thorough education in intellectual dissent."[37] It was a discovery Harold and Viola Isaacs had already made at roughly the same time, in Peiping, where they had been putting together their translation volume of modern Chinese stories, *Straw Sandals*.[38] Snow, in the course of translation, came to realize that Russian writers like Gogol, Chekhov, Turgenev, Tolstoy, Pushkin and Dostoyevsky, translated during the years when the Russians were advising the Nationalist Chinese in Canton, had made a great impact on Chinese readers and writers, one that endured despite a Kuomintang ban on Russian literature imposed by Chiang Kai-shek.[39]

Inevitably, the Snows got close to the pressures under which students and intellectuals at Yenching were suffering. They sensed the presence of the White Terror even on that benign campus, infiltrated, as all universities were at that time, by Chiang Kai-shek's fascistic secret society, the Blue Shirts.[40] Although not much was yet understood in China about the nature of Fascism and Nazism, just then surging through Europe, Chiang Kai-shek had started a flirtation with the forces of European Fascism. Nanking was thick with German military advisers and Italian aviators, and Chiang appeared to be submitting to the pressures of Japan, ally of the Nazis.[41] Dr. Stuart, pro-Chiang though he was, nevertheless was troubled by this development. He asked Snow to lead a faculty debate on the subject—unaware that a number of students already belonged to a secret Fascist student organization.[42]

So the Snows made a systematic study of Fascism. They got their hands on a couple of Fascist texts, and discovered the link between Madame Chiang's Confucian New Life Movement and Mussolini's Vita Nuova. Both seemed to be social control experiments, based on herd manipulation techniques, that called for terrorist tactics to clean up the social facade. These revelations shocked the Snows into a new awareness of what was going on in the world and how events in Europe were acting on the Far East. "Most of the West was asleep," Helen Snow wrote, "while the Italians, Germans and Japanese were out to change the world."[43]

The Japanese had already begun to seep into China from Manchuria. North of the Great Wall, they controlled China by proxy. Japan had conquered both Manchuria and Inner Mongolia. Chiang Kai-shek's pro-Japanese military chief, Ho Ying-ch'in, had signed away the two provinces of Chahar and Hopei north of the Great Wall by converting them into a "demilitarized zone," administered by an old Nationalist warhorse named Sung Che-yuan.[44] The Japanese were not, yet, prepared to go to war against the Chinese, but they were ready to sever those provinces, Peiping included, from the rest of China. This was generally known to correspondents in China, and especially to Snow, who in the summer of 1935 paid a visit to Manchuria and Japan. But the Kuomintang censored the news now very heavily and it was all but impossible to cable this information overseas.[45]

A fatalism seemed to grip China. At Yenching, professors and students took it for granted that Japan would soon move in on north China. To the Snows, it was now urgently clear that ominous forces were swiftly assembling while the world slept. They moved back into Peiping. "The end of 1935 was the absolute nadir in China," Helen Snow wrote, "a time of living death, full of the carbon monoxide and methane gas of putrifying vegetation. Ed and I had each other, but we felt alien to the rest of humanity, at least to the part then dying in North China. We felt totally alone."[46]

One day in October, 1935, at 13 K'uei Chia Ch'ang, a swank residence the Snows now shared with a Swedish geologist named Dr. E. T. Nystrom, their number one boy came to the living room to announce a visitor. "It is a student from the Department of Journalism of Yenching University," the servant told Helen Snow. "His name is Chang Chao-lin."[47] He then ushered into her presence a tall, wide-faced, handsome young Manchurian who had once taken Edgar Snow's journalism course at Yenching, where he was now the head of the student union, recently secretly revived, despite Chiang Kai-shek's ban on student organizations. He had come to see her husband, to find out whether it was true, as he had heard, that the Chinese were about to relinquish north China to the Japanese. It was in the air. Beneath the calm surface of life in Peiping everyone was waiting. The Japanese had recently sent their master of intrigue, General Doihara, to Peiping, to issue an ultimatum to the Nationalist Chinese administrator, the hoary General Sung.[48]

Doihara, known as "Lawrence of Manchuria,"[49] had placed before General Sung ten million newly minted dollars, and urged him to declare his independence of Chiang Kai-shek.[50] Snow, in fact, had reason to believe that the rumor of Sung's imminent capitulation was not without foundation. The night before Chang's unexpected appearance at his house, Snow had received a visit from one of General Sung's aides, who had come to tell Snow that Sung was ready to cave in, after fruitlessly beseeching support from Chiang Kai-shek against Japanese aggression and receiving only the most ambiguous response. Snow had just returned from a trip to Japan and Manchuria. He knew that Japan was not yet ready for war. Doihara, he told Sung's aide, was bluffing. In a showdown, Doihara would back off.[51] He now described Sung's position to the Manchurian student leader. Chang Chao-lin began to weep.

"Crying won't help," Edgar Snow said. "We've got to act."[52] It slipped out. He had not meant to say it. He was a journalist. He was supposed to be neutral. In that brief moment, Edgar Snow committed himself to China, along with Helen, his wife.

Chang wanted to publish a petition full of demands addressed to Chiang Kai-shek. Snow disagreed. The Chinese press would ignore it; the foreign press would call it propaganda.[53] What to do? Helen Snow suggested a student movement, like the New Youth Movement of May 4, 1919.[54] They talked all afternoon, throughout the dying October day. Chang soon came back to see them, this time with friends. Inspired by the Snows' support, they formulated a plan. These students—mostly Christian or Christian-educated youth—were supposedly the cream of China's future. Many were the children of important government officials. As such, like the students of a later generation who protested on Tiananmen Square, they enjoyed a degree of immunity from official punishment.[55] They were ready for action.

The Snows gave themselves to this fledgling movement. Helen Snow, by temperament, was more engaged than her husband, who, as always, melted into the background and emerged from time to time to give advice. Helen Snow was passionately attracted to the fierce ideals of the students and to their youth. She decided to take a stand against Fascism. Perhaps without the fervor of his wife urging him to take a stand, Edgar Snow might not have stepped across the line that separates the foreign correspondent from the China Hand. "Now I know," he said to his wife as the student patriots plotted away in their living room, "why people like W.H. Donald, Putnam Weale, Tom Millard and other newspapermen mixed up in China's internal affairs in the past. You can't just stand by and watch a lady you love being ravished and do nothing about it. And Peking is a nice old lady indeed."[56] Edgar Snow thus defined his personal role as the knight gallant of China's destiny. China, in this, as in many other Western definitions, acquired a feminine persona, one helpless at that.

Helen, on the other hand, acted as the midwife to the student movement. She'd made a study of Chinese student movements, beginning with the May Fourth Movement. She'd been in Shanghai during the 1931–1932 student demonstrations, and she knew how powerful the students of China could be when they acted in concert. Publicity was the key to keeping a student movement alive in China. Helen Snow took a version of Chang Chao-lin's petition to Frank Oliver, the Reuters correspondent in Peiping, to see if he would publish it. "For the Right of Free Speech, Press, and Assembly and Against the Illegal Arrest of Students," was its title.[57] "Why, we couldn't possibly publish such a thing," Oliver told her. "It's nothing but propaganda."[58] She scented his hostility—Reuters was staunchly pro–Chiang Kai-shek—and she also picked up on the more sinister enmity of his Chinese assistant, who she suspected would shortly be reporting the manifesto to the police. Clearly, a demonstration had to be organized at once.[59]

Helen Snow's idea was to stage a mock funeral on the streets of Peiping, to announce the death of north China. The Chinese students didn't like it. "Nym is right about the demonstration, if not the funeral," Snow told them.[60] Once, in New York, an executive for Samuel Goldwyn had praised Snow's instinct for the dramatic.[61] Now, confronting the dubious student leaders, he told them that a display by unarmed students against Sung's phony independence movement could make all the difference. The students were still skeptical. They thought they'd be arrested—as Communists. Communist suspects were being rounded up by Chiang Kai-shek's Peiping gendarmerie and shot. Snow disagreed. He thought they could take the police—and the Japanese— by surprise. The key would be to persuade all the students in Peiping to join the protest. The Chinese press wouldn't dare report it, the students insisted. They'd have to, Helen Snow said, if *everybody* joined in. Snow promised to marshal other correspondents to the scene of the action. He would report it fully himself.[62]

This seemed to reassure the student leaders. They worked out among themselves a set of demands. They wanted both Sung and Chiang Kai-shek "to reject Doihara's ultimatum, to end civil war, unite all factions for resistance to save China, begin 'mass training and mobilization,' and give people freedom to know the truth and prepare for what was coming."[63] A citywide student strike and demonstration was timed for the ninth of December, the day before General Sung planned to declare secession from Nanking. The leaders of the newly formed All-Peking Students' Federation printed up leaflets and posters, assembled first-aid teams, mapped out a route of procession.[64] "On the eve of North China's greatest student demonstrations," Edgar Snow later wrote, "Nym and I stayed up most of the night copying out translations of the students' 'demands' to release next day to the foreign press."[65]

The Peiping police were utterly unprepared for the demonstration of December 9. The Japanese had ordered the vicious Third Gendarmes —a proto-Fascist goon squad run by Chiang Kai-shek's nephew Chiang Hsiao-hsien—out of the city. Chiang Hsiao-hsien and his Fascist gang had reported to Sian.[66]

This, in the opinion of Helen Snow, was a boon of monumental proportions.[67] No patriotic, anti-Fascist movement could have demonstrated on the streets of Peiping with the Third Gendarmes in town. As it was, eight hundred students gathered without opposition at a dozen points around the city and converged in separate columns in a parade to present petitions to high Kuomintang officials at their offices on Chang An Boulevard.[68]

This small but valiant show of protest was exhilarating to the four or five foreign correspondents who cheered from the sidelines. Their presence further confused the police, who held themselves in check. When a remnant of Chiang Hsiao-hsien's "leather jackets" finally arrived and charged the crowd with clubs, they were no match for the demonstrators. "A few rifles were fired in the air; the parade wavered but held," Snow later wrote. "Correspondents and cameramen closed in, hoping foreign witnesses would be enough to prevent a tragedy. We were."[69] Crowds of onlookers—"Chinese shopkeepers, housewives, artisans, monks, teachers and silk-gowned merchants applauded from the streets," Snow wrote. Even rickshaw boys joined the fray, shouting out anti-Japanese slogans that had been prohibited. The police lowered their rifles. Some of them joined the protesters.[70]

Students all over China responded instantly to the battle cry from Peiping. In Canton, students boycotted classes for a week to urge the government to formulate an anti-Japanese policy, while groups in Canton, Hankow and Shanghai telegrammed their support to the Peiping demonstrators.[71] On Friday, December 13, Victor Keen of the *New York Herald Tribune,* the only other American foreign correspondent of stature besides Snow at that time in Peiping, reported that the Japanese had dispatched a gunboat to Canton to quell an anti-Japanese demonstration by four thousand students. "Student agitation against Japanese efforts to foster autonomy in North China," Keen wrote, "which began in the Peiping universities several days ago, is flaming up in Hankow, Shanghai and Canton, and is threatening to assume proportions that may seriously jeopardize Sino-Japanese relations."[72]

On the sixteenth of December, the students of Peiping staged a massive demonstration. "More than 8,000 university and middle school students braved freezing temperatures and police brutality here today," Victor Keen reported, "to stage a dawn-to-sundown demonstration against establishment of the 'Hopei-Chahar Political Council,' which they believe means Japanese rule for those provinces under the guise of autonomy. Sixty students were wounded and many more were clubbed and drenched by fire hose."[73] Keen personally observed Peiping police in acts of naked brutality against unarmed students of a sort less mechanized than that employed more than fifty years later in Tiananmen Square, but shocking nevertheless. "As soon as the students were divided and widely scattered," Keen wrote, "police pursued lingerers into narrow alleyways and beat them unmercifully with leather belts and the flat of their swords. Many were injured, some, it is believed, seriously. This correspondent on numerous occasions saw as many as half a dozen stalwart policemen brutally beating a lone student. In two instances he successfully intervened to end the attack, as did many other foreigners witnessing the spectacle."[74] A third demonstration was held a week later. For the first time, the students demanded an end to the civil war between Chiang Kai-shek's Nationalist army and the so-called Red bandits, who were now operating out of their new stronghold in Shansi.[75] They called for a United Front against Japan. They received, in response, an outpouring of support from soldiers, police and government officials.[76]

The Japanese backed down. Student pressure forced the Kuomintang to take an anti-Japanese stand.[77] Now the students fanned out into the countryside to awaken the villagers of rural China to the threat of Japanese invasion.[78] The refugee students from Manchuria were among the most ardent campaigners. They made their way to Sian, to meet with their leader, Chang Hsueh-liang, the Young Marshal, who had Fascist leanings. He was the son of the harelipped Manchurian warlord Chang Tso-lin. He listened sympathetically. He was supposed to be fighting the Communists in Shensi, where he was based with his force of one hundred and fifty thousand Manchurian troops. Chiang Kai-shek had made him Vice Director of the Red Bandit Extermination Campaign. The Young Marshal was won over by their arguments. He stopped fighting the Communists. He made regular contact with the students, and invited them to Sian so that he could hear, in person, what they had to say.[79] Thus had the Snows and their Yenching friends altered the course of history in China.

Chiang Kai-shek had made it impossible for any information about the Reds to be published in China. His White Terror made the mere mention of Communism a matter of the gravest consequence. People caught with anything remotely resembling Communist literature were summarily arrested and shot.[80] Few, if any, foreigners had ever visited the Kiangsi soviets. Consequently, rumors had abounded in the foreign concessions concerning their supposed barbarisms.[81] In 1934, Chiang Kai-shek had thrown all his money and troops into yet another Bandit Suppression Campaign. This fifth campaign was very nearly a success, thanks to General Hans von Seeckt, Chiang Kai-shek's *General Berater,* or resident general adviser, who had created the *Reichswehr,* the German Republican Army. General von Seeckt had reorganized the Nationalist Army from top to bottom, instituted a central command system and helped to establish Chinese war industries with German financial assistance. He had masterminded China's military preparations for the fifth Bandit Suppression Campaign, although there is some question about whether it was von Seeckt or his military chief of staff, General Alexander von Falkenhausen, who devised the plan that almost finished off the Communists.[82] This plan called for a huge circle of concrete blockhouse fortresses to be constructed around the Red encampment from which the Nationalists would wage a siege. The villagers within the battle area suffered the most from this strategy. As the Sino-German machine ground forward, over a million Chinese peasants were decimated, along with their homes and villages.

The circle, however, turned out to be porous. This was not necessarily due to oversight on the part of the Nationalists. Owen Lattimore has written, "One of Chiang Kai-shek's tactics was to encircle a detachment of the Red Army, but not completely, leaving open an avenue of escape into a territory which did not yet acknowledge Chiang's authority. Then, in the name of pursuing the Reds, he would move his troops into that province. For Chiang, getting control of a hitherto independent province had a priority over exterminating the Reds who fled into it."[83] In October 1934 Communist guerrillas managed to slip through a cordon of blockhouses to the southwest. There is reason to believe that Chou En-lai, in negotiations, persuaded Lung Yun, the warlord of Yunnan Province, of the wisdom of letting the Communists slip through his territory to the northwest. The Communists moved through so quickly and unobtrusively that they were gone before Chiang could use pursuit as an excuse to send his armies into Yunnan. (It is quite possible that Chiang did not have enough troops to pursue this strategy anyway.)[84] Over eighty thousand men and women accompanied their harried leaders on an epic retreat into the raw and mountainous northwest. This exodus became immortalized in twentieth-century legend as the Long March. The Communists were accompanied by one foreigner. He was Otto Braun, a German-born military adviser sent by the Comintern who was supposed to be the Communists' answer to General von Seeckt. (It was Braun who had insisted on the disastrous military policy of positional warfare that nearly finished the Communists off in Kiangsi.) Almost exactly a year later, four thousand survivors arrived in Pao An, or "Secure Peace," a northern village in the brown, dust-caked hills of Shensi Province. There, under their leader, Mao Tse-tung, they set up camp out of reach of Chiang Kai-shek's armies.[85]

The hated Reds now consumed Chiang Kai-shek's every waking moment. He was fixated on exterminating them and, in so doing, he ignored the Japanese menace at the back door. He made the Young Marshal chief of his Bandit Suppression Campaign, and kept him thus in his tight grip, so that he wouldn't go dashing off at the head of his own troops and stir up trouble with the Japanese. The Manchurian troops, however, were ambivalent about fighting the Reds at the expense of ignoring the Japanese, who had driven them from their native soil. Besides, they were favorably impressed by the Communists. The Reds didn't leave them to die on the field after a battle, or execute them. They took them home. They talked to them. They urged them to join forces against the Japanese in a United Front. They pleaded passionately for this common cause and then sent them back across the lines.

Among those who were particularly intrigued by the Communists, and their ingenious survival, were the members of the China Career Service in the State Department who were on assignment in Peiping. The language attaché, John Stewart Service, O. Edmund Clubb (who, as vice consul in Hankow in the early 1930s, had written the first and only extensively researched Foreign Service field report on the Red insurgency), John Paton Davies, Raymond Ludden and others had developed a particularly keen interest in the subject. So had Colonel Joseph Stilwell, U.S. military attaché in Peiping. Stilwell told Edgar Snow, "Those Reds may be bandits, as Chiang says they are, but bandits or not, they're masters of guerilla warfare." He thought then that they had the kind of leaders who win. "I mean officers who don't say 'Go on, boys!' but *'come on boys!'* If that's the case," Stilwell said, "and they had enough of them, they could keep the Japs busy here till kingdom come."[86]

Snow was on good terms with the new, up-and-coming China Hands in the Foreign Service. They all cared deeply about saving China from dismemberment by the Japanese. A number of them, as the offspring of missionaries, had grown up in China, and loved it as their principal homeland. Others, like O. Edmund Clubb, had made a career not just of the Foreign Service but of China, specifically. Edmund Clubb was Snow's closest friend in China. He urged Snow to try to get up to the remote outpost in northern Shensi to find out more about the Communists. He thought such a journey would be of great value to Clubb and others in the legation.[87] In China, where the community of Americans was tightly knit, there was a constant exchange of information between journalists, missionaries and the Foreign Service officers. The missionaries brought valuable information from the interior. Journalists, especially those with contacts among Chinese, provided another perspective. O. Edmund Clubb depended for insight and detail on what Edgar Snow, among others, had to tell him, and filed informative, detailed reports to Washington based on irreproachable intelligence from his various sources.[88]

At regular lunchtime get-togethers in the Legation Quarter, Clubb worked on Snow to visit Shensi.[89] Not that Snow needed much persuasion. He had wanted to get up into Red territory in 1930, when he was in Shanghai working for Consolidated Press. He had also for some time wanted to make a study of the Communists. In 1934, he had signed a contract with his American publisher, Harrison Smith, to write a book about them. He had also applied for a Guggenheim Foundation grant to make a study of the Communists while he was at Yenching. He'd been turned down in favor of an applicant who subsequently came to China to make a study of the facial expressions of the Chinese.[90] Snow had proposed a trip to the northwest to both the *Loudon Daily Herald* and the *New York Sun* to "try and crack the blockade around the Communist-held areas."[91] Both papers backed him. The *Herald* offered to pay his expenses and a sizable bonus if he actually got through. The trouble was that without safe passage provided by the Reds themselves, travel into rebel-held territory was a risk no journalist could dare to take. No American reporter in China at that time had contacts among the guerrillas.

In the days immediately following the December 9 Peiping demonstration, a young Manchurian refugee student at Yenching named Wang Ju-mei[92] brought to the Snows' house at No. 13 a mysterious youth named Yu Ch'i-wei, who went by the anglicized name of David Yui. "He was fairly tall, pale, tired, ill-looking, and ill-kempt in his long Chinese brown wool gown, (most male students wore gowns then, a sign of aristocracy)," Helen Snow later recalled. "His handsome face was open and changed expression easily, but it was also aristocratic and you felt the self-assurance."[93] David Yui had what Helen Snow described as "Mandarin authority," even though he was only about twenty-four. "What was it?" she wondered. "Experience, I thought: this must be the real McCoy, a real live subterranean member of the Communist Party, or at least the Communist youth."[94] Helen Snow never asked David Yui if he was a Communist. The very acknowledgment of it would have been risky. The Communist Party in north China had been disbanded in August 1935; no Communist presence was even believed to exist at that time there.

The Kuomintang, in November, had received a telegram signed by Chu Teh, Mao Tse-tung, Ho Lung and three other Red Army generals, offering to refrain from seizing or attempting to seize any further territory under the control of the Nanking government, or any of its allies, provided that Nanking embarked on a policy of active resistance to Japanese aggression. This was not known at the time to either the Snows or their Yenching friends, although their subsequent call for a united front may have been formulated by David Yui. He had appeared on his own in Peiping—so Helen Snow concluded—in response to the December 9 demonstration. He had come north from the Yangtze Valley, where he belonged to a well-established and influential family. He had been a student at Peking University. Later, David Yui confided to the Snows that he had been imprisoned, in chains, for six months in Tsinan. His uncle, the national secretary of the YMCA, had performed the marriage ceremony of Soong Mei-ling and Chiang Kai-shek at the

Majestic Hotel in Shanghai, in 1927. This uncle had saved David from execution. Just before his arrest, David had influenced his lover, Chiang Ch'ing, to join the Communist Party, with what dire effects the world would only come to know in the 1970s, when, as the widow of Mao Tse-tung, she was eventually publicly tried and convicted along with her cohorts in the Gang of Four for her role in the Cultural Revolution. David Yui became a friend of the Snows. He was "patriarchal"[95] toward the Yenching student leaders. He was critical. He thought they were anti-Fascist when they should have been anti-Japan. He met them at No. 13 because it was the only safe gathering place in Peiping. He often used the Snow residence as a place of sanctuary. He and Helen Snow discussed Marxism. He was not altogether happy about her influence on the students—she encouraged their anti-Fascism—but he conceded that she was a good agitator. His role was to take the student movement in hand, to make it more professional. David Yui was more than likely operating on instructions from the Communist International, which was soon to promote the United Front in China. He was also a recruiting agent. His object was to bring the student leaders into the Communist Party, which he soon did, the following February, once their first important goal had been achieved. David Yui was the Communists' number two man in north China.[96]

David Yui was the only Chinese Communist in the Snows' entourage at that time. They'd never asked him if he was a Communist, but they were shrewd enough to know that he was. He came and went. In February, he informed the Snows that an important Communist had arrived in Tientsin. This turned out to be none other than Liu Shaoch'i, a member of the Communist Party Central Committee. Snow told David that he wanted to visit the Communists and asked him if such a trip could be arranged. On the twenty-fifth of March, David wrote to the Snows from Tientsin. His written English wasn't of the highest quality, but his message was clear. "The problem of Ed's shall be settled a few days later," he informed them. "One of the both men shall tell you this consideration. On this problem I have explained to them as possible as I can. I think they have no reason to refuse your requirement. I hope it shall be realized. Please write to me before your travelling."[97]

The Snows heard nothing further. When it was clear that neither of "both men" were going to contact him, Snow went to Shanghai to visit Madame Sun Yat-sen. He asked her to vouch for him and to forward his request to travel to the rebel land. He then returned to Peiping. On June 1, he wrote to L. M. MacBride, foreign editor of the *Herald,* to tell him that he was planning a trip to Shensi and Shansi, to visit the scenes of warfare between the Reds and government troops. As he explained to MacBride, such a trip was now possible due to a hiatus in the fighting, the result of a secret truce between the Young Marshal and the Reds. It might also, he wrote MacBride, be possible to enter the Red districts of Shensi and Kansu and meet the Communist leaders; "it will be a world scoop on a situation about which millions of words have been written, based only on hearsay and highly colored government reports."[98] A few days later, Snow received a letter from a Peiping professor written in invisible ink, to deliver to Mao Tse-tung. This contact also gave Snow advice on how to contact the Red underground in Sian. His trip, it seems, had been approved by Liu Shao-ch'i, on instructions from Mao himself, who had been encouraged to court greater publicity for his movement by Stalin.

The Snows were ready. They were convinced that the trip to the Red territories was now the single most important objective of their lives. It was an enormous, secret event. For Helen Snow it was the culmination of her covert ambitions; for Edgar Snow, it was that mystical opportunity for which he had so patiently been biding his time, perfecting his craft. "No one," Helen Snow later wrote, "including the Chinese, had any idea of just what kind of people the Red Armies represented. Someone had to find out, and no-one else could or would make such a trip. Then, too," she added, "we were intoxicated with power, all kinds of power: power to influence history, marriage power, and, though we would never use such a term, a high sense of spiritual power over and above all mundane things."[99]

Mao Tse-tung selected his public relations intermediary with great care. It seems likely that he was acting on instructions from Stalin brought to him by the brother of Mao's brilliant military strategist Lin Piao, who had returned overland via Central Asia from a sojourn in Russia. Stalin eyed the growing menace of Japan with shrewd misgivings. He had made money on a deal with the Japanese in 1935, selling residual Russian interests in Manchurian railways, but the last thing he wanted was to see the Japanese take over north China, where they would be poised to strike across his vast Asiatic frontier. He put his money on Chiang Kai-shek to begin with in the 1920s in order to build up an effective militarist in China as an ally against Japanese and British designs on Russia. Now Chiang appeared to be capitulating to Japan. Stalin wanted to develop a United Front between the Nationalists and Communists in China to resist Japan. But who *were* the Chinese Communists? Chiang Kai-shek's news blackout had successfully blocked the Reds from public visibility. At best, they were believed to exist, but only as bandits, whom Chiang was trying to exterminate. "We actually know nothing about the Communist movement," Nathaniel Peffer, a China journalist and scholar, wrote in 1935.[100] To change this situation, and force Chiang to drop his bloody fixation, required, as Stalin saw it, and as Mao came to agree, some dramatic public relations campaign that would give the revolutionists validity in the eyes of the world as a legitimate popular Chinese political movement. Such publicity would legitimize a Red Chinese call for a United Front, and could bring pressure to bear on Chiang Kai-shek from outside China to turn his military resources on Japan in concert with the Communists.[101] Stalin's motives were in accord with those of Mao, who wanted to fight Japan. Mao needed time, also, to rebuild his movement. The continued air and ground assaults by the Nationalists made it difficult. He knew he could use publicity, also, to build up his following, which had been drastically diminished in the flight from Kiangsi and the Long March. Given Chiang Kai-shek's successful censorship policy, assisted by Japan, such publicity could not come from within China unless it came from the English-language press, based mainly in Shanghai.

Mao needed for his purposes someone to project his story abroad who commanded the attention of a large cross section of readers, including world leaders. He needed someone who could make a noise loud enough to break the sound barrier Chiang had erected in China, and so alert Chinese, especially those who might then look to Mao for hope.

Snow was a writer with a large American readership, known firsthand to Madame Sun as a reliable journalist who was friendly to the cause of her late husband. She knew him personally to the extent that she had influenced his outlook on China's destiny. His work, and his role in the December 9 student demonstration, were ample proof to her that Snow could be trusted to convey a favorable account of the Red Chinese saga to a large Western audience, and she probably passed this conviction along to Mao and Chou En-lai.[102] Snow qualified for this assignment because he was not a fervent partisan of the Chinese Communist movement. He was a good choice, however, because he knew his way around Chinese politics and had shown himself to be an observant, intelligent reporter and an outspoken critic, also, of the Kuomintang. Just how lucky this choice turned out to be for both Snow and the Communists became apparent once he and Mao sat down together in Pao An.

Red Star Over China, Snow's stunning account of the Communist guerrilla movement, conveys the enchantment of a work of literary imagination about travels in magic or forbidden lands, and it continues to cast that spell even today. In this respect Snow had long since outstripped Richard Halliburton: as a romantic literary traveler he was in a league with W. H. Hudson, or the Mark Twain of *Connecticut Yankee* and *Huckleberry Finn.* As a literary device, he acknowledged but cut from his account his companion, George Hatem, the Lebanese-

American doctor who accompanied Snow on his journey from Sian into the Red territory.[103] We are left with the image of the lone Westerner, accompanied by a single muleteer—"He was to carry my scant belongings—bedding roll, a little food, two cameras and twenty-four rolls of film—to the first Red partisan outpost"—as they made their way along a small winding stream for four hours into "no-man's land" without a sign of human life. So begins the picaresque tale, as our hero meets his first Red guerrillas, is chased by "White bandits,"[104] encounters the cool, ubiquitous, bearded Chou En-lai, and makes his way to the stronghold of Mao himself.

In another day, in the hands of another writer, *Red Star* might have been a novel, or an epic poem. Snow, however, never entertained (at least not at this stage of his life) the ambition to write a novel. "Novels are such little things,"[105] Helen Snow observed in later years. This was probably the prevailing sentiment among the romantic realists of the 1930s. It was an age that glorified the personal adventures of aviators and foreign correspondents. Charles Lindbergh was still the American hero of the day, and Vincent Sheean's novelistic memoir, *Personal History,* had recently been a runaway best-seller in the United States. Edgar Snow thought it was "one of the best books he'd ever read," according to Helen Snow.[106] Sheean epitomized the elegant, world-weary foreign correspondent in all his sophisticated glamour; Edgar Snow, as he realized his own persona in *Red Star Over China,* added weight and depth to that heroic persona. Snow was graceful and modest, and had a single, great story to tell. A cursory glance at Snow's career, however, is enough to verify Snow as a romantic adventurer in search of a literary grail—inspired by the extensive reading of his childhood. He had not so long ago written his father, "I foolishly dream of somehow making apparent on paper," what he called "an expiring memory of golden, island happiness, of that simple, idyllic existence which all men believe once was, and devout persons absurdly believe will be again." It was a pagan quest, but one that required inner faith, and once he crossed the magic frontier and entered the forbidden kingdom of Mao Tse-tung, he was never in doubt that his dream would be granted.

To Snow, the rebel territory was an exhilarating throwback to the world of *Boy's Life,* where, once again, he could revel in the simple, innocent pleasures. In this respect, his adventure in Shensi was not a journey into the unknown, it was an enchanted visitation to the lost world of his youth. *Red Star* is as American as *Huckleberry Finn,* and Snow very skillfully draws parallels between China and America in his use of description, as, for example, when he calls Mao Tse-tung "Lincolnesque."[107] Yet it is Snow's own very warm, straightforward relationship with the reader, and the way he presents the Red territory as a place any American would understand, and acts as a guide to the entire experience, that gives *Red Star* the feel of an American adventure story in the manner, not of the Sheean cosmopolite, but of the Mark Twain raconteur. ("Ed, now this is just too idyllic," his friend Harry Price remarked one night after the book was published. "Well," Snow said, "I'm just telling you what I saw.")[108]

The Red encampment was like a clean, virginal, male sleepaway camp in stark, haunting frontier country, where the boys and their counselors slept in caves. The tawny loess hills, composed of layers of soft earthen clay, were ideal for the purpose of carving out caves for habitation. The local people had discovered this natural resource over the centuries, and now the Red guerrillas were taking advantage of it. In Pao An, the cadres rose at dawn to reveille. Throughout the day, up there in the clear highland atmosphere of the Shensi hills, the accent was on learning, on various kinds of drill, on sports and physical fitness. Bedtime came soon after sundown, with the bugling of taps.

Mao had found in Snow a Mark Twain who could thrill to his story, and who he was assured had the ability to write it up. For Mao sized up his American guest in the course of a series of interviews he granted Snow in his cave dwelling in the hills of Pao An, and discovered a sympathetic listener who eagerly identified with the story of the rebels. Mao possessed a passionate temperament and a literary imagination himself. He was fresh from epic adventures that equaled the bandit sagas out of classical Chinese literature that had enflamed his youthful ardor and in no small way had inspired his ingenuity as a rebel leader. It must have come as an unexpected delight to Mao that he was playing host to a kindred spirit, because it did not take him long to open up to his visitor in ways he had never done before and was never to do again.

Mao was unorthodox among his own followers. In fact, he made something of a fetish of his individuality in this Boy Scout world he had established. In Pao An, where good posture was de rigueur, Mao rambled around in a slouch. Tobacco was practically forbidden, but Mao smoked cigarettes luxuriantly. Soon, when the Reds had moved their operation to Yenan, Mao could be seen by passersby raking the soil of his own little tobacco patch, cultivating the tobacco he chain-smoked. He also kept a wife by his side when women were in scarce supply.[109] While most of the men in the Red territory wore their hair cut short, Mao's hair was almost shoulder length, during the 1930s, when he was a slender young man with the appearance of an Apache. In Yenan, he slept in a double bed on a mattress and springs, unlike his cohorts, who bedded down on traditional Chinese k'angs, heated brick platforms. Sleeping until noon, he stayed up through most of the night, and turned in at daybreak, just when everyone else was getting up. These differences distinguished Mao from his followers and his top leaders, men like Chu Teh and Chou En-lai, but they also served to further remove a man whose spirit already, as Agnes Smedley observed, "dwelt within itself, isolating him."[110]

Mao was not incapable of intimate friendship, and even late in life, bereft of male comrades, he maintained close relations with women, but the party system itself made it impossible for Mao to maintain supreme power and at the same time to enjoy unguarded friendships with his male colleagues.[111] That may be why he chose to confide in Edgar Snow. Snow got into the routine of making regular visits to Mao's cave, where the guerrilla leader invited him to join him for hot pepper bread, or compote made by Madame Mao from local sour plums. The meetings often lasted until dawn. Mao clearly seemed to enjoy them, Snow noted. It was a relief for Mao to put aside the black iron dispatch boxes full of official papers, and to disregard, for a few hours or more, the drifts of tissue-paper communiqués that piled up on his table. Initially, the conversation was theoretical, concerning Chinese and world politics. Snow had made up a long list of questions to ask Mao. The Red leader, who had not been interviewed before, had never seen such a list. Mao steered clear of questions that Snow had listed under the rubric of "Personal History." Instead, he concentrated on the questions Snow wrote out for his consideration on matters dealing with everything but his own life. Snow's meetings with Mao took place in the presence of a translator. Snow carefully took down the answers Mao gave to his questions, then wrote them up in English. Mao's translator then translated Snow's notes into Chinese for Mao, who corrected them.[112]

Snow pursued the subject of personal history. At first, Mao dismissed his own life and times as mere gossip, which he asserted had no place in the grander scheme of his great movement. Snow drew Mao's attention to the story of George Washington, and the lives of French revolutionaries in Carlyle's *French Revolution,* which had inspired the Chinese leader in his youth. Mao moved to settle the matter once and for all. "Suppose," he told Snow, "that I just give you a general sketch of my life? I think it will be more understandable and in the end, all your questions will be answered though not in just this order." "That's exactly what I want," replied Snow.[113]

In the nights that followed, Mao unveiled for Edgar Snow the story of his life, from its beginnings in Hunan to the present moment in his cave dwelling in Pao An. He told Snow everything as he recalled it, with a great deal of color and imagination. What makes this account of great interest to Mao scholars now are the things that he chose to emphasize, his omissions, and his reconstructions. Snow happened to visit Pao An at a time when there was a lull in the fighting between the Nationalists and the Red guerrillas. Though the Young Marshal was supposed to be at war with Mao, he was already making secret contact with the enemy. Mao therefore had an unusual amount of time to spend with Snow on his oral history. Never again did he take the time to relate his life story, or compose an autobiography. All subsequent works on Mao, including Stuart Schram's *Mao Tse-tung* and Ross Terrill's exciting biographical account, have had to rely to some extent on Snow's transcription for material on Mao's childhood, youth and political evolution, up to the early 1920s (other documents now available to scholars were until very recently inaccessible).[114]

Mao dwelt at some length on his unhappy relations with his autocratic father, a rich peasant, who tried to bully Mao into obedience by beating him. Mao fought back, and finally brought an end to the corporal humiliation when he threatened to commit suicide by drowning himself in the family pond. This taught Mao a lesson in the use of power. He also observed how his mother, of whom he was extremely fond, employed evasive tactics to defuse her husband's rage. She mollified Mao's father with flattery and disingenuous courtesies, and so avoided directly engaging his wrath. These were tactics that Mao found useful in his guerrilla warfare ("when the enemy attacks, retreat," etc.). Neither of Mao's parents had acquired more than a third-grade education. According to Mao, his father eventually made it into the peasant landlord category and could afford to send his sons to school. Mao acquired a very thorough education in the Chinese classics and, on his own, read voluminously, including works by the aforementioned Carlyle, John Stuart Mill, the German philosophers and Rousseau. In his youth Mao was also something of a roustabout in the countryside of Hunan and Hupei. After graduation from Changsha Normal School, he went to Peking, where he got a job at Peking University as an assistant librarian under Li Ta-chao. Here he made his first contact with other members of the New Youth Movement, and, although Marxism had not yet made its formal appearance in China with the arrival of Gregory Voitinsky, the Comintern agent based in Irkutsk, Mao joined the pre-Marxian ranks of the anarchist movement.[115]

Mao related his early history to Snow in detail, but of course it had all taken place years earlier, and he depended for his version solely on his own memory. Even so, it seems to have been a fairly accurate, or truthful, depiction of his youthful development. He went on, as he told Snow, to become a labor organizer in Changsha. He was a founding member of the Chinese Communist Party in Shanghai in 1921, and proceeded to work his way to the top of the peasant propaganda department in the Kuomintang. All this period of Mao's career is a trifle vague in the account he gave to Snow—at the time, his decision to work within the Kuomintang after Chiang Kai-shek's March 1926 Canton coup, when Chiang seized power over the Nationalist government, might not have squared too well with his reputation as Chiang's number one enemy, though of course in view of Chiang's stated pro-Communist outlook in Canton Mao's role was entirely justifiable.

Mao was on happier ground, however, when he was regaling Snow with his exploits in Chingkangshan, sometimes in the company of Chu Teh, sometimes with the help of P'eng Teh-huai. These were the early days of the Red guerrilla movement, after the failure of the Great Revolution. The story of the Kiangsi soviets was of course one of the mysteries of modern China—a story that Harold Isaacs had originally intended to explore after his move to Peiping in 1934. Mao now gave Snow a fairly detailed picture of bandit warfare in those myth-enshrouded mountains until, with the decision of the Comintern in 1933, the Reds sought a frontal engagement with the Nationalists beyond the sanctuary of their mountainous stronghold.

The Moscow-trained CCP leadership had by now sidelined Mao altogether; he was under semidetention at this point. The guerrilla strategy he had used to great effect against the Nationalists in the first four Bandit Suppression Campaigns had been abandoned. The new Comintern-directed strategy called for a monolithic assault for all-out victory over the Nationalists. By leaving their mountain redoubt, however, the Reds now faced a Nationalist campaign devised by the German generals, von Seeckt and Falkenhausen. Their ambitious plan called for the strangulation-by-blockhouse approach. The Reds' defensive warfare was overseen by Otto Braun, otherwise known as Li Teh, a former German schoolteacher educated in military science in the Soviet Union who had never had any previous military experience but who, because he was German, seemed to hold out the best hope of outsmarting the Germans on the other side.

Chiang Kai-shek's encirclement campaign almost succeeded in destroying the Reds. At the time (August 1934), Mao was evidently not a major policy maker. The decision to try to break out of the death grip of the fifth annihilation campaign was made jointly by Chu Teh, Chou En-lai and Li Teh (Otto Braun).[116] The secret march to the southwest that resulted in the Long March consisted of one hundred thousand men and women at the outset carrying with them all the worldly possessions of the Chinese Communist movement, including silver, factory machinery and an entire arsenal, most of which was discarded along the route in the early stages of the march. To make good their escape from southwest China, the Reds were forced to fight their way through four main lines of enemy fortifications, to then march northwest toward Szechuan, which they succeeded in doing at the cost of about one-third of their entire force.

As Snow wrote in *Red Star Over China,* "It was one long battle from beginning to end,"[117] a six-thousand-mile trek through hostile, often mountainous, wilderness under continual assault from the forces of Chiang Kai-shek, who personally supervised the pursuit. In the beginning—for the first few months—Mao, still on the outs with the Central Committee and laid low by malaria, traveled by litter and only began to assume a commanding role again after a devastating river crossing in northern Kwangsi Province that was made under heavy enemy fire and wiped out half the Red Army. Once again, the hapless German, Li Teh, was responsible. It was due to this fatal head-on collision that Mao was able to rally support and take control of the Chinese Communist Party at Tsunyi, a city in Kweichow that the Reds captured after a daring river crossing and cliffside assault on Kuomintang forces guarding the ferry. Here, in January 1935, the CCP Politburo held a famous conference, at which the Moscow-appointed leadership, including Li Teh, was discredited, and Mao emerged first among equals, so to speak, in the Chinese Communist command structure.

The Long March, under the inspired leadership of Mao, proceeded to unfold like some legendary escapade in one of Mao's favorite Chinese classics, *The Water Margin,* or *The Romance of the Three Kingdoms.* It was a grueling ordeal, a survival epic. Snow's account in *Red Star Over China,* as told to him by Mao and others, remains a masterpiece of compression and conveys better than any subsequent version the flavor of the adventure, perhaps because Snow never bogs down in laborious explanation and detail. He proceeds swiftly with the ever-diminishing band on its many feints and river crossings, its lighthearted quick-step up the Tatu River by torchlight and the astonishing conquest of the Tatu Gorges, when the main corps of the Red Army managed to pull itself across the river abyss over a bridge of chains against enemy fire, which the brave guerrillas then quenched by hurling themselves on the Nationalist gunmen when they reached the other side. On they went, into the treacherous bog of the northwestern grasslands, where yet again thousands of men and women perished, sucked into the oblivion of the concealed marshes, a sea of mud relieved only by island clumps. Those who survived the fate of drowning in mud then had to cope with malnutrition, foot rot and a diet of poisonous grass. Truly, after such an ordeal, Shensi was a promised land.

The object of Snow's book, however, was not simply to relate the autobiography of Mao and sketch the epic of the Long March. One night, musing on the title he would give to his book, Snow decided to call it *I Went to Red China.*[118] His goal was to tell all he saw of the promised land. What Snow has to say about it all is by and large full of wonder and admiration. Snow stayed in the Red territory altogether for four months. This was hardly enough time to get beneath the surface of the new regime, for example as it affected the life of the peasant population of Shensi. Yet it can be said that if Snow found little to criticize in his sojourn, that's because at this stage there was scant evidence that peasants were being mistreated, or forced into submission, since for the bulk of the population the arrival in Shensi of the Communist guerrillas brought a great improvement in the quality of life. Snow, of course, had spent years observing the living conditions of the Chinese peasant under the Kuomintang. His experience in Pao An is comparable to that of the Western reporters who later, during World War Two, traveled to Yenan from the Free Chinese capital of Chungking. In both instances, the character of the Red headquarters was so vividly spartan and cheerful in contrast to that of Kuomintang China that it was almost impossible not to be enthusiastic about it. Snow, however, was not, as he was later accused of being, "soft" on Communism. He may have seemed soft on Communism from the point of view of right-wing American senators in the 1950s, but not in the eyes of the Communists. They thought he was liberal and progressive as a person, and an honest reporter, but he made them nervous when he tried to explain things in China by relating events from a Marxist perspective. "The point is,". Chou En-lai told Owen Lattimore in Chungking in 1941, "that Snow is a man who, by temperament and by intellect, never in his whole life will understand what Marxism is."[119]

Once he had interviewed Mao, and other Red leaders, Snow went on the road for many weeks with the Red Army, traveling into northwest China. "On the road" is used here as a manner of speech only. Often he was riding a black Mongol pony across the open plain, accompanied by Fu, his interpreter, and George Hatem, the American doctor with whom he had entered the Red territory. Snow was impressed by the iron discipline of the Red Army (again, in contrast to the shoddy and abusive treatment of the Nationalist Army conscripts). "A remarkable thing about RA," he wrote in his notebook, "is that perhaps it is only revolutionary army in which order and cleanliness and respect for property are fully maintained."[120] He was struck by the absence of looting and burning and pillage. He saw no violence inflicted on the local farmers, no instances of rape, both of which were frequently visited upon Chinese villagers by Kuomintang troops. The women in the villages where they stopped for the night, Snow noted, "look upon the soldiers as their friends and protectors."[121]

They traveled through spectacular countryside. "The way led

through grassy meadows spotted with wild flowers, purple and pale green asters, some very large and beautiful thistles and a crimson flower dark as blood in the green hills," Snow wrote in his notebook. "Gazelles were still numerous and overhead the sky was thick with eagles, enormous birds with a wing span of four or five feet—or were they bustards? There were many larks, red-winged blackbirds, magpies and thrushes; the meadows thronged with birds. Great clusters of pampas grass grew on the softly-rounded hillsides that are so pleasant a contrast with the ugly broken-up landscape of Shensi. Here one saw herds of three or four hundred sheep, goats and cows, and occasionally a herd of wild horses, very far in the distance. High in the air we saw two great eagles fighting over a carrion of some kind, tearing at each other with their wide claws, striking the air and their big wings fanning in fury."[122]

Snow was soon famous throughout the Red territories. A banner at the entrance to Yu Wang, a Muslim city in Ninghsia Province, proclaimed, "Welcome the American Internationalist to Investigate the Soviet Regions." He was given a "grand entry" by a bugle corps as he entered through the gate of the massive city walls. "Inside the city the troops of the 73, 75 and 78th divisions were lined on the streets by companies," he noted, "coming to attention for salute as we passed, then singing songs and shouting slogans. I felt," he added, "like a generalissimo with his prick out."[123]

The soldiers of the Red Army were proud and moved to have him among them. When soldiers of the Fifteenth Army left Yu Wang, their commander bade Snow a fond farewell with tears in his eyes. "He gave me a black snuff bottle before we left," Snow wrote, "apologized because he had nothing better, said that the men of Fifteenth Army wished me to have it so that I would not forget them. It had once belonged to a Mongol prince and was famous throughout the district among the peasants."[124]

In late September, Snow was back in Pao An as a guest resident of the Waichiaopu, or Foreign Office. He continued to collect biographies of Red commanders and various officials. He also lived what he called a "holiday life," riding, bathing, playing tennis. "There were two courts," he wrote, "one set up on the grassy meadow, clipped close by the goats and sheep, near the Red Academy, the other a clay court next door to the cottage of Po Ku, the gangling Chairman of Northwest Branch Soviet Government. Here, every morning, as soon as the sun rose above the hills, I played tennis with three members of the Red Army Academy: the German Li Teh, Commissar Tsai, and Commissar Wu. The court was full of stones, it was fatal to run after a fast ball, but the games were nevertheless hotly contested. Tsai and Wu both spoke Russian to Li Teh, whose Chinese was fragmentary, while I talked to

Li Teh in English and to Tsai and Wu in Chinese, so that we thus had a trilingual game."[125]

Snow had also brought with him to the Red Territory a pack of cards. He introduced gin rummy to Pao An. "For a while rummy was the rage," he wrote. "Even the women began sneaking up to the Waichiaopu gambling club. My k'ang became the rendezvous of Pao An's elite, and you could look around at the candle-lit faces there at night and recognize Mrs. Chou En-lai, Mrs. Po Ku, Mrs. Kai Feng, Mrs. Teng Fa, and even Mrs. Mao. It set tongues wagging."[126] Poker became the next craze—started by the Snow tennis foursome. The game moved on alternate nights between Li Teh's hut and the Foreign Office. "Into this sinful mire we dragged such respectable citizens as Po Ku, Li Ko-neung, Kai Feng, Lo Fu and others," Snow recalled. "Stakes rose higher and higher. One-armed Tsai finally cleaned up $120,000 from Chairman Po Ku in a single evening, and it looked as if Po Ku's only way out was embezzlement of the state funds. The poker players ruled that Po Ku could draw $120,000 on the Treasury provided Tsai used the money to buy airplanes for the non-existent Soviet air force. It was all in matches, anyway—and, unfortunately, so were the airplanes Tsai bought."[127]

Snow departed Pao An on the twelfth of October to make his way out of the magical kingdom back to Sian, thence to Peking. "I left Pao-An at nine this morning," he recorded in his diary, "bound for the highway to Sian. Mao Tse-tung was still asleep, but everyone else came out to say goodbye. They walked me through the city gate and as far as the Red Academy, where General Lin Piao was lecturing a class in the open air. He and the cadets rose and shouted: 'Peaceful good road, Shi Lo T'ung-chih! Ten Thousand Years!' The t'ung-chih meant 'comrade' and was courtesy-talk, but I felt depressed as it occurred to me that not many of these youths had a long life ahead."[128]

There were ominous signs emanating from Sian that Chiang Kai-shek was about to embark on a new anti-Red campaign. Secret police had come into Sian from Nanking to tighten the blockade, and it was now impossible for trucks to get through it on the Sian—Yenan highway without undergoing a thorough search by the Kuomintang. Helen Snow had come to Sian with the intention of joining her husband in Pao An but had returned to Peiping, partly on the advice of the Red Army liaison man in Sian, who warned that her presence in the city could draw attention to Snow, now possibly on his way out, whose films and notebooks, if discovered by the Kuomintang, would be confiscated. As it happened, Snow almost lost them anyway. A week after his departure from Pao An, he rode into Sian hidden in a Kuomintang truck, accompanied by a Manchurian officer. When he got off the truck,

Snow realized that the sack containing his diaries, notebooks, interviews and the first photos ever taken of Red China had been thrown off the truck at an area depot twenty miles back, along with sacks full of broken army rifles. "It was already dusk," Snow later recalled, "and the driver suggested that he wait till morning to go back and hunt for it. Morning! Something warned me that morning would be too late. I insisted, and I finally won the argument: At dawn, the drivers and the officer returned with the bag. They had no sooner arrived than the roads leading into the city were lined with gendarmes and troops," Snow wrote. "Generalissimo Chiang Kai-shek was paying a sudden call on Sianfu. It would have been impossible then for our lorry to return over that road to the Wei River, for it skirted the heavily-guarded aerodrome."[129]

Helen Snow had done her job and performed it with panache but she had also extended the boundaries of her role and that was the beginning of her undoing. As the official gatekeeper of Edgar Snow's career, Helen Snow was unsurpassed. "I created Ed," she once told an interviewer. "I trained him. He did not want to go out of his way to do all those things."[130] Helen imposed a discipline not only on her husband, but on herself as well. She repressed her own ambition, and set herself to the task of creating an attractive, efficient household on a somewhat confined budget. She also took the social heat for Snow, who, as Helen put it, didn't want to talk, and didn't like broken English.[131] Helen vented some of that repressed energy in her aggressive social encounters. She liked good conversation. She was brainy, and impatient with social trivia, but she was ambitious and willing to make the necessary sacrifices for her husband. She was, if not awfully well liked, certainly admired.

Then came the student protests, which were well outside the role of wife and manager. As it had in the lives of other China Hands, the cause became a crusade for Helen Foster Snow. She ceased to have a sharply defined sense of herself. This became an agony. It was mild at first because there was excitement for her in the student movement, and a sense of achievement. She threw herself into it. Then, when Snow went off by himself to Shensi to collect the fruits of their labor, Helen Snow was left alone to contemplate the bitter end of her part of the bargain.

Snow was reaping his reward, but where did that leave her? She believed in the utter importance, the greatness of his mission, and helped him prepare for it. She took him to the night train, and stood under the starry sky, waving to her husband as the train chuffed away in the direction of Sian. She had even remembered at the last minute to bring along his nose oil, so that the combined assault of the Shensi dust and the smoke from his Camel cigarettes wouldn't clog up his nostrils. Although in the years to come Snow privately acquired the reputation of having ladies in various Chinese cities who awaited his arrival, he was not in the profession of journalism for the solo flights it afforded. Unlike other foreign correspondents, he had met his wife in China and she went where he went. So when he got safely through the blockade he sent for Helen; she immediately left for Sian to join him, but as we have already noted, the risk of drawing attention to Snow's presence in Shensi was too great for her to attempt the next stage of the trip. She did manage to interview the Young Marshal while she waited in Sian, and in her dispatch he put out his first call for a United Front between the Communists and the Nationalists against Japan. This was a scoop of no mean proportions. It served as nothing else had since her marriage to stimulate the professional ambition that Helen Snow had long denied in the interest of promoting Edgar Snow's career. She had begun to sense her power on behalf of the students of north China. But time was beginning to run out on her China story. How was she going to make *her* mark? How was she going to write *her* great book?

Edgar Snow finally reappeared in November, nearly six months after his departure for the Red territory. Helen immediately set about helping him to marshal his materials into publishable form. She rushed his films down to Hartung, the German photography supply dealer, to get them developed. Word leaked out almost at once that Snow had been to the northwest. He held a hastily arranged news conference at the United States legation in Peiping, to announce to the world—and to Nanking—that Mao Tse-tung was prepared to call for a cease-fire in order to form a United Front. Chiang Kai-shek was furious. At first he tried to deny that any sort of Communist guerrilla government actually existed. When he could not discredit Snow, Chiang Kai-shek simply denounced him. In early December Chiang flew to Sian to personally command yet another Bandit Suppression Campaign, which he intended to wage with the help of Chang Hsueh-liang, the Young Marshal.

Chiang Kai-shek was too late. Chang Hsueh-liang had made peace with the Reds. He had also formed an alliance with the local Shensi warlord, Yang Hu-ch'eng. At daybreak, on December 12, troops under the command of Yang surrounded the Sian Guesthouse, where Chiang's bodyguard was quartered, and with some blood and gore took Chiang's men captive. Almost simultaneously, the Young Marshal's elite corps burst onto the grounds of the temple-hotel at the Hua-ch'ing Hot Springs at Lin-t'ung, outside Sian, where Chiang was staying. They shot and killed the reviled Chiang Hsiao-hsien, the Generalissimo's Blue Shirted nephew, lately commandant of the Peiping gendarmerie.

Chiang himself was captured in his nightshirt halfway up Tiger Rock, a stony outcropping in a valley behind the pavilion where he was lodging. The troops found him huddled in a crevice between Tiger Rock and the mountain behind it. He was minus his dentures, and refused to speak. Barefoot, feet bloodied, he was carried piggyback down the mountain in his nightshirt by one of the mutineers.[132]

The role of the Reds in all this was somewhat removed, but not very. Mao was eager to execute his old enemy. Stalin intervened, and ordered the Chinese Communists to broker Chiang Kai-shek's release. It was his conviction that the Reds were not by themselves strong enough to hold China together against the Japanese and that without the leadership of Chiang Kai-shek the Kuomintang generals would capitulate to the Japanese.[133] Chou En-lai came down from the Red territory to Sian to negotiate with Chiang Kai-shek, who promised to call off his Bandit Suppression Campaign and to form a United Front with the Reds in exchange for his release. With somewhat perplexing gallantry, the Young Marshal accompanied Chiang Kai-shek, Madame Chiang and her personal adviser, W. H. Donald, back to Nanking and surrendered himself to Chiang's custody. It was a form of filial atonement for the betrayal of Chiang, his leader. Chiang accepted the atonement, and kept the Manchurian prisoner for decades. (Well into his nineties as of this writing, he was removed to Taiwan when Chiang fled the mainland, and now lives there, a free man at last; he fared better than Yang Hu-ch'eng, the Shensi warlord, who was later arrested and held with his family until Chiang Kai-shek had them all murdered in revenge for the humilation he had suffered in Sian.)

All this happened while Snow was writing his story for the *London Daily Herald,* and preparing a version of his long interview with Mao for publication in the *China Weekly Review,* where, for the first time, the Chinese people could read about the Long March and the Red leaders in their stronghold. His book, however, was the major endeavor to which the Snows assigned their energies. Helen helped her husband get this project launched. It was Helen who recognized the value of the Mao autobiography as a historical document. Snow wanted to write it up as a series of encounters between himself and the Red leader, with dialogue lacing his own narrative. No reader, he thought, would want to labor through the unbroken first-person account of an unknown Chinese guerrilla leader, replete with incomprehensible Chinese names. In the case of other narratives his point would have had undoubted validity, but Helen was adamant on the subject of this particular autobiography. The documentary authority of an unbroken first-person account of his life by Mao Tse-tung greatly outweighed the transitory needs of his readers. It was like getting the story of the American Revolution from

George Washington at Valley Forge, she told Snow. "It's a classic," she protested. "It's priceless."[134] In this argument, Helen Snow prevailed. She claims to have personally typed out the autobiographical narrative in its final form. Helen raced through the process of preparing the manuscript of his book with her husband, but she could hardly contain herself long enough to do it. She was eager to go off to the rebel stronghold—now removed to Yenan, to the south of Pao An—and fill the place vacated by Snow. The original impulse that had brought her to China, to do what Edgar Snow did, only if possible even better, possessed her, especially now that here Snow was on the very edge of realizing his cherished dream.

Snow was baffled and annoyed by his wife's ambition. He was also recovering from a recent operation to remove kidney stones. Like Rayna Prohme, a little over a decade earlier, Helen Snow barely had the patience to nurse a sick husband back to health. Rayna, while Prohme recuperated in the courtyard of their house in Peking, managed to sign on with the Chinese Revolution. Now, as Snow recovered from his debilitating ailment, Helen prepared for her hasty departure to Yenan. Her plan was to interview the women of the Long March. Snow watched her go. Perhaps he was too weak to argue with her much about it. Perhaps, also, he did not care that much about whether she went or not. It was undoubtedly wearying to live with someone who had that much unrealized ambition. "At the last moment, Ed became silent and uncooperative," Helen Snow later recalled. "He refused to roll up my sleeping bag and complained about still being convalescent from the kidney stone operation."[135] He was unhappy about it, but he had work to do on his book. So he let her go.

Helen Snow had not foreseen the possibility that Agnes Smedley might somehow figure in her travel plans. Smedley was the writer and activist who had befriended Harold Isaacs in Shanghai until he failed to acknowledge Stalin in the pages of *China Forum*.

Agnes Smedley had already gone to Yenan, from Sian, in January, and was in residence there when Helen Snow arrived. Smedley had moved to Sian the previous fall from Shanghai. Things had not gone well for her in Shanghai. Bitterest of all had been her break with Madame Sun Yat-sen. Smedley was a woman of a highly sensitive nature, very much a creature of her compulsive instincts. If she had not been such a passionate, headstrong individual she never could have performed, as she did, in so many ways, as a helpmeet to the Revolution. In addition to her clandestine activities in Shanghai as someone who provided a haven for members of the underground, as a champion of civil rights and tireless proponent of revolution, she became a champion of the Red Army, and during the Sino-Japanese War, from 1937 to 1942, wore herself out getting medical help and supplies through to the soldiers of the Eighth Route Army of Chu Teh.

Smedley's loyalty was to her own inner voice and inevitably her relations with others suffered. This caused her terrible grief that manifested itself in physical ways, and she always endured great torment in the aftermath of interpersonal ruptures.[136] So it was after she parted company with Madame Sun. Ravaged by gastric ulcers, friendless in Shanghai, lonely and feeling wronged by the world, she gratefully accepted the invitation of a man named Liu Ting, a Red Army officer she had harbored in her Shanghai apartment for a period of time in 1935, to come north to Lin-t'ung. In September 1936, when Edgar Snow was still up in the Red Territory, Smedley went to recuperate and write at Lin-t'ung, home of the Hua-ch'ing Hot Springs. Liu Ting was the liaison between the Young Marshal and the Communists in Sian. Liu wanted a sympathetic, left-wing journalist in Sian to broadcast developments to the world, and this may be why he invited Smedley to come to Sian.[137]

Smedley wanted desperately to go into Red territory. Even though she had written a book about the Red Army and its campaigns in Fukien Province and Kiangsi, she had never actually been anywhere near it. She wanted to meet the Red guerrillas. It was Smedley who had urged George Hatem to go up to the Red territories.[138] Smedley had also promoted Edgar Snow's expedition, though she had not thought, one assumes, that he would get there ahead of her.[139] She was bitterly disappointed that Snow, and not she, had been the Western journalist chosen by the Reds.[140] However, Smedley was greathearted, painful though it was for her to be so constructed, and when Snow resurfaced in Sian in November, she set forth from Lin-t'ung to reconnect with him over dinner. The dinner was held at the house of a German dentist named Dr. Wunsch, another of Smedley's medical envoys to the Red encampment, and it was prepared by Ting Ling, a writer whom Smedley had saved from certain execution at the hands of the Kuomintang. Ting Ling had been kidnapped in 1933 by the Blue Shirts, who were tipped off to her whereabouts by her husband. Smedley had launched a relentless publicity campaign for her release in the pages of *China Forum*. Ting Ling, now on her way to the Red territories, was posing for a time as Dr. Wunsch's cook. Snow regaled them all with accounts of his visit to the Red Territory, further whetting Smedley's appetite to go there.

She did go there, but first she lived through the Sian Incident (which Dr. Wunsch did not: when Dr. Wunsch went to call on Smedley at the Sian Guest House, to which she had moved on the eve of Chiang Kai-shek's visit to the Hua-ch'ing Hot Springs, the dentist was gunned down at the entrance to the courtyard by Yang's roughneck troops).

The Young Marshal's troops captured the temple-spa at Lin-t'ung and broke into the guest house where Chiang Kai-shek's top commanders were billeted. Yang's men shot the place up, smashing and looting as they went. In the process they destroyed all of Smedley's worldly belongings, which seems not to have dented her morale (although the murder of Dr. Wunsch came as a dreadful shock).[141]

Smedley set to work caring for victims of the fracas. The wounded men and women lay on the stone floor, without blankets to cover them or pillows on which to rest their heads. Many of them still had open gaping sores, advanced cases of frostbite or crudely amputated limbs, mementos of Chiang's campaigns. Smedley was deeply moved by their stoic suffering. Besides ministering to the needs of these victims, Smedley also performed the service for which Liu Ting had invited her to Sian. In the evening she broadcast news reports from Sian to promote the cause of the United Front and the war against Japan. These broadcasts served to keep the pressure on Nanking to hold to its part of the bargain in the wake of Chiang Kai-shek's release. Smedley's fame spread in the United States, where her efforts, like the exploits of a character out of the Wild West, made good newspaper copy.[142] In China, however, and specifically in Sian and the surrounding countryside, Smedley's broadcasts enraged the American missionaries. They hated the Reds and to them Smedley was a Communist traitor. In Sian Smedley aroused the animosity of people who later fanned the flames of anti-Communism at home; they sought to pillory Smedley as one of those who had helped America "lose" China to the Reds.

Not surprisingly, Smedley had an explosive, volatile effect on the lives of the people in Yenan, when she finally got there. Smedley had a way of inserting herself forcibly into the personal lives of her friends and then inciting them, when possible, to battle, if not to revolution. Domestic harmony was not her thing: she seemed to oppose it in her own life, and in that of her friends. She was a radical and a feminist who believed that women should be free, like men, to speak their minds. She did not mince words if she saw men she knew oppressing women and she was just as likely to turn on the women, if she felt like it. In Yenan, Smedley was received by Mao, Chu Teh, Chou En-lai et al. as an honored guest and friend of the Revolution. She loved it up there. Yenan was an old fortress town centered around a hill station formed by an appendage of the Great Wall. The town was nestled between cliffs and a river ran down past it at one end that provided natural irrigation in the otherwise sere, bare brown landscape of northern Shensi. It was a landscape not unlike the mesa and dun earth plain of Smedley's own spartan and impoverished childhood in the American West. It inspired her to sing the cowboy songs she had memorized so long ago in that faraway land like "The Streets of Laredo" and "She'll Be Comin' Round the Mountain." It may also have inspired her to introduce dancing to Yenan.[143]

Here is where she ran afoul of the women of Yenan, the wives of the leading cadres who had accompanied their husbands on the Long March. Smedley, by the very force of her nature, was not content in Yenan to live quietly in her cave as a foreign guest. She decided that what Yenan needed was a little more life. Indeed, it was a dusty and lifeless place, only recently taken over by the puritanical revolutionaries as their new capital. Smedley knew from her Colorado youth how to put a little zip into a one-horse town. With the assent of Mao (who perhaps felt he would need to know how to dance on future state visits abroad), Smedley established dancing classes in the abandoned Catholic church at one end of town. These she conducted to the music supplied by some old square dance records and a gramophone she'd ingeniously managed to lay her hands on up there in that barren place. Soon Mao and other revolutionary leaders were showing up in the early evenings for lessons given by Smedley and her translator, the young and very becoming, sophisticated actress and divorcee Lily Wu.[144]

The women of Yenan were incensed. None of them were interested in dancing. Some of them couldn't dance anyway because their feet had been bound in childhood. These women saw Smedley as a saboteur who was undermining the unwritten code of marital conduct in Yenan. Very likely, unbeknownst to herself, this was precisely what Agnes was doing. The Yenan wives in their caves were by all accounts indifferent to their men. They tended not to enhance their own sexuality or appearance since they had been through all hardships with them as equals. This might have argued for Smedley's sympathy, but her heart was with the men, because, through and through, Smedley was a boy-crazy romantic. The Yenan wives were aroused to antipathy by the way Smedley had seduced their husbands into tripping the light fantastic down at the Catholic church and they also didn't like the way she spent hours and hours interviewing their men in her cave, which was right next door to the cave of Lily Wu, her best friend, who naturally attended the interviews as Smedley's translator.

All hell was on the verge of breaking loose in Yenan by the time Helen Snow finally got there. It took some time for her to figure out what was happening, even though it was clear to her as soon as she arrived that Smedley was living in a state of semiquarantine and was highly distraught, if not actually paranoid. Some of the behavior that Smedley exhibited at that time, Helen quite correctly assumed, was provoked by Helen's own arrival. Smedley was by nature unable to conceal her feelings. She was not happy about the appearance of Helen

on her turf. Already her feelings were hurt that Edgar Snow had preceded her in the estimation of the Red leaders and walked away with
the spoils before she ever got near them. Now along came Helen, whom
she had always looked upon as a lightweight. She did not know Helen
terribly well. Her friendship was really with Snow, whom she had
helped along the way during their early years in China together, and
whom she considered to be her equal. Naturally she looked down on
Helen and it galled her that the Red leaders were giving this neophyte
the VIP treatment when they should have known better. It was insult
added to injury that she had to endure the presence of this other American woman at a time when she was herself living as a pariah in Yenan.[145]

In fact, a strong alliance with the newcomer might possibly have
helped Smedley's cause. Helen was in need of an ally. She was shocked
to find herself in a place entirely unlike what her husband's glowing
accounts of Pao An had led her to expect. She had anticipated a clean-
swept, exhilarating encampment aglow with vitality and rude health.
Instead, what she found in Yenan was a dusty, rat-infested corner of
China where morale was severely tested by tuberculosis and the black
plague, carried by a population of ever-proliferating fleas. Helen was
almost immediately attacked on arrival by dysentery brought on by the
diet, which caused a drastic weight loss. Her illness was compounded
by severe culture shock.[146] Smedley insulted Helen before the Red leaders by making disparaging references to her good looks and her makeup,
as if to say that no woman who paid so much attention to her appearance
could possibly be a true friend of the Revolution. She also told the Red
Chinese that Helen was a bourgeois housewife. She seized the small
amount of money Helen had brought with her to Yenan—one hundred
dollars—and pocketed it and never returned it.[147] She also, or so it
seemed to Helen, tried in various ways to sabotage her.[148] Clearly
Smedley was in a peculiar state, even for her. As time went by, Helen
began to find out what had been going on in Yenan, and her assessment
of Smedley acquired a certain clinical detachment.

Mao, it seemed, had taken to stopping off before work every day
for chats with Smedley in her cave. Mao was not Smedley's favorite
leader. The journalists all had their special favorite and hers was Chu
Teh, about whom she eventually wrote a book. Mao didn't respond
very well to her, or so she sensed. She detected an evasive quality in his
behavior, in the way he avoided her eyes when he spoke to her. At first
she decided that he was soft, and somehow effeminate, an "aesthete,"
as she put it. Men who were what she called sissies had no appeal for
her. But she decided on closer acquaintance that the Red leader was
simply "spiritually isolated."[149] He was a poet, a literary man, a romantic, as she herself was a romantic. She encouraged him to learn how to

dance, and paired him off with Lily Wu. Their talks in Smedley's cave were of a wide-ranging nature. Mao seemed to welcome an opportunity to talk about things he perhaps had not had much time to contemplate in the years of warfare that preceded this new, brief hiatus between his truce with the Nationalists and the coming war with Japan, a time that allowed Mao the luxury of reading, writing and dancing. "Mao often came to the 'cave' where I lived with my girl secretary," Smedley wrote, "and the three of us would have a simple dinner and spend hours in conversation. Since he had never been out of China, he asked a thousand questions. We spoke of India; of literature; and once he asked me if I had ever loved any man, and why, and what love meant to me."[150]

Lily was of course present in her role as interpreter during Mao's discursive forays with Smedley. What was this phenomenon of which the poets Keats and Shelley wrote called romantic love? Mao asked Smedley. It was something outside his frame of reference. Had she ever experienced such a thing? What was it like? Before long it became quite clear that Mao was addressing his thoughts as much to Lily Wu as he was to Smedley. He began to exchange poems of a not altogther revolutionary nature with Lily Wu who conscientiously tried, with some success, to match the singular, bold artistry of Mao's calligraphy in poems of her own making. Mao's noonday visits to Smedley's cave did not go unobserved by Mao's wife, Ho Tzu-chien. Not only had Ho Tzu-chien accompanied her husband on the Long March, she had given birth to his child en route. She was proprietary about her husband, and became among the fiercest of the square dance critics. Smedley, though she does not seem to have known it, was already in hot water with the women of Yenan. Now here she was actually brokering a love affair between Ho Tzu-chien's husband and Lily Wu.[151]

Late one night in July, when Helen Snow had been in Yenan for over two months, disaster struck. According to Smedley, after she had gone to bed, she heard the familiar shuffling sound of Mao's footsteps in the cave next door. In the next moments catlike shrieks pierced the night. Smedley rushed to Lily Wu's cave to find Mao sitting on the edge of her bed fending off the blows of his wife, who had followed her husband to his assignation. Ho Tzu-chien was beside herself, screaming at Mao, who endured the abuse for a while in silence before he struck her a blow and told her to stop. Ho Tzu-chien then rushed toward Lily Wu, who was cowering in a corner, grabbed her hair with one hand and scratched the side of her face with her fingernails. Smedley intervened. She was the next one to field the fury of Ho Tzu-chien, who hit her and accused her of bringing her imperialist ways into the rebel stronghold and undermining local standards of morality. Smedley countercharged. She slapped Ho Tzu-chien and told her that *she* was the counterrevolutionary. She declared that Ho Tzu-chien was not worthy of being the wife of the chairman of the Chinese Communist Party. At this point Mao dressed down Ho Tzu-chien. He announced that Smedley was right. There was nothing wrong with his visit to the cave of Lily Wu, he said. She was by her suspicious, jealous actions guilty of counterrevolutionary behavior, and he ordered her to return to the house. When Ho Tzu-chien refused to go willingly, Mao ordered his guard to escort her home. It took two guards to wrestle Ho Tzu-chien from the cave of Lily Wu and march her back to Mao's house, along a route of curious onlookers, now awake, who peered at the strange procession from their own dwellings.[152]

Mao's marriage turned out to be irreparably damaged. Ho Tzu-chien left Yenan, and eventually went to Moscow for some "reeducation." Lily Wu's life was also damaged. She, too, soon left Yenan, after burning all Mao's poems. They never met again, so far as is known. Agnes Smedley also found herself persona non grata in Yenan after this episode. Smedley determined to leave Yenan, but it was impossible for her to do so once she suffered a serious injury to her back from a fall she took off a horse in mid-August.

At the same time, Helen Snow was having troubles of her own getting out of Yenan. For Helen, Yenan was no magical kingdom. She had planned to dash up there for a month at most, get her interviews and return to Peiping. Instead, she found herself trapped, unable to leave. She'd imagined that she'd be able to hitch a ride on some Red Army truck on its return trip to Sian, but there turned out to be no such vehicle available. She thought she'd found a rare chance to leave one day when a carload of American journalists—Owen Lattimore, Philip and Agnes Jaffe, and T. A. Bisson—arrived in Yenan, chauffered by Effie Hill, a Swedish mechanic who had been the driver of the great Swedish explorer Sven Hedin in the Gobi Desert. They had slipped through Chiang Kai-shek's cordon sanitaire outside Sian on the pretense that they were planning to visit a famous nearby mountain. Helen implored them to take her back with them in their car, but they were afraid to do so, because by now Helen was on a wanted list in Sian. They were unwilling to risk being seen in her company on the return trip from their alleged jaunt. "It showed a distinct lack of friendliness," she wrote.[153]

After that, the rains came. "The roads and bridges between the two cities were washed out in heavy downpours for weeks and remained so until fall," Helen later wrote, "so I was stranded in Yenan until September."[154] Yenan was not the kind of environment suited to someone of Helen's disposition. She was willing to wear an army uniform like everyone else, but couldn't bring herself to give up lipstick. The chief entertainments in Yenan, group singing, meetings, speechifying and, thanks to Smedley, dancing (in groups), were things she abhorred, and she hated performing in public, which all visitors to Yenan were expected to do. She declined to participate, and found that as a result she wasn't very popular. Altogether, there were three foreigners in residence in Yenan in addition to Helen and, with the exception of Dr. George Hatem, they were a miserable lot. Helen had made her peace, more or less, with Smedley. "Except during her black spells," she recalled, "Agnes Smedley had a special charm, even wit and humor. I used to climb the hill to her cave in Yenan just for the pleasure of hearing her refer to Chiang Kai-shek as 'that feudal bastard.' "[155] The other two foreigners, Dr. Hatem and Otto Braun, or Li Teh, the German adviser, were not, like Helen, at all favorably disposed toward Smedley. Otto Braun wouldn't speak to anybody by that time except Hatem, who took care of him in his illness, because he felt that it was too dangerous to talk. Hatem cheered up Helen Snow when he came to visit her on his rounds by singing, very loudly, under her window, "Arise, ye prisoner of starvation!"[156] But he refused to help Agnes Smedley after her horseback injury until, finally, he was persuaded to do so by Helen's tearful importunings. Even then he wouldn't actually speak to Smedley. It was the same old problem already noted by Viola Isaacs. Both Hatem and Otto Braun said that she "told lies" about them.[157]

Finally, Mao himself ordered Smedley to leave, with or without a bad back. "Agnes was not very brave," Helen Snow maintains to this day.[158] Her situation was extremely dangerous. In her state of paranoia, however, she resorted to stratagems that could only be called desperate, if not actually mad. It is Helen Snow's belief that Smedley sent the telegram to Edgar Snow that she later saw on his desk in Peiping signed in her name, calling for him to come to Yenan—for the purpose, Helen believes, of rescuing Agnes.[159] Although she had communicated with her husband about her plight, Helen Snow has no recollection of sending such a message herself. Some of the letters she did write to Snow, however, which she entrusted Smedley to mail for her, never reached him. It was Helen's suspicion, moreover, that Smedley was also keeping correspondence, including cash, mailed by Edgar Snow to Helen from Peiping. "About this time, communications seemed to be impossible though my husband did not know this," Helen Snow noted. "I wondered later if Agnes kept the money, as sometimes my mail was sent through her in case I had already left."[160]

Smedley and Helen Snow finally left Yenan together, on the seventh of September. The rains had stopped. "When the morning of

September 7 dawned," Helen later wrote, "I was so deathly sick I could hardly get out of bed."[161] It was, however, not an opportunity to be missed, since another one might not have presented itself again for weeks. It turned out to be a grueling, twelve-day, two-hundred-and-fifty-mile journey by horse and mule. The two women were accompanied by an armed guard and about thirty Red soldiers and three wives, including Chu Teh's wife, all of whom were going to the front to join the war against Japan. For part of the journey Agnes Smedley traveled on a stretcher, carried by five bearers. In addition to these servants, she was also attended by her personal bodyguard and a boy orderly. Yet according to Helen, Smedley had her eye on the bodyguard who had been assigned to Helen Snow, a hero of the Long March named Sun-hua. "The first moment Miss Smedley got a glimpse of my muscular, healthy new bodyguard," Helen Snow recalled, "her eyes brightened and she took a second look. I well knew what was in her mind. All during the trip she coveted her neighbor's manservant, but there was a limit to the Christian Girl Scoutism I had practiced all summer trying to be friends with this irascible, complicated person, who was charming one minute and impossible the next. My suitcase and my one hundred dollars she might have, but my bodyguard? Not until the last mile to Sian had been traversed."[162]

It took great courage and spirit for Helen Foster Snow to make her own journey to the Red territory after the return of her husband from his great adventure, and out of this ordeal she retrieved a work of permanent value. She had accomplished what she had set out to do: she interviewed Mao, Chu Teh and Chou En-lai, and she conducted over sixty-five other interviews, many of them with the women of Communist China, including Ts'ai Ch'ang, whom she likened to Rosa Luxemburg, K'ang K'o-ch'ing (the "Red Amazon"), wife of Chu Teh, and Liu Chien-hsien, a militant feminist who had been a close friend in Wuhan of Rayna Prohme. Ever after, Helen Snow would look back on her trip to Yenan as an achievement. Out of it she produced a valuable contribution to the documentary record of the period, which she called *Inside Red China.* Many people over the years, women especially and in particular those who knew her at the time, have criticized Helen Snow for competing with her husband, as though she ought to have been sufficiently satisfied to be the wife of Edgar Snow. "Why didn't she greet him with open arms and enjoy his accomplishment, instead of dashing off to Yenan herself?" This observation was typical of Helen Snow's critics, and came from one who had known her quite well in Peiping. "She was trying to *outstrip* Ed."[163] However, when she first went to China, it was not her ambition to be Snow's wife. Marriage to

Snow was, in a way, a detour for Helen Snow. Though never trained as a journalist, Helen Snow possessed the vocational drive of a born writer and journalist. Until she made her dash to Yenan, she had never truly asserted herself. For this she was resented, even by her mild-mannered husband, but the courage of her solo mission to Yenan was in the effort she made to be true to herself.

Photographs of Helen Snow in Yenan show her to be someone quite unlike the woman with smartly parted hair who gleams with assurance from poses with her chic Kansu greyhound, Gobi, in pictures taken during the Peiping years. In Yenan her hair is even a different color, lighter, and she looks younger, less formidable. She has lost the Mary McCarthy look of knowing malice and appears more earnest. Appearances can be deceiving, but the photographs correspond to Helen Snow's own description of the change her personality underwent. In the course of this episode she endured much discomfort, fear, anxiety and physical distress with, it must be noted, a certain élan. She was trapped in Yenan for months without knowing whether word of her captivity had ever reached her husband. She put up with life in a small, backward society of people with whom she had never come into such close proximity. She suffered a drastic weight loss from the diet and the dysentery she immediately acquired on arrival in Yenan. Although she never wrote the "one great book" for which she had nurtured such ambition, and always felt she had squandered her opportunities to do so on other projects, including those of her husband, nevertheless, Helen Foster Snow finally broke free. The price she paid for this triumph was ultimately very high. By the time she got back to Sian, she was no longer the self-assured person, impatient to act on her own, who had left her husband alone at home to finish his book by himself. She was tired, ill, shaky and unsure of herself. Coincidentally, the world as she had left it six months earlier was gone forever.

In July, while she was up in Yenan, the Japanese had occupied Peiping. The undeclared war between Japan and China had erupted after an encounter on July 7, between a Japanese patrol and Chinese troops stationed at a garrison at Lukouch'iao, near the fabled Marco Polo Bridge, eight miles south of Peiping. The Japanese had provoked the incident by performing maneuvers well outside the area where legation troops were permitted by treaty to operate. The Chinese had opened fire on the Japanese, who had then called in reinforcements. Exactly one month later, on August 8, the Japanese made their triumphal entry into the city of Peiping. "Through all the morning a long column of troops, trucks and tanks filed into the city through Yung Ting Men (the South Gate)," Graham Peck wrote, "parading up the central avenues before they divided to occupy the barracks vacated by the Chinese. I went out of the city with the Red Cross that day and missed the more spectacular parts of the procession, but I did get back in time to see the tail end of it. Up Hatamen Street was rolling a thundering column of trucks loaded with food and ammunition. All of them were draped with coarse netting in which cornstalks and foliage had been woven for camouflage; even the grim dust-covered drivers wore on their helmets small nets like lettuce bags, into which leaves and grasses, and sometimes flowers, were twisted with an unexpectedly coquettish effect." This procession was embarrassing for an American, Peck observed, "as it demonstrated that the mechanized army traveled entirely in American motor-cars. Also, a good proportion of the trucks were piled high with cases of a well-known American gasoline."[164]

Edgar Snow had by this time completed work on his book, and mailed it overseas. He was not particularly concerned about Helen's prolonged absence, nor indeed was there much time for that, since he was busy covering the battles that had begun within the environs of Peiping between the Chinese and the invaders. Like other foreigners in Peiping, Snow was also occupied by the effort to help Chinese friends, in his case university students and professors, who were on the enemy's blacklist. Snow helped them flee Peiping disguised as coolies, beggars or merchants. Some of his former students from Yenching joined guerrilla organizations that sprouted almost immediately in the countryside outside the city, and Snow allowed some Manchurians in league with them to operate a radio transmission system out of his house.[165]

Once the Japanese had actually occupied Peiping, however, there was little further news of import to write from north China. Snow's employer, the *London Daily Herald,* ordered him to leave Japanese-occupied China and report on events from Shanghai, the next battlefront. In early September, after waiting for months to hear from his wife, Snow received the telegram she claims she never sent, of which the only part that got through was the message "All right. Best you come here." By then, the rail lines between Peiping and Tientsin, damaged during the fighting, had been repaired, and it was now possible to leave the city. Snow packed up his household and stored the belongings that he and Helen had accumulated over the years of their marriage. He then departed for the coast on the roundabout journey to Sian, accompanied by James Bertram, the young New Zealand reporter, and Teng Ying-ch'ao, the wife of Chou En-lai, who had been recuperating from tuberculosis in the Western Hills, and who traveled with Snow and Bertram as far as Tsingtao disguised as the Snow family amah.[166]

Since she had never sent the telegram urging her husband to come to Sian, Helen Snow had no reason to expect him to join her there, and so she boarded a train for Peiping. As it happened, Snow and Bertram arrived at the Sian Guest House after an overland journey by train from Shantung Province only to find that Helen had left for Peiping that morning. An urgent telegram was dispatched to her train, summoning her back to Sian; by nightfall she and her husband were at last reunited. They traveled together to Shantung, which was as yet untroubled by the war, and there they relaxed together for a few days on the golden sands of Tsingtao, the smart resort on the China coast that had once been the pride of the Germans.

This was to be their last idyll in China. Snow went to the battlefront, Helen paid a final visit to occupied Peiping. In November, she rejoined Snow. Back once again in Shanghai, six years after her first date with Edgar Snow on that torpid day so calm with foreboding, Helen Snow could only regret the loss of her insouciance, the provocative youthful charm that had bewitched the journalist from Missouri. She now looked back on the early days of her marriage and yearned for the person she once had been. So did her husband, who, she wrote, "never got over his horror that I had changed from 'perfection' into whatever it was I was becoming."[167]

The ominous wave that had cast its shadow across China for so many years crashed at last on its shores and rushed inland. The wreckage was evident in the aftermath of the Japanese invasion. "There were miles of devastation along the Whangpoo River," Helen Snow recalled. "Japanese freighters were already loading looted machinery and scrap iron for the home islands."[168] Shanghai, all but the foreign settlements, was in ruins. Flames continued to lick the city long after the conquerors had moved on to the capital at Nanking. The Chinese, once again, had put up a valiant resistance. For months, they had held out under incessant bombing raids by Japanese planes (and at least one unintended bombing by their own).

The Japanese were enraged by this Chinese resistance. They had counted on a quick victory. They were furious when Chiang Kai-shek failed to submit the way he had seemed to promise he would. When finally they battered their way through the walls of Nanking, the Japanese found that Chiang and his government had escaped up the Yangtze River. While his new capital was being readied in Chungking, deep in Szechuan Province, Chiang waged a rearguard defense from Wuhan. Incensed that Chiang had eluded their grasp, and further maddened that the world was applauding China's heroic resistance, the Japanese released a terrible lust for revenge on the survivors who were trapped in Nanking. "Wholesale looting, the violation of women, the murder of women, the murder of civilians, the eviction of Chinese from their homes, mass executions of war prisoners and the impressing of able-bodied men turned Nanking into a city of terror," wrote Tillman Durdin in an eyewitness report for the *New York Times*. "The killing of civilians was widespread. Foreigners who traveled widely through the city Wednesday found civilians dead on every street." Years later, A. T. Steele, who had driven up to Nanking with Durdin in a borrowed Chevrolet, estimated that anywhere from a hundred thousand to three hundred thousand people died in the rape of Nanking. He recalled seeing people being shot in groups of a half dozen on street corners.[169] And Durdin wrote, "Just before boarding the ship for Shanghai the writer watched the execution of 300 men on the Bund. The killings took ten minutes. The men were lined against a wall and shot. Then a number of Japanese, armed with pistols, trod nonchalantly around the crumpled bodies, pumping bullets into any that were still kicking." A large group of military spectators, navy men from warships anchored off the Bund invited to watch, "apparently greatly enjoyed the spectacle," Durdin wrote at the time. "The capture of Nanking was the most overwhelming defeat suffered by the Chinese and one of the most tragic military debacles in the history of modern warfare," he concluded.[170]

From Nanking, Japanese troops marched westward. Meanwhile, Japanese air force bomber pilots, like angry hornets, ran raids up the Yangtze, bombing indiscriminately, and provoked more censure in the West when they sank the USS *Panay*. What they did not provoke was any military reaction from the other Powers. Despite the carnage, and the ferocity of the Japanese invasion, Edgar Snow predicted that the war would eventually ruin Japan. "For a score of what seem to me sound reasons, Japan has already lost the war and her attempt to conquer China," Snow wrote his father. "The deeper the war goes inland," he observed, "the more inextricably Japan flounders in the mind of China, and the greater becomes her impotency to withdraw."[171] He also foresaw the entry into the war of the United States, although he predicted that it would happen no later than 1940. "Increased Japanese provocation," he wrote his father, "together with increased Anglo-American armaments will result in a bolder and more decisive stand, eventually leading to war, as Japan's war base tends to weaken because of heavy inroads on her replenishable war reserves, the shaky economic structure (and increasing inability to withstand a joint boycott or move for sanctions), and deeper and more hopeless involvement of Japan's army on the mainland, etc."[172]

Edgar and Helen Snow were both outraged that Chiang Kai-shek and the Shanghai establishment had fled upriver and left China's industrial equipment behind, intact, for the Japanese. In abandoning China's light industrial machinery, they had only further enfeebled its resistance, for there was no industrial base in the Chinese interior. During the years when it might have been possible for him to do so, Chiang Kai-shek had failed to develop an industrial base with which to manufacture armaments for a war effort and otherwise to create a productive counteroffensive that would prevent Japan from taking over the economy of rural China, where there was active resistance to Japanese occupation. Instead, the Japanese were now poised to manufacture goods in China to sell to the Chinese. This seemed all wrong to the Snows. Rewi Alley thoroughly agreed. Snow had met this New Zealander on his visit to the famine in northeast China nearly a decade earlier. Alley was now the factory inspector for the International Settlement. He and the Snows had formed the habit of eating Sunday lunch together in Shanghai. Over roast beef, they vented the anger they felt about Chiang Kai-shek and his mistakes. Helen Foster described Alley as a man who "personified the best in British civilization—Irish-English poetic sensitivity, physical culture, sports, love of nature and hiking, most of all the Puritan ethic —not only the work ethic but also the conscience, as well as the identification with honest, working people." Alley was a Boy Scout, "a natural socialist, in other words with healthy instincts and emotions."[173] His frustration fueled his rage against the Nationalists and the Japanese, who had laid waste to industrial Shanghai.

Helen Snow was struck by the force of Alley's outrage. One day, on a tour of the factory districts, it dawned on her that with his energy and ability, and his political outlook, Alley might be able to establish industrial cooperatives throughout China, small factories, owned by the workers themselves, that would remain small and mobile. These cooperative enterprises could be set up in villages. Her idea had been inspired by a dinner party conversation with the British consul, John Alexander, and now she tried it out on Alley. There must, she told him, be "a people's movement for production, and the only way to get that is to have the people organize and manage themselves, linking their production units up together. Industrial cooperatives are the answer!"[174]

Rewi Alley accepted the challenge at once. He and Edgar Snow threw themselves behind the China Industrial Cooperatives, or CIC. When he wasn't out reporting the war (after the publication of his Yenan reports, the London Daily Herald had made him its Far Eastern correspondent), Snow devoted himself to the CIC and so did his wife. "Rewi was the indispensable man," Helen Snow has written. "He went out into the villages and got the work moving by sheer force of effort and personality, though constantly harassed and sabotaged by the opposition."[175] Alley was the organizer, and the Snows raised money and support. The virtue of the cooperatives was that they were not Communist-inspired or Communist in structure, and it was hard for anyone on either end of the political spectrum to take issue with them.

The Snows, assisted by a committee of volunteers, overcame Nationalist Chinese corruption and indifference to line up the Generalissimo and
Madame Chiang behind their cause; Madame Sun Yat-sen also became
a supporter through her organization, the China Defense League; and
so did Mao Tse-tung, who agreed to let Rewi Alley set up cooperatives
in his territory.

Much of the success of the industrial cooperative venture was due
to the rising star of Edgar Snow and the success of his book, *Red Star
Over China*. Snow was amazed by his own success. *Red Star* was, in the
words of Snow's biographer, "a monumental book," that "for many
intellectuals was the single best book of China reportage they ever encountered."[176] It ranked with *The Good Earth* by Pearl Buck as one of
the two memorable China books of that era. Fifty years later, at a
New York dinner party, this writer met a woman from Chattanooga,
Tennessee, who could recall how *Red Star* became her family's bible.
The book's immense popularity was of perhaps greater import in
China, where it appeared in both Chinese and English editions. Many
Chinese first learned of the guerrilla movement in the Red territory
when they read Snow's Mao interview, first published in abbreviated
form in *China Weekly Review,* then subsequently in an official National
Salvation Association edition, and in pirated versions. *Red Star Over
China* inspired young leftists and liberals and students to leave in droves
for the Red territory. It had given Mao Tse-tung precisely the local and
global publicity that he had hoped to harvest when he first invited Edgar
Snow to Pao An. Now Snow was himself a famous figure in China.

The book influenced a number of important people in their thinking about contemporary China, one of whom, Sir Archibald Clark
Kerr, was the new wartime British ambassador to China. In 1938, Clark
Kerr could be found either in Shanghai, at the serenely palatial British
government villa, or in Hankow, where Chiang Kai-shek, and many of
the principal figures in the United Front, had alighted, including a cross
section of Communist leaders, who for the time being had parted company with Mao Tse-tung in order to join forces with the Nationalists.
Although Mao, alone among his colleagues in the Politburo, was holding out for a separate command in the northwestern provinces under
Communist control, Chou En-lai, Wang Ming, Po Ku and others could
be found in Hankow, fraternizing with their recent enemy. Hankow
was an intimate and clubby place, for that brief moment. "History,"
Christopher Isherwood wrote, "grown weary of Shanghai, bored with
Barcelona, has fixed her capricious interest on Hankow but where is she
staying?"[177] Isherwood had made a journey to China with the British
poet W. H. Auden, on assignment from Random House and the British
publishing house Faber and Faber, and found himself in Hankow in

1938. It was an interim time, between the Spanish Civil War and the invasion of Poland by Hitler, when the Yangtze Valley was the only front in the world where the war against Fascism was being actively fought. Once again Wuhan, China's industrial triple city, as it had been in 1927, was under a spotlight. "This is the real capital of war-time China," Isherwood observed in the book he and Auden subsequently wrote, which they called *Journey to a War*. "All kinds of people live in this town—Chiang Kai-shek, Agnes Smedley, Chou En-lai, generals, ambassadors, journalists, foreign naval officers, soldiers of fortune, air men, missionaries, spies."[178] It was in this climate of unity—known as the "spirit of Hankow"—that Sir Archibald Clark Kerr, at the urgent behest of Edgar Snow, persuaded the Generalissimo and "Madame" to endorse the CIC. From Hong Kong, on August 28, 1938, Snow wrote to J. B. Powell in Shanghai: "I spent many wearying hours in Hankow talking about our cooperative scheme, and had the satisfaction, before leaving, of seeing it definitely launched. The present plan is operating under the Executive Yuan.* An Industrial Cooperatives Commission has been created, with Rewi Alley as adviser, under Dr. Kung."[179]

Indeed, the great peril now was that Madame Chiang and H. H. K'ung, her brother-in-law, would altogether take over the CIC and siphon off for their own, personal use the funds supposedly earmarked out of China relief money for the CIC. Luckily, the Snows quite inadvertently found a route around this danger in 1939, while they were in the Philippines. There, they met very rich overseas Chinese, who were willing to put large sums of money directly into the CIC coffers, much to the chagrin of Madame Chiang, who never liked to see money destined for China elude her grasp.

The Snows' China adventure as a couple came to an end in the fall of 1938, when Helen Snow went to live in the Philippines, where she raised money for the CIC and worked on her writing. Snow made a long trip by himself to the interior of China in 1939, and visited Yenan, which had been bombed to smithereens by the Japanese. The Communists had been driven to live entirely in caves, with a spartan stylishness. Snow revisited Mao and inspected the war effort against Japan. Then he rejoined his wife, in Baguio, where he completed his next book, *The Battle for Asia*. It was time, however, for them both to go home, if such the United States could be called. Home, for the Snows, was a time and a place to which they could never return.

In December 1940 Snow saw his wife off at Shanghai on a ship bound for the West Coast. "Our first priority was to escape from the

---

* The bureaucratic instrument through which Chiang Kai-shek ruled China.

East before Japan made us prisoners of war," Helen Snow wrote.[180] Snow had planned to return to the United States via Europe as an accredited war correspondent on assignment for the *New York Herald Tribune.* He was tired and depressed. He had dark circles under his eyes and had lost a lot of weight. When Helen departed he was suddenly alone. Separation and loneliness triggered guilt and remorse over the state of his marriage. He decided to skip Europe, and flew across the Pacific to meet Helen in California.

On January 13, at Midway Island on a stopover to the United States by Pan Am Clipper, Snow confided to his diary: "Surely this whole period must remain the darkest in my life. Never have I been through the depths of dispair [sic] in which my own role has appeared so altogether despicable and contemptible." He took himself to task for failing to appreciate his wife, to value her and understand her. "How early and how quickly I forgot the struggle I FOUGHT TO WIN HER and how quickly I gave up the effort to keep her after the first victory," he wrote. He blamed himself for never giving Helen enough money, for complaining about her extravagances, "because I blamed everything on the purely sexual relationship (my own fault) and took no account of my own role in the cause of its failure; because of my niggardliness about money she spent on work done for other people; because. . . ."[181]

Snow's sense of failure as a husband was undoubtedly aggravated during the war to come, for in it he was often separated from his wife for long stretches of time as a war correspondent in China and the Soviet Union. The Snows' marriage barely survived the war before it collapsed altogether in bitter acrimony. Yet there was a reprieve. And when his Pan Am Clipper landed in California, Edgar Snow discovered that he was the most celebrated journalist in America, if not in the whole world.

Teddy

TEDDY WHITE, a world-class correspondent and political journalist of great renown, author of more than several best-selling books that suffuse the reporting of current affairs with historical meaning in the course of lively narrative, learned his craft as an apprentice in wartime Chungking. He was the only American reporter of note who was spawned in that backwater.

Unlikely creature, unlikely place.

In 1939 when White was fresh out of Harvard and first went there, Chungking was the last place on earth that any self-respecting journalist would have wanted to be assigned to with the possible exception of La Paz, Bolivia. It was not just remote, which of course is why Chiang Kai-shek selected it as a wartime capital. It was also a fairly unpleasant place. To this day you wouldn't choose to go there unless you wanted to board a cruise boat for the downriver trip through the Yangtze River Gorges, soon to be dammed. Now, in the last decade of the twentieth century, Westerners spell Chungking Chongqing, and pronounce it Chongching. It is a huge city, modern by Chinese standards. The core of the city still hulks on the steep crags that rise up from the rivers Yangtze and Chialing, which flow together at its prow, so to speak. Almost nothing, however, remains of the city Teddy White first beheld in April 1939, when it was a medieval town of squalid huts and rank back alleys that stank of the fecal matter that flowed along the streets in open gutters that fed into the Yangtze and befouled the riverside towns and cities hundreds of miles downstream, and killed the Japanese in Hankow, or so some people in Chungking liked to imagine at the time.[1]

The modern metropolis of Chongqing flows from this center for miles in every direction into the countryside; when Teddy White went back there forty years later he couldn't even find the site of the Press Hostel, which for nearly six years most foreign correspondents and even some Chinese journalists called home.[2] He could still see the caves that the Kuomintang hollowed out of the cliffs with spirited enterprise in order to create shelters from the Japanese bombing raids that decimated much of the city in the summers of 1939, 1940 and 1941. The caves are still there, with their cross-hatched gates, monuments of a sort to Chungking's noblest moment in recent history. Nowadays the city on earth Chungking most resembles, to my mind, at least, is Pittsburgh, Pennsylvania, especially in the gritty humid haze of summer heat. In 1939, no such grandeur, however besmeared with grime, could have been attributed to Chiang's fortress. To get there, you had to fly in, from Hong Kong. You could only make the trip under conditions that were absurdly hazardous: planes bound for Chungking took off from Hong Kong at 4:00 A.M. to elude the Japanese and flew "blind" up through the gorges of the Yangtze onto a spit of sand covered with smooth round flat stones in the middle of the Yangtze, which served as a landing strip when the river was running low. (After the floodtides of summer and fall, planes landed at the military air base outside the city at Peisheyi.)

Passengers were restricted to just over two pounds of luggage, but since their own weight wasn't included in this allowance, people often arrived on the mid-river island wearing several suits of clothing and many layers of underwear. "I put on boots and Chinese padded coat over my dress, and a fur coat over that and carried an overcoat some fond papa was sending his son up here," Emily Hahn, a young *New Yorker* correspondent, wrote to her family from Chungking after her flight there from Hong Kong in 1939.[3] No enlightened American felt altogether comfortable about being carried up the vertical cliffside stairs on a litter by Chinese coolies, and many refused to be borne this way to the summit, but it was probably the wisest way to assault the city, since the steps were slippery with ooze and slime and invariably cluttered with garbage. Owen Lattimore, the journalist and Central Asian scholar, was invited to serve as an adviser to Chiang Kai-shek. He discovered upon his arrival in Chungking that when he refused this simple form of conveyance, his greeters felt constrained to go by foot also. For men of status, this concession amounted to a loss of face. Lattimore decided it was best to submit himself to the moral discomfort.[4]

Teddy, as Theodore H. White was known throughout his long professional career, felt no such discomfort. He accepted the white man's burden with good cheer and a certain wide-eyed wonder, for, as a young man putting some distance between himself and an impoverished Jewish background in the Boston district of Dorchester, he could truly enjoy its novelty. Few of his colleagues in the Chungking press corps flourished in that grueling climate as Teddy did. Most American reporters didn't even go to Chungking for any but the briefest of visits until after Pearl Harbor. As citizens of a neutral power, they stayed on in occupied Shanghai, Nanking and Peiping. So did most of the American

businessmen in China and many U.S. diplomats. These cities were the
hives of commerce and activity in China, even after the Japanese occupied coastal China. Nobody wanted to live in Chungking. Shanghai,
Teddy had discovered, was glutted with out-of-work reporters cooling
their heels at the Astor House bar. He'd gone there on the advice of his
Harvard tutor, the China historian John King Fairbank, who seems to
have thought that Teddy would do better as a journalist in the manner
of Edgar Snow, whom Fairbank had known in Peiping, than he would
as a historian, even though such a career was Teddy's first choice.[5]

Teddy was game. He was up for anything. He had tremendous
intellectual energy and curiosity. Irrepressible is the word that would
best describe him. He was like a brilliant Jewish leprechaun, tiny, with
elfin feet, glittering spectacles, and beetle-black hair. He was entirely
unprepossessing, as the photojournalist Carl Mydans has observed,
until he started talking, which he always did right away.[6] Teddy was
Fairbank's first tutee. He was a day student at Harvard, what they used
to call there a "meatball," and although he was very bright and well
brought up by highly intelligent, scrupulous parents, he had none of
the polish of "St. Grottlesex," (St. Paul's, Groton, Middlesex all compressed into one vaguely pejorative term connoting old-school snob-
bery). This is very likely why Fairbank steered him away from the
groves of scholarship in the direction of newspaper work. He was a
terrific student. He absorbed an enormous amount of Chinese history
under Fairbank's tutelage, and learned enough Chinese to navigate the
Chinese hinterland on his own when he finally got there.[7] Teddy set
out for China in high spirits, armed with letters of introduction from
Fairbank. In Shanghai he was forwarded on to the Kuomintang by J. B.
Powell, the great benefactor of American journalists in China. Powell
recommended Teddy to Hollington Tong, Vice Minister of the Chinese
government Ministry of Information (MOI), who was looking around
for someone who could help him handle American journalists in
Chungking under the prevailing conditions of censorship.[8]

Teddy, at the age of twenty-three, arrived in Chungking to work
as a propaganda official. His job was to feed stories to the foreign press
that had been concocted by a team of writers in the MOI.[9] He had great
fun doing this. A. T. Steele had a long memory and didn't hesitate to
recollect this aspect of Teddy's career with a grandee's disdain.[10] Steele
was among the very few journalists of stature who was occasionally in
Chungking to receive Teddy's handouts. Tillman Durdin, the *New York
Times* correspondent and his wife, Peggy, also a journalist, were both
present, but they became and remained Teddy's great champions. Unlike Steele, they never held Teddy's sins against him.

They were comic sins. Mostly his underlings at the Central Publicity Board invented fictitious Chinese victories for publication abroad. The purpose of this was to promote the cause of China in the United States, in order to work up economic support for the war against Japan. No self-respecting journalist was fooled by Teddy's bogus press releases, but very few of the reporters based in Chungking were able to get to the front to challenge these stories. Most of them were lacking funds to travel, and, besides, it was impossible to go anywhere outside Szechuan Province without permission from the government. Journalists in Chungking were virtual prisoners of the Nationalist government now.

It was hard to get to Chungking as a correspondent. You had to be accredited to a major American news outlet to obtain permission to go there from the Chinese government, unless you knew how to get there on your own by land and, once there as a freelance, could make ends meet. Once you got there, you were a member of the club.

Mel Jacoby was probably Teddy's best friend in Chungking. Mel is recalled as a man of intelligence who on occasion made incisive observations about the China scene. As correspondents, he and Teddy began on the same rung at the same time in Chungking. When he first arrived, Teddy's most secure accreditation, quite apart from his MOI job, was the letter he carried around from Thomas Winship, "boss" of the *Boston Globe,* which assigned him the privileges of a "special correspondent." Melville Jacoby had the same sort of arrangement with the *San Francisco Chronicle.* He, too, was just out of college. All he wanted to do when he graduated from Stanford was to go back to China, where he'd spent an undergraduate year as a student at Lingnan University in Canton. He wasn't like Teddy, except insofar as they were both Jewish, and they were both clean-cut boys who steered clear of booze and bordellos, such as there were in Chungking, which under Madame Chiang's New Life movement was rather suppressed in spirit. Most of the reporters found some kind of outlet for the tension induced by Chungking, called "Chungkingitis." The UP correspondent, Pepper Martin, for one, who was built like a rhinoceros, was famous for the way he shook the mud and wattle structure of the Press Hostel with the violence of his lovemaking. He actually managed to import a mistress from Nanking. "There were not very many bordellos in Chungking," Martin later recalled, "but you could always go to a massage place."[11] Jack Belden, who at the time was a wire service reporter, mainly drank: he was known to pull the shades down in his room at the Press Hostel and drink himself into a stupor for days on end. You knew when he was ready to socialize when he raised the blinds.[12] Teddy and Mel were different, and they became soul mates. They were a Sancho Panza–Don

Quixote pair: Teddy was short, voluble and brightly observant; Mel was tall, lean, with a dark-haired handsomeness humanized by a baleful, bloodhound expression. In contrast to Teddy, Jacoby was reticent. In some ways, he was genuinely modest, although Emily Hahn remembers him as someone who was insufferably arrogant, perhaps because of the very winning, leading-man appeal he couldn't help exhibiting. She recalls him as someone who swaggered.[13]

Emily Hahn was a free spirit from St. Louis who wrote blithe pieces for *The New Yorker* from Shanghai in the late 1930s during the Japanese occupation. She had come to Chungking in the winter of 1940 in pursuit of the Soong sisters, Madame Sun Yat-Sen, Madame Chiang Kai-shek and Mrs. H. H. K'ung, about whom she was writing a book. She stayed in Chungking for some months, and by her very presence made it seem like the right place to be. Although she enjoyed Teddy White, she also found him, and Mel, to be immature for her sophisticated tastes. It was, however, for those very characteristics that Emily Hahn rather deplored in Mel Jacoby that Teddy White held him in some awe. Mel was everything Teddy wasn't. Not only was Mel tall, dark, handsome. He also came from a background of immense wealth, which he was in the process of living down as much as he could. Most people in Chungking were unaware of this fact about Mel Jacoby. Nothing in his demeanor suggested that he had grown up in a house at the end of a five-block-long palm-lined driveway off Hollywood and Vine. He was a descendant of early Los Angeles settlers on the side of his mother, whose maiden name was Stern. His father had died during Mel's childhood, and Mel had grown up on the estate of his grandparents, who were land barons. It was a smothering environment made even more so because Mel's mother, Elsa, had become a Christian Scientist, and she imposed her beliefs on her son. The atmosphere improved considerably for Mel, the only begotten son and heir and favorite beloved grandson, when Elsa married Manfred Mayberg, proprietor of the German Seed Company in the San Fernando Valley, another land baron. Mel acquired the knack of slipping through life as inconsequentially as possible from an early age, unencumbered by accoutrements of conspicuous consumption, including cash, which, as a prince of the realm, he could manage without, although in the Far East it was occasionally noted that Jacoby was unaccustomed to the habit of carrying the stuff, which was odd, but contributed to his appeal.[14] Mel began his career as a journalist on the *Stanford Daily*. He was a year behind Annalee Whitmore, who also worked on the *Daily*. She thought he was attractive, but noted that he was not socially active and lived alone. As a Jew, he was barred from joining any of the fraternities.[15] China provided Melville Jacoby with an alternative to the lavish but smothering world of Beverly Hills and the anti-Semitic precincts of Stanford. In China, he found that anti-Semitism existed hardly at all, and there wasn't much wealth either.

At the time Teddy White was employed by the Ministry of Information criticism in general of the Kuomintang was muted. War now justified the most stringent censorship. Every dispatch was routed through the MOI. Hollington Tong's chief watchdog in the early Chungking days was a onetime University of Missouri journalism instructor named Maurice Votaw. Another member of the so-called Missouri Mafia in China, he was a dour, cadaverous chain-smoker. Mo Votaw killed anything critical of the Kuomintang that came across his desk.[16] But in the beginning, there was a great deal of sympathy anyway among American reporters in Chungking for the Nationalist regime. The United Front had demonstrated a stirring resilience in the face of the barbarous Japanese machine, all alone and without the support of any nation but the Soviet Union and a handful of German advisers. Chiang Kai-shek had led the Free Chinese, the Chinese who had fled subjugation by the Japanese, on a trek to safety deep within western China. They had carried with them, like beasts of burden, whatever was portable of their national possessions, including industrial equipment and university archives.

This was far from being the whole story, but it was a good story, and it was one that the small band of foreign newspeople in Chungking was inclined to report. It became a nobler story still when the first Japanese bomber squadron appeared in the fresh blue sky over Chungking on May 3, 1939, two days after the sun had finally burned off the winter fog. Teddy was there. Two days later they returned—twenty-seven black beasts of the air spread across the sky, wing tip to wing tip —and dropped their load on the city in scarcely more than a minute, or so it seemed to Teddy, huddled in the rocks by the river in the twilight with a colleague from the MOI. When it was all over, he climbed back up to the city in the darkness and witnessed the holocaust. "One could hear the bamboo joints popping as the fire ate the bamboo timbers; now there was noise, women keened, men yelled, babies cried," Teddy later recalled. "Some sat rocking back and forth on the ground, chanting. I could hear screaming in the back alleys; several times I saw people dart out of the slope alleyways into the main street, their clothes on fire, then roll over and over again to put out the fires."[17]

The city of Chungking was utterly unprepared for the aerial onslaught. The citizens of that faraway place lived in another century. They had never before beheld such aircraft; had never imagined terror of this sort from the heavens. The savage violation of innocence perpetrated by the Japanese created among the citizens of Chungking and all others present a certain esprit de corps. The energy was demonstrated in the speed and efficiency with which the slick, modern-minded mayor, K. C. Wu, a Princeton graduate, set about digging those shelters. That summer, the Japanese planes came back time and again. Much of the city was destroyed. Out of the blackened ruins, the people of the city kept resurrecting it, and meanwhile a system of alarms was established that gave everyone enough time to get to the nearest shelter before the bombs fell.

War came to Chungking before it darkened the skies of Europe. This did not increase the desirability of Chungking as a place to be. Journalists did not flock there in any greater number to be on hand to witness its daily immolation. Besides Durdin, the only U.S. correspondent of note resident in Chungking was Robert P. Martin of UP, a former varsity end for the University of Washington and a graduate of the Columbia University School of Journalism, who was otherwise known as Pepper Martin.

Perhaps because Henry Luce, the founder and publisher of *Time* magazine, was the son of a China missionary and grew up in China, *Time* had a personal stake in China. *Time* was the first American publication besides the *New York Times* to perceive a need to have someone based in Chungking filing regular reports. In June, a month after the bombings began, John Hersey, who was also the son of a China missionary, was hired by Henry Luce to be the Far Eastern editor of *Time,* and flew into Chungking to find a reliable informant among the local reporters. This was Teddy White's big break. Durdin and Martin both recommended him to Hersey, who then hired him. Teddy continued to work for Hollington Tong for another six months, but by the end of July he was making more money as a *Time* stringer than he had earned in months of work for the MOI. Furthermore, the assignment wasn't very hard. *Time* didn't want spot news. Teddy was hired to write "mailers," reports the magazine could use as background material for articles. "I should try to tell not what had *happened* but what was *happening,*" Teddy wrote. "This is the essence of the difference between daily and magazine journalism."[18] He churned out mailers for *Time* at night, after putting in a day's work at the MOI. As an employee of the MOI, Teddy was in a better position than most to know that only mailers escaped the censor's eye. Mailers were subject merely to self-censorship by their author. "Take old Daddy Kung, for example," Teddy wrote John Hersey, referring to H. H. K'ung, who was married to Ailing, Madame Chiang Kai-shek's eldest sister. H. H. K'ung alternated with his brother-in-law T. V. Soong as Chiang Kai-shek's finance minister. He was considered corrupt, but not awfully bright. "There's a man I should have written about and never dared—that old, fat, double-chinned, pot-bellied bastard. The seed of Confucius."[19]

This was Teddy's start in life as a journalist. First, he apprenticed with the government of China as a disseminator of misleading information, and from this beginning went to work for *Time*. He never passed through the intermediate stage of reporting spot news on a deadline, and unlike other Chungking reporters of that time, he didn't have to eke out a marginal living as a news beggar feeding off the scraps of questionable handouts he himself had helped to manufacture.

The China Hand's lot throughout the war remained for the most part a marginal, embittering career experience, but not for Teddy until the very end when Whittaker Chambers had taken over as foreign editor and Teddy was on the outs with *Time*'s Foreign Office. But even then Teddy didn't bail out. The one time in the history of China when that country became a prolonged cause célèbre, an ongoing saga, in the United States, it did so mainly because a god of the press, Henry Luce, happened to have a personal stake in the story. His publications promoted it, lavished attention upon it and in a sense re-created it for the American public so that people could understand it as a simple parable. Gods can do that. It was Teddy's luck to be snapped up the way he was on a moment's notice into a realm where his career and his personal life partook of myth.

Other reporters in China also got jobs with the Luce organization, sporting briefly on the lower slopes of that corporate Olympus. Jack Belden, for one. Teddy helped both Belden and Pepper Martin get jobs with *Time,* and he also assisted the mythic Mel Jacoby. Jacoby became a player in Teddy's legend. Belden was a legend unto himself. He made his reputation as an independent war reporter in China between 1937 and 1942, and then as the author of a truly stunning book about the loss of Burma, *Retreat with Stilwell,* a work now forgotten, but a masterpiece never forgotten once read. Belden was a brilliant, temperamental writer who later covered the war in Europe for *Time,* but it was not a happy arrangement. Among Belden's un-*Timely* vices was his affection for colorful language. "As for Jack's four-letter words," Teddy wrote a *Time* editor. "Well, Jack is Jack. If he wants to say fuck, shit and piss, that's his business. If you can't publish them because of law, I should suggest substituting the Chinese equivalent which gives it an oriental flavor and means nothing to the American reader. For example. Wherever he says 'fuck,' say 't'sao!'; where he says 'his mother' say 'ma ti pi'."[20] Belden was not a team player, and *Time* really couldn't tolerate a star not of its own making. "They say he's a prima donna," Annalee Jacoby wrote Teddy in 1944, when Belden was covering the Allied invasion of Europe for *Time*. "He's number four in France; he should take what's left after Wert [Charles Wertenbaker], Bill Walton, and Bill White choose their assignments, and he's not happy about it."[21] Pepper Martin ducked the legend business altogether, was a first-rate journalist, and passed uneventfully through the Luce enterprise and on to *U.S. News & World Report*. Teddy, though, became a legend of *Time*'s own making. Because Luce was so engaged in the story of China from 1940 to 1949, the consequential story of this particular China Hand in wartime, the most enduring and the most notable, is also the story of a Luce Hand.

Teddy may not have guessed that he'd been co-opted by Mount Olympus, but John Hersey was the first tip-off. Hersey was the Hermes of Time, Inc., a fleet-footed messenger for Luce. He came to Chungking on winged feet. "This week," Teddy wrote his mother in June 1939, "concurrently: Mr. Carter of the IPR [Institute of Pacific Relations] flew into town; and with him he brought a young milkling lad: John Hersey. John Hersey is now his secretary; but when John Hersey gets back to New York he is going to become Far Eastern Editor of the magazine *Time;* that is because John Hersey had the right kind of parents and the right kind of luck; and in addition to the fact that he went to the right kind of school and is very goodlooking and tall and very attractive personally and is truly intelligent; but nevertheless he never held down a real job before and is green; but he is the Far Eastern Editor of *Time* and is being sent out to the Far East with Mr. Carter to look the situation over. Yes."[22]

Teddy was right in every way about John Hersey except for the crack about Hersey's job experience. Hersey had put in a few years as a *Time* writer. Also, if it counts, he had served as a secretary to Sinclair Lewis. For Hersey, however, employment as a Luce protégé was a foregone conclusion dating back to the time when, as a Yale undergraduate, he visited Luce for a job interview. He was fated to start off in life as Luce's heir apparent. He came from Luce's particular stratum: China missionary offspring, or "mishkid," Hotchkiss, Yale. He was also Skull and Bones, vice chairman of the *Yale Daily News* and a member of the Elizabethan Club, all Yale distinctions of a high order. Following his graduation he had spent a year at Cambridge, for buff and polish.[23] Hersey went to work at *Time* as a junior writer in 1937, and after Luce rediscovered him, he was as chummy as anyone could be with a man whom Alexander King, another Luce employee, described as a "timberwolf kind of man" with "cold, pale-gray eyes that hardly ever participated in his rare smiles."[24]

Hermes touched Teddy's shoulder with the golden staff and vanished once more into the stratosphere. In a way, Teddy didn't altogether revel in his good luck. *Time* wasn't exactly what he considered first-class in the way of a periodical. The following year he had his eye on Durdin's job with the *New York Times*. He would have seized instantly the chance to work on board the great gray battleship.[25] Also Teddy might have felt out of place at *Time* because he came from a mildly socialist point of view. So, however, did others who put in their years at Time, Inc., and some, like Dwight Macdonald, who wrote for *Fortune*, were further to the left than Teddy ever was. Teddy signed on without much of an inkling that from this solitary and modest beginning in a backwater of no distinction, he would rise to the very heights of the corporate press world and that his passions would involve him in a tale of epic proportions from which he would retrieve fame, fortune and some honor. He did, however, grasp the importance of securing himself a place on the Luce masthead. A mere Chungking stringer could easily fall off the lower slopes. Without waiting any longer than he absolutely had to, Teddy set out for Shensi to get a firsthand look at the Sino-Japanese War, which he now could afford to do on a Luce pay scale. He went with the blessings of his employers, Hollington Tong and the MOI ("my prying had begun to annoy them").[26]

Teddy won the admiration of the Time, Inc. editors with the dispatches he sent back after the Shensi trip. He showed the kind of flair they liked in their correspondents. He'd been riding horses with the U.S. embassy career officers on the south bank of the Yangtze just outside Chungking and this stood him in good stead in Shensi, where he spent days on horseback riding through the war-ravaged terrain where no correspondents ever went. ("Can you imagine Teddy on a horse?" Shelley Mydans, a journalist and the wife of Carl Mydans, wondered out loud in later years.[27]) He interviewed Communist and Nationalist soldiers alike and wrote copious notes by candlelight after dark. He made a thorough inspection of the damage inflicted by the Japanese in southeastern Shansi, and witnessed the Communist guerrilla campaign to capture rural China, as they "taught people how to defend themselves and kill," making "the countryside an environment of hate for all invaders."[28]

Time could not have asked for a better man than Teddy White to do the kind of reporting they wanted. The Luce system of journalism operates like an intelligence bureau, and so it is not surprising that dispatches from their correspondents in the field read like reports filed by OSS or CIA agents. In his mailers Teddy wrote reams of colorful first-draft copy off the top of his head loaded with incident and chock-full of facts. Above all else, Luce believed in the inviolability of facts. In addition to the clever manipulation of the photographic image as symbolic statement, Luce's achievement was the use to which he put facts in his publications so that they represented what he wanted them to. Luce introduced a new and sophisticated sleight-of-hand to the practice of "objective" journalism. Teddy's raw material and stream-of-consciousness narrative could later be shaped, cut and polished by writers in Time, Inc.'s New York editorial offices. So it was with much of the stuff Teddy wrote from China, although his report from Shensi was so lively *Time* ran it in a highly condensed version edited by John Hersey under Teddy's byline, the first time any foreign news reporter employed by *Time* had been so honored. "The *Time* treatment of Sian was unusual," Hugh Deane, a young *Christian Science Monitor* reporter, who was in Chungking from 1939 to 1941, later reflected. "They made his reputation by making him a part of the story."[29]

Teddy wrote with a historian's attitude. "Professor Fairbank singed him with the brand of history," one astute observer has noted.[30] While most China reporters wrote their stories in their heads on their way to the telegraph office and threw their notes away as soon as they'd filed their dispatches, Teddy not only kept his notes but expanded on them when he got back to his room at the Press Hostel, which of course was exactly what the *Time* correspondent was called upon to do.[31] Generally speaking, material filed by *Time* correspondents was meant strictly for corporate use as the raw stuff of articles. Teddy was never happy about that practice. He circumvented it by using his material as the raw stuff of the books he wrote, including his first effort, *Swords into Ploughshares,* written for Random House in the winter of 1940, which was never published. In January he wrote John Fairbank "Re the trip north in August: *Time*—the suckers—were very much impressed by my work; and offered to offer me a retainer in Chungking to act as their correspondent,—retainer plus payment would give me an income of 75–100 gold dollars a month,—which is affluence in Chungking at the present rate of exchange (even after the familial contributions deducted). Which I took."[32]

Teddy White was simply fabulous at the role. *Time* generated a sense of drama and importance among its employees that other corporations, including the *New York Times,* couldn't match. Part of it was money. Luce spared little expense to get what he wanted out of his correspondents (not to mention writers, editors and researchers). His outfit could afford it. Moreover, the *Time* correspondent was supposed to be more than a mere journalist. In Chungking, Teddy White was now the representative of the empire of Luce. "Invitations come to *Time*'s China correspondent," Teddy later recalled, "particularly from the diplomatic colony, where the exiled envoys to this half-forgotten Asian war spent their evenings entertaining each other and picking each other's brains for shreds of information."[33] As an envoy, Teddy was supposed to be on an equal footing with members of the Foreign Service community. Henry Luce staffed his publications with graduates of Ivy League universities so that they could match members of the power elite in wit and social polish, and Teddy had the right credentials, even if he utterly lacked the white-shoe manners. He was thus resented by embassy officers on the south bank, who didn't like the way he shared his notes with the Soongs but not with them.[34]

Teddy thought the people at the embassy were anti-Semitic. He sensed that they disliked him, and he may have been right. "He was thin-skinned, pushy," Jack Service says.[35] Service, who was third secretary at the U.S. embassy from 1941 until 1943, when he was transferred to U.S. military headquarters in Chungking, didn't think Teddy had a sense of humor.[36] According to Pepper Martin, U.S. embassy officials were particularly incensed when Teddy returned from Shensi because he had not informed them that he was taking the trip. "He did not tell the embassy," Martin recalled, "because he didn't *care* for those people." Generally speaking, the people on the south bank didn't like any of the journalists very much, with the possible exception of Edgar Snow, who visited Chungking in 1939.[37] "There was something snotty about those guys in the embassy," Pepper Martin later recalled. "It was the south bank versus the other side of the river. They used to complain, 'The problem with you correspondents is that we give you everything we have and you give us nothing.' " Actually, Martin asserted, the correspondents didn't have the sources the embassy had, except for the Communists. "Embassy people were reluctant ever to go over and talk to the Communists," Martin told me, "because they didn't want to arouse the suspicions of the Nationalists that the U.S. wanted to put the Commies in power."[38]

After his early horseback riding picnics with the embassy crowd, Teddy steered clear of the U.S. Foreign Service officers, especially in the prewar period. He found the British far more hospitable, and less out of touch than the Americans. Nelson Johnson, the American ambassador in Chungking, had first come to China before the fall of the Manchus and could recall how, as a young Chinese-language student in Peking, he had violated imperial protocol to steal a glimpse of the Empress Dowager Tzu Hsi's funeral cortege. Johnson was good-natured, but he maintained that state of mind by isolating himself with a few aides in his villa on the south bank. Johnson emerged only on rare ceremonial occasions. He loved pomp. In Peiping, as U.S. minister, he made use of the diplomatic privilege that allowed him to be met at the train station by a full-dress Marine Corps band and his entire diplomatic staff whenever he returned from a journey outside the city of more than a day.[39] The British ambassador, Sir Archibald Clark Kerr, out in his embassy on the bluffs overlooking the Chialing River, well removed from the frequently bombed city proper was, from the point of view of the press corps, the most valuable contact in the diplomatic community. He was a very different breed of cat from Nelson Johnson. Joseph Alsop, who was attached to General Claire Chennault's staff in China during the war, once observed that Clark Kerr was "one of those rare men who positively enjoy danger."[40]

Archibald Clark Kerr was a modernist and a Scottish aristocrat, who had joined the British Foreign Office in the days when diplomats were expected to have a large private income. His father had contributed an allowance on Clark Kerr's behalf. Clark Kerr had served all over the world. As a young man he'd been assigned to Persia. He'd also served in Washington in the years before World War One under James Bryce and Sir Cecil Arthur Spring-Rice, two great British diplomats of the old school. Clark Kerr had been a highly successful ambassador to Iraq, during the period immediately following the formation of that state, when the British wanted to maintain their influence there. He had also been assigned to Central America and later to Chile, where he'd met Tita, his wife, a beautiful, tiny, blonde siren, a "Pocket Venus," as Emily Hahn called her.[41] Teddy White described Clark Kerr in a mailer as a "tall (six foot) stern, angular-faced Scot. Scottish he is to the very bone and core of him—his iron-gray hair, his felicity of spoken expression, his rough gray tweeds, his nervous tenseness that paces him back and forth during an interview, the awkward impression of sincerity he gives, all bespeak the stock from which he springs."[42] Sir Archibald and Tita were the very model of what the British Foreign Office wanted in a diplomatic couple. They cut a glamorous path through the diplo-jungle. Sir Archibald exuded the air of amateurism that W. H. Auden observed was the quintessence of diplomatic comportment, seeming always to be a man of leisure, available for the cosy chat. His sympathies, insofar as anyone could divine them, were inclined toward the Communists, whom he had first come to know quite well in Hankow.

Beneath the surface glamour of their union, however, Clark Kerr and Tita were not at all the supremely well-matched couple they gave every appearance of being. Sir Archibald, up there at the red-pillared villa Chiang Kai-shek had loaned him on a headland above the Chialing, indulged his appetite for youthful male lovers. "Everybody knew about the stream of young Chinese boys who passed through the British embassy," Tilman Durdin recalled not long ago.[43] (It was not, however, a facet of himself that Sir Archibald shared with Isherwood and Auden, who, while guests of the Clark Kerrs in Shanghai, relaxed from the rigors of investigating child labor in the Dickensian factories of

Hongkew by visiting male brothels. "Every evening when they met Archie and Tita for pre–dinner cocktails, Archie would ask what they had been doing that afternoon," Isherwood wrote. "If they had been to the bathhouse, they had to invent something. Archie accepted their lies without comment, but a certain gleam in his eye made them wonder if he was playing a game with them." Isherwood thought they were probably tailed as a routine security measure. "Of one thing they felt certain," he wrote, "if Archie did know about the bathhouse, he wouldn't be in the least shocked."⁴⁴) However she may have felt about this, the fiery Tita was not without her own resources. She eventually ran away for awhile with Bill Hunt, an enormously successful, rugged American businessman in Shanghai who printed the Nationalist Chinese paper money, of which there was a very great deal more than there should have been at all times.

Teddy White came to know Clark Kerr extremely well. He was drawn anyway to powerful older men. This was one of Teddy's characteristics during the China years (and ever after, to judge by his subsequent relationships to men of power, especially presidents). It accounts for the bonds he formed with other powerful older men besides Clark Kerr, chief among them Generals Stilwell, Chennault and Douglas MacArthur. The simplest explanation that comes to mind for this need is that when Teddy's father died when Teddy was fourteen years old, a strong source of approval and affection was rudely annihilated. Teddy was forced to assume some of the burdens usually assumed by the man of the family and to contribute to his family's welfare. He sold papers every morning on a streetcar run in Dorchester before he went to school, and even deferred college for two years to help support his family. Later, at Harvard, he sought out the advice and encouragement of John Fairbank, who became his mentor. In China, Teddy found that men of eminence were equally drawn to his warm and youthful attentiveness, which bordered on veneration. It was a kind of charm. In Chungking, and later in prewar Manila (where, in the fall of 1940, he first met General MacArthur), Sir Archibald Clark Kerr, Claire Chennault and others could spare the time to talk at great length with Teddy, to respond to his rapt inquiries.⁴⁵

The result was that Teddy quickly found his way into the confidence of such men. What was at the time probably a personal alliance later became a professional weapon in Teddy's arsenal, as his relationships with men of power, especially with presidents and presidential candidates, became a major source of his professional success. The early father-son relationships paid off professionally in other ways as well. The long hours he spent up at Clark Kerr's residence were an important part of his education. In Clark Kerr, Teddy found that one of the most distinguished, sophisticated professional diplomats in the English-speaking world was willing to make himself available for long tutorial sessions. Unlike many men in his position, Sir Archie does not in any way appear to have been a snob. "He was a sad man," Annalee Jacoby Fadiman recalls, adding that at the same time the diplomat was "quick, humorous, lighthearted and great company."[46] A Scottish highlander with a strong sense of tribal roots, he was never broken, as the sons of upper-class British families often used to be, by the brutal public school experience. This was because Clark Kerr suffered some kind of lung ailment as a child and instead of attending school, between the ages of eleven and twenty-two he traveled on the continent with a tutor. He studied at Bonn University, but took no degree. Sir Archie had a sense of humor. He scorned bridge playing, which was a staple form of entertainment on the diplomatic circuit, and loved the sound of bagpipes. He ducked a commission in the British army and volunteered in 1917 as a private in the Scots Guards, "because I preferred to be buried to the sound of the pipes, than to the tune of the fife and drums," he told Teddy.[47] All this endeared Sir Archie to Teddy, who wrote it up for *Time*'s files.

In the dismal winter and the summer of blistering heat and bombardment that followed in 1940 Teddy succeeded in his appointed role as *Time* correspondent because he absolutely refused to let the place defeat his spirits. As a correspondent this took some doing. First of all, Chungking was shut down in wintertime. There was no news to send out. The Japanese weren't running many raids over Chungking, which was enshrouded in the all-pervasive, cold, dripping fog that descended on the city in late autumn and lingered, holding it in a chilly state of permanently overcast gray until May. It was a demoralizing climate in which to live, never quite warm enough for comfort, always damp. There were steep, crowded, alleyways reeking of rotted, fly-coated meat and decaying fish and always the putrid odor of backed-up sewage. It was like some isolated, oversized Hopi village of years past. There was no green to soothe the eye. It was a city of gray and black, for all the houses had been painted black to camouflage them against aerial attack. It was treacherous, too. The streets of Chungking were slippery underfoot when not actually ankle-deep in mud.

The worst of Chungking for a reporter, however, was the news blackout imposed by the Ministry of Information. Censorship could be tolerated by the Chungking press corps for a while in the interests of Chiang's war effort. In 1939 journalists were willing to lay off the Chinese government, and to overlook the more glaring examples of government incompetence. After a year of being locked into this oversized medieval fortress town deep within provincial China, with little

outside news to distract them, the journalists found themselves stagnat-
ing in a political quagmire but unable to do anything about it. As Teddy
wrote Fairbank, "the longer one stays here the more confused one becomes."[48] There were three stages, he wrote. At first, all you saw were
the dirt and filth. "During the second stage you accept the dirt and the
filth and see the good, the heroic, the new striving to break through in
the country," he wrote. "In the third stage, one sees behind the good
and the heroic, to the corruption, graft, intrigue, administrative stupidity, cowardice, and greed of its officials. And one begins to doubt."
With the doubt came the frustration. "I think I know more about what
is happening in this country than any man in town other than Durdin
of the *Times*," Teddy wrote. "But it is impossible to make use of this
knowledge. It burns within . . . but it stays right there . . . we can't
say what we know today, because it may injure a people whom we are
trying to help; and tomorrow no-one will be interested in what we have
to say; and it won't be true anyway."[49]

Teddy wasn't as hog-tied by this situation as his colleagues, since
he wasn't trying to drum up spot news. He kept himself busy generating
mailers. Like everyone else, Teddy also whiled away hours in the bomb
shelters. It was amusing to note, Emily Hahn wrote home to her family,
that people in Chungking hated the Japanese "mostly not for what we
ought to, the death and the waste, but for those long, dreary hours
underground, and the interrupted sleep on moonlight nights."[50] The
elegant diplomatic wives of Chungking wore their jewels and furs into
the dugouts for safekeeping and sweated it out more profusely than
anyone else in Chungking. When the raids were on, everyone in
Chungking had plenty of time to run for their assigned dugouts. Spotters all along the route the bombers took from Hankow kept Chung-
King alerted to the progress of the Japanese bombers by telephone.
Signals mounted on poles at the crest of the city and at various other
points were used to inform the citizenry of impending raids. Triangles
were hoisted to signify that the Japanese had left Hankow, discs went
up as the aircraft drew near. When the balls went up you had to drop
everything and scamper down into a cave to sit, sometimes in the company of rats, in airless chambers sometimes for up to three or four hours
until the buzz of the planes sounded and the bombs fell with an earth-
shaking thud and the bombers departed. In the caves, dimly lit by
peanut oil lamps, people socialized. On one occasion Teddy made the
acquaintance of the Chinese mistress of a Belgian attaché. This led to
his first sexual encounter, two days later, when he met her for a rendezvous at a Chinese hotel. ("The meal we ate was good," Teddy later
recalled, "but the experience was disappointing. The windows of the
bomb-racked hotel had been replaced by greased paper; Chinese waiters

poked their fingers through the paper to peek in; we went to bed; I fumbled at her; my inexperience was obvious; and she wailed, in Chinese, 'You're nothing but a little boy.' "[51])

Like everyone else, Teddy suffered from "Chungkingitis," but apart from his disappointing deflowering he did not submit the way his colleagues at the Press Hostel did to lurid diversions. He was a workaholic. "He worked like an eager beaver," Service recently recalled.[52] "He was at work as much of twenty-four hours as it was possible to be," Carl Mydans recalled.[53] This, as much as anything, probably accounts for his great success. Just as, at Harvard, it had earned him a *summa cum laude*. Certainly, it helped him to stay healthy, when his colleagues, in the summer of 1940, all seemed to succumb at once to a variety of maladies. "There was Eskelund of the A.P. who got tuberculosis and dysentery," he wrote home, "Marcuse of Havas who got streptococcus infection, Pierard who had a nervous breakdown, Martin who contracted syphilis and Mel Jacoby whose resistance was so weakened by the heat and the raids that he fell for the first malarial mosquito who bit him."[54]

The years between 1939 and 1942 in Chungking were of a very special sort, although not of a sort to be looked back upon with longing, exactly. "Chungking was a backwater if not a dog house for the Americans who were sent there on regular jobs," the travel writer and painter Graham Peck wrote in *Two Kinds of Time,* his book on wartime China. "The south bank businessmen might live in the remains of nineteenth-century treaty port grandeur, complete from frogged liveries for their sedan-chair coolies to a pantry supply of BB shot to roil sediment out of their bottles for boiled drinking water, but they were little more than caretakers for their firms' property. The State Department men might enjoy the protocol and prestige of station in an alleged national capital but they could not avoid the uneasy feeling that the real work was done, and the careers made, down in the greater occupied cities. It was the same with the correspondents; there was a certain glamour to be had from residence in the most-bombed town in the world, but they knew they would not really be getting ahead until they were called back to the coast."[55]

Most members of the foreign press were housed in a state of semi-captivity two or three miles from the center of town in the Chungking Press Hostel, which Hollington Tong had built in the summer of 1939 next to his offices, where he could keep an eye on them and their work. "When I went there to live in the early autumn of 1940," Peck wrote, "it was a sort of field, fenced in with bamboo palings and fringed with banana trees, holding two little timber and wicker dormitories from which the summer bombings had blown so much of the mud-plaster that the correspondents liked to mutter they were going to send down to Hong Kong for a goldfish bowl—'so we can get some privacy around here, dammit.' "[56]

Besides Peck and Teddy White, the other reporters, who numbered fewer than a dozen, included Jim Stewart of AP, Guenther Stein, a Swiss reporter who contributed to the *Christian Science Monitor,* Jack Belden, Betty Graham, for whom, as the sole female correspondent, Hollington Tong had chivalrously erected a separate dwelling, and Karl Eskelund, Pepper Martin's assistant, a handsome Dane, whose father was the personal orthodontist to the king of Siam. Pepper Martin was another frequent inhabitant. Not so Emily Hahn, who, when she came to Chungking for her extended stay in 1939, spent a great deal of time at the Press Hostel but refused to actually live there. "I wasn't tempted in the first place by the exquisite discomfort of the Press Hostel," she wrote in *China to Me,* "nor in the second place by the jolly, quite maddening lack of privacy that prevailed there, nor in the third by the worse-than-primitive plumbing. (We used to have better plumbing facilities in the Congo than obtained at the Chungking Press Hostel.)"[57]

The Press Hostel was eventually bombed by the Japanese in 1941 and rebuilt to improved standards. In the new, reconstructed version European meals were served twice a day. In the early years, however, correspondents subsisted on a constant diet of mediocre Chinese food. For most of the reporters, it was a miserable situation, to be ever under the watchful eye of the infinitely civilized Mr. Tong and spies from Chiang Kai-shek's secret service, often unable to obtain the funds necessary to hire translators or researchers, and fed doctored news from the MOI. Nevertheless, Chungking correspondents made the most of their semi-house arrest. They often dressed up to dine in jacket and tie, which they did at round tables in the Press Hostel mess, where Teddy White, as Carl Mydans recalls, used his chopsticks to fend off other diners, preventing them from plucking forth pigeon eggs from the communal soup until he had completed his discourse of the moment. There was an esprit de corps among reporters at the Press Hostel. As correspondents in China always have, they talked with great agitation nonstop about Chinese politics ("like a bunch of schoolboys,"[58] as a later observer at the Nanking Press Hostel pointed out) and gladly shared information with each other to a degree rare among correspondents competing in the field. Pepper Martin came to believe that the cooperative spirit that evolved among journalists in Chungking was a distinct contribution to the business of foreign news reporting, and an important aspect of the China Hand legacy.[59]

Teddy had won the approval of the *Time* New York office as the acting Chungking correspondent, but he had not, yet, won the full

confidence of Luce and company. This he proceeded to do when *Time* sent him on a swing through Southeast Asia that included French Indochina, Thailand, Malaya, Java (then part of the Dutch East Indies), the Philippines and Hong Kong. It was a lonely, tedious, fact-finding expedition, but it was an important and fundamental part of his on-the-job training. "My technique is this," he wrote his friend Butsy Schneiderman. "I get to a new town, hit the hotel and look around at the city. I go into the shops and price the goods and see whose goods they're selling, how they carry themselves, how the people act, sniff the air, ride in the rickshaws. Then I go to the American Consulate or Ministry and see what the office knows. If the American Consulate helps me, my work is very easy; if it doesn't (as in Hanoi) I have a tough time. At the American Consulate I line up with the local big-shots, find out who knows what and who the government's key man is. Next I go to the government press bureau and check myself in."[60] After making these contacts, and meeting with local journalists, Teddy was then ready to line up interviews with officials, a process that usually took a week. Teddy was often depressed during this extended trip, he wrote Schneiderman, because his work seemed so futile. "It seems almost pointless to spend so much time and energy as I do just to fill one and a half columns of *Time* Magazine every month (in a good month)."[61]

Teddy's tour deepened his beliefs. He saw the Japanese in action in Vietnam, where they had bullied the French colonials into letting them use North Vietnamese air bases for bombing raids into south China. In Batavia, in the Dutch East Indies, Teddy interviewed Saito, the Japanese consul general, at a time when the Japanese were using the threat of force to extort oil concessions from the Dutch. "Saito was a bundle of nerves," Teddy wrote Schneiderman. "He's a slim, cadaverous, wiry little man and he paced back and forth in his office, almost shrieking at me—'What do they expect us to do? One hundred million people to starve up there on those rocky islands? We won't do it. If you Americans cut off oil from us, we must have the oil from the Indies. And we will have it, too.' And more on this same theme. He scared me with his intensity and I realized then for the first time what is driving the Japanese on."[62] This didn't make Teddy like the Japanese. Indeed, his travels in Asia reinforced his hatred of them, a hatred now identified in retrospect as Japanophobia, but not recognizable as such at the time. Few correspondents felt as vehemently about the Japanese as Teddy, who "regarded the Japanese as his personal enemy," to quote Pepper Martin.[63] "I found them repulsive in the openness of their ambition and the coarseness of their manners," Teddy later wrote.[64] "He had an awful lot of prejudices," said Martin, who greatly respected Teddy as a corre-

spondent. "He thought the war was being fought against *him*. He took the war personally. He was the most Japanophobe guy I've ever met. After the surrender in Tokyo Bay we flew back together and he was calling the Japanese 'those dirty bastards.' "[65]

Although he didn't know it at the time, Teddy also made contacts that would prove of great value in the years to come, on his solitary swing in the autumn of 1940. The most important of these was General Douglas MacArthur, whom he interviewed in Manila. "The Napoleon of Luzon," MacArthur was then rather disdainfully called. He appeared to have put his best days behind him, as he vaingloriously entertained the illusion that America's future would be decided outside his window, in Manila Bay, and that he would command that destiny. A press spokesman in Manila told Teddy that MacArthur was a mere field marshal in the Philippine army, not even worth seeing. Teddy thought otherwise. Since few others shared this opinion, Teddy had MacArthur all to himself. Two years later he recalled the scene for David Hulburd, his editor at *Time*. "I think he was wearing slippers," Teddy wrote, "but I remember he had no stockings on and how thin and spindling his bare legs looked as he paced back and forth. First he served me orange juice and then he started to talk. We talked about the military angles of the article for half an hour or so, he talking, I listening. Then by that time he was in full voice and roaring out his opinions on all the world and on all strategy in great organ tones. I needled him about his relations with Mr. Quezon to see if I could get a reaction and I did . . . then he got going on MacArthur and the Philippines. How he was defending the United States by defending these islands just as if he were standing in the soil of the United States itself. He was here doing his duty as he saw it. I don't know whether he rang Old Glory in on me then or not, but you could practically hear the bugles playing as he got up to the peak. . . ."[66] This interview made a great hit at *Time*.

While in Manila, Teddy was hired by *Time* as a full-time staff correspondent on full salary. *Time* cabled him a bonus of one thousand dollars. "When I reached Hong Kong," Teddy later recalled, "en route back to China, there was also an invitation to join the staff in New York, whenever I wanted. My instructions were only to return to Chungking, to stay at least through the spring of 1941, until Harry Luce, the distant owner of *Time,* could come to visit China, his birthplace—and I, as *Time* correspondent, might serve as his escort."[67]

In early 1941, the time of the New Fourth Army Incident, the United Front began to deteriorate, and, not surprisingly, so did the United Front in the Chungking Press Hostel. The harmony of the Press

Hostel was finally broken by arguments between those who favored the Kuomintang in the war against Japan, and those who sided with the Communists in an undeclared war launched against them, unexpectedly, by the Kuomintang, in southern Anhui Province, when Kuomintang forces surrounded remnants of the New Fourth Army and set about the business of mowing them down. It was a massacre perpetrated in cold blood against Red troops who were attempting to withdraw northward under their leader, Yeh T'ing. In the course of it many innocent civilians lost their lives. Meanwhile, the mood and atmosphere of murky wintertime Chungking was poisoned by the insidious presence of ubiquitous spies, who infested every corner of Chungking. Some were the agents of Tai Li, Chiang Kai-shek's spymaster. Others operated out of the headquarters of the CC Clique, a faction in the Chungking bureaucracy named for Chiang's right-wing political protégés, Ch'en Li-fu and Ch'en Kuo-fu, who were brothers. Other spies worked for the military faction, and then there were all kinds of spies working for private individuals. As a Chinese friend told Owen Lattimore, Chiang Kai-shek's American adviser, "The life in Chungking is terrible. Unless you are in a very favored position, the secret police keep tabs on you, preventing you from having an adequate sex life."[68] Corruption was now endemic to the scene, which was a shocking state of affairs to new arrivals from the United States, who knew nothing of the malaise that was rotting the foundations of Chiang Kai-shek's regime, thanks to censorship and the Kuomintang public relations effort abroad. The only image of China that was getting through was the gallant one, the brave and stalwart China, alone and isolated single-handedly fighting off the Japanese.

Mel Jacoby, as Teddy's heir at the MOI, was instrumental in the daily work of putting forth this successful propaganda. He helped to write and broadcast material from a Chungking transmission studio, XGOY, which was picked up in Ventura, California, by a ham radio operator, a dentist named Dr. Charles Stuart. Mel's clearly enunciated radio broadcasts, punctuation marks included, were transcribed by Dr. Stuart and then mailed out in the form of typescripts, to MOI publications, and other subscribers. This process saved the Chinese government the cost of using cable services, but it was also an amateur operation. In early 1941, Hollington Tong sent Mel Jacoby back to the West Coast to see Dr. Stuart about improving the transmissions. Once in California Mel Jacoby was swiftly entwined in the gossamer web of the Luce enterprise spun now in the environs of Hollywood, where John Hersey had been sent by Luce to find someone on the West Coast to send to Chungking as a representative of the United China Relief, a fund-raising outfit he'd set up in partnership with Madame Chiang Kai-shek to recruit money and supplies for Chinese war victims, especially children.

The person who wanted this job more than anybody was Annalee Whitmore. She was the slightly older editor of the *Stanford Daily* who had found Mel Jacoby "very attractive, though quiet." In the words of one who had known her in high school, Annalee was "dashing."[69] "You could say she was petite," Carl Mydans, the *Life* photojournalist, told this author years later. "She was electric; she was brilliant, bright, quick."[70] She was a screenwriter from Piedmont, California, whose father was a banker. He also built airplanes, and raced them. Annalee had always been the apple of her father's eye. When she was a child, he delighted them both by taking Annalee on afternoon spins in his private plane. He also raced cars. He taught Annalee she could win anything she set her mind on. This turned out to be true. In 1937, after she graduated from Stanford, Annalee set her mind on Hollywood. She got a job at the stenographic department of MGM typing screenplays. Briefly, she was an assistant to F. Scott Fitzgerald. "He was almost absent," she later said. "By that time," a year before he died at the age of forty-four, "Fitzgerald was ill, shaky, forgetful, depressed." He tried to dictate to Annalee, but had trouble concentrating his thoughts. Her chief errand for Fitzgerald, she recalled, was to select a matching compact and cigarette case on his behalf as a birthday present.[71] Swiftly, Annalee went from typing screenplays to writing them. In 1939 she was the youngest studio screenwriter in Hollywood. She co-wrote *Babes in Arms,* a musical starring Judy Garland and Mickey Rooney. After that, Annalee was off and running. MGM gave her a seven-year contract.

But then she set her mind on China. It was a war zone, and she wanted to go where the action was. To do this, however, she had to obtain permission from the U.S. Department of State. She tried and failed to get a permit to visit China for the *Reader's Digest.* What to do next? A friend told her that Mel Jacoby was back from China. "Maybe he can give you some idea of how to get a permit."[72] Mel agreed to meet with Annalee at a bar on Wilshire Boulevard. He thought he could help. He knew John Hersey, had met Hersey in Chungking, and now got word to Hersey that Annalee was available for an assignment in China. He arranged a dinner with the Luce envoy. Hersey also heard about Annalee's ambitions from David Selznick, a movie mogul and co-director with Luce of United China Relief. Selznick was a son-in-law of Louis B. Mayer, as was Mervyn LeRoy, for whom Annalee had worked on a movie called *Ziegfeld Girl.* Hersey happened to be looking for someone who would go to China without salary, and in Annalee he found the person he was looking for. This was the beginning of a complicated China love story, shadowed with tragedy. It was a real-life movie, worthy of a talented Hollywood World War Two movie scenarist.

Hersey recommended Annalee to Luce, who hired her, sight unseen, from his headquarters in the Chrysler Building high above Manhattan. Simultaneously, Annalee fell in love with Mel Jacoby. She no longer found Mel merely attractive. "I thought he was wonderful," she later recalled. She was fascinated by his elegance. She was fascinated that he was diffident and modest, that he wore clothes of the very best material, carried no cash yet was able to acquire a Rolleiflex camera effortlessly, without stealing it, although exactly how he managed to do so remains a mystery to her. Annalee was in thrall. She went with Mel to visit Dr. Stuart and his secretary. Actually, she wanted to accompany Mel back to Chungking. This, however, was not possible, even to one as determined as Annalee, because the State Department had not yet given her a green light, and Pan Am wouldn't permit her to fly without an O.K. Instead, she accompanied Mel to San Francisco on the Southern Pacific train he took with his mother and stepfather, the Manfred Maybergs, who were sending him off to China on a Pan Am Clipper.

When Mel boarded the airship in San Francisco, Henry Luce and his wife, Clare Boothe Luce, were already on board. Together they flew to Hong Kong. Nobody seems to know whether Mel was aware that the Luces would be on the flight. It is known that when the Pan Am Clipper landed in Hong Kong, Luce had hired Jacoby as the China correspondent for *Time* magazine.

When Henry and Clare Boothe Luce flew into Chungking and landed on the little sandbar in the Yangtze River, Teddy was there to greet them, at the plane, wearing shorts and a stained sun helmet. It was unquestionably one of the crucial moments of his entire career as a journalist. Henry Luce may or may not have known this, or very much cared. On the basis of Teddy's dispatches he'd already decided to promote his career. Still, the very sight of Teddy awaiting him at the foot of the gangway may have given Luce a moment's pause. "What an odd-looking person Teddy was," Carl Mydans, who happened to be in Chungking at the time with his wife, Shelley, many years later recalled.[73] In his pith helmet and shorts, behind the glittering spectacles, Teddy would have been very hard to size up if you were Henry Luce. But then Teddy immediately would have started to talk. "He was funny-looking," Shelley Mydans added, "but once he started talking you never again thought about what he looked like."[74] Carl Mydans agreed. "He was one of the most lovable men you would ever meet," he said. "He had a fireworks of a mind. You were captured by his dynamism."[75]

Right away, on the sandbar, Teddy called him Harry. This was the absolute summit of presumption. Carl Mydans, who had no trouble calling most people by their first names, confided, "Every time I started to call Luce by his first name my tongue froze."[76] People who worked at *Time* lived in terror of Henry Luce. A sudden, unexpected meeting called by Luce was known as "the Terror," "the Rack" or "The Last Judgment."[77] "He expected immediate answers to his questions," one of his biographers has written. "His intensity was compelling. He demanded complete attention."[78] You also had to be like an electrical generator to keep Luce tuned in on what you were saying. He loved abstract information, and when he heard new facts, or received knowledge that was new to him, the Press God's face lit up. The trouble was that his employees found after the jolt of a new fact had passed, he lost interest in you, his mind racing off in quest of the next zap. None of this in any way bothered Teddy White. He was a dynamo. He never stopped talking to Luce, feeding him new information Luce had never heard before, bolstering his verbal reportage with historical insights, impressions, analogies, new names. ("Names," he once wrote, "are to young reporters the money in the bank; they are credit references; they lead to other contacts, other sources; their invitations translate into circles of acquaintances, thus stories."[79]) He talked nonstop all the way up the slippery, vertical steps to the top of the Chungking bluffs, one sedan chair to another.

As a talker, Teddy managed to sideswipe Chiang Kai-shek's plans for the Luces in Chungking. The occasion of the Luces' visit was important for the Chiangs, almost an occasion of state. Henry Luce was Chiang Kai-shek's ally in the United States. He did not want Luce to get any wrong ideas while he was in Chungking. The whole visit was carefully arranged, down to a Potemkin Village outside Chungking, where Luce was entertained in the house of a simple landowner-farmer who just happened to be a warlord in exile from Anhui Province.[80] In Chungking, the Luces were house guests of H. H. K'ung, Madame Chiang Kai-shek's brother-in-law, and Chiang Kai-shek had already by the time they got there made arrangements for them to tour Chungking by limousine, one of which he'd released from his private stable for their convenience.

Luce was oblivious to Chiang's designs—he'd descended on this whirlwind visit from Olympus—but Teddy was not. He was there to act as Harry's guide and that was what he set out to do. He convinced Harry to forget about the limo and spend his Chungking days exploring the alleys and byways in Teddy's company. Clare Boothe Luce was off with Madame, but in the evenings he told Clare what to look for, and what to ask permission to see. It was on Teddy's advice that Clare insisted that her hosts fly them up to the Yellow River front. This was not something the Chiangs were at all interested in doing. They did not want the Luces straying too far afield. When they flew up to Loyang on one of their China air force planes, they sent Hollington Tong up with them to keep their attention riveted on the important things. (This was not, of course, how the then Vice Minister of Information put it in *Dateline China,* his memoir: "Realizing the risks involved," he wrote, "the Generalissimo asked me to accompany the Luces, for he did not wish to see them stranded at any point along the way, or to be the only victims in case of an accident. If foreign visitors were to crash, good manners demanded that a Chinese representative crash with them."[81]) On the ground, however, slippery and muddy even in May, no MOI official was required to be along while Teddy cast his charm around the enchanted Henry Luce.

Teddy took Luce everywhere, and told him everything he knew. He told him things he never would have filed in a million years. About the greed of "Daddy" K'ung, the evils of Tai Li, who was Chiang's Himmler, and the inside story of the New Fourth Army Massacre down in Anhui Province, a story that Teddy had painstakingly put together with the help of Chou En-lai, whose offices in Chungking were in the same strange ramshackle building at the end of a gray alleyway that housed Tai Li's deadly operation. There was enough to fill an entire month or more of nonstop mailers stored up by Teddy in his three years of intense Chungking residence and field trips, the latest of which, to the front of southeast China, he had just completed.

Teddy knew things that others hadn't seen or heard by the very virtue of being the Luce man in Chungking. The standard excuse the Kuomintang used to refuse reporters permission to visit the front was safety. The Kuomintang claimed that it didn't want to have to be responsible for foreign lives. The Luce reporter was different, however. "They couldn't think of anything that could happen that would be dangerous—because of Henry Luce," said Carl Mydans, who, as a Luce photographer, was in a position to know.[82] Teddy, with his curiosity, his remedial Chinese and his energy, was full of information about rural China, stuff Henry Luce, the old mishkid, could not hear enough about. Teddy knew this. He was bright. He knew how to play to father figures. He loved the game. He had rehearsed it already with Sir Archibald, and MacArthur, and now he played the game flawlessly with Henry Luce. Clare Boothe Luce planned to do some writing on China and she, too, relied on Teddy. This was extremely beneficial for Teddy's career. "Teddy stuck close to Clare Boothe Luce and it helped him to get to New York and a permanent job," Till Durdin recalled not long ago. "He told her what to write."[83]

"Luce made quick decisions but he had good judgment," Carl Mydans pointed out in later years. "He knew how to pick people."[84] As Teddy recalls it, in his memoirs, two days before his departure Luce turned to him, "in that peremptory half-stammering speech of his, asked me if I could be packed and ready to leave in forty-eight hours. I asked him why and he coughed out that I was going home with him to New York. He did not ask me whether it was convenient to leave China at that time or what my plans were. He had decided that I was to be the Far Eastern Editor of *Time*. Now. So thus, three years after graduating Harvard, I would be returning home to my family in triumph."[85]

Annalee Whitmore flew into Chungking from Hong Kong soon after Henry and Clare Boothe Luce departed with Teddy White. She'd come across the Pacific in a Norwegian freighter, finally, and her arrival now in late May was characteristically dashing. The appropriately named Royal Leonard, an American pilot who had flown the Prince of Wales around the world, invited Annalee to co-pilot his CNAC (China National Aviation Corporation) plane on the flight up to Szechuan. Along the way he told her, "You've got to see Kweilin. The mountains there are one of the great sights of China. I'll show them to you." The moon by then had vanished, and they landed in Kweilin on a bumpy road and trundled along it to look at the famous pointed hills. The plane got stuck in the dark but Royal Leonard found a peasant to dig the tire out. When Mel came down to the sandbar the following morning to meet her, Annalee was drinking tea with Royal Leonard beside the plane under an awning. "Mel was a little put out," she later recalled.[86]

As a representative in Chungking for United China Relief, Annalee worked for Madame Chiang Kai-shek. She also wrote copy for Hollington Tong, who was running United China Relief for the "Missimo," as Madame Chiang was sometimes called. Annalee was fond of Madame Chiang, even though she found her to be quite high-handed. Annalee noticed one day when they were visiting a tea house that Madame Chiang smoked cigarettes in complete disregard of signs, posted by her own New Life Movement, bearing the stern injunction, WE WILL NOT SMOKE. Annalee pointed the signs out to Madame. "Oh that's for the people," Madame breezily replied.

"It was still a honeymoon," Annalee later said of that time.[87] China was still the lonely victim of Japan in the early summer of 1941. The war in Europe was now in full swing and occupied the attention of all the Westerners in Chungking, who eagerly and anxiously listened to all the bulletins coming in on shortwave radios. They all felt trapped and far away in the humid vale, sweating out the last summer of the Japanese bombing raids. That was the summer when the Press Hostel was bombed.

In 1985, on a visit to Chungking with a group of China Hands, Annalee recalled the *Three Castles* cigarettes they used to smoke, and the rats, and the snake they released into the Press Hostel Garden to eat the rats. "How could we have had such a good time?" she wondered out loud as the bus wove its way through the outskirts of the city from the airport at Peisheyi. "Now, when we talk about it, it doesn't seem like much. But we were young and you came up to this place that was constantly bombed. There was a real spirit and of course in 1941 there was just a handful of Americans in Chungking and we had just the little that we were allowed to bring up from Hong Kong. That had to include summer clothes and winter clothes and evening dresses and carbon paper. I don't know how we did it. We'd get mold on our shoes, green and velvety, but we'd just wipe it off."[88] At first, Annalee lived up at Chialing House, a somewhat raffish hotel but a decided improvement on the Press Hostel. She'd made a conquest of Mel, immediately. So much for Betty Graham, lone female journalist in the Press Hostel, who had made Mel the object of her passionate yearning, even as she was pursued by the love-sick Jack Belden "through five provinces," as Teddy White put it. It was not the last of Betty's unlucky forays into the jungles of love. She soon left again for the front, but never came back. She traveled with the Eighth Route Army, and accompanied Red Chinese forces into Shantung after the war, dressed in a People's Liberation Army uniform. She ended up in Peiping, following the Communist takeover, passionately in love with Alan Winnington, a left-wing British writer. When Winnington jilted her, Betty committed suicide.[89]

Annalee and Mel dined together every night at Chialing House until, in July, Annalee moved into a mission compound with a good chef, and they ate together every night there. Annalee had planned to leave Chungking on the first of July, but various errands kept her busy well past that deadline. In the fall, *Time* and NBC, for which Mel was doing regular broadcasts, decided he should go to Manila. The tempo of war had heated up. The Japanese were acting up down in the Pacific. The emphasis of their hostility seemed to be shifting to the Philippines, and Chungking, because of a worsening censorship problem, was no longer a particularly useful news center.

In the autumn, Carl and Shelley Mydans, and then Mel, left for the Philippines. Manila was where the Japanese were expected to strike, when the time came, and the time was imminent. The United States had declared an embargo on all goods to Japan; President Roosevelt had raised the ante by belatedly denying the Japanese shipments of petroleum and steel, and he'd made them unwelcome in the Panama Canal. The Japanese had already expanded their aggressions in the Far East, emboldened to do so by the Nazi invasion of the Soviet Union which tied down the Russians, and effectively prevented them from interfering with Japan's grand design. (In 1941, Stalin had signed a nonaggression pact with Foreign Minister Matsuoka of Japan, similar to one he'd made with the Nazis, which undoubtedly further liberated the Japanese from a fear of Russian interference in the Far East.) The Japanese regarded the American presence in the Philippines as a special threat to that design. The Philippines were an American dagger pointed at the heart of Japan. Although the Japanese had been negotiating with Washington and continued to do so right up to the eve of Pearl Harbor, Roosevelt anticipated war with Japan. He had dispatched the U.S. fleet to Honolulu as a warning to the Japanese. Meanwhile, the Japanese had begun to interpret the U.S. embargo as a threat to their survival. General MacArthur, though he was to prove tragically ill-equipped when attack came, fully expected the Japanese to hit the Americans first in the Philippines. He was on the alert, even though the American navy and air force commands were not.

Manila was the place to be. It was not safe, since it was right in the line of anticipated attack, but if you were a young correspondent like Melville Jacoby, you couldn't have been in a better place. He wanted Annalee Whitmore there beside him. In November, he sent a message to her in Chungking. He asked her to come down to Manila and marry him. "If you don't come now, you won't make it," he warned her.[90] She flew to Hong Kong and boarded a China Clipper at Kai Tak Airport for Manila. The one after that was the last. It was bombed in Manila Harbor. Mel married Annalee as soon as she got off the plane. "I wore a wild little nylon knit with palm trees and ukeleles on it," she later recalled.[91] Carl and Shelley Mydans were best man and matron of honor.

Between Thanksgiving and New Year Carl and Shelley Mydans and the Jacobys lived at the Bay View Hotel in Manila. The omens of war were in the air and on the ocean. Japanese bombers flew out to the Philippines from Taiwan and back again. A huge steamer from Japan arrived in Manila Harbor to evacuate Japanese civilians. On December 9, the day after the Japanese attack on Pearl Harbor, which, in Asian time, had taken place on December 8, Japanese planes bombed Manila. The Old Town was decimated. Gasoline made a torrent of fire on the Pasig River as it flowed through downtown Manila. MacArthur disappeared. Nobody knew where he'd gone. It was assumed that he'd set up command headquarters on one of the as yet defended islands. He was certainly not in Manila. What to do? Carl and Shelley and Mel and

Annalee burned all their notes and flushed them down the toilet. On hindsight this seemed like a rather hasty decision to Carl Mydans. Much of the material concerned China, however. If they were captured, he had reasoned at the time, written observations sympathetic to China might have been used as incriminating evidence against them by the Japanese.[92] As it happened, Carl and Shelley Mydans decided to stay in Manila, and were captured on January 2, 1942, by the Japanese and interned along with two thousand other American prisoners of war, at Santo Tomás University.

Mel and Annalee Jacoby, accompanied by an Associated Press reporter named Clark Lee, set out by night on a small boat bound for Bataan, a peninsula which was still in the hands of American and Filipino troops. In the night, the sky was lit up by flares and exploding bombs. "It was like every Fourth of July you've ever seen packed into one,"[93] Annalee later recalled. At dawn they were close by the island of Corregidor. Their captain pushed his passengers off on a leaky skiff. Air raid sirens were screaming when they reached the dock at Corregidor. There, the military police told them to stay in a shelter. "We were in effect under arrest," Annalee recalled.[94] She'd brought along cans of corned beef and beans, and a box of crackers, and these supplies sustained them until some GIs happened along who escorted them to shelter in a nearby ditch. From there Annalee and Mel, together with Clark Lee, made their way to the hospital peninsula on Corregidor where, as it happened, General MacArthur was hiding out with his staff, along with President Quezon of the Philippines, and many of the residents of Corregidor.

For the next two months, the three reporters lived in tunnels under the hospital with MacArthur, his wife, Jean, and Arthur MacArthur, their son, who at that time was six. Sometimes they would leave the confinement of the tunnels during the day when it was safe to sit outside. Otherwise they were prisoners in the stuffy, airless underground corridors.[95] MacArthur was convinced that American convoys were on their way with fresh troops. It was only a matter of time before the reinforcements would arrive, he thought. Meanwhile, he had enough men and planes to hang on to both Bataan and Corregidor. He refused to allow the reporters to send out dispatches until, one day, he realized that the convoys he had so counted on to come to the rescue had bypassed Bataan and Corregidor. They had steamed on down to Singapore on instructions from Roosevelt, it turned out, who had appointed MacArthur Pacific Allied Far Eastern commander with headquarters in Australia, only to abandon him to the Japanese. "Once he realized nothing was coming, MacArthur let us go ahead and file," Annalee in later years remembered.[96] Mel thereupon cabled vivid eyewitness dispatches back to *Time* on the war in the Philippines. (These dispatches formed the basis of John Hersey's wartime best-seller *Men of Bataan,* a sore subject with both Mel and Annalee, who thought *Time* owned the rights to the material and wanted to use it themselves. *Time* let Hersey have their cables to write his book, however, and offered the Jacobys four hundred and fifty dollars for their research.[97])

The journalists made several trips back and forth between Corregidor and Bataan.

Eventually, the MacArthurs moved to Bataan, and so did the three reporters. Mel and Annalee shared a house with Clark Lee. General MacArthur visited them there, and asked them all sorts of questions about China. He discoursed at great length about the death of Empire. "General MacArthur spoke in paragraphs," Annalee recalled, "and he always used exactly the right adjectives."[98] No help was coming for the men on Bataan. MacArthur was soon ordered to abandon them for his new headquarters in Australia. Before he departed by PT boat from Bataan, he called Clark Lee and Mel Jacoby into his office. "I've got a little cattle boat for you," he told them.[99] He was sending a pool of Britishers down to Australia, and he offered them passage, along with a letter of instruction addressed to any military personnel they met along the way who could assist them in their flight.

Mel and Annalee proceeded to enjoy a delayed month-long honeymoon, not exactly of their own choosing, as they made their way down through the Philippine archipelago. The cattle boat put to sea only at night. By day, it lay to anchor off remote island beaches concealed from overhead Japanese spotters by overhanging tropical foliage. At every stop the islanders feasted the honeymooners. Local boys brought them coconuts as they basked in the sand.[100] It was a movie. Just who was scripting it they did not know. On the remote island of Cebu they stayed for ten days in an abandoned beach house, where they slept on folding cots. The *Dona Nati* put into Cebu while they were there. Four ships, including the *Dona Nati,* had been sent from Australia loaded with rations and bullets for General MacArthur's men. These relief missions had been sabotaged by the Japanese. All the ships had been sunk except for the *Dona Nati,* which arrived, finally, with a supply of an antimalarial drug for American troops hiding out in the jungles of the Philippines. From Cebu, the *Dona Nati* was scheduled to return to Australia. The Jacobys received permission to board the *Dona Nati,* which they had to do by climbing up the cargo nets of the great freighter, bloodying their knuckles as they went.[101] "Land looked good," Mel cabled Time, Inc. when they arrived in Brisbane. "Everything in Australia looked good, from the first Allied plane to the green trees and lawns."[102] He and Annalee flew to Melbourne. MacArthur was already there.

So was Teddy White. He was now the China-Burma-India (CBI) theater war correspondent for *Time*. At corporate headquarters in New York Teddy had welcomed America's plunge into war after the Japanese he hated had bombed Pearl Harbor. "We were gleeful," he later confessed. "I most of all. In that first hour none of us knew how badly the American fleet had been damaged at Pearl Harbor. But it was the right war, a good war, and it had to be fought and won."[103] He'd been restless in New York and was overjoyed to be back in the East. He set out by boat for Singapore in early 1942. He'd expected to set up his post there, but Singapore had swiftly fallen to the Japanese, and he'd gone on to Australia, where he was reunited with his old friend Mel Jacoby, and first beheld Annalee.

Days after his arrival in Melbourne, Jacoby was invited by MacArthur's chief of air operations, Brigadier General Harold A. George, to fly with him to Darwin. The purpose of this reconnaissance trip was to find out whether the northwest coast of Australia was vulnerable to Japanese attack from New Guinea. The general and Mel were friends from Bataan and Corregidor days. Mel decided to go. Along their route to the northwest, they picked up an American "hitchhiker," a GI returning to his post from leave, whom General George, mistakenly it turned out, thought was on his way to the U.S. base at Alice Springs. The general ordered his pilot to land at the Alice Springs airfield. When a staff officer explained to George that the hitchhiker was going on to Darwin, the brigadier general told his pilot to land there anyway, because he wanted to visit the base. George's party stayed overnight at Alice Springs. The next morning, all set to depart, General George and his assembled passengers, including Mel, stood beside their aircraft and watched a P-40 land at the far end of the field. A second P-40 came in immediately behind it. Turbulence in the air, created in the wake of the first P-40, detached a propeller from the second plane.

Carl Mydans told me the story as he had heard it soon afterward up in Manila. According to this account, which Mydans insists is correct, the propeller "walked," in great giant steps, right across the field to Mel and cut him to pieces before it crashed into General George's plane, killing all the bystanders, including the general.[104] Annalee had just put her hair in rollers when someone knocked on her hotel room door the following morning. It was Colonel LeGrande Diller. He made her sit down on a bed. "They're all gone," Colonel Diller told her. It was the twenty-ninth of April, 1942.[105]

Mel Jacoby was the first American correspondent to die in World

War Two. "I still haven't gotten over Mel's death," Teddy White wrote to David Hulburd at *Time* from a ship bound for India on June 14. "It's almost ridiculous, Dave, to have been bombed in Chungking, in Hanoi, in Cochin-China, in Manila, in Corregidor by the enemy—and then to be killed by your own countryman under your own flag."[106] Teddy, as Mel's best friend and as the newly returned Luce CBI correspondent, had taken charge of Mel's funeral arrangements. "I took hold of arrangements when Mel died," he wrote Hulburd, "had him cremated and later had one of his Bataan friends take me up in a plane and we strew his ashes over the Pacific."[107] Teddy also took charge of Annalee. "Annalee," he wrote Hulburd, "is coming to New York and I know you will like her as much as I do. She's swell . . . she'll be in to look you up first thing when she gets to New York. I've written to Harry under separate cover about Annalee, and I presume he'll get the note shortly after this. I suggested that we try to take Annalee on our staff. She's an excellent correspondent and her contacts with the High Command and all MacArthur's men here are A-1. She also has magnificent contacts in China and the Philippines. After you've met her you'll be able to see what I mean about her ability."[108] Teddy's campaign to bring Annalee back to China as his colleague had already begun, although she had not yet left Australia. She had remained Down Under for a few months to file for *Time*. White's assessment of Annalee's attributes was shrewd. She possessed many of the qualities *Time* was always looking for. Luce probably knew this, since he had already hired her sight unseen for United China Relief. Teddy, however, had fallen in love with Annalee.[109] It remained unstated, but it glowed just beneath the surface, and added meaning to his new, enlarged role as a journalist in the Far East.

Teddy wasn't destined to be a war correspondent in the sense that someone like Jack Belden was clearly meant to be. As a war correspondent in Chungking in the late summer and autumn of 1942, Teddy White was simply back where he'd begun. But now he was a big frog in a backwater. He was dean of the Chungking press corps. This was no great distinction. With the possible exception of Brooks Atkinson, the *New York Times* drama critic on assignment to the CBI theater, who was to earn a reputation in China for his literate and balanced dispatches, the journalists gathered in Chungking were not "the top of the barrel," to quote Joseph Alsop.[110] Those reporters were mostly in Europe, in Alsop's opinion. There was no good reason to assign first-rate journalists to Chungking. Censorship made it almost impossible, as always, to get the story out, and the real story was more and more focused on the vicious politics festering in the Kuomintang. You couldn't write about that. You couldn't write about inflation. You couldn't write about how the unhealthy reproduction of paper money, an invention of the Chinese, was making the task of shopping more cumbersome for those who could afford to do it at all, since prices had risen astronomically. (In 1939 a rickshaw ride in Chungking cost sixty cents; by 1942, the price was four hundred dollars in Nationalist Chinese currency.[111]) The old Chungking joie de vivre was gone, Teddy discovered; nobody could afford to throw a party. Teddy complained about that, to David Hulburd. "The price situation isn't the only thing that's changed about Chungking—it's developing a spirit quite different from that it formerly had," he wrote on December 2, 1942.[112]

By now the Japanese had turned their attention away from Chungking to fight the Pacific war. "In the old days under the bombings and the blockade it used to be the most heroic city in the world—as London used to be during the blitz. But now it is no longer being bombed and it plods along dully worrying about food and housing and when they're going to get supplies; it's an uninspiring picture of unrelieved hardship that has lost its vividness—even misery when continued too long loses its glamor."[113] Perhaps the only improvement in Chungking was the Press Hostel itself. "The Press Hostel has been completely renovated since I left and they are now serving us foreign food at breakfast and dinner," Teddy wrote Hulburd. "*Time* may be interested in knowing," he added, "that the Chinese government is building in the middle of our hostel compound a beautifully landscaped garden full of flowers and semi-tropical shrubs known as the Melville Jacoby Memorial Garden."[114]

This was all very well, but where was the story? Until the arrival in the summer of 1942 of the American Volunteer Group, General Claire Chennault's Flying Tigers, it was a discouraging assignment according to Pepper Martin, who was back in Chungking. Once the Flying Tigers, reassembled as the Fourteenth Air Force, arrived with their B-25 bombers, things picked up; correspondents could go along on bombing missions against the Japanese in Indochina and Burma. According to Martin, however, "no matter what happened in China it was always a defeat. I know that's what bothered Teddy. We weren't seeing any wins."[115] The bombing missions were an escape from the monotony of the torpid CBI theater, and Teddy came to enjoy the super-amusement-park thrill of sitting in a cockpit and watching a target down below miraculously go up in smoke. Teddy often escaped from Chungking and went down to visit General Chennault's outfit, which was based in Kunming. Teddy and other reporters sought relief from professional stagnation by flying on bombing missions with the Eleventh Bombardment Squadron, which specialized in hit-and-run strikes. Pepper Martin accompanied fourteen bombing missions; Teddy, Martin told me, made more.[116]

In 1942, Teddy wrote a letter to his family in which he described his first bombing raid. "I've sat through many a bombing both in dugouts and out; but this is the first time I ever sat upstairs and watched the bombing from above. A bombing is a remote and abstract thing when you watch it from the bomber. It is a matter of calculation and exhilaration. You watch the target creep up through the great shiny panes of the nose of the plane, you ride on the line as if you were fixed on a railroad track, and you scarcely notice when the bombs have gone except that the ground below seems to flower in great blossoms of white and red explosions. And then you feel almost giddily excited when you get away and all the enemy planes come pouring in on you and you watch them go down in flames and nothing happens to you."[117]

Teddy's real war was elsewhere, however, and it was only just beginning. His war was in a dimension slightly removed from the terrestrial one taking place. The conflict was brewing up within the hermetic confines of Time, Inc. This war, in which Teddy would be the central combatant in the China theater, prefigured the Cold War and the McCarthy debacle of the 1950s. It was a global war, involving all the brightest foreign correspondents at Time, Inc. In China it would involve the Generalissimo, Madame Chiang, Generals Stilwell and Chennault, and Ambassador Patrick Hurley, the "courtesy general," whom Roosevelt first sent to China as a personal envoy in 1944.[118]

The antagonist in this war was Henry Luce. The beginnings of this ever-deepening conflict between Teddy and his boss could have been foretold at the outset of their relationship in 1941. By then Luce already had taken an early and influential stand in the ideological face-off that would preoccupy the postwar world. He had declared himself around the time of the 1940 presidential election, when President Roosevelt defeated Wendell Willkie, Luce's candidate. Luce hated and was much hated in return, by Franklin D. Roosevelt. Nevertheless, Luce had come to the conclusion that the United States would have to enter the war in Europe. In this regard he was at odds with isolationists in both parties, including his friend Joseph P. Kennedy, Roosevelt's ambassador to the Court of St. James. Luce set forth his terms in an editorial in *Life* magazine entitled "The American Century," in which he not only exhorted American enterprise to think globally, but also predicted America's role as an armed guardian of free enterprise against "tyranny." This editorial, published in February 1941, was a clarion call to American capitalism to seize the initiative in the postwar world and profit from the availability of newly liberated markets and resources. It was a call to a new, American imperialism. It was Luce's somewhat grandiose vision of a postwar victory.

One of the regions of the world Henry Luce envisioned as a postwar bonanza for American imperial investment was a liberated Asia, and the linchpin of Asia was going to be China. He knew how foreign capital could take control of China's resources because he'd grown up there when China was still prey to superpower designs. Like Stalin, Henry Luce recognized the value of having a strong ally in China, and, again like Stalin, the person he thought was best equipped to keep it strong was Chiang Kai-shek.

By April 1941, when he visited Chungking, Luce had already made a big investment in Chiang Kai-shek through United China Relief. He had personally invested sixty thousand dollars in an organization made up of eight charitable outfits in the China fund-raising business that he had strong-armed into joining forces. He'd persuaded men of international prestige, Thomas W. Lamont of J. P. Morgan and Company, David Selznick, Wendell Willkie among others, to serve on the board of the UCR. He had raised a quarter of a million more from *Time* subscribers, to whom he'd mailed out a letter of personal appeal. This was a start. United China Relief grew into an enormous missionary fund, committed to a free, Christian China that would take its place in the American Century as an enemy of Japanese and Communist tyranny. In 1941 when Henry Luce toured Chungking on foot with Teddy White, though he had taken his stand on how he wanted the postwar world to shape up, he had not yet embarked on his holy war against Communism. The rebels in Yenan did not yet appear to constitute a serious threat to the postwar stability of China, and Russia had not yet emerged as a global threat to the Luce concept of American postwar supremacy. In 1941 Luce could listen raptly to Teddy White's critique of the Kuomintang because they shared a belief that Chiang Kai-shek was the best leader China could provide. As the Far Eastern Editor of *Time* between June and December 1941, Teddy was a frequent guest at the Luces' house in Greenwich, Connecticut. He found editorial work frustrating, but he was, nevertheless, Henry Luce's protégé. He could influence the way Henry Luce saw things concerning China. Because of Teddy White, Henry Luce could look at the Chiang regime with some detachment. A year later, despite the commitment to the Chiangs and United China Relief, Henry Luce continued to rely on Teddy White as his China informant.

By early 1943 he was further removed from his correspondent in China, though more dependent than ever on his views. Luce had planned to visit Chungking in 1943, and he'd applied for permission to do so as a war correspondent. As a publisher and editor, he was denied permission; on the grounds "of the extreme stringency of transportation," credentials were not being issued to "publishers, editors and executives who wish to make visits to combat areas."[119] This was a bitter blow to Luce. He appealed to Army Chief of Staff General George C. Marshall, then to Secretary of War Henry L. Stimson and finally, in person, to President Roosevelt. To no avail. Luce believed that FDR had personally devised the order to spite him. By now, Luce had begun to fashion his ideological hatred of the Soviet Union into a political instrument of war.

This was the moment when Stalin had held his ground and turned the tide against Hitler. To the Allies Stalin was a hero, "Uncle Joe"; his earlier pact with Hitler was forgotten. Suddenly the Russian and American people were comrades-in-arms, if not comrades-in-politics. Luce, however, saw a giant of evil proportions rising up, looming over Eastern Europe. In the Democrats, he perceived a weakness for Communism. He began to make his publications, in which editorial comment was always smoothly and anonymously blended in with the news story, vehicles for his anti-Communism. In religious wars, issues are always black and white. To Luce, Godless Communism was evil, Christian capitalism was good. He was choosing sides already, and ultimately China would become the scene of a holy war in which from Henry Luce's point of view Chiang Kai-shek would have to emerge victorious. Anybody who thought otherwise was going to have to pay a big price.

Teddy didn't know that this was going to happen. He was still Henry Luce's man in China, trying his best to tell the story the way he saw it, in spite of all the local obstructions. In fact, to do his job the way he was sure Harry would have wanted him to do it, he used his prestige and his travel allowance to circumvent Hollington Tong's closely maintained supervision. In February 1943, Teddy made arrangements to go up to Honan Province with a Press Hostel colleague of his named Harrison Forman, who was reporting for various publications in Chungking, including the London *Times*. Teddy was acting on a well-informed hunch when he went up to Honan. A famine was raging up there and he'd heard rumors about the corruption and stupidity of the famine relief effort during the winter, but he'd been skeptical. Like all China Hands, however, Teddy read the Chinese press or had it translated for him. When *Ta Kung Pao,* China's most prestigious independent newspaper, was suppressed for three days after hinting at the scandal taking place in Honan, Teddy smelled a story. "It was as if the White House had closed down the *New York Times* for exposing graft in the WPA," Teddy wrote Hulburd.[120]

In Honan, an American Catholic missionary, Bishop Thomas Megan, took Teddy and Forman on a tour by horseback of the famine, through a dying countryside. It was a reprise of Edgar Snow's experience at Seretsai in 1929. Like Snow, they saw starving people eating bark from trees. Teddy saw plump, sleek dogs dining on hastily buried corpses. He heard stories of cannibalism, stories about villagers who had strangled their children and eaten them. In Honan, clusters of starving villagers wanted to pull him off his horse, presumably so that they could eat the horse. As a Japanophobe, Teddy placed the blame for famine on the Japanese for having invaded China in the first place. In order to stop the southern advance of the Japanese, Chiang Kai-shek had cut the Yellow River dikes and switched the river's course, thereby changing the ecology of north China. Honan was suffering from a drought and no longer had the Yellow River spillways as a backup resource to irrigate the fields. But this was not the scandal.

The scandal was that the government wasn't supplying any relief. Chiang Kai-shek was taxing the Chinese farmer out of existence and siphoning hundreds of millions of dollars from the U.S. Treasury to pay for the war, but his own currency was worthless. If Chiang had paid his soldiers with worthless paper money, they would have deserted. Instead of paying them, Chiang was letting them live off the land. Grain that ought to have been supplied to the starving Honanese from surplus yields in other provinces was going instead to the army. In Honan, army warehouses bulged with surplus grain, but the only food that reached the starving people came via the black market. Only a fraction of the two hundred million Chinese dollars appropriated for famine relief got to Honan. People were selling their children to brothel keepers who had gone up to Honan from other provinces looking for cheap bargains.

Teddy, as always, wrote detailed notes. He didn't wait to file his story from Chungking, although he expected it to go there when he sent off the first two of three dispatches through the telegraph operator in Loyang. All material cabled abroad from the provinces was supposed to be routed through the censor in Chungking. For some reason, however, Teddy's shocking Honan revelations went straight to New York. They never would have reached *Time* if they'd gone through Chungking, but due to the "anarchy," as Teddy called it, that prevailed in Honan at the time, or perhaps thanks to a telegraph operator equally scandalized by the famine outrage, Teddy's story landed on the pages of *Time* magazine. It happened that Madame Chiang had recently arrived in New York to embark on a good-will tour on behalf of United China Relief. She was horrified to see Teddy's story ablaze on the pages of *Time*. She confronted her friend Henry Luce and ordered him to fire Teddy White. Luce refused to do it.

"I went and am sorry now that I went," Teddy wrote Hulburd. "I have been mentally sick ever since I came back,—nervous, depressed, unhappy. The story is unbelievable even now, and can't be fully told till after the war. The army was extorting grain from the peasantry by force; people were selling children to pay taxes; there were dead bodies on all the roads; I saw dogs digging corpses out of sand pits, and dogs dismembering dead refugees on the highways. The provincial government under threat of the local military was trying to keep the story quiet, trying to prevent anybody from sending news out. The Chungking government had sent not a single man into the heart of the famine area, Chengchow, to investigate for itself. There had been $200,000,000 appropriated by the Central Government for famine relief in Honan. I tried to track it down—but practically none of it had got to the people's mouths." [121]

Teddy returned to Chungking like a man possessed. He decided to raise hell. He went to see everyone he could, including Madame Sun and H. H. K'ung. He saw the minister of economic affairs. He got the town all churned up. The minister of war, Ho Ying-ch'in, demanded that Teddy pay him a visit. Teddy and Ho argued passionately. Ho denied that peasants had turned surplus grain, shipped in from other provinces to feed the starving Honanese, over to the army. Teddy insisted that he had spoken to peasants who had done so. Teddy told Ho that his generals were misreporting figures to him from up there.

"The thing wound up with my seeing the Generalissimo himself," Teddy wrote Hulburd. "The old boy gave me twenty minutes. He was as he always is completely impassive and expressionless, sitting in that great chair in the dark room saying nothing all the time, only grunting assent and dissent. First he didn't believe my story about the dogs digging bodies out of the sand. Then I made Harrison Forman show him the actual pictures of dogs digging bodies out. That woke him up. Then I told him about the army taking the people's grain and the old boy said it was impossible. I said it had actually happened. Then he started to believe me and started to take notes on place names and dates of our trip. He took them down himself on his own little pad.

"Well, all this meant hell for the men who had been handling relief. Mostly they were CC people and ministry of finance men. The Generalissimo has one simple remedy for that sort of graft when it can be gotten to his attention—stand them against the wall." [122]

The Honan famine story was important because it was the first crack in the facade that the Chiangs, with the help of Henry Luce, had been presenting to the world. Teddy provided a glimpse of the kind of corruption that was eating away at China's power structure. In May, after some soul searching, Luce published a major piece by Pearl Buck in *Life* that was sharply critical of the Chiang Kai-shek government. He ran it mainly because he didn't want to be accused of misleading the American people. He was already parting company with the craft of reportage, however. "But just think, Teddy—the great fact is that Chungking is still there!" Luce wrote his China correspondent after he'd decided to run the article by Pearl Buck. "That's the fact you have to be concerned about explaining . . . you have always had immense faith in China and in the Generalissimo . . . perhaps you felt that you had communicated too much faith—or a too easy faith. I simply write to say you need have no such fears. It is still the faith—and not the defects of the faith—which it is most of all important to communicate."[123] Faith was engaged in a struggle with truth, the battle lines were now being drawn by Henry Luce. Teddy White was still, in his eyes, a true believer, a disciple.

Teddy, however, was beginning to entertain serious doubts about how *Time* was handling the China story. The turning point in how China was being perceived by American readers came in mid-1943. Ironically, this happened just as popularity for the cause of the Nationalist Chinese reached its zenith in May and June of 1943, after Madame Chiang made her highly publicized tour for United China Relief. Her tour ended in Hollywood in a blaze of floodlights at the Hollywood Bowl where China got the full treatment from a star-studded cast, thanks to David Selznick, who was on the UCR board of directors. Teddy White's Honan story had been published and was followed by the Pearl Buck article. That summer, two more articles that were highly critical of Chiang's regime blew the myth of China's virtuous pathos to pieces. One was an article in the newsletter *Far Eastern Survey* by T. A. Bisson. The other was an article published by the *Reader's Digest* in August in which the military correspondent, Hanson Baldwin, asserted that China was not a nation but a geographical expression. The piece by Baldwin roiled the waters of both Chungking and Washington because it reflected long-standing disillusionment with the Chinese military by GIs in Kunming.

In the fall of 1943, Teddy began to take some flak for *Time*'s rather arrogant ad hominem treatment of U.S. policy-makers in China who failed to follow the Luce line. Teddy was not happy in this role. One instance concerned Clarence E. Gauss, a Foreign Service China Hand who had replaced Nelson Johnson in 1941 as the United States ambassador to China. Gauss had been trying to use American aid as a bargaining instrument to bring about democratic reforms in China. The Chiangs didn't like that, and they made their feelings clear to Henry Luce. On November 12, Teddy wrote David Hulburd, "Last spring we wrote a column on Ambassador Gauss. We cut his gullet, we left his windpipe dangling in the air—we said that he couldn't speak Chinese, implied that he was surly and unpleasant and incompetent. We wound up by saying that no one would be more surprised than Mr. Gauss himself if he came back to China. Well, Dave, Mr. Gauss is back in China now, he is still the American Ambassador. And when your Chungking correspondent goes to the American Embassy now he wears earmuffs and gloves to keep from freezing."[124] Teddy was not at that point convinced or even aware that perhaps Luce himself was responsible for the Gauss column, or of the direction that *Time* was beginning to take. He had not yet found himself in dispute with Luce. But he did have qualms about the *Time* executive staff. Teddy had persuaded *Time* to sign on Pepper Martin, who had gone to New York in October 1943 to work in the home office. In November, Teddy warned Martin, "*Time* includes some of the most artistic knifers-in-the-back in the business: there are dozens of career men in the outfit all of them bound for the top and not too particular about the kinds of deals they have to make on the way." He warned: "Watch yourself, keep your mouth shut and play it close to your chest."[125]

Meanwhile, things were going from bad to worse in China. Civil war was beginning to break out between the Communists in Yenan and the Nationalists, and Chiang Kai-shek was beginning to give serious thought to the idea of bombing Yenan with U.S. air supplies. It had also begun to look as though some sort of collaboration between the Nationalists and the Japanese occupation army might be in the works, with the understanding that after the war the Japanese would help defeat the Reds. This was certainly in the air, if not in the works. Teddy wrote three articles on the subject of the Nationalists and the Communists, because the Ministry of Information had issued a statement in October that seemed to imply that the subject of Communism was no longer taboo. Teddy submitted his articles to the censors. They killed two of them. Teddy was furious. He was also in need of a break.

In January 1944 Luce brought Teddy back to New York, where he proceeded to write a long, critical piece on China for *Life*. He lambasted the Chiangs, the conservative CC Clique under the two Ch'en brothers, and the secret police, who up to that point had not been acknowledged in the United States, although they had turned Chungking into a paranoiac's worst nightmare. He pointed out that Chiang had used some of his best troops to seal off the Communist armies in Shensi and had prevented medical supplies from reaching the Communists. He criticized the United States for failing to provide Chiang with adequate military supplies with which to fight the war, and he predicted the coming civil war. "You have written undoubtedly the most important article about China in many years—perhaps ever," Henry Luce told

Teddy after he had read it in draft.[126] Teddy replied, "I was scared as Hell, Harry, at what I thought would be an inevitable clash between my conviction and your policy."[127]

In between bombing raids and disputes with the Chinese government, Teddy had continued to think about a future that included Annalee Jacoby. Annalee had returned to the States in the summer of 1942. She had gone directly to New York, where the *Time* management was still distraught about Mel's death. They wined her and dined her and Henry Luce invited her with a group of senior correspondents and editors out to his house in Greenwich, where the talk was mainly of Australia, "with Annalee making enormous sense," David Hulburd wrote Teddy. "But I think under that smile and that cheerfulness there's a good deal of brooding. Certainly she's in a highly emotional state underneath, but where it is divided between Mel and MacArthur and the war and Australia is hard to say."[128]

Annalee wanted to go back out to the Far East, to the China-Burma-India theater. Women were not yet being allowed out there as war correspondents, however. Instead, she returned to Hollywood, where she still had four years left on her MGM contract. Three months later she abruptly left Hollywood and returned to the East Coast, to her family's home in Bethesda, Maryland. Her father was chief of evaluation of the Federal Housing Administration in Washington, D.C. It was there, finally, that Annalee began her serious mourning. She spent a great deal of time chopping down trees, by her own account.

"I'm greatly worried about Annalee," Teddy wrote Hulburd, his editor at *Time,* in April 1943, after his return from Honan. "I learn privately that Annalee is living in Washington, stays with her parents, refuses to see anybody, does not answer letters, has stopped working on her book."[129] He wrote, "I feel to a certain degree responsible for her, partly for herself, partly for Mel's sake. I wish we could dope out some way of getting herself out of her tailspin. I can't do a damned thing about her because she answers no letters she receives from China. But if someone from the Washington office could call her up some time and check on her, or if she could be persuaded to go to work in some one of *Time*'s offices somewhere in the States or abroad—I think that would be a great help."[130]

White kept writing to Annalee, to cheer her up and feed her Chungking gossip. China, he wrote her on May 3, 1943, was "full of war correspondents, including Bob Bryant that exuberant stud who used to peddle his wares at the Hotel Australia, Melbourne. . . . No news of Til Durdin or Peggy, but Brooks Atkinson here for the New York Times who is my idea of one of the finest men in the world, perfect company . . . Harrison Forman, that son of a bitch, still working for the London Times . . . Nina and Spencer [Moosa] now remarkably ensconced as dead [sic] and matron of the Press Hostel carrying on tirelessly and learning finally to love each other dearly and tenderly . . . Newsreel Wong moved into press hostel with wife cum daughter cum son. Awfully hard on him bringing up two adolescents at the Press Hostel, when nightly Pepper Martin and other good friends entertain beautiful and bosomy maidens immediately upstairs. . . ."[131]

On the East Coast, Teddy sought out Annalee. He roused her out of her depression. Originally, he had urged her to join Time Inc. Indeed, he had a job picked out for her as a writer of "Time Views the News," but she had been reluctant to take on the job, and instead, accepted an offer to work in Washington. Both Teddy and Annalee had really hoped that she would be offered a job as his assistant in Chungking. The decision to forgo the "Time Views the News" job was based on that expectation, and White fully intended to work on Hulburd, while Annalee proved her stripes at the Office of War Information. By April he had declared his love for Annalee, who was then living with her mother in a house she had bought in Larchmont (Annalee's father had recently died). Annalee had agreed to spend two weeks in his company, after he returned from Boston, where he had gone to visit his family. "Personally, too, it is a highly pleasant thought that every day of the working week you will be so close to me," he wrote. "I don't know how conspicuous you wish our love to be—as for me I wish to yell it from the rooftops—but even without attracting undue attention it means we have a long vista of lunches and cocktails and other rendezvous stretching away."[132]

Upon his return, Teddy found much to his distress that Annalee had decided to accept the job on "Time Views the News" after all. This meant the disruption of Teddy's fantasy, and the end of his projected two-week idyll. "The news you gave me caused me to gulp," he wrote Annalee. "It is very strange how in human affairs one can consider a course of action, then discard it, and when forced back to it in the end find it highly disconcerting. So with this. . . . And I have said again and again,—here will be two weeks of vacation entirely yours. All night, every night I have told myself that in x-number of days I shall be back with Ann; somehow it has been the understream of all the past week and a half. And I have said again and again,—here will be two weeks which will be a remembrance forever; even if the girl never marries me those two weeks will be mine. I find myself, in trying to write to you the things I feel, peculiarly stumbling and halt and I've been lingering over that last sentence for a long while. People grow older and the years have a way of spinning themselves out and straining the bitterness from hurt wounds; but sweetnesses and joys last so much longer and ache more persistently; and I want you now in May and in spring no matter what the eventual cost to myself or to you (which is egotistical). . . . Well, that's a hell of an introduction to what should be a congratulatory cable. And now, to prove to you, how very resilient I am, I shall turn on my heel like the ringmaster at the circus, and show you all the good things about your present job, and why my original advice, to take it, was sound and well-considered."[133] Annalee went to work at *Time,* and she and Teddy set in motion the process of obtaining Annalee government permission that would allow her to join Teddy in Chungking. In June, he returned to China.

When Teddy returned to Chungking after the publication of his article he fully expected to be treated as a persona non grata by the Chiang regime. To his surprise, Kuomintang officials greeted him warmly. The people who gave him a cool reception, much to his dismay, were other China Hands, journalists and Foreign Service officers who had grown to despise the Kuomintang. They felt that Teddy was one of the few journalists covering China who knew how bad things were under the Nationalists and had it in his power to publicize them on a grand scale, in a Luce publication. Indeed he had accused the Kuomintang of combining "some of the worst features of Tammany Hall and the Spanish Inquisition."[134] He had identified the Chiangs as the source of China's decay. Yet the antidote he had recommended was just what Henry Luce was lobbying for: increased American assistance to the Chiang regime, he wrote, "with force at the moment on a scale far greater than we have done for the past two years."[135] Teddy could not bring himself to suggest that there might be an alternative to the Chiangs. No wonder Luce had praised the piece and run it as written.

The reason for the extreme bitterness that Teddy's *Life* article aroused had its origin in the deterioration of China's military situation during the five months of his absence. During that time, Japan had put the Chinese army to flight in Honan. The Japanese had begun a terrifying, swift advance to the southeast, toward Kweilin, where General Chennault had constructed a base for the Fourteenth Airborne with money he'd received and supplies flown over the Hump—the air route over the lower Himalayas from India that provided the only Allied access to Free China. Meanwhile, inflation had paralyzed Chungking. Teddy had returned to a deeply anxious atmosphere bordering on panic. The Americans' chief objective in the Far East was to win the war. In their present state, the Nationalists were clearly not capable of performing as the pillar of strength that President Roosevelt liked to say they were. To advocate pouring more money and arms into the Nationalist Chinese sink hole was obviously sheer folly.

When the United States entered the war, the primary task before the Allies was to defeat Germany in Europe and North Africa. This was how General George C. Marshall, chief of staff of the U.S. war effort, saw it. Marshall did what he could for MacArthur in the Pacific and the war was prosecuted with vigor on all fronts, but the war plan was to defeat Hitler in the West first and then turn the hose full blast on Japan in the East. In the Far East this plan was not altogether appreciated. To journalists and military men alike, especially Americans, the war against Japan was of paramount importance, yet the Allied commanders out there had to fight tooth and claw to gouge money and personnel out of a war budget already stretched to its huge limits. To the American war strategists in Asia, China was deemed important strategically because that corner of China that was still free provided the only available land base for an aerial war against Japan.

In the war against Japan, there soon came to be two schools of thought about how scarce American money should be dispensed in China. One of these schools held that the money should be spent to train Chinese troops in the techniques of modern warfare in order to defeat the Japanese who had already occupied Chinese soil, to seize land first and then strike at the Japanese heart from the air. General Joseph W. Stilwell carried the spear for this school. Stilwell had served in China as an army engineer in the 1920s, and had again been assigned to China as a military attaché in the 1930s. It has been said that General Stilwell was cursed with China. He could read and speak Chinese, knew the Chinese people well, and understood the terrain of China. Stilwell's command was two-fold: he was commander-in-chief of the China-Burma-India theater, and he was also commander of U.S. forces in China. He had been routed by the Japanese in Burma in 1942, but he had marched out of Burma into India with the remnants of the American and Chinese force he had commanded, the heroic feat memorialized by Jack Belden in *Retreat with Stilwell*. It was Stilwell's intention to reverse his defeat, open the Burma Road with Chinese soldiers he was training in India, and then take back the rest of China from the Japanese. American supplies and military men were being flown at great expense and effort over the Hump, a "skyroad 525 miles long," as Teddy White described it, across the eastern Himalayas and the forests of northern Burma.[136] Stilwell thought that the military supplies being brought in should be used for his proposed ground war.

Major General Claire Chennault represented the second school of thought about how to defeat the Japanese from land bases in Free China.

Chennault was a buccaneering retired U.S. Army Air Corps officer, a onetime daredevil stunt pilot who had barnstormed a living for himself around America in the peacetime years following World War One. He was described by Owen Lattimore as "perhaps the most brilliant trainer of fighter pilots of his day." Lattimore also asserted, "Chennault himself was a simple-minded man."[137] Chennault had hired himself out to Madame Chiang in the 1930s and at her behest had fashioned a mercenary air force of American flyers who called themselves the Flying Tigers and flew airplanes with noses painted to resemble the visages of attacking tiger sharks. Chennault disbanded the Flying Tigers before World War Two began, reenlisted and received a commission in the U.S. Air Force. He was attached to the Nationalist government in 1941, assigned to reassemble a new, American volunteer air force to fight the Japanese. Known as the American Volunteer Group, or AVG, it was incorporated after Pearl Harbor into the American war effort as the U.S. China Air Task Force. As such, it was inducted into the U.S. Army, and served under the command of General Stilwell. Chennault, however, was accustomed to his own command, and he was encouraged to play that role by his friends, Generalissimo and Madame Chiang Kai-shek. Chennault, and his school, believed the key to winning the war was air power. It was Chennault's passionate conviction that money for China should be spent on shipping air force matériel over the Hump, and on building air bases in western and southwest China from which to carry out air strikes. Chennault believed that he could defeat the Japanese single-handedly in the air, if only Roosevelt would supply him with the necessary bombers.

The Chiangs urged Chennault on. They disliked Stilwell, who intensively questioned the fighting quality of the Chinese troops. He also insisted on taking personal command of the Chinese armies. Chiang Kai-shek understandably opposed this idea, as the Russians from their own, bitter experience could have told Stilwell. Chiang had always set severe limits on the control he allowed foreign advisers to exercise over his forces. The Germans, von Seeckt and Falkenhausen, knew this. The truth was that Chiang Kai-shek personally controlled only a few divisions. Some were under the command of warlords who operated independently of Chiang. Still others were Communist, and to bring them into the war effort under the command of Stilwell so that he could improve their fighting skill was unacceptable to Chiang.

The Chennault vision of early, flashy, easy victory in the air appealed to Chiang and his wife. They lobbied ceaselessly in Washington for the Chennault option. They undermined Stilwell whenever possible. This was not hard to do because Stilwell, nicknamed "Vinegar Joe," was a prickly, plainspoken man who abhorred political infighting.

Chennault, and the Chiangs, had a very effective operator in the smooth T. V. Soong, who had access to Harry Hopkins, Roosevelt's key assistant, and through him and others like Joseph Alsop, Roosevelt's cousin, they pushed for planes and money. When Madame Chiang made her triumphal visit to the United States in early 1943, she too became a powerful voice for the Chennault forces. She enlisted the support of Henry Luce, who began to undermine Stilwell in *Time*. Stilwell and Chennault became bitter antagonists. The story of their behavior, their separate efforts to fight the war against Japan from China, was Teddy White's chief occupation as a war correspondent from the time he returned to China in 1942 until he finally left China in 1945. He admired both men at different times. He became close to both of them. He earned the affections of each. He was drawn, first of all, to Chennault, whose argument for striking Japan's sea power and land bases from the air was seductive. For a long time, Teddy was a Chennault fan. Stilwell was arguing that a less flashy course would be required if the air war was going to work. The Yankee commander of Allied forces in the China-Burma-India theater held that unless the land bases on Chinese soil were secured under his command first, the Japanese would retaliate against U.S. air strikes by knocking out American air force bases in Free China with their army. Stilwell's argument made sense, but it was obscured by the dazzle of swift victory that Chennault promised. There was another hitch: the Chiangs didn't want to use their own troops against the enemy. They wanted the United States to defeat the Japanese for them, so that they could use the troops Stilwell had led out of Burma and was training in India, at Ramgarh, against the Communists after the war.

By May 1943, Chennault and Stilwell had reached a Mexican standoff. Which one would get the better part of U.S. supplies being flown over the Hump? Roosevelt was persistently lobbied by Chennault's people in Washington, on the advice of Joseph Alsop, who was now attached to Chennault's headquarters in Kunming. Joseph Alsop had been a close associate, before the war, of T. V. Soong. At that time the slick Soong was China's representative in the United States and was energetically greasing the pipeline for the half-billion Treasury Department handout that kept the Chiang-Soongs from bolting the Allied cause before the war. The Chennault people outmaneuvered Stilwell's advocates, and the president gave the better part of the tonnage to Chennault.

Teddy later claimed that by then his sympathies had begun to shift to Stilwell. As perhaps they had—personally. But he was now trapped in a box canyon. In his memoirs he writes that he had begun to believe that the Chiangs were incapable of governing China. This was written in hindsight. He never said or wrote any such thing at the time, although many others were vociferous on the subject. Teddy tells us that he'd begun to see things in a new light after his visit to the Honan famine. He never suggested, however, that China might do better as a nation under Communist rule, and this was the heart of the matter.

During the five months that Teddy was in New York, in 1944, it had begun to look as though perhaps some sort of rapprochement with the Communists *was* advisable. Foreign Service advisers on Stilwell's staff and in the U.S. embassy were suggesting this course as an option as early as 1943. Just exactly how Marxist were the Communists? How allied were they to the Leninist objective of world revolution, to the overthrow of capitalist societies? Were they, in principle, anti-democratic, part of a monolithic movement operated out of the Soviet Union? The evidence compiled from field reports by competent, reliable China Hands like John Stewart Service and John Paton Davies seemed to suggest that the Chinese Communists were a local guerrilla operation independent of the Soviet Union, less concerned with international Communist objectives or with the establishment of a workers' state than with a classic, Chinese-style restructuring of society in the countryside. Indeed, after the death of the 1927 Revolution, the Chinese Communist movement had gone that way. Stalin had reinforced this notion in conversation with Averell Harriman, Roosevelt's wartime ambassador to Moscow, when he asserted that the Chinese Communists were "margarine communists."[138] He also called them "radish communists," red outside and white inside.

In fact, not a very great deal was known about the internal workings of the Communists. This, as we've seen, was an issue between the embassy staff and the journalists: information was scarce, and each side of the river thought the other was hoarding it. Nobody had been up to Yenan since 1939, and almost all reliable information about the Reds was fielded in Chungking by Chou En-lai, one of the smoothest public relations artists of this or any other century, whose press attaché was the tall, willowy and sympathetic beauty, Kung P'eng, of whom Eric Sevareid wrote, "She was a beautiful woman, but in her presence the male-female feeling all but disappeared, replaced by a sexless awe and admiration."[139] Nobody in either the press or the embassy was going to learn much of substance from them about the make-up of the party power structure, internal party disputes or the long-range objectives of Mao Tse-tung, who was inscrutably changeable. John Paton Davies, who had been seconded to Stilwell's staff from the embassy, had suggested to Vinegar Joe the idea of opening a U.S. consulate in Yenan, for the purpose of getting to know the Communists better, with the ultimate objective of bringing them into the Allied war effort and, to use Owen Lattimore's term for it, "patching up" the United Front.[140] This idea came on the heels of Chou En-lai's invitation to the United States to send visitors to Yenan.

It had long been Stilwell's contention that the Japanese could not be defeated without the help of the Communists. He'd been impressed by their fighting skills back in 1935, when he expressed his vivid admiration in conversations with Edgar Snow. He wasn't at all deterred by the politics of the Yenan guerrillas. It seems in retrospect that U.S. advisers in China, and Stilwell himself, were determined to believe the best of the Communists in their zeal to achieve their war goal of defeating Japan. John Paton Davies has admitted as much.[141]

Unquestionably, however, by portraying the Communists in an unrealistically favorable light, the Foreign Service officers gave ammunition to the pro-Chiang China lobby, which had lined up on the side of Chennault. The profoundly important, delicate matter of U.S. relations in China with the Nationalists and Communists, so vital to the postwar role of the United States, came down to a struggle between the pro-Chiang China lobby and Stilwell. By late 1944, the Stilwell camp included the China Hands in the U.S. embassy, Stilwell's own staff and most of the journalists in Chungking, including Teddy White. Thus, an affair of state, which should have been handled by experts with professional detachment, subsequently became a hot issue in the nasty postwar fight shaping up in America.

The journalists had by and large formed a favorable impression of the Communists quite independently of the Stilwell faction. They were disgusted with the Kuomintang and the Nationalists by 1944, when Chiang's government reluctantly permitted a group of Western and Chinese journalists to visit the Communist stronghold. The Western journalists, struck by the clear, pure mountain air of Yenan and the Boy Scout atmosphere of the place, were favorably impressed by the contrast to Chungking.[142] The difference in climate seemed to symbolize a spiritual contrast between the two camps. Needless to say, visitors were not encouraged to venture down any side streets on their own. On a later visit, Tillman Durdin did just that and encountered some unexpectedly rough treatment at the hands of Red cadres, which gave Durdin a glimpse of that side of the Red encampment that most of his colleagues had not seen.[143]

The journalists were flattered, à la Edgar Snow, with photo opportunities and interviews with the top dogs. Although the 1942 Rectification Campaign in which an altogether unlikely and well-intentioned Trotskyist writer named Wang Shih-wei was persecuted (and subsequently executed and cannibalized) came up in press conferences, the journalists gleaned almost nothing on their visit about the internal political developments that had turned a purge by Mao of the pro-Soviet influence of Wang Ming—his Stalinist foe in the party—into an anti-writer movement. By then, unsavory party hacks had secured Mao's favor and held important subordinate roles in his hierarchy. It might have been difficult for outsiders to know that a gangster element was already exercising authority in the Communist Party but not impossible. It's just that the wrong outsiders went up to Yenan.

Neither Anna Louise Strong nor Agnes Smedley could have been counted on to take an unbiased look at how things stood in Yenan, although Smedley might have ascertained the state of things from her old friends Ting Ling and Mao Tun. As a devout Communist sympathizer, however, she might not have wanted to believe anything ill of her former Yenan hosts. Despite their earlier treatment of her, she had never exhibited any animosity toward the Communist leadership in Yenan. Edgar Snow was no skeptic, either. Among the journalists assigned to the China-Burma-India theater, only Harold Isaacs, in my opinion, could have made a reasonably educated appraisal, without bias, of how things stood in Yenan. Isaacs arrived in Chungking on July 28, 1944, on assignment for *Newsweek.*

"I'm afraid I'm really a sentimental dope," he wrote. "But the first sign of Chinese peasants working in the fields, their backs bare, their heads under broad round hats, of the women carrying load for load with the men, of the grinning children—oh the children!—forgive me, it almost made a tear start up." Isaacs wrote this in the first minutes of his return to China after an absence of nearly a decade, and thirteen years after the Yangtze River journey that had given his life such meaning.[144] Much had changed since then. The dynamic, radical enthusiasm that had inspired *China Forum* and the anger that had fueled *The Tragedy of the Chinese Revolution* had long since mellowed. He'd been a stalwart Trotsky man in New York when he'd settled there on the Lower East Side with Viola. By the late 1930s, however, he'd drifted away from the Trotskyists. In 1940 he put radical ideology behind him when he stopped working for Havas and joined CBS as an editor and writer. In 1943 he left CBS and went to work for *Newsweek.* He was a white-collar man employed by a middlebrow institution at a satisfactory salary when he showed up in Chungking as the *Newsweek* CBI correspondent. It is striking to read his correspondence from wartime China and find so few traces of the old outrage.

Isaacs was biding his time. This was a transitional decade for him. As a wartime correspondent for *Newsweek,* Isaacs's talents were under-employed. This might have given him heartburn. Quite the contrary.

Although he entertained no illusions about his magazine, which was a pale competitor of *Time,* he worked hard and filed voluminously. As he wrote to his editor at *Newsweek,* self-education was his primary purpose for being where he was. It was quite enough for him to have a good job that enabled him to look around the theater. He was even a little rusty on China, and he took advantage of the reputation that he brought with him to ask and listen. He'd already made his name as a China Hand. This was the advantage he had over his chief rival, Teddy White. He was almost a generation removed from Teddy. The pundits in residence, people like F. McCracken Fisher, Richard Watts, Graham Peck of the Office of War Information and George Atcheson and Everett Drumright over at the embassy, all knew who he was and received him with respect.[145]

Isaacs also had some friends in Chungking from the old days, notably Madame Sun Yat-sen, whom he called Susie. Madame Sun had come up to Chungking from Hong Kong on the eve of the Japanese takeover. She lived in a two-story gray brick house in the middle of town. Her presence was a source of continuing discomfort to all the other members of her family. Her younger sister, Madame Chiang, was married to the man Madame Sun liked to mockingly call the Generalissimo, and whom she held in such contempt. Her sister Ailing had a reputation for getting rich off various schemes related to the government, and this sister, too, Madame Sun must have held in disdain. Her younger brother T. V. Soong had also long since abandoned the principles of her late husband, Dr. Sun, in the pursuit of power. "She was sitting in judgment on them all," one observer has recalled.[146] She was in steady communication with the Yenan delegation in Chungking and received visitors from America, who came bearing gifts from her admirers abroad. She was in a virtual state of house arrest, however; Chiang Kai-shek had supplied her with a limousine, but if she used it to visit anyone she ran the risk of putting her host under a cloud of suspicion. "The basis we had established of a rather thorogoing mutual personal confidence was almost immediately re-established," Isaacs wrote Viola, after he'd paid his first visit to his old Shanghai patron. "At first glance she seemed scarcely changed for the ten years that have gone by. A little stouter but still very beautiful. 'Have you any friends?' I asked her sometime later during our talk. 'None as good as you,' she said."[147] But she had changed, he found. She had lost some of her own revolutionary edge. "She's probably right, from her own pt of view, to avoid having to account for her attitudes because I think they have passed over into a kind of mixed up haze, filled with anomalies and contradictions. She still works for the Yenan people but refers to 'disagreements.' "[148] She talked with Isaacs about the Communists, whom he referred to as "the folks of the promised land."[149] "Susie's position about them," he wrote Viola, "is a little fuzzy and criss-crossed with curious contradictions. She can sometimes adopt an attitude of rather uncritical partisanship, but she will also make sharp allusions to the past, to the flip-flips, to the quality of their integrity . . . of which she does not have a very high opinion."[150]

On one occasion Madame Sun asked Isaacs to be her escort to the Czech Independence Day celebration, attended by the Chungking diplomatic corps and the top brass of the KMT. As they stood in the receiving line with U.S. Ambassador Clarence Gauss, General Ho Ying-ch'in and others, Isaacs asked her, in a low voice, how she could stand such things. She replied, "What do you think I asked you to bring me here for, then? I need help in this two-faced business."[151] She told Isaacs over dinner one night that she wanted to flee "after the war, although whether she meant from China, or Chinese politics, is unclear. She wants out," Isaacs wrote Viola. "And in expressing it she sometimes says sharp things. 'I don't want to get mixed up in another 1927 —I don't want my personal feelings subject to anybody's orders.' There was more of the going back," Isaacs wrote Viola. "The rather bitter laughter at the sentimental romanticists who see 'love' in her marriage. She was more of a daughter, an acolyte, an amenuensis [sic] . . . and carrying the weight of it ever since has been her cross."[152]

All this ought to have given Isaacs a superb vantage point. Teddy was not the only other first-string journalist in Chungking. Others, Brooks Atkinson for instance, were around and about. Yet Teddy, despite his youth, comported himself as if he were the most important correspondent in residence, and it was a great relief to some in Chungking that now at last a good counterweight to Teddy had appeared on the scene. "I have gathered from a number of people, ever since my arrival in CBI, that my arrival was looked forward to by not a few people mainly because they seemed to expect I would provide some sobering competition for the arrogant White," Isaacs wrote Viola. "He's quite a shrewd and intelligent character but his manners have suffered, I fear, from lack of what he would regard as worthy competition. And in many matters he's almost adolescent. It is easy to understand why he is disliked by the other correspondents. He came into my room the other day quite unsolicitedly to 'fill me in on the "situation."' There's no question about his grasp of things. I don't know about his understanding."[153]

Teddy was aware of Isaacs's reputation. Indeed, before setting out for China he'd gone at the suggestion of John Fairbank to visit Isaacs, in the hope of getting some advice on how to proceed as a freelance reporter in China. Isaacs was only able to tell him to go there and find out for himself since there was no tried-and-true way to do it.[154] Now Teddy was roughly where Isaacs had been a decade earlier, in the very fire of his youthful ambition. Isaacs had no ax to grind with Teddy, although he did not hesitate to criticize the much debated *Life* article. He'd read the article, finally, he wrote Viola, in an old back issue he'd picked up at field headquarters down in Kwangsi. "Got into a brief discussion with Ted about it . . . challenged its premises, told him in my nicest blunt manner I thought it fundamentally dishonest. He admits the disproportions [but] justifies them on the grounds that that was the only way to get some bits of the truth into a Luce publication. He further suspects, I fear, that he is a prime mover in shaping American public opinion. White is well-informed and he has a hard kind of intelligence."[155] Isaacs told Teddy that his basic criticism of the piece was its failure to relate the Kuomintang mechanism to the social structure of the country.[156] Teddy brought no social attitude toward the social problems he discussed. "I think the article pretty accurately measures White, however," Isaacs wrote Viola. "Ready to turn up a fifth ace anytime rather than lose a hand." He asked Teddy to take a red pencil and underline all the passages he did not believe. "He looked at me peculiarly: 'That's a funny request,' he said, 'I believe everything in the article, only of course not all the truth is there.' "[157]

In most ways, it seems, Harold Isaacs was well equipped to tell the China story as it was. He should have provided a useful counterfoil to Teddy White. It would have been to the advantage of American readers if he had. The two big stories yet to come out of China in 1944 were the stories of the so-called Stilwell crisis, and the near-miss in Yenan, when the United States lost its best chance to establish a relationship with the Communists. In both instances, Harold Isaacs's contribution could have been of great value; in each instance, alas, he was thwarted by circumstances beyond his control.

The story itself is well known: Chennault may have wounded the Japanese, but he fell far short of achieving what he had claimed he could do. Roosevelt was no longer enthusiastic about him. Meanwhile, the Japanese were eating up southeast China on their way toward the southwest. Chiang Kai-shek was under increasing threat from the Japanese. Roosevelt was tired of being nagged for money—a billion dollars—and aircraft. Stilwell, meanwhile, urged Chiang to send troops from Yunnan to the west bank of the Salween River in Burma to hold the line there against the Japanese. Chiang opposed this, he was determined to save his troops so that he could use them to fight the Reds once the United States defeated Japan. He kept threatening to make a separate peace with Japan, but this was just a scare tactic. Marshall forced him to put his Yunnan troops into action by threatening to withhold Lend-Lease money.

Through T. V. Soong, Chiang persuaded Vice President Henry Wallace, who came through Chungking in the spring of 1944, to ask Roosevelt to send him a "personal representative" to help him handle political and military matters. On the advice of Joseph Alsop, Wallace also recommended that Stilwell be recalled. The War Department shot this down. General Marshall was discouraged by the desperately poor performance of Chiang's troops but was still counting on defeating the Japanese from mainland China. He and the Joint Chiefs of Staff urged Roosevelt to demand that Stilwell be placed in command of all Chinese forces. On July 6, the president radioed Chiang, asking him to place Stilwell in command of all forces, Chinese and American, including the Communists. Chiang replied that he would do this, but stalled for time. President Roosevelt decided to send a personal representative.

For this job, General Marshall and Secretary of War Henry Stimson recommended Major General Patrick Hurley, a self-made millionaire from Oklahoma, who had been the floor manager for Herbert Hoover at the 1928 Republican Convention in Kansas City. Hoover had rewarded Hurley for his efforts by appointing him Secretary of War, at a time when war was far from anybody's mind. In that capacity, on Hoover's instructions, he had ordered Douglas MacArthur to disperse the Bonus Marchers in the summer of 1932 in Washington, D.C. Although he was a Republican, Hurley subsequently smoothed the way in Congress for bipartisan war legislation that Roosevelt had initiated. He had also won recognition as a negotiater in 1932 with the Mexican government, after it appropriated some U.S. oil companies. Hurley managed to secure a hefty settlement for those oil companies. "The former Oklahoma cowboy who struck it rich," Dean Acheson called him.[158] To Joseph Alsop, he was a "curious figure," whose white mustachios and upright carriage gave him "something of the appearance of a nineteenth-century riverboat gambler."[159] Hurley was dispatched, along with Donald Nelson, the recently deposed head of the War Production Board, whom Roosevelt wanted to get out of his hair. (Roosevelt was a master at rendering scarce people who had begun to bother him, and sending them to China was one of his favorite methods.) Hurley was supposed to negotiate with Chiang to bring about Stilwell's total command of Chinese troops. Stilwell gave Hurley a prospectus of the changes that he wanted to enforce. These changes were unacceptable to Chiang. They would have been unenforceable, and they would have brought about Chiang's downfall.

Chiang rejected Stilwell's changes on September 12, 1944. Stilwell went down to Kweilin with Chennault right after, to supervise the destruction of the U.S. air base there before it fell to the advancing Japanese. He came back to find that Chiang, panicked by the Japanese thrust, wanted to withdraw troops from the Salween front. This undoubtedly perturbed Stilwell enough to back-channel a complaint to Marshall, who was at the Octagon Conference in Quebec with President Roosevelt when, on the sixteenth, he received Stilwell's message urging a quick decision by Chiang on his overall command. Did he also include the draft of a note for Roosevelt to sign, addressed to Chiang in very stark language? Joseph Alsop believed he had, and told me so.[160] Roosevelt immediately ordered Chiang to keep his forces in play in Burma and to "place Stilwell in unrestricted command of all your forces."[161] Stilwell, as the senior U.S. military officer in Chungking, was required to present the radio message to Chiang himself.

However, he should not have interrupted Chiang during a meeting he was holding with Hurley and T. V. Soong and his top officers in order to hand it personally to him. If Alsop is correct in his assumption, Stilwell began to read the radiogram out loud to Chiang. Such behavior would have caused Chiang to suffer an intolerable loss of face, as Stilwell, an old China Hand, surely realized.[162] In any case, he'd appended a Chinese translation of the message to the English text. The message was "hot as a firecracker" as Stilwell himself put it. Clearly, Stilwell's feelings of resentment toward Chiang were out of control. "The harpoon hit the little bugger right in the solar plexus and went right through him," he wrote afterward in his command journal. "It was a clean hit, but beyond turning green and losing the power of speech, he did not bat an eye. He just said to me, 'I understand' and sat in silence jiggling one foot."[163] Stilwell's message was not crafted to assuage Chiang. It was also gratuitous, since it made no new demands. Mainly, it heaped blame on Chiang. Alsop claims that when at last Chiang was alone with Soong—after the departure of Hurley and the scheming subordinates—he burst into tears. This is not hard to imagine: Chiang was known to lose himself in tantrums, throw teacups around and even chew the rug when properly enraged.

Chiang proceeded to "knock the persimmons off the tree," to borrow Patrick Hurley's expression.[164] On September 24, he handed Hurley an aide memoir demanding Stilwell's recall. This document, strange as it may seem, was drafted by none other than Joseph Alsop, who was pressed into service by T. V. Soong. Hurley found the language of the aide memoir (a rewrite of Chiang's own version) too harsh and Chiang Kai-shek agreed to tone it down. Hurley sent it off to Roosevelt on September 25. The president, faced with a demand by the Chinese head of state, had no choice. He had to acquiesce. He wanted to replace

Stilwell in China but keep him in Burma, to split the CBI command, but Chiang Kai-shek would have none of it. Roosevelt then decided to recall Stilwell and to replace him in China with General Albert C. Wedemeyer, whom Alsop described as a hater of Communism and whom he claims he recommended as a replacement.[165]

"It was a hot and sultry autumn in Chungking," Teddy later recalled, "itchy and wet; rumors flourished, begat and multiplied as they can do only in a community with no open communications system, where anxieties and heat incubate rumor to fever. Yet . . . out of all the blur of rumors, I could begin to range in on some very large shapes that were indisputably real: We Americans would be forced to a choice. The choice was being forced on us by the Japanese. They meant to wipe out our continental base on the mainland, and we were apparently compelled to choose between Chinese Communists and Chinese Nationalists to hold that continental base."[166]

It was all but impossible to get information about what was actually going on in Chungking. That was problem number one that reporters had to cope with. It might have been better to be a novelist in Chungking than a reporter. "The truth lies in tiny disembodied bits of fluff hanging across this or that luncheon table or around an open bottle of Chungking vodka, over an empty flat table and under short, uncomfortable chairs in somebody's Chinese living room," Harold Isaacs wrote, "around a steaming pot of noodles in a dirty restaurant on Chung Shan Lu, in crinkled brows or passing smiles of mutual understanding, in quiet talk with this one or that one—Full bodied it exists only outside where you go and see it and touch it and smell it. And even there you have to put it together to recognize it. And there are all kinds, this man's truth and that man's truth—sliced up and reassembled they make the third man's truth and so on. Nobody ever knows for sure."[167]

Problem number two was that once reporters obtained information it was impossible to do anything with it. Teddy, however, gradually began to understand from unofficial contacts in the U.S. Army headquarters that Stilwell had reason to believe that he would soon be commander-in-chief of the Nationalist Chinese army, personally in command of thirty Chinese divisions, with absolute control over the Lend-Lease aid to China, which he planned to share with the Communists, whom he intended to incorporate within his new Chinese army. That Teddy only came to know *this* much about what was happening, and only at the end of September, is an indicator of just how battened-down the hatches were in Chungking. Only when the chips had fallen did he discover what few others knew. Teddy found out what had happened because in his bitterness and tight fury General Stilwell summoned Teddy and Brooks Atkinson to his headquarters above the Chialing to tell them what had happened. This was in itself an act of insubordination, a breach of discipline, for Stilwell was pledged to an oath of military secrecy. He went even further, however. He gave Teddy and Atkinson open access for the four days leading up to his departure on the twenty-third of October to the "eyes alone" cable traffic his office received from Washington. He wanted them to tell the story, when it was all over, "the way it really was."[168]

He informed the reporters that he was going to be relieved of command within the next few days. That was how they got the story. Nobody else got the story besides Teddy and Brooks Atkinson until after Stilwell had flown out of China accompanied by Atkinson, who broke the story, and "irrepressible" Darrell Berrigan, as Edgar Snow called the UP reporter who had seen the worst of the Burma fiasco as Jack Belden's companion.[169] Atkinson took Teddy's story with him, an important piece of history-in-the-making, which would have done great credit to Teddy and *Time* had it ever seen the light of day. It was a story in which Stilwell emerged as a hero and, of course, *Time* could not accept Teddy's version, which cast Chiang Kai-shek in the light of the corruption, decay and tyranny that were swiftly undercutting his regime. Instead, as Teddy later wrote, "Luce had my full report of the Stilwell Crisis in hand when he let the story be edited into a lie, an entirely dishonorable story."[170] The editor was Whittaker Chambers. The message that he twisted into the story was that America *must* support Chiang, or lose China to Russia. Later, Teddy reflected, "The story had the tone of apocalypse and, as usual with apocalyptical stories, had the forces and the future all wrong."[171]

Harold Isaacs's dispatch on the Stilwell crisis was not subjected to the grotesque revisions that Teddy's story suffered at the hands of the perfervid Chambers, but it did not fare much better. Isaacs was not among the elect few who were close to Stilwell, although he had interviewed him, traveled with him and liked him. "Seemed to me a pretty tired and discouraged man," Isaacs wrote in his notes on September 9, after an off-the-record press conference with Stilwell.[172] The next day, in a letter to Viola, he noted, "He has a mild manner, his voice not at all as leathery as he looks. His fourth star makes him a dignitary but I don't think he feels much like one (. . . He's an unmincer of words. The thoughtful military man is in a tight squeeze out here)."[173]

Isaacs knew little about the Stilwell crisis until Stilwell was on his way back to Washington. Isaacs then proceeded to put the story together with the help of his contacts in the U.S. embassy and the U.S. Army. The chief frustration for Isaacs was the news blackout on the story imposed from Washington. Even after Stilwell was in Washington and the news of his recall was released, no news directive came through from the War Department to Chungking for another six or eight hours. When the directive of what news could be released about Stilwell's recall arrived from Washington, Isaacs's copy was butchered by the U.S. military censor, Upshur Evans, because the directive stipulated that only the terms of the announcement could be filed. When he took what was left of his story to Hollington Tong, his old employer on the *China Press* back in 1931, Tong announced, "It's out of my hands. It must go to a higher authority."[174] Which meant that it had to be translated into Chinese, sent across town and checked over by the "higher authority." When it finally went out, his story had been cut from 1,660 to 300 words. "Screwed, blewed and tattooed," as Isaacs put it.[175] Ultimately, what Isaacs called the War Department's "unscrupulous cover-up political censorship"[176] made no sense whatever, since the *Times* had gone ahead and published Atkinson's story on October 31. Atkinson gave the Stilwell crisis the full treatment. He was scathing about the U.S. decision to recall Stilwell. Icily, he wrote, "Relieving General Stilwell and appointing a successor has the effect of making us acquiesce in an unenlightened cold-hearted autocratic political regime."[177]

The decision to recall Stilwell had profound implications for the war effort. Atkinson took note of this. He pointed out that Stilwell's recall was a signal that the United States had decided to discount China's part in a counteroffensive. China was no longer of strategic importance in the war against Japan. In the week of October 23, 1944, combined United States air and naval forces effectively put the Japanese navy and air force out of business at the Battle of Leyte Gulf, in the Philippines. Now, the war against Japan could be waged from the Pacific. "The battle of Leyte Gulf was perhaps the greatest naval victory ever," Teddy told me in a conversation we had in 1982. "It happened the week of the Stilwell crisis, which meant they could put China on the back burner and leave her there forever."[178]

Isaacs was furious about his treatment at the hands of the censors: U.S. and Chinese. However, the truly unkind blow had already been delivered by the Ministry of Information when he was refused a *huchao*, or permit, to visit Yenan. By October, every other important journalist in Chungking had visited the Promised Land, as Isaacs called it, except for Isaacs and Teddy White. On October 15 Chiang Kai-shek put a ban on any further visits to Yenan by journalists. Nevertheless, Teddy White was granted a *huchao* because he had applied for it months earlier, before the ban was announced. Isaacs had not gotten in under the wire. A visit to Yenan by Isaacs would have compensated for much of what had happened, including the editorial castration he received at the hands of *Newsweek*. Even if he had not been able to write the experience up to his satisfaction for the newsweekly, it would have provided valuable material for his subsequent book, *No Peace for Asia,* which was based on his wartime investigations and postwar travels in Asia. In addition, Isaacs's impressions of Yenan would have proved useful in the light of his experiences in Shanghai in the early 1930s and his extensive knowledge of the Chinese Communist Party. Here was one foreign correspondent with the kind of background that could have proved invaluable, not only to his readership but to people in the Foreign Service in Chungking and members of the U.S. Observers Team already in Yenan. The so-called Dixie Mission had been in residence up there since August, appraising the Chinese Communists, and deliberating the strategy of supplying them with weapons in order to bring them into the Allied war effort against the Japanese in China. Alas, despite appeals to Ambassador Clarence Gauss and Hollington Tong, Isaacs had no luck. In the course of trying to obtain a *huchao,* however, Isaacs had a couple of revealing encounters.

The strangest encounter Isaacs had over the *huchao* was with Major General Patrick Hurley, who had remained in Chungking to broker a coalition agreement between the Communists and Chiang Kai-shek. Hurley has been described by those who knew him at the time as someone with misguided confidence in his own gifts as a personal mediator. China was way over his head. Furthermore, China was a nation and, indeed, a civilization, about which the president's special envoy was only superficially informed. By the time of Stilwell's recall, Hurley had already shown a tendency to cave in to whichever party at the moment he happened to be negotiating with. Worse was yet to come. On October 24, when Isaacs went to see him in his quest for a *huchao* to visit Yenan, he was only in the early stages of the bewilderment and paranoia that would seriously beset him later. "Called him this morning," Isaacs wrote Viola, "he sent his car over, and I started promptly to give him the situation."[179] Isaacs then proceeded to give Viola a report on what happened next. "Utterly without warning he pounced on me," Isaacs wrote, "deliberately twisted everything I tried to explain to him, accused me of asking for a special personal favor, flew into a temper— made one ugly accusation which made me leap to my feet in chest-tight anger—got us into some heavy exchanges (Hurley: 'I'm an old Oklahoma mule driver and I'm not taking any shit.' Isaacs: 'General Hurley, don't make the mistake of thinking I'm a mule.'). It was like a session with the mad hatter. Nothing made any sense whatever. I might have been talking in Urdu for all he seemed to understand. I patiently tried explaining and reexplaining. He just as consistently misunderstood. The man is engaged in negotiations about which he apparently has an out-of-the-world conception. He is either a senile idiot or just senile or just an idiot. Or possibly one of those creatures whose mind does not begin to function before 9 a.m. There were some fantastic bits of business (Hurley: 'You come in here and ask me to get embroiled with the Generalissimo for you and then when I won't do it you'll go back and write shitty things about me, I know you fellows.' Isaacs: 'General Hurley, I don't know anybody I'm less interested in writing anything about. I think this matter is of interest to your negotiations. If you don't think so, then that's that.' Hurley: 'It isn't so at all. It's not the press that's banned. It's you and you want me to go to bat for you on it.' Isaacs: (—all over again—'the facts are these general . . .'). I left wondering if it all could really have happened the way it did happen. Had seen Hurley before, in fact had no reason to expect this outburst. I had acquired no high opinion of the man's intelligence and had seen ample signs of age—but none of senility. The level on which high policy is made . . . when you get a look at some of the people making it . . . fully expresses the quality of those policies. I don't know why I should feel flabbergasted. Surely I have no right to be surprised at anything anymore."[180]

Isaacs had none of Teddy's good luck in Chungking, and was forced to spend too much time fumbling with authorities. His Stilwell story, as published, was a great disappointment to Isaacs, who had finally circumvented the censors by flying over the Hump and sending the full, uncensored dispatch out from India—much to the anger of the MOI. He complained in a letter to his editor, Chet Shaw, that all but the cold facts of the story had been removed, all of the background material that put the firing of Stilwell in context, so that, as Isaacs put it, the story lost all its *significance*. Worse yet, the editors inserted in his story an alleged quote by Stilwell calling Chiang Kai-shek "an ornery little bastard."[181] Isaacs had neither seen nor heard the quote, he'd never filed it, but had to take the brunt of Hollington Tong's fury, and that of other Chinese officials who saw the story and appealed to Stilwell's successor, General Albert Wedemeyer, to cancel Isaacs's accreditation. Wedemeyer replied that "he believed in freedom of the press and would take no action against any correspondent that would abridge that freedom."[182]

It was this kind of development that prevented Isaacs from playing a more useful role as sage. He probably understood the Reds better than the Foreign Service officers, who had been charmed by them in Yenan and tended to credit them with more idealism than they possessed. He visited Chou En-lai at Communist headquarters in February. "Chou is a stocky man," he wrote, "with a strong featured face and soft, jet black hair—he faintly reminds me, in looks alone, of Lo Hsun,★ without the little webs of wisdom around his eyes and mouth. He talks English somewhat haltingly but always with great vigor. Impatient with quiet conversation he springs up from his chair and stalks up and down and if he stops balances himself on his soles and toes."[183] He could see through Chou En-lai, and the game the Communists were playing. The Communists wanted to "push" Chiang Kai-shek into "democracy," he wrote Viola on the tenth of February, 1945, after this Kremlin-style session with Chou En-lai at his headquarters between midnight and 2 A.M. "They want to hang onto the chance of American friendliness. They want to tack and maneuver. They want to play 'realistic' politics. They breathe 'democratic' virtue against the one-party evils of the CKS [Chiang Kai-shek] dictatorship—they are for, I believe, a coalition with everything to the right of them extending out to CKS—but they would be ruthless, I'm certain, if there was anything to the left of them. But," Isaacs continued, "they do have great virtues as compared to the KMT —the kind of virtues that make them so readily acceptable to 'liberal' Americans who, unfortunately, do not make American policy. I think some kind of power lies ahead for these people—but will be all bound up in the way the Kremlin decides to lay its hands on Asia and on the future of the U.S.–KMT tie-up. The interests of the people will fall down in the middle, as always."[184]

Isaacs summed up his impressions of the Communists this way: "These are people who have totally and completely abandoned any principled political base. They maneuver like diplomats and military intelligence agents. They play with the notion of 'democracy' and 'people's power' just as unscrupulously as the KMT or Stalin does. They are also shrewd, bold, and smart and they exploit to the fullest their realization that mass support is a whip hand in anybody's political game. They are efficient. They are ruthless. They will play any card any time. They will play for and with anybody if it will serve their ends. They are much to be counted on. They are much to be feared."[185]

Teddy was there in Yenan when Patrick Hurley suddenly appeared out of the sky with no advance warning. It was one of the most spectacular uninvited arrivals in the history of international relations. All the important Chinese Communist leaders barreled over to the airfield post-haste in order to be there when they got word that a plane bearing Roosevelt's personal representative had landed after making the usual

★ Isaacs's friend Lu Hsun, the great twentieth-century Chinese writer who died on October 19, 1936.

double pass up the valley and back to approach the landing field. Hurley had come to Yenan bringing an agreement okayed by Chiang Kai-shek that he was confident Mao Tse-tung would sign.

Hurley had composed the document himself. It was a three-point agreement, which would unify the armies of China, grant supremacy to Chiang Kai-shek and legalize the Communist Party. Hurley had also rewritten the Three People's Principles of Sun Yat-sen so that they now read something like Lincoln's prescription for democracy in the Gettysburg Address. Hurley's unexpected arrival in the Red stronghold was supposed to be a dramatic, bold gesture. In this purpose he succeeded. He stood in the doorway of his plane before the assembled leaders of the Chinese Communist movement, resplendent in his uniform, bedecked with ribbons, white hair glistening in the sharp sunlight, the very model of a modern major general, six feet three inches tall, white regimental mustache included, and let out a Chocktaw war whoop. The weird, high-pitched screech echoed in the surrounding canyons in the silence that followed.

Teddy witnessed this spectacle, and played a part in what followed. What followed was a climax, a different kind of climax than what it was believed to be at the time, but nevertheless one of immense importance to the history of the twentieth century. Hurley had never in his life met Mao Tse-tung until his impetuous flight landed him on Communist soil. Yet he was without any doubt that he would be able to charm Mao into signing an agreement that handed control of his troops and territory to Chiang Kai-shek. John Paton Davies, the Foreign Service officer who had been on temporary assignment to Stilwell, and whose brainchild the Dixie Mission was, happened also to be on hand for Hurley's surprise visit. Davies let Hurley know on the afternoon of his arrival what he thought were Hurley's chances of pulling off single-handedly an agreement with Mao based on Davies's calculations. Hurley did not appreciate Davies's implication that this effort was doomed to fail, and told him he thought Davies should return to Chungking the next day on the plane that had flown Hurley up to Yenan.[186]

Hurley reserved his greater wrath for Teddy White, however. Eager to please, Teddy had taken it upon himself to inform Hurley that Mao had confided to him that he would never sign an agreement with Chiang Kai-shek. Hurley put this on record. "Theodore White, correspondent of *Time* and *Life* told me that he had just talked to Chairman Mao and Mao had told him that there was not any possible chance of an agreement between him and Chiang Kai-shek. White told me reasons why Mao should not agree with the National Government. White's whole conversation was definitely against the mission with which I am charged."[187] Hurley was furious with Teddy, but not as angry as Mao was when Hurley told him that Teddy had passed on what Mao had told him, presumably off the record. Or assumably so, as Davies might have put it. This anger was relayed to Teddy by Huang Hua, Mao's spokesman. It finished Teddy with the Communists.

Mao wanted to do business with the United States. He lectured Hurley at some length on the long-standing antagonism between the Reds and the Nationalists. Hurley was somewhat chastened. He invited Mao to rewrite his proposal, and so Mao did. He came up with amendments that called for a coalition government, a united high command, which would include the Communists, and for Lend-Lease equipment to be distributed to the Communists. Hurley not only agreed with these changes, he even added a few of his own, including a proposal for freedom of speech and, with a Rooseveltian flourish, freedom from fear and freedom from want. It was now a five-point proposal, which Mao and Hurley both signed in duplicate, one for Mao to keep and one for Hurley to take back on the tenth of November and present to Chiang for his signature. Mao was jubilant. He placed great faith, evidently, in the personal representative of the president of the United States.

Altogether, Hurley spent three days in Yenan, and then flew back to Chungking. Teddy and Chou En-lai both returned with Hurley to Chungking. Teddy was pretty much persona non grata in Yenan. Chou En-lai, who was returning with Hurley in the event that Chiang signed the five-point proposal, barely spoke to Teddy en route. In Chungking, Teddy filed a euphoric story about the unity at last achieved, which proved to be wishful thinking when T. V. Soong, China's new foreign minister, took one look at the revised proposal. "The Communists have sold you a bill of goods. Never will the National Government grant the Communist request," he told Hurley.[188]

This was the beginning of the end for all manner of things: it was the beginning of the end of any true hope that the United States could ever detach itself from Chiang Kai-shek and make a rapprochement with the Communists; it was the beginning of the end of the State Department careers of the China Hands who had dared to suggest such a rapprochement; it was the beginning of the end of General Hurley's sanity. Hurley lapsed into futile rage, which he directed primarily at those whom T. V. Soong, hissing into his ear, told him had sabotaged his efforts. John Paton Davies was the chief culprit. Once, six months after their return from Yenan, and after he'd been appointed ambassador to China, Hurley turned on Teddy White. He called him "You goddam seditious little son of a bitch."[189] Senility had long since set in, as Isaacs had noted.

By now, Annalee Jacoby had joined Teddy in Chungking as a correspondent for Time, Inc. Soon after she arrived, Annalee agreed to play hostess at a banquet Hurley gave for top Chinese brass and members of the government during the Stilwell negotiations. Annalee stood beside Hurley and identified Chinese dignitaries for him as they came through the door. All went well for a time. T. V. Soong was present and sat on Annalee's right. After dinner, however, Hurley stood up and toasted Annalee, whom he called "my tall, blonde goddess of a bride." This might have deceived some of those present, except that Annalee was a brunette, at five feet three inches petite even by Chinese standards. Hurley proceeded to ramble on about the children they'd brought up and their long married life. He even rhapsodized about their wedding night. "Afterwards everyone filtered out in an embarrassed way," Annalee later recalled, "and because of this lapse into premature senility in full view of most of the Chinese government, I think a lot of rather fearful things happened."[190]

The beginning of the end of Teddy's relationship with Henry Luce was also at hand. It came with Teddy's return to Chungking from Yenan, when he read an official Japanese news service summary of his Stilwell scoop and discovered to his horror that Whittaker Chambers had rewritten, and distorted, his account. Although he threatened to resign, Luce persuaded Teddy to stay on as his China correspondent, but then tried to restrict him to writing "good-fashioned Time news," as he put it.[191] As an example of the kind of reporting he wanted Teddy to do, Luce sent him an excerpt from a London bureau cable on England's two-thousandth day of war: ". . . yellow crocuses bloomed, daffodils sold for dollar and half per bunch, Commons passing bill making rear lights compulsory on bicycles."[192] Henry Luce was now deeply engaged in his holy war against Communism. He no longer wanted the China story as it appeared to the pro-Mao and anti-Chiang Teddy; he wanted to write it in New York as he knew God would have written it, whether or not that was how it was happening. Teddy let Annalee Jacoby cover Chungking for him. He would have enjoyed staying on in the Press Hostel just to be in the room next to hers, because he was still in love with her, but that wasn't working out either. Perhaps in a compound wherein the garden was enshrined to Annalee's late husband, Teddy should not have expected too much of Annalee. Somehow, he had not succeeded in replacing Mel in her affections as he had dreamed of doing. He went off to cover the Pacific war.

The Communists refused to believe that Hurley's policy was the same as the policy of the U.S. government. By the time Chou En-lai held his Kremlin-style interview with Harold Isaacs in February 1945, Chiang Kai-shek had taken Hurley hostage to his position. Chou En-lai asked Isaacs if the "Hurley policy" would persist—"i.e. playing the game for CKS," Isaacs wrote. "I said there was no such thing as a Hurley policy. There was only a Washington policy, a White House policy. He didn't want to accept that," Isaacs wrote. "When I said that Washington was committed to sustaining CKS even at the expense of American military policy in China and would see it thru that way, he stopped his pacing and stared at me.

" 'Then in that case we would have to count on the United States helping the KMT to beat us.'

" 'I think so,' I said.

"He threw up his arms. That was ridiculous. 'Then we couldn't do anything. We couldn't get anywhere,' he exclaimed.

" 'Not if you're making it depend on US friendliness,' I said.

" 'That's impossible!' he cried. 'Why the only way we can get ahead is to hold hands together and go forward together as far as we can. Of course, as you say, we must depend on our own strength which is the strength of the people, but you've got to be realistic too.' "[193]

Mao Tse-tung and Chou En-lai made one more serious attempt to negotiate with Chiang Kai-shek in the immediate aftermath of the war before they took up arms against the Nationalists. When Hurley personally brought Mao by plane from Yenan to Chungking in August 1945, there was some hope that a power-sharing arrangement could be worked out and civil war averted.[194] Mao was willing to split the spoils of victory with Chiang. He was willing to let Chiang have the Yangtze Valley, and everything south of it; but he insisted on taking north China, including the Yellow River basin, for himself. Chiang wouldn't hear of it. He continued to hold fast for a unified China under his overall command in which the Communists would be welcome to play a part. Chiang had the victorious all-powerful American army behind him, ready to ferry his troops to north China to occupy territory surrendered by the Japanese. This agreement by the United States to use its resources on behalf of Chiang Kai-shek was all but a fait accompli, a feat of the Washington China lobby, which had put money and influence into it.

Teddy was back in Chungking after the exhilarating experience of watching the Japanese surrender to the Americans on board the USS *Missouri*. In the mounting confusion of postwar Chungking, he was aware that forces beyond anyone's control were shaping the destiny of China. Chiang's stand, with the United States behind him, meant that the door was closed for Mao. He could expect no support for his movement from an America that had opted to join forces with his enemy. Teddy, along with others in the U.S. press corps, was dismayed by this turn of events. The journalists, who had tried to report China as they saw it, began to find themselves on the side of the bad guys from the point of those who now exercised the real power in China, the U.S. military. "They aren't there, those Communist guerillas you say are there," a brigadier general shouted at Teddy after a briefing. "They're a fiction of the American press. They haven't got the guns and manpower to keep those railways closed. Their only strength is what the American newspapermen tell Americans about them. Guys like you and Edgar Snow, who talk about the Communist guerillas and their areas —you guys are what makes their strength. They aren't there, I tell you; they exist only on paper."[195]

Teddy knew they were there, and so did Henry Luce, who ran a cover story on Chiang Kai-shek written entirely by Whittaker Chambers, who completely ignored the copy filed by Annalee Jacoby from Chungking. "I think we're finished. I think it's hopeless," Annalee wrote Teddy in September. She had heard about the Chiang cover story, although she hadn't seen it, and from what she'd heard, she knew it stank badly of Luce's prejudice, as served up by Chambers. "[Luce] won't listen open-mindedly to anything, and I want to quit soon with a bang." She urged Teddy to quit, too, writing, "they're so deep in this insane Russo-phobia that no logic is possible, no fact will be believed, your honesty won't be trusted."[196]

Teddy won the prize. He had to share it, in the end, with Annalee Jacoby, but that was all fair and good, because she'd helped him win it. Together they wrote the book that broke the whole story of Chiang Kai-shek's corrupt wartime regime. "He asked me to help him because I knew things he didn't," Annalee told me years later.[197] They pulled it off by sitting down as soon as they got home in the fall of 1945—he in New York and she in Larchmont—and hammering out alternate chapters, which they mailed to each other for revision. This was a job loaded with hidden perils for both of them. Teddy, as a writer, was a product of the Luce school of reporting. He was used to filing long, fact-filled, unedited, profusely written off-the-top-of-the-head mailers, or, during the war, no-expense-spared radiograms, so that always, throughout his life, his writings had about them an unshorn quality. He presented facts in a language that just managed to avoid being hackneyed. It was his own prose. "He gushed purple prose," Annalee Jacoby, who took on the task of editing Teddy, recalled in years to come.[198] This wasn't much fun. When she did edit his prose, Teddy turned into Rumpelstiltskin. Also, he forgot to tell Annalee that he'd arranged with their publisher for his name alone to appear on the cover of the book. To be sure, this was arranged before Annalee became his co-author, but until she discovered it somewhere in the contract, Teddy had been prepared to cut her out of getting full credit. That didn't sit well with Annalee, and, at the last minute, it almost wrecked their collaboration.

To complicate matters, Teddy was too enamored with Annalee. He had fixated on her the day he met her in Melbourne, Australia, in the company of Mel Jacoby: love at first sight. He'd angled to bring her back to China for *Time* in order to conquer her affections, which turned out not to be available. Somehow, working on their book at fever pitch, they managed to surmount these problems, because Annalee kept her distance. When she didn't, trouble loomed, as my father remarked in a letter: "Teddy is working very hard on his book with Annalee Jacoby. He writes it and then she crosses it out, according to the impression I got from listening to them at it one afternoon."[199] Annalee later recalled: "We had knock-down drag-out fights. Teddy over-wrote. Words poured out of him like water out of Niagara Falls. There was too much rhetoric, too many purple passages. He made my writing better and I certainly made his better. He hated being cut. Every sentence was a jewel."[200]

The matter of sharing credit came up a week before they were due to submit the manuscript to their publisher. Teddy apologized to Annalee. A new contract, he assured her, would be drawn up. "Personally," he concluded, "I guess we've come to a dead end. I can't see any way out when the book is finished but just separating to make our separate lives. Even now as bitter as you may feel I want you to know my basic feeling is unchanged, still as it was in 1944 and 1945. Please let's not have bitterness to mar our memories after the book is published. The old Chinese saying was that the finest of feasts must come to an end. I'd like to remember the high spots, the successes and cooperation, rather than these melancholy twilight months now."[201]

Their book was finished in the spring of 1946. In 1941, Teddy had signed a contract with William Sloane, their publisher, before Sloane had his own imprint. At the time, Sloane was visiting Chungking and was a vice president at Henry Holt. After the war, Sloane left Holt to start his own publishing firm and because he wanted White's to be his first book he bought Teddy's contract from Holt. He was determined to ensure its success. Nobody doubted that it would be a good book. As far back as 1943, in the Press Hostel, Israel Epstein, a colleague of Teddy's, forecast that Teddy could contribute "the biggest and most reliable set of facts."[202] This proved to be prescient. Teddy and Annalee's book was also timely. Teddy wanted to write it at breakneck speed to change U.S. policy in China. This worked to their advantage, financially, because in 1946 the American public was still receptive to the China story, and therefore so was the book-marketing business.

Teddy's unrequited ardor for Annalee had one quick final chapter. Teddy had transferred his affections to a *Time* researcher by now, the graceful and charming Nancy Bean. Suddenly, at the time their book was published, Annalee experienced a change of heart, and told Teddy she wanted to marry him after all. "This shook the hell out of all three of us," Teddy wrote the Durdins. "I damned near went crazy. After 2 or 3 weeks of perpetual emotional crisis and after Nancy had made up her mind to get along without me—and I still hate myself for the pain and hurt I caused her—Annalee changed her mind once more and decided she didn't want to go through with it. I feel very small, very dirty, very ignoble, and quite lost about it all."[203]

It was all part of Teddy White's rough passage into selfhood. His love troubles, and his sudden, unwelcome transformation into a pundit, had made him sadder and wiser. The roughest part of the passage, however, was the break with Henry Luce. Teddy loved being Henry Luce's fair-haired boy in China. The part about going out to Greenwich to spend weekends in the company of people like Lord Beaverbrook and Vincent Sheean was not the only side of the relationship he valued; what he treasured was the closeness, the long philosophical correspondence, the "Dear Harry-Dear Teddy." He loved the intimacy with this larger-than-life man. He saw no ignominy in it at all. To his credit, he never ceased to appreciate Henry Luce's intelligence, and there is reason to believe that he never quite got over his affection for the man who had raised him to such precipitous heights.

There came a classic moment, however, when Teddy had to walk away from the relationship. This happened when he had finished his book and was all set to go back to work at *Time,* as Moscow correspondent. By then, Whittaker Chambers had been relieved of his post, and a veteran correspondent of the European war, Charles Wertenbaker, was the new foreign editor. Wertenbaker had already approached Teddy about the Moscow assignment, and Teddy wanted it. Wertenbaker then sent word to Teddy that Luce wasn't sure he wanted to send Teddy to Moscow.[204] Something was amiss. Full of filial pride, Teddy had sent Luce the manuscript of his book. He thought that Luce would feel correspondingly proud of him. Luce, however, felt cheated. He was jealous. "He felt that all too many of his bright young men had used *Time* as a personal mount, had galloped to fame on the magazine's back," Teddy wrote. "Young John Hersey, for one. He was breaking with Hersey; it was unclear from Luce's words whether he had fired Hersey or Hersey had quit. But Hersey had told Luce to his face that there was as much truthful reporting in *Pravda* as *Time Magazine*."[205] Luce was enraged with Hersey because he had gone out to China on assignment for *Life* in early 1946, and then had gone on to Japan, where he'd collected the material for *Hiroshima,* and sold that brilliant piece of writing to *The New Yorker,* which published the entire, short work in a single issue.[206] No, he wasn't happy about Hersey: Hersey was now famous, quite independently of *Time* or *Life.* Now here was Teddy, promising to do the same sort of thing with *his* book.

On June 26, Teddy sent Luce a dense, three-page memo, forcing him to make a decision on the Moscow assignment. The next day, Luce summoned him to his office on the thirty-third floor of the *Time* building in Rockefeller Center. There, they had a highly emotional session: work for the family firm, do things my way, or get out. Luce challenged Teddy to accept his role as a *Time* employee, a Luce underling first, a luminary second, if it came to that. Teddy maintained he was a foreign correspondent, not a desk man. Luce fired him, on July 13, the day that Teddy learned his book had been acquired by the Book-of-the-Month Club.

The president of the Book-of-the-Month Club did the authors a further service when he suggested a new title, *Thunder Out of China,* under which it rode to glory.

Alive
in Our Hearts

I KNEW NOTHING about Barbara Stephens until I was older, and then, what I was told hardly amounted to very much. My father never mentioned anything about her, ever. China, to him, was a closed book. He revealed almost nothing to any of us about his private life there and he said little about his family to people he knew in China. My mother told me about Barbara Stephens, and what she knew, she had learned from Graham Peck when we lived in Cambridge, Massachusetts, during the worst year of my parents' troubled marriage. "I don't know why he behaves this way toward you," Graham told my mother the night they went out together to hear Lena Horne. "Barbara was very much like you. Same kind of person: wore loafers and yellow Brooks Brothers sweaters."[1] According to my mother, my father had been madly in love with Barbara Stephens in China, and then she had mysteriously disappeared. That's how I heard it.

My father's life in China was an enormous gray mystery. In the years that preceded Nixon's visit there in 1972, China was beyond reach. Yet because our father went there in 1943, and stayed there until 1948, and made his name in China as a foreign correspondent for the *New York Herald Tribune* and *The New Yorker,* the great gray impenetrable realm, from which he reappeared briefly in 1946, loomed as an unspeakable presence in our southern California encampment, where we seemed to live in a state of suspension, awaiting word of his return. When he came back in 1948, he brought us presents: intricately carved red clay boxes with black lacquer inside, Chinese and Tibetan rugs of thick nap and rich design, rubbings, a small white, ivory bear that fitted snugly in the palm of my hand. Treasures from the East! So the scent of China entered our lives as a sort of mystical reprieve, and lingered, long after he once again disappeared back into the Orient, where he remained, with occasional return visits, until 1954. Our mother went to visit him in China, in 1947. This undertaking lasted six weeks, and I knew very little about it at the time, since I was then five. I suppose because my father had gone there, and in so doing had put the well-being of our family in jeopardy, that China assumed for me the dimensions of a serious, but necessary emergency. In that sense, China was an extension of my father. He was invoked by my mother at times when his absent authority was called for, and somehow this led to my assumption that China was a symbol of his importance.

It was necessary for him to be in China. That was my understanding. He'd gone there during the war with the Office of War Information, and he had remained there, I assumed, because China was immensely important. The idea was that Dad would eventually return and that when he did life would return to normal. The war would really be over at that time. Meanwhile, we waited, and nothing else was of commensurate importance, including our mother's dinner dates with other men. The fiction was interred only when, in the early 1950s, our parents divorced, and our mother remarried. Life got a fresh coat of paint. The emergency was over.

By then, China was in my father's past. He had stayed on in Asia to pursue his career as a foreign correspondent for *The New Yorker*. Although China faded as a source of urgent anxiety, and our attentions were now fully occupied elsewhere, China remained off-limits. The China of wartime chaos and treasure and dimly heard festivities assumed a darker hue in my imagination. When I was in my twenties, traveling in Mexico with my father just before he took his life, I spoke with him at some length, on the drive from Oaxaca to Mexico City, about China. For some reason he tried to tell me about Nelson and Hurley, those two wartime emissaries of President Roosevelt to Chungking. I recall very little of this tangled discourse, except that Dad described Donald Nelson as a "butter-and-egg man."[2] I never quite understood exactly what this expression meant, but my father's use of language was very effective, and I certainly caught the drift. Because I've never had occasion to try to use the expression myself, I'm still not quite sure what he meant. Donald Nelson wasn't very important to China, as it turned out, and while in the course of my own long immersion in matters concerning twentieth-century China I have learned much about Hurley, Nelson remains, for me, a "butter-and-egg man."

That very afternoon when we got back to Mexico City, Dad received word in the mail that Graham Peck had died. He turned to tell me from where he was standing with his back to the main entrance of the Hotel Genève, after quickly scanning the letter he held in his hands. "Graham died," he said. He never said another word to me again about Graham or, if my memory serves me correctly, about China. Two months later he jumped, or fell, to his death from his sixth-floor room at the Genève to the sidewalk below, much to the grief of a great many people, and the matter of China, blacker, more opaque than ever, was for a time out of reach.

Graham Peck was a great China Hand as I came to appreciate, and so was my other godfather, Preston Schoyer, whom Dad had met during the war in Fukien Province. For this reason, I have always felt that my father gave me a relationship to that part of himself that was connected to China, perhaps because he went there when I was a year old and never really came back. China was his special bequest to me, so to speak. I have also felt, however, that my father—my own existence quite to one side—was an agent of destiny in the lives of many people. He possessed some unusual psychic power, and this made him a force in the lives of all kinds of people. It also gave his China reporting a formidable prescience. He had ferocious mental acuity and never hesitated to express the force of his convictions. He had the looks of someone from another planet, a cosmos where brain power had a certain malevolent ascendancy over everything else, an impression that was accentuated by the size of his head and the construction of his forehead. He resembled William and Henry James, who were double cousins on his mother's side of the family. He had a big head and a round face, but otherwise was slight of build until he set out to develop his physical powers. Starting in his childhood my father liked to roam the countryside of his "aboriginal setting," as Henry James once called the countryside around Salisbury, Connecticut, where Dad's mother had put down stakes as a young woman. Later in Marin County, where he lived before the war, and then in China and in India, he walked for hours, even for days at a time, and built up his physique so that in later years, although he remained quite short, he acquired an impressive thickness, and you would never use the word slight to describe his appearance after he had been in the Far East. He was fair-haired, and possessed large, deep-set eyes of an astral blue that glowered under his large brow and ragged blond eyebrows. He had a jutting lower jaw that tended to emphasize the thickness of his lower lip. In times of mirth, his smile was a rictus of sheer ecstasy. He had what is called "presence."

He had an emphatic way of speaking. He could insist in an overbearing manner on how things should be done with a ruthless, and sometimes rueful, clarity. In time, he became a religious seeker, a practitioner in his Eastern years of Buddhism, who insisted on doing things in ways that seemed quite often eccentric. As a practicing Buddhist, for instance, he never wore leather, and carried suitcases made of wicker, and called for scrambled eggs when others were dining on roast beef, or some other meat dish. One correspondent who knew him during his Buddhist phase recalls that Dad often wore a necktie instead of a belt to hold up his trousers. At other times he used a piece of rope. He was vehemently loyal to his regimens. Keyes Beech, the veteran war correspondent, was present on the occasion during the Korean War, when

Dad refused to wear the life preserver, called a Mae West, required by the U.S. armed services on military flights from Japan to Korea because they had leather patches on them. According to Beech, the flight sergeant said to my father, "If you don't mind, Mr. Rand, will you just let it lie on your lap?" "I can't," my father replied. "I'm a Buddhist." "Well," said the flight sergeant, "I'll be a son of a bitch."[3] He threw Dad off the flight, so that he was forced to take the ferry from Fukagawa to Pusan, which was a matter of no small inconvenience. Dad could be violent in carrying out ritual, especially when intoxicated. In Greece, where it is the custom to smash glassware, he took immense pleasure hurling drinking glasses onto a terrace. Otherwise, however, the violence that was within him was severely withheld, expressed only in his eyes, or in the controlled fury of his emphasis.

Like Graham Peck, who was also a Yale man, my father was a drinker. You could drink to a certain madness in China and never seem odd. As misfits in Yankee Connecticut, my father and Graham were both suppressed in their respective ways and for their own respective reasons. Graham, as it happened, was gay. This never came out when he was in China, but being in China enabled him to express himself more openly in other ways, by getting drunk, for instance, and singing arias from Chinese opera. In China, where everything seemed delightfully irregular, Graham, like the other China Hand misfits of his own and earlier times, my father included, could escape the conventional confinements of his own country. In Kweilin, Graham lived above a whorehouse, which beautifully suited his sense of irony. He knew all the prostitutes by name and had probably slept with many of them, according to Teddy White, who, like many of Graham's China colleagues, refused to accept the reality that Graham was gay. Whether or not Graham was gay, or straight, was of slight concern to my father. He and Graham shared a strong misogynist streak, in any case. In Graham, this hostility toward the female of the species was expressed in various ways, usually with a wicked wit that my father and all Graham's male friends greatly enjoyed. He had a prodigious memory, which enabled him to file away a number of off-color stories and limericks. The contents of Graham's scatalogical file would suggest that he was horrified by the sexual side of women. In Cambridge, when Graham came to live with us while my father helped him finish *Two Kinds of Time,* my mother recalls that Graham and my father were like two naughty boys. "Graham was an imp," she recalls. Graham was the wit—"It was gay humor, you know"—and my father, as she put it, "lumbered along beside him, frightfully amused."[4]

My father stressed the masculine side of himself to the exclusion of anything that might be considered feminine. When drinking, he was capable of expressing great passion for women, but he had a very hard time relating naturally to women, and, indeed, throughout his life much of his anger was directed toward women. It was an anger he had trouble expressing, except obliquely, and it was frustrating, also, because on a deeper level he hungered for feminine companionship. But he never liked any woman to walk at his side on his long country jaunts, unless she could maintain his own brutal, nonstop pace and, in so doing, prove her worthiness as his equal. Most women, my mother included, walked behind him. In China, where he walked a great deal, Dad found that the Chinese had already invented a term for this person: she was a walk-behind woman.

His ability to accept people and situations of any kind—as long as they didn't directly interfere with his independence—was one of the qualities that made my father a great reporter, and a man who was often ahead of his times. But he yearned to express himself as an artist. His mother was an artist of renown, as were her Emmet cousins. Art was held in high esteem in the Rand household when he was growing up, by his mother and her family. It was not, however, held in very high esteem by his father, who placed a great emphasis on manliness, as might be expected of someone of his day and age, threatened as he was by his wife's independence of spirit. Masculine inhibitions concerning self-expression forced my father, I think, to deny himself the supreme pleasure of self-expression; it was the side of him that he allowed certain others, Graham, for one, and myself, for another, to exhibit in his stead. He made a connection between me and Graham, then he made my connection to Graham somehow a connection to him. Some of the things I liked, drawing, for instance, and painting and writing, were all things that Graham did professionally. Dad saw that connection, and after he made it, I think, I became as a child more acceptable to him than I had been at the outset (infants and small children he found to be an intolerable distraction, in general). It was prescient of him to make that connection with Graham, since at the time I was only four or five years old and, as it happened, I believe I shared a certain sensibility with Graham. Otherwise, successful artistic expression was associated in his mind with the women of his family. He feared the compromise it might make on the masculinity he prized in himself, and this fear eventually became a serious block to his periodic efforts to write fiction.

Graham went to China in 1935, after his graduation from Yale. He and my father were a year apart at Yale, but never met each other as undergraduates. Graham was a friend of John Hersey, who could recall visiting Graham's suite at Trumbull College sometimes in the morning to find him lying still fully clothed from the night before, sound asleep on the couch, with an open book facedown on his chest and a half-empty bottle of bourbon beside him on the floor. Graham was the son of a hairpin manufacturer in Derby, Connecticut, who "hated his father," as Pepper Martin once recalled.[5] And this was yet another characteristic he and my father had in common. Peck senior was a spry, wily, short bright-eyed man of whom Graham lived in terror. He called his father "sir," and always stood up when the old man came into a room. The elder Peck ran a Dickensian outfit, according to Israel Epstein, who visited Graham in Derby after the war. Peck senior's hairpin business had been almost destroyed by the advent of the bobby pin, Epstein recalled. On his tour of the hairpin factory, conducted by Graham's father, he and other visiting China Hands observed with interest the writing stands at which accountants were forced to do the bookkeeping and billing without the comfort of sitting down. Graham's father employed Polish immigrants at the factory and at home, and Epstein can recall how the Peck's Polish housekeeper used to shield Graham and his drinking habits from the old man by warning him whenever his father was on his way up the front walk. Needless to say, his Victorian father was fiercely at odds with Graham's witty, phlegmatic temperament. After he graduated from Yale, Graham won a trip around the world by boat in an artist's contest sponsored by Ivory Soap, and so secured for himself his ticket out of the Land of Steady Habits. This was how he came to be in China.

According to John Hersey, Graham earned money on his cruise ship by making crayon drawings of the passengers. As he circumnavigated the globe, Hersey later recalled, Graham continued to drink to his heart's content. "He wrote letters to me on his trip, and I could tell he was drinking," Hersey asserted, "because as it progressed his handwriting grew rounder and ever more expansive."[6] In Tientsin, Graham jumped ship. He wrote about this in his first book, *Through China's Wall,* which tells the story of his early sojourn in China. One photograph taken at the time, in Peiping, shows Graham as a smooth, plump, brown-skinned youth, dressed in white shorts, white knee socks, jacket and bow tie; his hair is soft and curly. His eyes, peering out of a soft face, are those of a wicked, precocious boy. Graham had a wit, fine and razor-sharp, that he applied to good use in his descriptive passages about his encounters throughout China with all kinds of people. It was peculiarly suited to capture the ephemeral subtleties of Chinese civilization. Graham learned Chinese and he learned by heart whole arias from Chinese opera, which he used to sing out loud when his inhibitions had been sufficiently loosened by distilled spirits. He never intended to stay as long as he did in China. He settled down in Peiping, lived luxuriously in a Manchu palace on practically nothing and enjoyed himself, although he soon came to realize that he had barely penetrated the real China, and set about turning himself from a tourist into a true traveler-explorer.

For a season, Graham lived in Peiping, then he traveled to Mongolia, lived for a summer in yurts with Mongolian tribesmen on the wide open grasslands, and after returning to Peiping made his way via Shanghai and the Yangtze Gorges to Szechuan, vaguely hoping to follow the route of the Long March. He got as far as the Tatu Gorges before he turned back. He managed to be in Peiping in July 1937, at the time of the Marco Polo Bridge Incident and the ensuing Japanese invasion, which he described in a characteristically original manner (some of which I quoted in an earlier section of this book).

Graham made most of his crayon portraits in the course of these first early China travels. He had enough to hold a large exhibition in Peiping in the summer of 1937.[7] These are studies of various Chinese, including Mongols, whom he encountered on his journeys. As an irreplaceable record of people in their remote setting at a time now altogether gone, they more than justify the Ivory Soap investment. Reproductions of these paintings accompanied the text of *Through China's Wall*, which Graham also illustrated with line drawings. The book was published to modest acclaim in 1940 by Houghton Mifflin. By then Graham, who had made a visit home to the States, had returned to China, this time by ocean liner across the Pacific. Teddy White recalled how impressed people were when Graham Peck came out into the Press Hostel garden waving a check from Houghton Mifflin. "He was a hero," Teddy later said. "None of the rest of us had ever heard of getting two thousand dollars for a book."[8] *Through China's Wall* has been recognized as one of the very few travel accounts of China that conveys something of the palpable essence of those days. Robert Payne, the author of more than a few highly regarded books on China himself, called it "one of the two best books about China." The other was Graham's second book, *Two Kinds of Time*.[9]

Graham met my father around this time, during his second China sojourn. By the time of their meeting, the war with Japan was in full swing. Graham had been living in a cave in Loyang—he'd driven there from Szechuan Province with Rewi Alley, who was busy in those days setting up his first China Industrial Cooperatives. When the Japanese bombed Pearl Harbor, Graham returned to Chungking and signed on with the Office of War Information. When Dad got to Chungking, in May, 1943, where he had been sent by the OWI, Graham was already living at Chialing House, the home of a number of colorful people, including the Dilowa Huktu, the Mongolian "Living Buddha," who was a friend of Graham's. "The Living Buddha sang cowboy songs from Mongolia," Emily Hahn, another early resident, later recalled, "and imitated the sounds that cows make when they are being milked."[10] In that steamy early summertime, when Chungking swarmed with visiting U.S. emissaries, Graham was one of the bright lights of Chungking. He and Dad struck up a fast friendship almost the moment my father flew into the wartime capital, in May 1943.

Dad cultivated a rugged exterior manner and physique, but he was a sensitive, introspective loner, "an odd fish," as Joseph Alsop once put it.[11] Although he had an unusual ability to form bonds with men and women of all sorts, he was particularly attracted to souls of similar sensibility to his own. Graham was a soul-mate. He and Dad were Dionysian in spirit, or at least in spirits. They fashioned their own variation of Yale-in-China, which was a singular departure from the earnest version, incorporated in 1902 as the Yale Foreign Missionary Society, downriver in Changsha. Graham taught my father a great deal about China in those early Chungking days. He also, I suspect, initiated Dad into a love for the Chinese. Although Dad had attended Groton and Yale, and had circulated in the not unsophisticated playrooms of rich San Francisco society, he still had not yet altogether shed the rural outlook of a Connecticut country bumpkin.[12] He fell in love with Chinese ceremony, which often combined an elaborate, witty and civilized ritual language with an earthiness that appealed to his sense of humor. He loved the subversive anarchy that lurked just below the civility of the Chinese temperament; it matched the wild impulses just below the puritanical manhole cover of his own character. Dad and Graham could revel in Chinese anarchy. It gave them both great pleasure, for example, to watch Chinese Nationalist soldiers marching out of step.

In the two years that followed Dad's arrival in Chungking, he and Graham became fast friends. Graham was based for a time in Kweilin, until it was abandoned to the Japanese, and Dad was more remotely situated in the mountains of Fukien Province, where he ran a listening post, but they managed to connect fairly often. Their experience in the OWI was exteremely important in the lives of these Yalies-in-China. Graham, given the task of running the OWI operation in Kweilin, evolved into an advocate of using propaganda for the unusual purpose of telling the truth about American war aims in China. To that effort he contributed a system of visual aids as a propaganda resource for use among illiterate Chinese. Toward the end of the war, when he was based in Chungking, he also wrote an analysis of Chinese press accounts of the first visit to Yenan made by Western and Chinese journalists under the auspices of the Chinese Ministry of Information. He lost his soft, boyish looks, and came to look slightly Chinese. He became something of a legend among Americans and Chinese in the wartime capital. He was, as it turned out, at his zenith. And my father had also found the atmosphere in which he could truly flourish. He found it in Yung-an, in a setting far from the war, where he set up his OWI listening post. There, behind enemy lines, where no Japanese soldier would ever set foot, he discovered the freedom to run things his way, and to live by his own rules. Appropriately, Yung-an means "Perpetual Peace." These circumstances matched almost perfectly the arcadia of his countryside boyhood.

Many coastal Chinese had fled to Yung-an, and my father was able to hire a Foochow chef, who prepared food that was considered the best of any U.S. outpost in that part of China. He ran his outfit at night. This involved interception of longwave Japanese radio messages from the coast, and the relay of intelligence to Chungking. He also oversaw a team of translators who turned out a Chinese version of U.S. propaganda for distribution to local Chinese newspapers situated throughout southwest China. He was a night owl by nature. " 'Early to rise, early to bed, makes a man poor, foolish and dead' is my preferred version of that particular adage," my father once wrote.[13] In Yung-an, he worked at night, and took naps during the day. He slept in a bedroll, fully clothed, the way the Chinese did, to stay warm. He roamed the local hills by himself, but he was not without companionship when he wanted it. He ate with Chinese friends in the local chop shops when he went to town and made use of the local bathhouse.

Dad managed to sustain this way of life uninterrupted for nearly two years, before the chaos of peace broke into his life. In several ways the OWI equipped him for his later work as a journalist in China. He took daily lessons in Chinese, learning it well enough to travel by himself in rural China and make himself understood. This was an acquisition of wartime service that later recommended him to the *New York Herald Tribune* as a China correspondent. He also gained experience of lasting value as the author of field reports for Military Intelligence that were considered of very high quality by the authorities for their grasp of the complexity of the political situation in southwest China. Military intelligence has to be detailed and exact. It required in this instance a sophisticated understanding of local society, provincial government, the Communist guerrilla movement, secret societies and bandit activities, not to mention Kuomintang politics, which were byzantine.

My father fell afoul of the Kuomintang in a big way in the late spring and summer of 1945, which was an aspect of his initiation as a China Hand. It effectively ended his Yung-an idyll when not long before the end of the war a Chinese reporter on his staff was arrested by agents of General Ku Chu-t'ung, commander of the Third War Zone, in which my father operated. Yang Chao, the reporter, and his assistant, Chow Pi, had been dispatched by my father to gather intelligence in a region well known to be under the control of the Reds. What my father very likely did not know was that Yang, although not a member of the Communist Party, may have handed over information to the Communist New Fourth Army about the Third War Zone at a time when civil war was breaking out in rashes all over China. On their return from Red guerrilla territory, Chow Pi was seized by the Nationalists. He immediately tipped them off to the activities of Yang. General Ku's men came for Yang later, after he had returned to the OWI compound. Because my father was away, they seized Yang and took him off for questioning. In an unguarded moment, Yang managed to stroll out of his confinement and make his way back to the compound, where he sought asylum from Ku Chu-t'ung's men. By then, my father had returned. The laws of extraterritoriality no longer prevailed, however, as they had for most of the war in areas commanded by Americans in China. Under those laws, Chinese employed by the U.S. war effort had not always been subject to Chinese jurisdiction. Usually, they were considered to be within American jurisdiction. In 1944, however, at the request of Chiang Kai-shek, extraterritorial legal protection for Chinese, along with the entire system of extraterritorial rights, had been abolished by President Roosevelt. The law now compelled my father to hand Yang Chao over to the local Chinese military authorities. He did so with great reluctance, and only after he was granted visitation rights so that he could monitor Yang's treatment.

Almost immediately, he had second thoughts. He tried through U.S. channels in Chungking to have Yang released. Yang's arrest, however, was the first instance under the new agreement between the U.S. and Chinese governments in which a Chinese had been forcibly removed from the sanctuary of his American employer. For Chiang Kai-shek, it became a test case of newly restored Chinese jurisdiction. This was bad luck for Dad, but far worse luck for Yang Chao, whom General Ku spirited off to Hangchow, where, to extract a confession, his jailers tortured and beat him, ultimately to death.

The Yang Chao affair was one of the first aspects of my father's experience in China that I encountered in the spring of 1982, just after my fortieth birthday. My wife and I were living in upstate New York, in a rather large Greek Revival house behind a white picket fence in Spencertown, New York, which we had rented for the winter. The purpose of this retreat was in part to enable me to give up alcohol in a state of relative isolation, although I must add that we were not in isolation from relatives, one of whom, my father's brother Jake, lived not far away in Salisbury, Connecticut. It was there, in Jake's warehouse, that I found the black file cabinet containing the memorabilia of my father's China experience. Even now, as I write, I can feel the strange combination of dread and curiosity with which the sight of that black metal cabinet filled me, as though I were confronting some live thing all compressed into those drawers, so carefully packed away by my father. It was the black beast itself of his China life. I opened that first, top file cabinet drawer with morbid excitement. Obviously I was tampering with my father's secret life. He had long since taken his own life, but I felt then a primal fear. I still have moments of uneasiness as I sit upstairs here at home in Belmont, Massachusetts, in the attic, writing this account. Even now when I am alone in the house, I am afraid my father might be waiting for me downstairs, in my son's room, back from the dead. It is as though by writing about this buried world I am calling him from the grave, broken and bloody from his terrible fall.

I understood almost immediately what a nest of snakes it must have been to my father, who had packed it away. Never had I imagined, however, that you could pack so much paper into one of those containers. Letters, clippings, hundreds of onionskin pages and carbons of OWI dispatches on thin, brown wartime Chinese paper had all been tightly, carefully filed away. I came upon my parents' China correspondence, also carefully preserved in carbon copy, sentences scissored out by the military censors to excise any mention of my father's whereabouts. In the bottom drawer I found a black cardboard scrapbook of my father's *Herald Tribune* newspaper clippings, along with packets of photographs, and reels of negatives. The China adventure was buried alive in this black metal vault, nibbled away by field mice who had left tiny, hard droppings in between the otherwise excellently preserved pages of documents.

I had no guiding principle, at the time, to direct me as I withdrew this compacted material from the black metal file. I made my selections at random. I took some of it with me back to Spencertown, where I unloaded it in the back living room. I left the rest at Jake's. Then I went back to Jake's and took more of this looted history out of the file cabinet. By now the sickly past had come to life, much as the sickly life of China had burst into movement in the summer of 1945 when Japan surrendered and the coma imposed on normal living by the occupation finally lifted. In Salisbury and Spencertown, papers multiplied, and danced in the spring breezes. I seemed to spend my days driving back and forth between those two places, transporting boxes of material. I had done some reading; I knew some China Hands; I had visited others in Hong Kong. I was not uninformed about the world, long lost, that now rushed into my life. One day I made a day trip over to Cambridge on the Massachusetts Turnpike to retrieve some of Graham Peck's papers, including a 1936 Peiping telephone book and a photograph album that I had prematurely given to Boston University. I also consulted in

Cambridge with John Fairbank. On that brief lunchtime visit, Fairbank supplied an intensely vivid impression, standing up outside on his lawn in the sudden swelter of late May, of what it had been like just at the end of the war in sweltering Chungking and Shanghai.

Yang Chao, Fairbank told me, had been beaten to death in prison. Red marks found on his body when it was returned to his wife attested to this. Nothing my father had done, including the pilgrimage he made to Hangchow to see General Ku Chu-t'ung in the fall of 1945, Fairbank insisted, could have saved Yang Chao. The Communists had made a cause célèbre out of Yang Chao's murder at a rally in Jessfield Park in Shanghai, but my father had escaped censure for his role in the episode, at least until after liberation, when, in absentia, he was accused by the Chinese during the anti-rightist campaign of having been a spy. About Barbara Stephens, however, Fairbank could recall nothing whatever.

To this day I find it baffling that he drew such a blank on her name, he who was possessed of such an excellent memory for detail. She arrived in Chungking as a clerk-typist for the OWI in 1945. Her letters indicate that she knew Fairbank at the time. Furthermore, she was memorably beautiful, surely the most dazzling of the half-dozen young American secretaries who flew into Chungking at the end of the war. John Hersey remembered her, but then he had taken a trip with her from Peiping to Lanchow in 1946 by train. He had spent days in her company with Graham Peck and their Chinese friend Yeh Teh-chuang. Yet for all that, even Hersey's recollection seemed somewhat sparse. Barbara was, Hersey recalled, high-spirited and funny. She had what he called "a manic turn of mind." She laughed a great deal, Hersey said.[14]

Most photographs fail to capture Barbara Stephens's vibrancy. I found among my father's papers a number of photos of Barbara, and the only one that suggests her vitality was a picture taken of her in Sinkiang Province, on a brilliant day, on a visit to a place called Yiachi, where she can be seen sitting on the railing of a footbridge with a baby on her lap. A small boy stands shyly at her side. A feminine face peers out from behind Barbara, and perched against the railing across from them is another young Chinese woman. Barbara is wearing a loose white blouse, sleeves rolled to her elbows, black slacks and sandals. Her bright golden hair is an expression of her youthful energy. She wears it loose, and shoulder length. In the foreground, the footbridge is flanked by short, whitewashed pillars, each of which holds a pot of flowers in bloom. Behind Barbara, on the far side of the footbridge, in front of a gateway and on either side of it, against a whitewashed wall, fifteen men in military costume, and three women, not in military attire, are standing in a row. Barbara wears a radiant smile. She is the very picture of dazzling health. She is the object of the photographer's eye.

By the time that picture was taken, on the nineteenth of July, 1947, Barbara was a sophisticated woman, intrepid in her self-confidence. She had traveled in trucks and army vehicles around the entire province of Sinkiang, across deserts and through mountain passes, in bitter cold and baking heat, usually the only woman among Central Asian Muslims who spoke only Turkic. She was on a self-appointed assignment to investigate little-known evils that the Nationalist Chinese were visiting upon their Turkic subjects in that remote region. By then, she was an avenging angel.

Nevertheless, when she first arrived in Chungking at the age of twenty-one she made an impression sufficiently striking to inspire a photo essay by the photographer Jack Wilkes that was subsequently published in *Life*. This episode she later wanted to live down, mainly, I suspect, because it earned her passing celebrity in China. "*Life* goes on a date in Chungking," it was called. It typecast Barbara as a girl-next-door on a date with a visiting American journalist named Palmer Hoyt. It was a quintessential *Life* magazine conceit: a pair of all-Americans who just happen to find themselves in Chungking, having a romantic encounter.[15]

There was anger beneath the deceptively placid loveliness. Barbara Stephens grew up in Westchester County, and attended Hunter College, according to her Chungking photo-date, Palmer Hoyt (better known these days as the author Edwin P. Hoyt).[16] Her father had been a corporate executive. According to Hoyt, grief over the breakup of her parents' marriage while she was still in college had moved Barbara to join the OWI and apply for the China assignment. She landed on her feet in Chungking, and in due course had decided to stay on in China once the war ended, although the decision to become a freelance correspondent came later. As she began to penetrate the mysteries of Chungking, Barbara met members of the press corps who were quartered at the Press Hostel. She also socialized with some of the Red Chinese in Chungking, and soon got to know Chou En-lai. She also made friends with Kung P'eng, Chou's beautiful press attaché. This did not make its way into *Life* magazine. Graham Peck discovered Barbara sometime in the summer of 1945. He connected swiftly with her sense of the absurd, and her capacity to knock back Chungking B, as the local gin was called. Together with Graham's friend Yeh Teh-chuang, whom they called Lao Yeh (Lao being a Chinese term of affection, which, literally translated, means "old"), they formed a trio of merrymakers, and practiced what Graham called Pure Discourse.

Graham encountered Pure Discourse while perusing the *China Handbook,* which he describes as the "Kuomintang's package of facts suitable for foreigners."[17] As he wrote in his second book, *Two Kinds*

of Time, Pure Discourse "was a kind of ritual behavior which must have been invented in many countries in prehistoric times, but I think it was first given that name in China, several centuries ago, when a group of Taoist intellectuals started a splinter movement or cult to protest against the state religion—Confucianism—which was passing through a very formal and corrupt phase."[18] It was the habit of these rebellious Taoists, known as the Seven Sages of the Bamboo Forest, to stroll together in the heat of the afternoon in a bamboo grove where they recited poetry, played the lute and drank wine. The Seven Sages ended their strolls in a state of silent harmony, at one with the unnameable, and proceeded to drink themselves into a serious stupor in which they became blissfully indifferent to the world and achieved intimacy with Tao.[19] Not surprisingly, since under the Kuomintang Confucianism was passing once again through a very formal and corrupt phase, the *China Handbook* took a highly disapproving attitude toward Pure Discourse, distinguished as it was by "Drinking to excess, nihilistic behavior, denying all the ritual and moral code of Confucianism, ridiculing and insulting the people of the world in every possible manner."[20] It was a definition Graham found perfectly suited to his own behavior, not to mention that of my father, who showed up in the late summer of 1945 in Chungking, where he, too, indulged in no small amount of Pure Discourse, with Graham, Lao Yeh, and Barbara Stephens. They all spent a long weekend together *"sunging,"* as the Chinese call seriously festive celebration. Dad didn't see any of them again after that for a few months. He went back to Fukien Province and from there traveled by boat down to the coast on the Min River, a trip he wrote up for *The New Yorker* as an account of what it was like to deal with Japanese and Chinese officialdom immediately after the war. For a time he stayed in Canton, where he set up a United States Information Agency station. Then he went up to Hangchow, where he endeavored unsuccessfully to see General Ku Chu-t'ung about Yang Chao.

By this time, my father was supposed to be back in Marin County. That was my mother's point of view. She was alarmed because Dad kept putting off his return while the husbands of all her friends were coming home from war. First there was the USIS in Canton to launch. Next he had to attend to the matter of Yang Chao. Finally, his OWI superior, William Holland, wanted him to make an exploratory visit to Formosa. All these things made it necessary for my father to stay on in China a while longer. He was reluctant to turn his back on China. China was now an all-consuming interest. He had a tendency to preoccupy himself with immediate circumstances and then, when he moved on, to put them emphatically behind him. China was the present tense in his life, whereas San Francisco, and especially the *San Francisco Chron-*

icle, where he had worked until he received his China commission, were of the past. He had broken through to a new and bigger reality. China was also a source of deep joy to him. He had made many friends there, Chinese and American, and his American friends all felt passionately involved with China.

In Yung-an my father had changed. He had expanded. In a way, he had become his eccentricities. He felt he could no longer fit back into a domestic role, even an unconventional one. Something definite seems to have happened to him, also, in the months just before and after the victory over Japan. Earlier in 1945, he had sketched a scenario in which our family would move to New Mexico to live, possibly because of all places in the United States it most closely resembled China. This idea was forgotten in the weeks and months that followed. His letters were fewer and further between. Perhaps the Yang Chao business had awakened him to a new immediacy. The sudden outbreak of peace also probably made him have to face the prospects of returning home as he had not until then had to do.

It also opened up a whole new world of opportunity for a journalist. The postwar China story was about to begin. My father was unquestionably aware that he was now superbly well qualified to cover it and make of it his career. In Shanghai, in November, he reconnected with Barbara, Graham and Lao Yeh. Shanghai was pandemonium. It was now a chaotic city, which at one and the same time showed signs of the prosperity it had enjoyed during the Japanese occupation and of terrible disrepair and decrepitude, also in part due to the Japanese occupation. When Owen Lattimore visited Shanghai in the months immediately following the war, he noted that "the show windows of big shops on Nanking Road were stuffed with American electrical equipment which had become very short in the United States, and car sales places were full of shiny American cars." These were all 1941 cars—preserved, Lattimore deduced, in sealed warehouses by Chinese collaborators during the Japanese occupation.[21] The Japanese had torn the guts out of the city, however, right down to the light fixtures and the spigots in Broadway Mansions, home of the foreign press corps. It was a raw, unheated city. The large houses in the French Concession and the outlying suburbs, built at the height of prosperity on spacious suburban lawns by Western colonials, were in a state of appalling neglect. Coastal Chinese who had fled inland from the Japanese now seemed to be pouring back into Shanghai, and the streets were jammed with people and livestock and cars and trucks honking their way through the melee.

Meanwhile people were fleeing Chungking by any possible means. By the end of 1945 the Nationalist government was beginning to reestablish itself in Nanking, and every available truck, riverboat and China

Air Transport plane out of Peisheyi Airport was packed with travelers escaping from that confined and fetid city at long last. Barbara Stephens managed to get down to Shanghai on an errand for Chou En-lai's press attaché, Kung P'eng, and her husband, Ch'iao Kuan-hua, later the Chinese foreign minister. They had entrusted Barbara with the mission of delivering their infant son, Ti-ti (whom Barbara described as "pretty much of a wild indian,")[22] to Kung P'eng's family. She soon returned to Chungking. But Graham Peck and Lao Yeh were en route to Peiping, and in November, in Shanghai, they all engaged in more Pure Discourse. My father was also in Shanghai. Neil Brown, who had been Dad's chief radio operator at the listening post in Yung-an, was there, too. He was trying to get back to the United States. After Barbara had returned to Chungking, my father wrote her a letter in which he described his efforts to see Neil Brown off on a flight from Shanghai. I quote from it here at length because I think it excellently conveys the flavor of Shanghai at that time, not to mention that of Pure Discourse.

"Graham and Yieh finally left on Tuesday morning by ATC after considerable fumbling around," he wrote. "At least I think they left, because I haven't seen them since. Presume they are now in the land of snow and dust. I wanted to go sleep on their floor and see them off properly. Graham said that was a nice idea, but that it would really be better for them to catch the plane without hindrance, so I finally gave in. It was bitter cold that night, and the last I saw of Graham he was tightly done up in Tibetan clothes in a pedicab outside the Great Eastern, bowing regally and repeatedly to me with a glowing red face. I didn't see Lao Yieh in the evening, since he was off on a mission to present Miss Sun with a bicycle and withdraw from her life. A few days before he had been threatening to buy Graham's mother a fur coat, which I suppose I would have had to wear home, but G talked him out of this. It is now," Dad wrote, "only 2:15 p.m., and the office is deserted. There is a great crowd in the street between here and the Palace, and I think that Marshall or the Generalissimo or both will soon draw up. The crowd includes MPs, Chinese police and soldiers in various uniforms but all scratching their ears, and a big slug of middle-school students who just rounded the corner, also planes overhead. Two of the middle-school students have battledores and shuttlecocks with them, so most anything may happen. I will be a cinch to miss it, though, since I don't like to stand by the window forever, at least not without the right company. You had better read about it in the papers. (A man just got off a streetcar with a dozen and a half shiny tin horns in his hand.)"

He continued, "We also saw Neil off on Sunday. This took the whole day off and on, and was done in relays. At one point Graham gouged my hand open with a sliver of glass he had made out of a tumbler, and Sophie had to get me all up in slings and cross hatches, or thought she did. At another they started discussing my sweater in an unpleasant way. Graham said it wasn't a sweater but a brassiere, and this went on for a while. Finally Sophie said that it would look better under my shirt than over it, and made me retire and change it around that way. Have clung to this style ever since, and am now about to dig through my baggage for a clean one. Actually, of course, Neil never got away, but is still holed up in his apartment waiting for a plane (Thursday). For various reasons I have been pretending he isn't there, but will break down and go back for another today or tomorrow if the situation remains."

Back to the window, he then wrote, "It turned out to be Marshall. Ed Rauch happened in a little while ago, and for some reason I had a bottle of whiskey around so we took up a watch at the window. Presently some MP jeeps and motorcycles showed up with a car bearing a five-star license in their wake. Marshall and Wedemeyer and a man in 4F clothes, who I imagine was an Embassy running dog, got out. They waved and saluted to what sounded like a Yale football song coming from a band across the street and then vanished into the Cathay Hotel, where they should now be powdering their noses." And it went on.[23]

The next act was about to begin in China. General Marshall had just arrived in China as the envoy extraordinaire of President Truman, who had sent him there with the hope that he might be the one person who could mediate a truce between the Nationalist Chinese and the Communists. It was December 20, 1945. While my father was writing his letter to Barbara, General Marshall was upstairs in the Cathay Hotel in a suite with General Wedemeyer, the successor in China to General Stilwell. They met for two hours and, although nobody knows exactly what went on between the two men who had been extremely close to each other, Leonard Mosely, a biographer of Marshall, recounts that their friendship was ruptured forever by the exchange. "You have come here on an impossible mission," Wedemeyer told Marshall in the opulent surroundings of the plush suite overlooking the Bund and the leaden sky and the windswept sea lanes of the Whangpoo, while the great man unpacked. "Wedemeyer," Marshall replied, his face red with anger, his eyes flashing, "It *is* going to work! I *am* going to do it! And what's more, *you* are going to help me do it![24]

By the time he got back to Marin County in January 1946, my father had already made up his mind to find a job as China correspondent for a major American daily. Nothing could have prevented this effort, including a pregnancy that became apparent several months later. It enraged Dad that my mother, in his view, had chosen to add this extra dimension to their complex marital relations, but he did not let it stand in his way. I doubt that my mother, unhappy though she was about losing him again so soon to China, was entirely opposed to this career move because he made such a strong argument for his case, which was essentially that China was about to provide its big professional opportunity. He helped my mother move our family from Marin County to a large, white Spanish colonial revival house with a red-tiled roof on the northern outskirts of Santa Barbara, and then set off for New York to seek his fortune.

In New York, he got together with Yang Kang, the *Ta Kung Pao* correspondent and Yang Chao's sister. He also visited Virginia Stephens, Barbara's mother, who had converted to the Church of Christ Scientist. It was on this expedition that he looked in on Teddy and Annalee, while they were writing *Thunder Out of China*. He reported on all of this to Barbara. "I went to Teddy White's apartment in NY one afternoon," he wrote, "and found him and Annalee Jacoby collaborating noisily on his (or their) book. I withdrew into the next room for an hour or so and caught up on some magazine reading I wanted to do, and then later we went out to dinner. She asked me if I knew you & spoke very warmly of you (perhaps you don't know it, but you have a lot of real friends around & about). . . ." Dad also visited his friend Richard Watts, and in the same letter he wrote her about that. "At the moment he is just about the most authoritative and respected American reporter of the current situation in China," my father wrote Barbara, "a situation that he watches closely from a lookout on the second floor of a 5th Avenue apartment house. . . .[25] Watts, his friend from OWI, had worked for the *New York Herald Tribune* and now he secured an interview for Dad with Joseph Barnes, who at the time was the foreign editor. The *Trib* already had a reporter in China, A. T. Steele, a China Hand of long standing, but Barnes wanted someone who wouldn't have to cover the day-to-day story out of Nanking, who could roam around China and provide a more panoramic picture of the Chinese scene, and he hired Dad to be the *Trib*'s roving China correspondent. In June, Dad sailed for China out of San Francisco aboard the *Marine Lynx*, a converted troop transport ship that the passengers called the *Marine Jinx*, and the captain called the *Latrine Stinks*, at least according to my father. Now that he was safely sailing away once again in the direction of China, he wrote to my mother in his customary chatty, informative manner, full of the affectionate badinage that so completely failed him when he was actually in her presence.

I don't think he had the slightest idea what the future held in store for him or his family, as the *Marine Lynx* churned its way across the Pacific to China. He would soon, with the birth of my sister Diana, in

September, be the father of five children. He suggested to our mother that a visit by her to China in the wintertime would be a good idea. He was given to making unrealistic proposals, thoroughly worked out in his own mind but often without consultation with those for whom the proposals were being made. "How about making it this winter?" he wrote. "The winter in Shanghai is a little colder than in Calif., though I don't know about Nanking, but it is nice then."[26] The winter in Shanghai is bitterly cold at times, not very Californian. He was idealizing, just as he was idealizing a reconciliation with my mother. Dad was prepared, as a matter of good conscience, to bring his wife and family to China, but on another level he probably doubted that Mom would seriously entertain the idea. He would have hated combining his family life and his China career that way. He wasn't equipped any longer to live a conventional family life.

"Your father didn't do anything the rest of us didn't do," Keyes Beech once said. "He just did it more spectacularly."[27]

Beech told me in 1982 over lunch in Washington with Pepper Martin about the time he first met my father in the Far East. It was in Shanghai that Beech went up to my father's room at Broadway Mansions and knocked on the door. When beckoned to enter by Dad, Beech beheld my father sitting up in bed, "blood on his head, blood on the bed, blood here, there, everywhere," Beech recalled. "There was a bottle of bourbon beside the bed. We both wondered about where the blood had come from, and decided that your father had been rolled the night before, since his wallet, watch and so forth were missing."[28] It was characteristic of Dad to go out and get rolled. He did it repeatedly throughout his life. It could have been New York, or Lima, Peru, or Boston, where, one night, in late 1962, he was arrested for carrying on too boisterously at a neighborhood bar while waiting for a late train to New York. He was taken off to a local precinct, then shifted to the security of the central jail downtown, where he was detained for questioning in the Boston Strangler case.

But drinking and whoring were considered standard recreational diversions by the correspondents of my father's time in the Far East. Not everyone indulged them, but many did. Elizabeth Purcell, an Australian who worked at the *China Weekly Review* in Shanghai in the late 1940s could recall how, after dinner one night with my father and Bill Powell, who was now the editor and publisher of his father's old periodical, the two men announced to her: "We're going to a cat house." This was not long after my father had returned to China. "I was furious," she recalled. Then, at four o'clock in the morning, Elizabeth, who lived in Broadway Mansions with her husband, John Purcell, a *Life* magazine reporter, got a phone call from the fourteenth floor. It was Powell, calling from my father's room. "You've got to help us out, Chris is in terrible shape," he told Elizabeth. "I swept down in my nightgown," Elizabeth told me years later, "and found one Chinese girl all covered up and in bed, another one on a chair. Your father was absolutely unable to move. He sat in a chair babbling nonsense and laughing, which I must say was most annoying, and Bill kept going from one Chinese woman to the other, saying 'Get your clothes on, get your clothes on.' Bill, you see, was rather straight, except for your father's effect on him, and he was in a complete panic."[29]

One reason why Dad wanted to stay on in China was to live the unencumbered life. In postwar China he felt free to do whatever he wanted, whenever he wanted to do it. This could mean staying holed up for days in his room in Broadway Mansions, as Jack Belden did, or drifting for weeks around China on the backs of trucks taking in the countryside and staying at local Chinese inns. It was what made him such a model student of China. As Arch Steele put it, unlike other journalists who were there, himself included, Dad "got into the soul of China." He had, according to Steele, "that inner fire, that inner intensity."[30] It was the great experience of his life, and he spent the rest of his years, one way or another, trying to recapture it.

By now, Barbara was in Peiping. She had been thinking about leaving China, and had written to my father in Marin County to tell him so. "You say you may leave China by early summer," Dad had at once replied. "Why is this? Do you regard that vast and puzzling country as a mere finishing school? Am afraid I can get into this matter only on professional grounds at the moment, but that is grounds enough." He thought that Barbara really entertained a basic grasp of China, and that she could handle a news job. "If you really want to come back and marry some nice young man and settle down," he wrote, "then that is that of course, but if it is anything else I don't see why you don't take counsel with your small pointed jaw for awhile and see if you don't come up with a different idea."[31] Which Barbara did.

It was during this period in Chungking that Barbara got to know the Communists. "I had a number of opportunities to see and talk to most of the Communists," she wrote Dad, "as I had dinner there a few times and they came to our place to a couple of parties. I was tremendously impressed by General Chou [En-lai], personally, and he is a very attractive man. I talked to him, General Yeh [Yeh Chien-ying] and the rest of them during several evenings, though not too vociferously as their English is a little more than halting. They always greeted me with great acclaim as the 'girl who took the baby to Shanghai,' " she wrote, "and although it pleases me of course, I am a little sad to think that my pictures in *Life* are my only claim to fame among the Communists and with everyone everywhere else in China. I might say the glory is a little hollow; just a little of course."[32]

In March 1946 Barbara made her way to Peiping. There she joined forces with Graham Peck and Lao Yeh, and the small group of foreign journalists in Peiping. Reunited, they practiced a certain amount of Pure Discourse. Both Graham and Barbara kept my father posted on this while he was still in the States. For a short time when she first got to Peiping, Barbara actually moved in with Graham and Lao Yeh. "I stayed at their house for three weeks," Barbara wrote, "and we had a very fine time falling through the paper walls every night and destroying the crockery. But people began casting all kinds of aspersions and when I went to Shanghai and found I was notorious there I came back and moved."[33] On her brief trip to Shanghai, Barbara had obtained a job as a stringer for Agence France Presse, and when she returned to Peiping, she moved into a house of her own, near the Forbidden City, in a quiet neighborhood four houses away from her friends. "The sun shines more sunnily here and the breezes blow balmier and it is generally a pleasant location," she wrote my father. "I have a courtyard with cherry and pear blossoms and a front yard with the same. I sit in it more than is wise or sensible but it is very pleasant. . . ."[34] "China was a place for free spirits," Arch Steele once told me. "It was such an easy place to live and operate in. You could do almost anything you pleased, and you could do it on very little money. The situation opened up opportunities for getting involved. It spoiled people." He added, "No one who's lived in China for any length of time can ever be as happy or content or interested in life anywhere else. It was contentment in itself. It had everything."[35]

Even for those days, at that time, Graham and his merry band quickly earned a reputation for their bohemian ways. Barbara, Edwin Hoyt recalled, "was extremely 'wild' as we would say in those days."[36] "I remember one time," Hoyt wrote, "I had been in Korea for the UP, and I came up to Qingdao in a PBM and somehow got invited to Dick Service's house for lunch. He was U.S. consul there then. I met a navy captain at lunch. We were talking about where I was going. I said to Peking 'to see my girl.' 'Who is that?' 'Barbara Stephens.' He laughed sourly. 'From what I hear, she's everybody's girl.' " He was in love with her, he wrote to tell me, and so were Graham and Lao Yeh.

The wife of a China Hand recalled that Barbara would calmly eat tomatoes and other uncooked vegetables at the Wagons-Lits Hotel in Peiping, while others feared dysentery. "She was at home in China the way I would be at home in Chicago,"[37] this acquaintance recalled.

Barbara was completely at home in smoky local Peiping restaurants, she added, where groups of China Hands gathered for long lunchtime feasts of Peking duck and sweet and sour pork. She wore no makeup and was the type of adventurous soul who would bathe in a Chinese river without a moment's hesitation, no matter who happened to be present. She even brandished a "trusty" thirty-eight.

Men fell madly in love with Barbara, but John Hersey insisted that her relations with with Graham Peck and Lao Yeh were strictly platonic. He, too, was in Peiping that spring. "In Peking the general tendency was to stay where you were," Hersey said. "It was beautiful and there was so much to talk about. Conversation about real aspects of life went off into speculations about philosophy."[38] Because Pure Discourse was their bond, what they really liked to do together was talk, drink and eat, more or less in that order. Meals were endless, Hersey recalled, and went on from five or six in the evening until four or five in the morning. Dishes brought by a servant were often ordered in from a local restaurant. According to Hersey, the amount of drinking that went on at Graham's house was prodigious. Mostly they drank pai-kar, the Chinese version of white lightning, distilled from kaoliang. After ten years, Graham continued to make it his spirit of choice because it was cheap and plentiful.

Peiping was a gilded lotus land. The city was in glorious flower. It was aswarm at that time with Americans: marines, United Nations officials, journalists, consular officers, all en route somewhere else, or based there temporarily. This gave the newly liberated city an air of festivity and excitement. The food and drink were plentiful then, thanks in part to the Japanese, who had started truck farms in the nearby countryside, which produced excellent fresh fruit and vegetables. "Peiping was like ripe Camembert," an American China Hand said to me years later in Hong Kong.[39] It was the beginning of Lao Peking's last great flowering as a walled city, baking at that time in the summer heat of the North China Plain, fragrant at night with ancient jasmine scents and the pungent smells of Peking cooking, odors richly underscored by the night soil being transported daily out of the city in honey pots, as the containers for human excrement were called, to be used as fertilizer in the surrounding farmland. It was the ideal setting for Pure Discourse, as my father wrote in a "Letter from Peiping" for The New Yorker in 1947. "There is a difference of time element, or of precision, between Peiping and the more Westernized Chinese cities," he observed. "It isn't obvious, but it grows apparent as you stay on here. People aren't so apt to make appointments for sharp hours, and then rush to keep them. It is more customary to tell someone that you will be around to see him in due course; and then eventually to go, at some time when he is likely to be in, and to stay and talk at length, perhaps for a few hours." Dad, like Graham, was unable to resist alluding to Pure Discourse in his narrative. "The spirit of Pure Discourse is strong here," he wrote. "Men like William Blake, who seemed queer in places like London, would not seem queer in Peiping."[40]

The hot and heavy story at that time was the cease-fire negotiation that General Marshall was brokering between the Nationalists and the Communists. Manchuria had been the sticking point for Marshall. Both the Communists and the Nationalists needed the rich agricultural and industrial resources to sustain their civil war efforts. The United States did everything in its power to help the Nationalists to reoccupy north China, but were powerless to get them into Manchuria while the Soviet Red Army was there, and the Red Army had not departed on a dime. That the Soviet Red Army was there at all was a product of the Yalta Conference, held in February 1945, which had so much to do with the subsequent Cold War and the immense tangle of hostilities that troubled the twentieth century in the half century following the war. At Yalta, Roosevelt still thought he might need the Russians to defeat the Japanese, and he prevailed upon Stalin to turn his attention to that end once the war in Europe was won. Stalin, in a basically one-on-one agreement with Roosevelt, arranged to send troops overland into Manchuria after the hostilities in Europe were over, with the objective of helping the United States subdue the Japanese in Manchuria and, if necessary, in the Japanese archipelago. This plan was deemed necessary at the time by Roosevelt, who took scant notice of the historical implications of an agreement that would allow the Russians back into territory that had always held an appeal for them, if only because Port Arthur in Manchuria could provide them with a warm-water naval base in the Far East. It was like letting the fox into the henhouse to give the Russians free access to Manchuria. Moreover, Roosevelt did so without first consulting Chiang Kai-shek.

After the death of Roosevelt in April 1945, Chiang was left to make the best of a deal that he knew would all but lose him the northeast to the Communist Chinese, since the Russians would undoubtedly give them a leg up in Manchuria. But Stalin had been an ally of Chiang's in decades past, even up through World War Two. Besides, Stalin was not prepared to back the Communists one hundred percent. He looked with suspicion on the Chinese Communists. In exchange for agreeing, on paper, to help the Nationalists reclaim Manchuria upon Soviet withdrawal at the war's end, Stalin exacted heavy demands of Chiang, which were written into an agreement, the Sino-Soviet Pact. Recent evidence has come to light, according to one Chinese political scientist with whom I have spoken, that in 1945 as part of the Sino-Soviet Pact they signed on August 14—the day hostilities in the Pacific ended—T. V. Soong gave Stalin Outer Mongolia, among other things exacted by the Russian leader, in exchange for Stalin's protective assurances toward the Nationalists after the Yalta Pact allowing Russia into Manchuria to help win the war against Japan had been foisted on Chiang Kai-shek. In this version of the Sino-Soviet Pact, Stalin agreed to work *only* with the KMT, and agreed to occupy Manchurian cities until the Nationalists got to them.

Marshall wanted to send teams of observers into Manchuria to ensure that neither Communists nor Nationalists would obtain the upper hand there. He had already obtained a cease-fire between the two sides throughout China, and as the Russian army withdrew in March he wanted to extend the cease-fire to the northeastern territory. The Communists, thanks to the Russians, were already strongly entrenched in Manchuria. The Russians had stonewalled the Nationalists, denied them assistance when at last their forces moved into Manchuria, a violation of the spirit, if not the letter, of the Sino-Soviet Pact (although by prearrangement with the Nationalists Stalin did keep his troops in Manchuria until the United States had flown the cream of Chiang's army up to the northeast). "During the final weeks of the Soviet occupation, Nationalist officials pleaded for advance information concerning the evacuation schedule and sought to elicit a Soviet commitment to relinquish control to the Chinese government alone through a formal transfer of command responsibilities (the Chinese term is chieh fang)," writes China scholar Steven I. Levine. "However, the Russians refused to make any adjustments in their withdrawal schedule. As they had from the very outset, they declined to shoulder any part of the burden for the Nationalist takeover bid."[41]

Soviet policy in Manchuria tilted the balance of power decisively in favor of the Communists in China, although this was not fully understood at the time. It doomed Nationalist hopes of reclaiming the northeast, and it was the beginning of the end for Americans in China. The situation was thick with irony. Roosevelt had invited Stalin to join the war against Japan via Manchuria without first informing Chiang Kai-shek, and by the time Stalin set out for Manchuria the war with Japan was already won. By letting the Russians back into Manchuria, the Americans were dooming the prospects of the side they wanted to win in China.

The civil war was under way mainly in Manchuria by the time my father got back to China. The Russians had finally withdrawn from Manchuria, taking with them entire Japanese factories built and then abandoned. (In one famous instance they departed with an entire hydroelectric plant.) Chiang Kai-shek had airlifted his own armies across China to the northeast with the help of the U.S. Air Force. He did this in the spring of 1946 against the advice of the Americans, who thought he should first concentrate his troops in Shantung Province below Manchuria and give himself more time to launch an assault. As it was, the Reds were already in the Manchurian countryside and under Lin Piao they waged a brilliant guerrilla campaign against Chiang's best, American-trained troops, who were cut off north of the Great Wall from their line of supplies. They suffered horrible casualties when Chiang refused to order a retreat back to Shanhaikwan, behind the wall, as Ho Ying-ch'in, his chief of staff, had begged him to do.

By the time my father started reporting on China, the Marshall mission was foundering. Treaty talks were in process during July but they were deadlocked, and a resumption of civil war seemed imminent. In the sweltering summer heat of Nanking, and up in Chiang Kai-shek's cool mountain retreat at Lushan, General Marshall negotiated a temporary truce. "It was a holding action," Pepper Martin later said, "nobody called it that, but that's what it was."[42] Marshall continued to mediate between the Communists and the Nationalists, but he turned his efforts more and more toward the creation of a Chinese National Assembly and a constitution. The Communists made him a target of propaganda, pointing out that he was acting simultaneously as a "mediator" and "military adviser" to the Kuomintang. The United States had thrown its weight behind Chiang Kai-shek. Therefore, Marshall's influence as a mediator was ultimately untenable. In any case, neither Chiang Kai-shek nor the Communists were interested in what Marshall had to offer. Both Chiang and Mao were inclined to reject any constitutional democratic system unless they had total control over the machinery of government, a contradiction in terms.

The Communists stayed at the negotiating table for quite a long time. They had asserted an interest in democracy. They had sought a rapprochement with the United States in the fall of 1946, but when Chiang Kai-shek, richly supplied with U.S. military equipment, began to attack them in north China, it finally became clear to the Communists that America had chosen sides. They got ready to pack up, and resume the civil war in earnest.

When my father returned to Shanghai from Peiping, he wrote Barbara, "I haven't thanked you enough for the pleasure you gave me in Peking, and in fact I can't." He told her that he'd returned to Shanghai short of sleep and out of touch with the news, but this was okay, he wrote. He cloistered himself in his room for two days, alternating between a sleeping bag on the floor and his oversoft bed. "One of the floor boys makes very good scrambled eggs with tomatoes, and I lived off those," he wrote. "By reading a few days' output of Shanghai papers, translation services etc. you can get right back into the swing of things."[43] He was alarmed, however, to hear by radio message from Barbara that she was planning to leave Peiping almost immediately on a long expedition by herself to Sinkiang Province. Quite why Barbara had decided to do this remains a mystery. Possibly it was a journey inspired by the visit she had made earlier that year to Lanchow with John Hersey. Somehow, she had learned about the Nationalist abuse of the Sinkiang tribespeople, and her passions had fastened on this as yet untold story. Perhaps also only Sinkiang could have satisfied Barbara's need to prove her capabilities for travel on a mission rife with peril for even the most intrepid of seasoned journalists.

Sinkiang is China's most far-flung province, over two thousand miles from the coast, a vast Inner Asian territory the size of Europe, surrounded by a ring of jagged mountain ranges many of which at that time had not been properly charted. It's a region of mountains, deserts made of gravel, and oases watered by mountain streams fed by the melting snows of the Pamir and the 'T'ien Shan ranges, to the south and east, and the Dzungaria range in the north, which marks the boundary between Sinkiang and Mongolia. Valleys became populated as the result of an east-west trade route, and civilization sprang up early in the oases, especially those of southern Sinkiang, where Buddhism, transported over the mountains of India, came to flourish and from there found its way eventually into China proper. The Chinese had never really settled Sinkiang, although off and on they had ruled it for over two thousand years. Thus, Sinkiang was never either culturally or racially a part of China. In the fall of 1946, Sinkiang was populated mainly by Uighurs, Turkic-speaking Muslim farmers, and nomadic tribespeople known as Kazakhs, who migrated with their sheep and goats from the Dzungaria mountains, where they lived in the summertime, down to the plain in the autumn. Originally, the Chinese colonized Sinkiang in order to protect their northwest flank against the encroaching Huns, also known as the Barbarian Horde. In the late nineteenth century, the region became a buffer against the encroaching British in India and Afghanistan, and the Russians.

In the twentieth century, three different Chinese militarists had ruled Sinkiang in succession, all more or less autonomously, all more or less brutally. The last of these, Sheng Shih-ts'ai, had maintained power for eleven years by skillfully cultivating the support of Stalin, who helped him to develop education and improve communications. Sheng had also given the local inhabitants of Sinkiang a degree of autonomy, but when World War Two occupied the attention of the Russians elsewhere, Sheng was forced to lean on Chungking. He became harshly repressive, and suspicion drove him to imprison and torture many of those whose lives he had earlier enhanced through education. Sheng Shih-ts'ai was eased from power in 1944. (He is said to have bought himself a cushy job in Chungking as minister of agriculture and forestry with a huge payment, in gold, to the Nationalist treasury.)

The Turkic-speaking people of western Sinkiang, with Soviet military assistance, subsequently rebelled and, although news from Sinkiang was very hard to come by, the situation had far-reaching implications because it involved a potential conflict between the Nationalists and the USSR. Vague rumors had been reaching Peiping about the state of this rebellion and the threat of a global confrontation in Inner Asia. Barbara Stephens had decided to investigate this ill-defined situation and to get to the bottom of horror stories she'd heard about atrocities the Kuomintang was visiting on the Turkic people. She had ended her arrangement with Agence France Presse and was now on a modest retainer from *Life* magazine, which had agreed to foot the bill for her adventure in exchange for the story.[44]

"I was alarmed to hear that you are leaving Peking so soon," my father wrote her at the end of August. "I knew you said it would be early in September, but I was counting on the usual supply of headwinds." He was planning a trip up the China coast to north Kiangsu by LST, an amphibious transport vehicle operated by an agency of UNRRA and CNRRA, the postwar United Nations relief agencies that often provided journalists with transportation around China by plane, truck and boat in the course of their massive relief deliveries. It was Dad's intention to return to Shanghai by September 10, he wrote Barbara. "My idea of heaven would be to find you in Shanghai when I get back from my trip, or soon afterward, but probably this is too much to hope for."[45] She came sooner. In the first week of September, she flew down to see Dad in Shanghai, then flew back to Peiping to complete the final arrangements for her overland trip to the west. A few days later, Dad was up in Nanking. He wrote her to say, "At least it is quiet and peaceful without you around, and I suppose that ought to be regarded as something."[46] He filled her in on some Nanking gossip. He also wrote, "This Parting at Morning is hard on the old fibers, but I guess it is the only thing, especially for an average man. It is also good training for one's eventual career in hell." He wanted her to send him a photograph. "Perhaps you will agree that you should come through on your promise to give me a small picture of yourself," he wrote. "Those *Life* ones simply don't make the grade. Frankly," he added, "I don't want one in a padded suit with a lot of camels in the background either. Just something nice and simple." Although he and Barbara would have yet another rendezvous in Hankow, in October, Dad did not know it and his letter to Barbara from Nanking was in the nature of a farewell. "Please drop me a line now and then, and tell me how you are doing, plus a little about your childhood etc.," he wrote. "If you hear angels churning the air overhead on this trip of yours you will know who sent them."[47]

Barbara traveled west from Hankow to Chungking, from there to Chengtu and thence to northwest China, where she lingered for six weeks before traveling on to Sinkiang by truck. On Christmas Eve, before her departure across the desert, Barbara wrote Dad, "It is so cold here that your toothbrush becomes a bristly ice cube before you can get it in your mouth and tears in your eyes from the wind freeze on your glasses. My face and hands are black from the cold & dirt & it would be impolite to mention how long it's been since I had a bath." She was anticipating the upcoming truck ride to Tihwa, the capital of Sinkiang, with a certain detachment. "They tell me," she wrote, "that 1/2 of the people going there die of the cold on the way or get killed by bandits (Khazakh) so I am greatly looking forward to the trip."[48] More than three weeks later, she sent Dad an account of the journey. "After spending a week in Hami closely guarded and watched over by a very fatherly Chinese general who did everything but hold my hand and whisper sweet nothings in my ear, I arranged for transportation in a military truck, and replete with body guard, footmen and a sack of dried Turfan raisins took off across the Gobi for Tihwa and places unknown."[49] This leg of Barbara's journey was a six-day truck ride. "The trip," she wrote, "was cold and interesting if you like snow and deserts and soldiers and two bowls of undecorated mien (noodles) per day and assorted k'angs [Chinese platform beds] of both heated and unheated varieties with Turkis, Mongols, Chinese and Tibetan truck and mule drivers for bed companions. Having gone unbathed for a number of months, I did not feel the cold so much despite my very inadequate clothing; I hadn't spoken or heard a word of English in a month or two so through necessity had become very fluent in Chinese, or at least fluent enough to interview everyone from Chinese and Turkie officials to truck drivers and inn keepers and soldiers all along the way."[50] In Tihwa Barbara was a guest of John Hall Paxton, the U.S. consul, and his wife, Vincoe, a former missionary nurse. Both of the Paxtons were teetotalers. Barbara got around this by sneaking off every night with a State Department courier "to deliberately and without any hilarity, polish off a bottle or two of vodka," she wrote Dad. "But," she added, "these secret orgies aren't fooling anyone as any dope seeing our grey faces in the morning at breakfast would know that something is up."[51]

Altogether, Barbara spent seven months in Sinkiang. In January, she flew to Ili, the hotbed of the autonomous region, and after extensive interviews with people there, she returned in bitter weather to Tihwa. "I just returned from a 3 week trip to Ili the other day and had a very interesting and exciting trip," she wrote Dad on February 24, "although I had a triple guard most of the time—a personal bodyguard, one who slept outside my door, and one who stood, armed, on guard at the place I stayed in." In Tihwa, she reported, tension was running high. "Things have been a little tense around here the past two or three days," she wrote, "and the streets are lousy with soldiers and mps and cops and the consulate guard has been reinforced from 1 to 12. I have it from my spies however that it will all blow over provided it doesn't explode first which is unlikely."[52] Meanwhile, Barbara wrote, "I am trying to learn Turkic, which is just like Turkey's Turkic almost but am pretty much stuck on the first two words which are *salaam* and a noise you make which sounds more like hoossh than anything else and which is likely to arise where you can't use it and be very much to the point."[53]

At first, with or without Turkic, it was hard to get any information at all. "The political situation," she wrote, "and practically everything else in the province is very interesting and also just about impossible to find out about. Nobody knows anything about anything or else they all think they know all about inquisitive correspondents and are just keeping their traps shut. In fact people look at me very suspiciously when I ask any kind of a question, except maybe how much? and what time is it? which I have learned in Turkic, and it makes me think that no one has been doing much questioning around here lately."[54] Graham Peck wrote to my father on April 8 to tell him that he had received a letter from Barbara. Graham was back in Derby, Connecticut, where he had gone to live with his parents while he worked on his book. "Barbara sounded terribly belligerent: fed up with her trip but determined to go through with it, somewhat aware that she was going to enjoy having done it after she had done it, but hating every minute of Tihwa where (on March 22) she had already been delayed three weeks by floods."[55] By then Barbara was feeling lonely and isolated. "Never receiving any mail from home or seeing a familiar face is taking its toll on me," she wrote my father, "and I get so lonesome sometimes off in the middle of the desert that I would even be happy to see your homely face around the next sand dune."[56] Loneliness notwithstanding, Barbara planned to stick to her plan, which called for her to be back in Shanghai in June.

In the meantime, as soon as she could, she headed for Kashgar. Kashgar is situated on the western edge of the southern sector of Sin-Kiang, which is known as the Tarim Basin. To get there, Barbara traveled overland across the Taklamakan desert, then south along its lower rim to the oasis of Ho-t'ien, and then back to Tihwa by truck, horses, mules and camels across long desert stretches in the heat of early summer. This expedition took four months. "One interesting thing about her travels in Sinkiang," my father later wrote, "is that almost all the people there are Moslems and are therefore unused to seeing women get out of the kitchen unless they have sacks over their heads. Against this background Barbara was even more of a surprise than she would normally be. She spent a great deal of time seeking out the Turkic people and listening to their complaints. Apparently like backward people in many places they have a deep faith in what will come of getting their story put before the American public, and they came to look upon her as a heroine who would help to deliver them."[57]

Much had happened in China since Barbara's departure in November for the northwest. The Marshall mission had collapsed, and General Marshall had returned for good to the United States at the year's end, leaving John Leighton Stuart, the former president of Yenching University, to carry on in his stead as the U.S. ambassador. Marshall appears to have invested great hope in Stuart, but by 1947 there was very little even he could do to influence events in China. The Kuomintang, thanks to extensive corruption, had rapidly alienated the middle class. Everyone in China, missionaries included, was by law required to turn in to the government whatever precious metal they happened to possess. In exchange they were given currency by now so inflated that to buy a bottle of beer in Shanghai you needed a wheelbarrow of Nationalist Chinese yuan. Meanwhile, the disaffected student population and the underclass of China had cast its loyalties with the Communists. One student informant in Peiping wrote the U.S. consulate, on January 6, 1947: "The Communist element is very strong. They have their numbers in every rank and file. Some of them disguised as maid servant, cook boy and rickshaw coolie."[58]

By May 1947, the Communists controlled the north China countryside. The question, then and now, however, was how much rural support the Communists actually commanded. Were they a small, elite command offering an alternative to the now all but discredited KMT? Or were they the avatars of a powerful nationalist movement that had swollen to great purpose in the countryside during the Japanese occupation? The failure of Mao Tse-tung's initial land reform movement in 1947, and his summary treatment of peasant landlords, suggests that the agrarian population was less than enthusiastic about the radical political changes urged on it by the Reds. The population was war-weary and ready to accept whatever peace bought, though not at absolutely any price as Mao recognized when he withdrew his land reform program.

This was the time of my father's most fruitful China reporting. No longer bound to the Marshall negotiations, he was free to wander far and wide in China. In the late spring of 1947 he described his state to Barbara: "having it very nice, wandering about China as my fancy dictates."[59] Under the circumstances, however, it was all but impossible for an American newspaper correspondent to cover the civil war from the Communist side of things. When it airlifted Chiang's troops to north China in 1946, the U.S. government alienated the Communist leadership. Journalists who had been on good terms with the Communists in Chungking now found themselves frozen out. (Jack Belden was the one American correspondent who actually got through the looking glass. He spent weeks at a time in Communist-held territory where he gathered the material for *China Shakes the World*.) My father covered the collapse of what he called non-Communist China. "Non-Communist China seems to be disintegrating in these months," Dad wrote Barbara on May 20, 1947. "There are recurring sharp economic crises, and riots and disorders all over the place. The government keeps issuing fancy emergency decrees that it can't possibly enforce, and it's making almost no progress on the actual battlefronts. Very sad."[60]

Putting the story together was a complicated business. The collapse of a government is one thing, but the collapse of an entire society is quite another. This was the situation that reporters faced between 1946 and 1949. China had been in social transition ever since the fall of the Ch'ing Dynasty in 1911. The Communists in various parts of rural China had been working away at the foundations of the old society from within. Kuomintang corruption had also been working its wonders, destroying through corrosion the system of government that held China together from the top down. After the war, much of China already functioned in a piecemeal way. The charade of democracy instituted by Chiang Kai-shek at the insistence of the United States, and other frantic machinations of Chiang and the CC Clique, were but one fraction of the story. The whole economic picture had to be understood and reported.

In a story dated September 18, 1946, my father wrote that "one of the leading factors now hindering Chinese economic recovery is a lack of shipping on inland waterways and coastal routes." Freight in China at that time was moved on waterways. "The whole fabric of Chinese commerce is based on this fact," he wrote. Coastal transportation also depended on shipping, since the only link between half a dozen major ports on the central and southern Chinese coast was water. The Japanese had all but destroyed Chinese shipping, however, and the remaining boats had been taken over by the government for military purposes. "The shipping shortage is clearly reflected in the current Chinese price structure," Dad reported. "Rice is short now in Shanghai, which lies at the mouth of the Yangtze River. At the same time it is very plentiful in Szechuan Province, near the headwaters of the Yangtze. Rice prices are ten to twenty times as great as those in Szechuan. Normally river transportation would tend to equalize these prices, but shipping is so tight right now that they have little effect on one another."[61] Foreign shipping might have helped to ease the problem, my father wrote, but hatred of prewar imperialism was exploited by Chinese shippers so that vessels flying foreign flags were banned from all but a few ports, like Shanghai.

My father's task was to fill in gradually the picture for his readers of what was happening to China. Spot news reporters were tied to Shanghai or nearby Nanking, the capital, to be on hand for late-breaking stories. Other papers had only one man in China to cover the big story in Nanking. The *Tribune* had two men in China, and in addition relied on the news services for spot news. This released my father to travel about and see things with his own eyes. He made this kind of reporting his specialty from then on. "One of the best aids we had in China was personal observation," he later wrote, "which was done by riding through the country in buses, wandering in alleys, consorting with soldiers and waiters, drinking with generals, sleeping in small hotels, and watching what people did all the while. For fun and education there was nothing like it."[62]

Even as he covered the breakdown of the Marshall mediation effort and the incipient civil war, my father began to make his way around central and southern China, to Hankow ("the greatest city of interior China is still flat on its back from the war and shows little sign of being able to raise itself"); to Hengyang, where famine had been so serious people had been eating clay, and where local farmers now suffered such serious epidemics of malaria and dysentery that they were unable to harvest the rice crop; and to Canton, where he reported on the presence of bandits and Communists in southern China: ("It is also just about impossible to draw a line between Communists and bandits throughout South China. Banditry has been part of Kwangtung's landscape for ages. It never dies out in the backward districts, and it increases greatly in hard times. Communists have proseletyzed among bandits, and the latter are inclined to call themselves Communists without much reason beyond the wish to increase their impressiveness.")[63]

Once fighting resumed between the Nationalists and the Communists it was practically impossible to visit the front. "I never even knew where the front was," Keyes Beech, who had been sent to China by the *Chicago Daily News* to cover the civil war, later told me.[64] The

Communists, of course, no longer welcomed American reporters in their midst. The closest my father got to the Communists was in March 1947 on a brief flight to Yenan when he accompanied the staffs of the Communist liaison officers at Nanking and Shanghai who were being transferred back to their own territory. ("Their clothing fitted the work they had been doing, which was to represent Communism in the big cities—the political, commercial and news centers of non-Communist China. It became incongruous the minute they reached Yenan, the rustic capital of an organization whose whole base is rustic. Typical sights there are camel trains and peasants in raw hide coats. Hundreds of cave dwellings look down from the cliffs around the narrow, primitive town.")[65]

Reporting the China story from the Kuomintang side was a negative way to tell it and inevitably made the Nationalists look bad in the eyes of American readers. By implication, American policy didn't look too good, either. At home, Henry Luce led the pack of howling pro-Nationalist China lobbyists. Other publishers felt the same way Luce did, to a greater or lesser degree. That made it harder to get the story of what was really happening in China across to readers. My father, however, had friends or admirers on the editorial staff who protected his work. Surprisingly, there was no censorship in China of foreign reporting after the war and most of my father's stories were printed as he wrote them, including his big scoop on the Formosa massacre. This was an account he wrote following a visit he made to Formosa in March with Bill Powell (who had resumed publication of his father's *Shanghai Weekly Review*). Dad and Bill Powell discovered that the troops of general Ch'en Yi, the Chinese governor of Formosa, had slaughtered at least five thousand Formosans in the streets and in their houses. The Formosans, who had lived relatively peacefully under Japanese rule for fifty years until it ended on VJ Day, had staged protests against their new Chinese rulers because the quality of life under the new regime had deteriorated so drastically. ("The Disorders that spread through Formosa early this month are now almost over, but the memory of them will remain for some time. The ruthlessness and treachery of the Chinese government in dealing with them has deeply shocked all neutral observers here," my father wrote on March 24, 1947. "The resentment of the Formosans, which has been mounting steadily, came to a head on Feb. 27 [sic] when the police of the government's hate monopoly bureau killed an old woman peddler in a roundup of contraband cigarette stalls. The people started demonstrating, beating up mainland Chinese and destroying the cigarettes and stocks of other government monopolies. Government troops and police for their part became panicky and started firing into unarmed crowds. The disorders spread from Taipei, which is the capital city in the north, to other parts of the island.'')[66]

My father didn't think of himself strictly as a newspaper reporter, and this may have helped him as a journalist for the *Herald Tribune*. Although he had put in his years as a journeyman reporter, he really considered himself to be a writer. He aspired to literary craftsmanship, if not artistry. While in China he began to write for *The New Yorker* pieces that reveal some of the descriptive intensity of his later work as a travel writer. By the time he went to work for the *Trib* he had also developed an original voice. He tried to observe people and scenes with a fresh eye, and he liked to put himself in unusual situations that would force him to think in new ways. He also had the ability to make unusual connections between things, a knack facilitated by a gift of almost total recall. What he liked to do, in city or countryside, was to go on extended walks and in the course of these walks he would stop, stand in one place, observe, cogitate and even compose in his head a description of what he was looking at.

His thinking, his observations, his methods of obtaining information were all his own, emphatically so. This was also true of his language. He coupled his own speech rhythms with a style comprised of simple country expressions and a vocabulary derived from his classical education at Groton and Yale. The result was like good conversation. This was reinforced by his practice of dictating his work to a secretary, which he began to do after an episode in Peiping of Pure Discourse when he fell off a wall in the Forbidden City and damaged his wrist. For quite some time after that he was compelled to wear a sling, which prevented him from writing by hand or using a typewriter. This in effect changed his writing style, for he discovered that the conversational quality of dictation improved his prose, which in turn made it difficult for his editors at the *Herald Tribune* (a "terrible bunch of butchers," according to Arch Steele[67]) to cut. Consequently, he continued, at least for as long as he wrote for the *Herald Tribune*, to dictate his articles to a secretary. After that, his dispatches were usually printed as he sent them. Through this method, he was able to reach his readership in a more personal way than many reporters do, and later, as a *New Yorker* correspondent, he maintained the habit by reading his pieces out loud as he wrote them.

As a writer and as a reporter, my father was highly conscious of his reader. In China he deeply believed that his readers were out there, beyond the hostile barrier erected by the publishing industry and the China Lobby in postwar America. He worked hard to develop a method and a style that would enable him to do this. He was like Edgar Snow in this respect. These men did not only write for the pleasure of self–expression. In my father's family, high in artistic accomplishment, there was always a customer. One reason my father floundered when he tried to write fiction, I think, was that while it was not in his ethic to tap the source of his personal demons and make music, he also had no audience for whom he could fictionalize his experiences, and be an artist that way. Eventually, his readership came to expect from him a certain kind of nonfiction, just as Edgar Snow's readers wanted a mix of personal adventure and high–class journalism that after the Cold War began, he could no longer give them. Such are the perils of having a readership.

Snow's career as a journalist died a lingering death. My father dreamed of taking on the mantle of Henry James, and venerated Hemingway, and wrote fictions destined for the closet shelf, and continued through the 1950s and 1960s to address the needs of his aging readership with an ever heavier heart as he searched for new subjects to write about for *The New Yorker*. "Every new piece I write is less challenging than the last one," he once told my brother Chris.[68] In China, though, he was in his prime, as a man and as a writer. He had a great story to write, and he figured out how to tell it in a powerful and original way. He broke through the barrier. He and his readers found each other. Once that happens, and the bond is formed, writers experience a gratifying power. Success is theirs while the relationship lasts: money, reputation, worldly acclaim, in some combination all follow. My father paid a big price for success because in achieving it he had to relinquish his home and his family. Guilt never left him alone for long in the years that followed. He went around the world as a Far Flung Correspondent trying to escape from guilt. He took to drugs and religion to escape it. Finally, he flung himself out of a sixth–floor window to his death. Yet who knows? He was beset with inner rage and grief. He might very well have lost his family without the moments of triumph he experienced. For, like all the China Hand misfits who are the subjects of this book, he experienced triumph, fleeting though that sensation may have been. A sense of great purpose and the success that came with it were a transforming experience for my father, if not an altogether liberating one. He made a name for himself in China. With it, he commanded attention and respect for the rest of his life. That was a solace, surely, of sorts.

Barbara returned to Tihwa, not in May, as she had planned, but on July 24. The next day she wrote to my father to thank him for sending her a packing box full of her mail. "I had not expected to spend so long in South Sinkiang," she told him, "but the communications are entirely outside the bounds of anything reasonable. I returned from Hotien alone

and having spent almost the entire 4 months in the company of Chinese
and Turkie's [sic] without more than a very few minute's opportunity
to talk in English, I was in a pretty strange state of mind when I got
here."[69] She brought back seven notebooks packed with testimony by
Turkie people about their mistreatment at the hands of the Chinese.
Barbara's "strange state of mind" alienated her. "I had heard there were
some Americans in Tihwa and for no reason was somewhat terrified at
the prospect of seeing so many foreigners all at once—I'd only seen 2
or 3 in about ten months and had gotten to the point where anyone
without slanting eyes and black hair looked funny," she wrote. "I
barged into the Consulate where a luncheon party was in progress and
felt so funny that I just mumbled a few words and hunted a dark corner
where I spent the afternoon. It is perfectly ridiculous, but I just don't
know what to say any more. I will have learned however by the time I
reach Shanghai and this gradual breaking in is merciful."[70]

Barbara was outspoken, however, on the subject of her investigations, and word of this reached General Chang Chih-chung, the acting
governor of Sinkiang, and his number two man, General Sung Hsi-lien.
Moreover, on her visit to Ili in April, Barbara was observed by the
British consul, Eric Shipton, who wrote in a dispatch that she held
strong, preconceived ideas of how the Turkies were being ill-treated and
that her observations were "undoubtedly" colored by her ideological
views.[71] Her travels were noted by others as well, and since she seems
not to have been afraid to express her views, it is not surprising that her
presence in Sinkiang raised a few eyebrows. John Hall Paxton, the U.S.
consul in Tihwa, later wrote in a report to the U.S. embassy in Nanking
that "what was perhaps a friendly warning for Miss Stephens had already been received (through a third party, purporting to have come
from Generals Chang Chih-chung and Sung Hsi-lien) on account of
her incautious and bitter criticisms of Chinese government practices in
Nanchiang (South Sinkiang)." Paxton added, "I suggested to the Chinese authorities that they avoid any attempt to persuade her to reduce
her criticism of the government activities as that might be expected to
add fuel to the flames of her attacks in her writings once she had returned
to the United States. I also cautioned Miss Stephens," Paxton wrote,
"to be extremely discreet in her remarks and writing until she reached
'safer' areas lest her information be suppressed by some 'accident' to her
person."[72]

Paxton's warnings were not lost on Barbara. "I have information
and certain facts to prove that the gov't has and perhaps intends to apply
a very rigid censorship on the 'enemy propaganda' I have and plan to
disseminate about Sinkiang," she wrote my father. "In fact they are not
at all happy about me and certain informed sources as they call them

speak of accidents etc. I am not intimidated but just to ease their minds I plan to get out of here as soon as possible, flying to Lanchow and going from there to Sian and from Sian by train to Shanghai."[73] Barbara's notebooks, according to Paxton, amounted to full documentation of her charges of Chinese misgovernment in southern Sinkiang. Despite Paxton's warnings and despite the offer made by Douglas MacKiernan, a consular intelligence official, to microfilm her notes, Barbara made no provision to safeguard her evidence. She decided to hang on to it until she had been flown to safety.

Clearly Paxton had her best interests at heart. He admired Barbara. "She was a very young woman—only 23—who had shown great courage in her travelling," he stated in his report to the U.S. ambassador. "She had greatly improved her Chinese by use in her travels and spoke it fluently and well by the time of her departure from Tihwa although she had had little formal study and knew nothing of the written language." She came to Sinkiang "rather over-inclined to accept with passionate assurance that if only the Chinese control of this area were removed the people would fare far better, even under Soviet domination which, she admitted, would probably follow," he wrote. When she came back from south Sinkiang, Paxton noted, "it appeared that she had seen enough of the terror inspired by Soviet undercover activities to feel that their control was not the ultimately best solution for the majority of the people and she seemed to favor gradually increased autonomy of the area under nominal control of the Chinese Government without the plague of Chinese officials that she felt were sucking the blood of the people." Paxton wrote, "I feel that her estimate, if the foregoing be a fair estimate of it, may not be far off the mark."[74]

In Tihwa, on the morning of July 29, Barbara boarded a Chinese air force C-47 transport plane, equipped with bucket seats, bound for Lanchow. Of the two pilots who flew the plane, one had received his flight training in the United States. The plane, No. 257, had been scheduled to fly first to Kashgar, before heading back to Lanchow. It had only gone as far as Aksu when reportedly it had developed engine trouble, and flown back to Tihwa to pick up passengers there for the return trip. The other non-Asian passenger on the plane besides Barbara was a British member of the Friends' Ambulance Unit named Brian Sorensen. Others aboard, according to Paxton's report, included Hsieh Yung-tsun, a secretary from the Tihwa Kuomintang headquarters, three prisoners and two Chinese artists, Han Lo-jan and Lu Feng, both leftists. "Han Lo-jan," Paxton wrote, "had been imprisoned until his 'conversion' to more approved views (Miss Stephens informed me that his real attitude had not been changed and that he opposed the Kuomintang as bitterly as ever, in fact, but had learned discretion)."[75] The wife and two children of General Hon Sang, commander of the garrison forces at Aksu, were scheduled to board the plane at Tihwa, but on the morning of the flight they failed to show up at the airfield, and the plane took off without them. It was understood later that General Hon's wife was "indisposed." There was one important KMT official on the plane. This was Major General Yu, chief-of-staff to General Chang Chih-chung. General Yu, however, disembarked at Hami, which was the plane's first stop.

The plane remained in Hami overnight. On July 30 it took off, but because of poor flying conditions it returned to Hami the same day. The pilots made yet another attempt on the thirty-first. The weather was good at the outset but may have grown turbulent and overcast after takeoff. The pilots were said to be impatient, at that point, to get back to Peiping, to their families. On August 1, Paxton cabled the U.S. embassy at eight o'clock in the evening: "Have just learned that Chinese Air Force plane transporting Miss Barbara Stephens (American freelance correspondent) and Brian Sorensen (English member of Friends' Ambulance Unit) has not been reported since departing from Suchow for Lanchow morning July 29th."[76] This was not entirely correct. It was last seen, as Paxton later reported, on the thirty-first of July. "Now learned that [not] missing until July 31st when it took off at 2:50 in good weather," Paxton telegraphed Nanking on the second of August. "Radio contact was broken at 4:50 p.m. about quarter hour out from Chia Yu Kwan Air Field in Kansu. This is rugged terrain and local Chinese air force authorities fear aircraft has crashed."[77]

Just exactly what happened to the plane remained a mystery for some time to come. The terrain over which the C-47 had vanished was rugged and weather conditions there were subject to sudden change. The search effort was necessarily a matter for the Chinese air force to pursue, and they appeared to be reluctant. On August 4, Paxton wired the American embassy in Nanking: "Only available information regards missing aircraft is that search plane merely returned to Hami yesterday and is not actually commencing patrol until today. This may have been due to weather out of Hami. It was clear here. Any news received from CAF headquarters would be appreciated."[78] By August 6, Paxton was clearly disturbed by the failure of the Chinese air force to launch a full-scale search for the missing plane. "Reference Tihwa telegram to Department 35 August 4, re missing plane with Barbara Stephens aboard," Paxton wired Nanking. "Subordinate of local Foreign Office representative informed me yesterday that while a single search plane was making occasional patrols for lost aircraft, CAF authorities seemed to be relying on eventual report by villagers on forced landing to District Magistrate. As their chief interest was in material rather than personnel, news might be long delayed. Little concern seems felt for possibly injured survivors as no important Chinese aboard."[79]

It was clear by the following week to Americans in both Nanking and Washington that Chinese officials were dragging their feet in the search effort. Barbara Stephens's mother in Arlington, Virginia, had been informed about the missing plane immediately. As days went by without any word, she put pressure on General Marshall, who was now secretary of state. On August 9, Marshall sent an urgent cable under his own signature to the Nanking embassy: "Mother's anxiety great and threatens publicity campaign force more positive action asserting Chinese search not sufficiently diligent and Dept remiss in urging efforts."[80] He directed the embassy to make stronger inquiries of the CAF. Meanwhile, John Melby, who was attached to the Nanking embassy, wrote in his diary on August 9: "Trouble comes in bunches. In the last two days some American soldiers in Nanking drowned two Chinese, apparently the outcome of some horseplay; in Shanghai another shot one; in Tientsin a Marine did the same thing. And in Sinkiang a Chinese plane crashed killing all aboard, including Barbara Stephens, a young reporter I had known in Chungking. She was a lovely girl. The Chinese are not even trying to get to the wreckage, saying that no one of importance was aboard; but there is reason to think there were some whom they are just as glad to be rid of on account of political activities they considered undesirable. A rather cryptic message from Barbara just before she got on the plane at Tihwa suggested as much and that she was following some lead for a newspaper story. Now we will never really know."[81]

The possibility of sabotage was finally directly addressed by Consul Paxton in his five-page, single-spaced typed report to the secretary of state on August 20. Paxton was disturbed by the foot dragging of the Chinese, who were reluctant to keep him informed about the search. They volunteered no information about the nature of their effort, and when Paxton made inquiries, he never received information other than that which he requested. It was evidently not unusual for the CAF to take their time searching for lost planes, and officials seemed to be waiting for villagers in the area to report signs of the missing C-47 in order not to use up expensive fuel in a painstaking aerial search over rugged topography. Nevertheless, it was the first plane lost in Sinkiang in four years, and local officials were notably evasive when the subject came up. "The possibility that the destruction of the plane and its passengers was desired, though wild, is conceivable, at least in this lawless area," Paxton wrote. "It is technically possible that a time bomb could have been placed in the baggage aboard the plane, set to explode when it was over the worst terrain and calculated to damage the steering mechanism so seriously as to make a crash inevitable, resulting in the almost certain death of all persons on the plane."[82]

Paxton described the warnings he had conveyed to Barbara, and observed that "Since the disappearance of her plane two casual enquiries have been made as to the whereabouts" of her notebooks. "In view of the absence of important Chinese reported aboard the plane at the time of its disappearance," Paxton wrote, "it is a conceivable motivation that a Chinese secret agent charged with the destruction of the evidence of Miss Stephens' first hand observations of Chinese malpractices (many of which, to judge from her own remarks, have been carefully concealed from Generals Chang and Sung) might have considered the loss of the plane to be unimportant compared with the accomplishment of his mission. If such an 'accident' were deliberately planned, that it was delayed until after her arrival at Tihwa, might be attributed to the certainty that any accident on the road could be expected to be subject to severe scrutiny and it would not have been easy to destroy evidence of foul play unless all witnesses were disposed of at the same time as was the case in the presumed plane crash," the consul speculated.[83]

"Your father was terribly shaken by the news of Barbara's disappearance," John Melby told me years later.[84] On July 28, the day before Barbara boarded the ill-fated C-47 in Tihwa, Dad had written a long letter that he had mailed to her care of the U.S. consulate in Tihwa: "It is a long time since I have written to you, but then so far as I know it is even longer since you have written to me (I never can be sure of this, because your letters come in at queer intervals and by queer means; how can I tell that there isn't a camel waiting downstairs with something?)" He wrote to tell her that he was suffering from prickly heat, that he had been to both Peking and Manchuria and was planning a trip to Canton and Macau that week with Bill Powell, Pepper Martin and Preston Schoyer, the novelist he had met in China during the war. "So far this year has been a Communist one here," he wrote. "It looks as if they might knock off Manchuria soon, and they are having pretty much their own way everywhere."[85]

He gave her as much gossip as he could. "Graham is evidently fine," he wrote. "He is living with his family in Derby, where there doesn't seem to be much pure discourse, and according to him no lying around drunk in the middle of the day, so he is making good headway on his book, which according to one rumor I have just heard may turn out to be two books." He told her that Arch Steele was away, and that he had the "freedom to roam about China at will." He urged Barbara to return. "It is certainly not my place to advise you about your movements," he wrote, "but it occurs to me that there are some people who are very fond of you who are waiting on the other side of the ocean. I haven't heard anything from your mother since I saw her in February of last year, though I have sometimes thought of writing to her. I dare say she will be glad to see you, even if you look like a camel or a Uighur." He had promised Graham to speed her homeward from Shanghai. He told her, "I am very much out of touch with you, and for all I know what you are doing may demand your attention for many months without let up. On the other hand it may be that since you have such a long life ahead of you, you might be able to spare a few months toward the spreading of happiness to those who need it in the bleak northeastern U.S.," he wrote. "Not having seen you for almost a year, how can I tell what you are after? If it is freedom, it strikes me you have established your claim to that, and no one can take it away from you. My own feelings toward you are not of much consequence and are not worth going into. You know how I will look on you always. Am looking forward to a chance to bat the breeze with you," he wrote. "Have you let your hair grow? God and the angels bless you, Barbara. Always as ever, and you know it."[86]

Dad headed up to Sinkiang on the fourth of September, a year almost to the day after his rendezvous with Barbara in Shanghai. The plane was still missing, and he assured Barbara's mother, by letter, that he would find out everything he could about its disappearance. He was due for a trip up to the region for his paper anyway (and subsequently the flight he made became the subject for a *New Yorker* piece he subsequently wrote called "Flight to Urumchi").[87] Barbara, though, was high on his list of reasons for going when he did, although he was not optimistic about finding her alive when he got there. "I have heard rumors that the plane came down safely in the desert etc.," he wrote Mrs. Stephens. "I would advise you not to pin too much on these. Rumors spring up around most events in the remote parts of China. But I can tell you more about this after I have been up in that country."[88]

One rumor had it, as Dad later wrote Graham Peck, "That the pilot was suspected either of Communist leanings or opium smuggling and had gotten the wind up and gone off to Outer Mongolia."[89] Another was that "several of the other passengers, including Barbara, were frowned on by the authorities and had therefore been taken off to some secret spot and confined."[90] Dad spent two weeks in Sinkiang. He couldn't find out any more about what had happened than was already known, including the rumors. "I believe rumors like this appear whenever anything noteworthy happens in Sinkiang," he wrote Graham. "When I was there I got the impression that the plane's disappearance could be easily accounted for by very bad flying, which is SOP [standard operating procedure] with the Chinese Air Force."[91] When he returned to Shanghai, still no sign of the wreckage had been sighted.

An offer of a thousand dollars had been made to anyone with proof of Barbara's whereabouts, however, and at the urging of the State Department, the Ministry of Foreign Affairs requested the air force to continue with the search-and-rescue effort.

The time had arrived, in early October 1947, for my mother's visit to China. Her trip had been in the offing for a long time. When writing to her on board the *Marine Lynx* in June 1946, Dad had raised the possibility of a trip that coming winter. This idea was proposed before my sister Diana was born in September 1946. As it happened, the birth was followed by a complication. Aside from the usual postpartum depression, my mother suffered a serious case of phlebitis in the legs. She survived this setback but it required a long period of recuperation, and a trip to China by Christmas time was out of the question. My father kept encouraging her, however, in his letters home. He wrote letters that were loving and at the same time defensive, if not burdened with guilt. He wanted my mother to accept his work in China. "I feel it's essential for you to see China and see me at work and form some opinion of the whole deal," he wrote. "As far as the job goes, it is still the best way I have ever discovered of applying my energy." He acknowledged that there were problems. "The complications between it and home are formidable, but worse things have been overcome before, and I think we can handle it if we try hard."[92]

That was in July 1946. In November, he wrote a long, tightly written review of his career for my mother in which he justified his decision to return to China. He conceded, however, that on his trip home after the war "I showed a great callousness to you and your problems." This was due to wartime experience, he told her. "That you shouldn't do it with a wife and many children in peacetime was something that hadn't filtered back into my head, though it has now as I have thought about it and talked to people and heard about the hair-raising things you have been up against." He acknowledged also that in Marin County his conviction that he could make the grade as a reporter in China had led to "a blind determination not to discuss anything that would interfere with my purpose." Now that he had succeeded, however, and was "too far gone in the writing business to try anything else," he was ready to talk with her about their future together, in the Far East, or elsewhere. "If we can get together and go over everything, preferably I suppose late at night, I am sure we will come out with an acceptable answer," he wrote my mother in December. "First I think you must really have a decent look at China, though. If after that you decide it's no go we can change the program accordingly. But I think the chances are very good you'd like it a lot and would feel it would be a good thing for the children."[93]

Here my father's instincts grievously led him astray. My mother's arrival in China aboard a Pan Am Clipper was inauspicious. With the single exception of a visit to Mexico and a trip to Algeria during her junior year at Vassar when she had been a student at the Sorbonne, she had not traveled to "backward" countries. She was not altogether prepared, therefore, to cope with the culture shock of postwar travel in the Far East. She flew from San Francisco to Shanghai. The plane trip was broken by a number of stops, including Wake Island and Okinawa, where airline officials opted to take on extra passengers instead of extra fuel, a decision that caused some anxiety over Shanghai, where the plane was forced to circle the airfield in a typhoon for half an hour. On the ground, people meeting arrivals were understandably nervous because a plane had crashed a week earlier in Shanghai during a typhoon. The pilots finally "found a hole in the typhoon," as my mother put it, and flew down through it to safety.[94]

My father was among the greeters. He was heavily under the influence of alcohol, holding a bunch of roses that had become crushed out of shape in the melee. The airport was a mob scene to a degree entirely new to my mother: screaming, chattering, sobbing people thronging the building to no apparent purpose, shouting in high-pitched Shanghainese, nobody keeping order. If the airport scene was a shock to my mother, however, the city of Shanghai itself came as a further disturbing revelation, with its bedlam, streets teeming with people and animals and cars.

Dad took her to Broadway Mansions, where she beheld the walls from which the Japanese had ripped the fixtures. She spent her most peaceful moments in Shanghai there, however, in the apartment of John Purcell. John worked for *Life* as a journalist and coordinator, and his wife, Elizabeth, worked for the *China Weekly Review*. My mother found the lugubrious wind that blew around the top of the tall building unsettling, and she recalled not long ago how on her first night in Shanghai my father took her to the Columbia Country Club with other correspondents and their wives. It was her first experience among China Hands in China. She discovered that what they liked to do, and indeed compulsively pursued, besides drinking, was discussion about Chinese politics. She was not, at that point, well informed on the subject, she felt unwelcome in their midst, and she thought she was unable to contribute anything to the conversation. She had also just crossed the Pacific Ocean on a sometimes harrowing flight. She went out on the terrace to have a good cry. The diners, eventually seeing that she was missing, launched a search for her. Afterward, word got around that when my father got back to Broadway Mansions he spent most of that night in a bathtub of cold water in a room across the hall. "He stayed in there so long that the next day his skin was all shriveled up, like a prune," one correspondent, Bob Burton, told me years later, in Hong Kong.[95]

Needless to say, my mother was not altogether as taken with the Chinese as Dad was. She liked them, but she did not like the way they spat and, as she put it, "threw food on the floor."[96] In Nanking she saw rats gnawing chicken bones on the floor of a restaurant where she was eating. This disturbed her. The food also took some getting used to. "All that rich Peking duck for lunch. God," she later declared, "I'm much happier with a plain sandwich."[97] In Nanking, she and Dad attended a luncheon given by Hollington Tong for the press corps, where she ate "Chungking" food for the first time, hot, chili-based Szechuan dishes. She had the beginnings of a cold just then, a sore place at the back of her throat. She was picking carefully at her food, and decided to try an innocuous-looking piece of lettuce, which turned out to be spinach marinated in Szechuan oil. "It was like an explosion, like dynamite," she later recalled. Her eyes watered, and she began to cough. The vice minister of foreign affairs, George Yeh, who happened to be sitting next to her, quickly got her some tea. The spinach, and the force of the explosion, had blasted away the sore spot.[98]

My father was enraged by almost everything my mother did or said in the presence of other correspondents. When she got to China, he had told her not to worry about her behavior or what she said when they were with his colleagues. "They'll all like you because you're my wife," he told her. Yet when she "got too chatty" at meals, especially on the subject of Chinese politics, he'd try to silence her by kicking her under the table.[99] Dad's behavior in China shocked my mother. He seemed brutal. She'd noticed his public irascibility for the first time in Shanghai, after they'd gone by pedicab to a White Russian restaurant. One of the pedicab boys had followed them into the restaurant to demand more money, and my father had berated him furiously in front of other diners. She didn't understand that these were the British colonial manners people who lived out in the world of Empire were apt to acquire. She objected to the way Dad and his friends treated the Chinese. For despite the sympathy that Dad and his friends, and, indeed, most correspondents, showed toward the Chinese, there was a tendency among them to mock the citizens of their host country. The familiarity of wartime bred a certain contempt for the Chinese, which was a part, unconscious though it may have been, of the colonial mentality, both British and American. Nor did my mother care for the correspondents as a group. "All told, they were a seedy bunch," she recalled. "They behaved together like a bunch of schoolboys. They never looked like much once you saw them over here in the States."[100]

My mother's impression of the journalists was formed in part by their behavior at the Press Hostel in Nanking. She knew nothing about Barbara Stephens, or about the tragic mystery of her disappearance. No one, including my father, had mentioned a word about it to her. While she and Dad were in Nanking, however, word came that the C-47 had been found. Wreckage of the plane had been discovered by searchers at a village called Wang Shih Kou in the Kya Ku Kwan Mountains some three hundred miles northwest of Lanchow. A telegram received by the Ministry of Foreign Affairs from the Kansu provincial government stated that, "The military plane which was missing between Hami-Kansu was discovered on a great mountain situation 80 Chinese *li* to the north of Chia Yu Kuan. This fact was ascertained to be true by officers sent to investigate on the spot. Besides, a gun and a diary and other things were discovered as proof. The body of the plane was destroyed by fire, though the number 257 can still be discerned on the tail of the plane."[101]

On the eighth of October, an assistant military air attaché at the Nanking embassy, Air Corps Major Kearie L. Berry, Jr., flew up to Chia Yu Kuan on a CAF plane. The bodies, twenty altogether, had been removed from the site of the wreckage to a temple near the air base and Berry was taken there to identify the remains of Barbara and Brian Sorensen, the Friends' Ambulance Service official. Their bodies were badly burned, but Berry was nonetheless able to identify them by taking measurements ("height of bodies, size of feet, etc.")[102] When word reached the Press Hostel that Barbara's plane had been found, the news created quite a stir, but nobody dared tell my mother what it was all about. Whenever she entered a room, people would stop talking at once and look at her. All she could pick up were veiled references to "Kazakhs." People would say something about Kazakhs, look at my mother, and then stop talking. Finally, Peggy Durdin, who ran the Nanking Press Hostel, took her aside and explained to her what had happened.[103] Barbara's name was never mentioned again. Nor does she recall that my father was visibly upset by the news that Barbara's body had been recovered, although by that time Barbara's death was a foregone conclusion accepted by everyone except possibly her family.

My mother stayed in China for five weeks. From Nanking she and Dad flew up to Peiping on a China Air Transport plane. For the novice, this was a hair-raising experience of the sort my father greatly enjoyed and my mother intensely disliked. Dad explained to her first of all that their Chinese pilot flew the plane right up into the air without properly taking off down the runaway in order to avoid gunfire. This by itself was unsettling. He next confided that on a recent flight cows had wandered up to the cockpit and poked their heads between the pilot and co-pilot. From the air, as they circled the Peiping airport for a landing, my mother could make out a pack of dogs leaping furiously about in a corner of the airfield. On the ground, she realized that the dogs were playing with a human head. Apparently an airport coolie had been decapitated by a propeller blade. Workmen at the airport had been able to retrieve the body, but they had not managed to get the head away from the dogs.

In Peiping, they went to the compound of Josephine and Jim Burke, a freelance writer who later became a star *Life* photographer. The Burke compound was part of a Manchu palace complex, home to other foreign correspondents, situated on Ta Tien Shui Ching, not far from the Forbidden City. Peiping was bitterly cold. The Burkes' house seemed primitive to my mother, who wasn't prepared for paper windows and the restricted warmth of coal-burning braziers, which heat the area immediately within their vicinity only, but fill the rooms with smoke. Westerners, especially, sometimes forgot to extinguish their fires and consequently suffered smoke poisoning and even death by asphyxiation in their sleep. My mother continued to wear the fur coat she had brought, but she shivered inside it. She also began to suffer once again from the cold that had been temporarily banished by the Szechuan spinach. She and Dad moved into the Wagons-Lits Hotel. There, all the steam that was supposed to heat the radiators came pouring forth from the spigots in the bathroom and this greatly improved her cold.

Apart from these discomforts, my mother enjoyed Peiping. It was a buyer's market at that time. The China Hands, she observed, were mad about buying things. My father invited curio dealers up to their hotel room to display their wares, received them with the great display of ceremony that had become an essential part of his manner when dealing with Chinese intellectuals and antiquarians, and then stood there while my mother picked and chose. On at least one occasion she visited the public market place, but she was put off by the ferocity of Chinese street people and by the pedicab drivers outside the hotel who fought and shouted among themselves over the clientele. Otherwise, she found the people of Peiping attractive, chic and bright, like Parisians. She also enjoyed the smooth, undulant rhythm of the rickshaw, and the padded sound rickshaw boys' feet made on the pavement as they trotted through the silent *hutungs*.

By now, the city was under siege. "We could hear gunfire all around the city after dark," she recalled. One evening, there was a panic. Word went out: "They're coming tonight." "They are not coming tonight," my father declared emphatically, and indeed they did not come that night or any night soon.[104] The plan the Communists had conceived was far more subtle, to take the city relatively peacefully, by slowly cutting it off from the outside world, which is precisely what they did. In 1949 General Fu Tso-yi, the Nationalist warlord, surrendered Peiping to the rebels without a shot fired. By then, CAT pilots, and fliers for China National Airways, General Chennault's converted wartime air operation, along with various other entrepreneurs, had made a fortune for well over a year in gold bullion flying the lucky rich out of north China.

I have heard Peiping described on the eve of the Communist takeover as "ripe Camembert" and "ripe Stilton," both.[105] Whichever cheese it may have resembled, the wicked old walled city was not deemed by my mother to be a suitable place at the time for bringing up children. That was her way of informing my father that she had no intention of moving our family to China. At a brisk glance, it was not the right environment for a family life, since a civil war was raging in the countryside, and soon such items as coal and sugar would be hard to come by.

A civil war was also raging within my parents' marriage, however. Like other wars, this one was about power. In China the power belonged to my father. He had long since abandoned the home front. China was his turf. When my mother came to visit, he took time off to escort her around. He was proud of his role in China and he wanted her to see him in it. He was also proud of her in the abstract. "I married a high-born lady,"[106] he once declared in his cups to Bob Drummond, a friend in Peiping. She was cultured, bright, well educated and extremely attractive. "Your father went way up in my estimation when I met your mother in Shanghai,"[107] Mary Sullivan, who worked on the staff of the *China Weekly Review* in the late 1940s, told me not long ago.

Dad wanted to show my mother off to his friends. He did not, however, want her to assert herself in any way. Partly, he had come to China to get away once and for all from domination. He had seen his own father dominated by his powerful mother. This was a situation that had aroused in him contempt for his father and a certain terror, a self-loathing, he had set about ruthlessly to correct. It was not, however, in my mother's nature to submit to his rather dominating ways. In China, though, there wasn't too much that she could do about him. In response to his heavy-handed method of calling the shots, she could retaliate. In photographs taken of Mom in China she often looks as though she might be biding her time, and one in particular, on the terrace in front of the Temple of Heaven in Peiping, shows her both watchful and glamorous. (The latter was a photograph my father carefully filed away in the black file cabinet.) She never looks happy in China and sometimes she even looks ravaged. She was losing this fight far away from home. She didn't exactly lose the war, though. The Nationalists lost the war. Dad lost China and my mother and his family, although he did make a name for himself in the process. My mother's visit to China was a hollow victory for Dad. The marriage was over when the visit ended, though nothing of the sort was conceded at the time. The China Hands all knew it. Mom's departure from Shanghai left both of my parents depressed, like two fighters who have sparred with each other to a pointless draw.

My father stayed on in China until the following June. He made an effort to gather the belongings that Barbara Stephens had left in various cities around China and ship them home to her mother in Arlington. He wrote to Mrs. Stephens in late November about his trip to Sinkiang, and the subsequent discovery of the plane. "It occurs to me you might possibly feel she got on that particular plane, rather than waiting for another one, because she felt she had no right to delay getting home any longer. I don't believe this is true at all," Dad wrote. "She had been considerably delayed on her Kashgar trip; long before it ended she had accomplished her objective, which I would guess was primarily to prove to herself what she could do and secondarily to gather material for a book; that was finished and she was determined on general principles to get moving; and my experience is that there would be no stopping her when she was in a mood like that," Dad wrote. Then he added, "Getting around China takes some qualities that few people seem to have, but that Barbara had in a high degree. Her mastery of the language was remarkable, for one thing. I suppose there were 100 or 200 people who came out here with the O.W.I. during the war, and not one of them (except a few who had been here previously) came anywhere near her in this. As you say, she was completely fearless. She was also very quick on her feet, and I believe could talk herself out of any situation that didn't involve a failing airplane. As you may have guessed, I was extremely fond of her, yet I never worried about her going off on that trip because she was so thoroughly able to take care of herself."[108]

Nothing to implicate the Chinese in a plot to destroy Barbara's plane was ever found. The case was soon closed. O. Edmund Clubb, the U.S. consul general in Peiping at the time, many years later told me that the Chinese were perfectly capable of blowing up a plane.[109] Barbara, in a letter to her mother written five days before she left Tihwa, wrote quite candidly of her situation. "Many of the things I must write are very damning," she wrote, "will gain me the eternal hatred of a great many very important, influential and powerful Chinese, which in itself is dangerous. I made the great mistake of sending a couple of stories out by Chinese post before I left Tihwa (early April) which were particularly fierce, thinking that they were honest in talking of no censorship—which shows what a fool I was. They were no doubt carefully read, probably held up, as I have had no word about them, which is strange, and which I certainly shall not treat lightly when I get out of this place and can write. The word has been carefully delivered indirectly to Paxton, the Consul, that the former Governor and the Military Commander here are very unhappy about certain very severe criticisms I have made of the Chinese government and asked if he thought censorship should be applied. They can't very well censor me or anything I write when I get out of Sinkiang, so there is only one way to do it and that is while I am here. Do not get any silly ideas. The Chinese have gotten over their violent means of 'complete' censorship of a person they don't like I am sure, although Paxton, who loves drama, talks much foolishness of getting out quick. This business is just a big pain in the neck, but just to keep from getting on their [word erased] I am getting out on the first plane which will probably please those in power immensely. If they try any funny stuff it will just make a better story for me and they've got more sense than that when they are wooing the American government. This whole business is enough to make you sick as a kitten.''[110]

Barbara was given a proper burial in Nanking, on December 22, on a cold, bright winter afternoon among the bare hills outside the city. Various friends, embassy personnel and journalists, including my father, were present. The service was conducted by Ambassador John Leighton Stuart. Barbara's friends Jim Burke, Bill Powell, Graham Peck, my father and Lao Yeh contributed the gravestone. Barbara's name, and her dates (1922–1947), were carved in English at the base. The marker was an elegant, tall rectangular marble slab. A message in Chinese, inscribed in vertical rows of Chinese characters, began: "She was young, brave, liked to talk, liked to drink. She had a husky voice. She is buried here." The translated inscription that follows reads:

> *You died and went back to the place*
> *Where you are from*
> *But we are still here in this bloody,*
> *Crazy, unlucky world.*
> *But as you know we will fight*
> *Forever without hesitation.*
> *We will never give up, and will*
> *Still drink vodka and laugh loudly.*
> *Go my dear child without worry*
> *You will still be alive in our hearts.*

Afterword

Arch Steele saw the end approach. He had taken a house in Peiping in the autumn of 1948 "for the duration," as he put it in a letter to my father, who at the time was a Nieman Fellow at Harvard University. Once, in Chungking, Steele had confided to Brooks Atkinson that he hoped to hibernate in Peiping for the rest of his life. This was not to be. "Like a sick old man who has lived a full but wicked life, Lao Bayjing is preparing itself for its next incarnation," he wrote my father. "The exodus from Peiping (to resort to the purple prose of the [Peiping] Chronicle) is 'rampant': Shanghai-bound planes are booked up until next March."[1] At that time those with the most to lose from a Communist victory were hastily taking flight. In December when the city came under siege, almost all foreigners in Peiping were urged to leave. The city was under mortar attack by the surrounding Reds; fuel, electricity and food supplies were all cut off. It lasted for six weeks. Fu Tso-yi, the general in command of Peiping, surrendered on January 22, 1949. When the People's Liberation Army marched into Peiping, few Americans were there to record the event, and when Mao Tse-tung proclaimed the People's Republic of China, on October 1, 1949, from the T'ian-an-men Gate, no American journalist was there to report it.

Nor were the China Hands made to feel welcome by the Communist leaders who had once befriended them in Chungking, Yenan or Hankow. The new leaders of China wanted to distance themselves from the correspondents. A few China Hands were still around when the Red avalanche from the north descended on the Yangtze Valley and the Communists crossed the Yangtze River and entered Shanghai. They were shocked when old friends like Huang Hua and Kung P'eng cut them dead on the sidewalk or crossed the street to avoid them. In their own country, the China Hands were prophets without honor. There, too, a cold, if not hostile, reception awaited them.

The aftertaste of China was bitter for many of the journalists whom I have written about in this chronicle. The reasons vary, but most of those who were dedicated to China suffered because they had lost the source of their inspiration and passion. Many, even though they might not have wanted to stay on permanently, would have continued to make China the core of their careers. For most China Hands, this was not possible, if only because there was no market for books and articles about China. After the war, and especially after the failure of General Marshall to mediate a successful arrangement in power sharing between the Communists and the Nationalists, Americans became disenchanted with the subject of China. It had become a symbol of American failure. Sick of war and confused by a peace that ushered in a more complicated world order, most Americans turned their backs on China.

At the same time, the idea that China had been "lost" to the Communists gained currency, especially when Ambassador Hurley returned to the United States in 1946 and began to spread the word on radio talk shows that certain members of his staff in China who had favored opening up relations with the guerrillas in Yenan had "lost" China. The anti-Communist movement was already under way in America, launched by the Republican Party, which was frustrated after years of Democratic rule in Washington. The Republicans found common cause with the China Lobby, a consortium of missionaries and business leaders, publishers like Henry Luce and Nationalist Chinese in the United States who fought bitterly on Capitol Hill and in the press for greater U.S. involvement in China's civil war on the side of Chiang Kai-shek. The Truman administration resisted the China Lobby, and after the liberation, Communist China became the most visible proof, besides Yalta, of how Roosevelt and the Democrats had allowed themselves to be "duped" by "Reds" in the Foreign Service and elsewhere. Anyone associated with China over the long haul who had not been staunchly anti-Communist and pro–Chiang Kai-shek ran the risk of being singled out and publicly exposed by the inquisition that followed as "soft on Communism."

Careers were destroyed, valuable expertise was jettisoned. A number of important China Hands in the State Department were purged on the basis of circumstantial evidence or no evidence at all, merely on unsubstantiated testimony that they had been somehow tangentially involved with American Communism. Not a single China Hand was ever found to have been disloyal in any regard to his country. One need only mention certain names to recognize the truth of the outrage: O. Edmund Clubb, John Stewart Service, John Paton Davies, John Carter Vincent. One result of the purge of China Hands was the disastrous U.S. involvement in Vietnam, a war that haunts us still.

If you had been a journalist in China during those years, the best thing to do was to stay out of the United States, and that's what most did, except for those who, like George Sokolsky and Freda Utley, offered spurious witness against their colleagues. Agnes Smedley remained adamantly pro-Communist to the end, which came in England where she had gone to live at the close of the decade. Anna Louise Strong continued to make Moscow her base, until Stalin expelled her in 1949 and she went to live and, finally, in 1970, die in Beijing, where she was considered something of an icon by those in power.

Edgar Snow, who never carried heavy ideological baggage, continued to see himself as a friend of the Communists. For over a decade after they came to power, however, the Communists did not see it that way. Snow was not allowed back in until the 1960s, when he wrote extensively, and fairly glowingly, of Mao's China. (Don't go there unless you pay your own way, was Snow's advice to Jack Belden.) Snow, too, became an icon of the Chinese, along with Anna Louise Strong and Smedley, in the Three S Society, which was formed in China to celebrate these friends of the Revolution.

Snow's career in his own country had long since ground to a halt. He was the most visible victim among his colleagues of the Washington smear campaign, with the exception of Owen Lattimore, McCarthy's number one State Department Communist, a former journalist and Central Asian scholar who had been Chiang Kai-shek's adviser in Chungking on the recommendation of President Roosevelt for a short period of time in 1941. Unlike Lattimore, Snow was never subpoenaed and brought before a committee and forced to answer false charges. But his name kept coming up in testimony and in newspaper columns, in all the whispering galleries. Snow was as American as the Missouri River, "but," as Laughlin Currie, Roosevelt's personal representative to Chiang Kai-shek and another victim of McCarthyism, later put it, "you never live down guilt by association."[2]

There were always other, contributing circumstances when the careers of journalists foundered after China. Snow found it hard to land other stories to write. He continued to cover Communism in Third World countries when perhaps he should have tried to find a whole new area of interest. What he had to say about the subject was far too complex and detached for his employer, the Saturday Evening Post, which was an essentially conservative magazine. When the magazine's editors tampered with Snow's work, he quit, which left him high and dry.[3] Coupled with his own career problems, the whisper campaign did him in and he eventually moved to Switzerland. On his occasional visits to Washington after trips to Mao's China (when nobody else was going there) he got the cold shoulder from the New Frontier and Johnson's White House. Ironically, it was Snow who first brought word that Mao would welcome Nixon. The tragedy is that sixty-two hours before Nixon flew to China on his historic mission of rapprochement, Snow died of cancer in Switzerland. He was attended by a medical team sent by Chou En-lai to ease the ending.

Others who were less obviously identified with the Chinese Communists fared better. Arch Steele retired in the 1960s after a career as a foreign correspondent covering other parts of the world, including the Middle East. Tillman Durdin continued to report from the Far East. So did Pepper Martin, Keyes Beech and my father. Dad covered the Korean War, along with Beech, Martin and others, but in the middle of it all he quit the *Herald Tribune* to freelance, mostly for *The New Yorker*. He wrote from Hong Kong, from Southeast Asia, from India, Pakistan and Nepal, and enlarged on his reputation as an Asia Hand. He generally preferred to avoid politics altogether. He walked, and observed, and sometimes took part in ritual events, and then wrote about what he had seen in a language that was always precise and original. In his travel pieces or essays for *The New Yorker* he always managed to illuminate part of the rich tapestry of a culture. His pieces on Asia have been collected and published in three books, *Hongkong: The Island Between*, *A Nostalgia for Camels* and *Mountains and Water*.

Teddy White turned his back on China altogether for many years after the publication of the book he co-wrote with Annalee Jacoby. This was calculated to avoid the guilt-by-association scourge. New York had dried up for him, and he was lucky to be able to start all over again in Paris, which became his base as he covered the Marshall Plan in Europe as a news service reporter. He arose like a phoenix in the early 1950s with *Fire in the Ashes,* his book about the regeneration of Europe.

The few, fortunate China Hands were those who could channel their passions elsewhere. By the time Harold Isaacs returned to Chung-King during the war, he had detached himself from the obsession of his youth. He was a different person when he covered the China-Burma-India theater for *Newsweek*. In the years that followed, although he edited and revised *The Tragedy of the Chinese Revolution* twice, he focused on other matters. In 1954 he went to work as a resident social scientist and writer at MIT where he also taught. The inquisition somehow passed him by. This is surprising. As a once passionate Trotskyist, he was one China Hand with a history of radical ideology. Indeed, in the late 1940s the China Lobby turned its gaze on Isaacs when he was still working for *Newsweek*. The organization sent a letter to his boss, Chet Shaw, who was not known for his liberal outlook, advising him to fire Isaacs. Shaw took the letter to Isaacs, told him to draft an answer and send it back for his signature. Isaacs was never bothered again.[4]

After about 1947 it was no longer possible to function in this country as a China Hand. This became very apparent to two gifted writers,

Jack Belden and Graham Peck, when their important books about China were published in 1949 and 1950. "I thought my book came out at a good time just when China fell," Jack Belden wrote Edgar Snow in 1964. "But McCarthyism killed reviews. I believe it was on about page 35 of the Sunday Book Section."[5] Belden was the author of *China Shakes the World,* which was the only book published after the war about the Red guerrillas in the civil war period (1946–1949). Few American journalists were welcome in the Red areas after the Marshall mediation effort failed and the United States was so clearly allied with the Nationalists. Meanwhile, the Nationalists made it impossible for the reporters to get anywhere near the front. Belden could, and did, and he wrote a passionate account of the civil war from the other side, as eloquent as his two other classic pieces of war writing, *Retreat with Stilwell* and *Still Time to Die.*

It didn't sell. In 1950, Belden returned to Harper and Brothers a royalty check made out to him in the amount of $28.07. In an accompanying letter to Cass Canfield, president of Harper, he wrote, "This check presumably represents royalties due from six months sales of "China Shakes the World," less $1000 already received for the period January to June 1950. It has been delivered to me three months later. I do not believe the sum is correct and even if, by Harpers [sic] complicated figuring it is correct, I find it not acceptable. I have thought of framing it as a reminder of the folly of writing books. But then I hardly need a tangible reminder."[6]

Belden never published another book. "He was a much more dedicated gambler than a writer,"[7] Pepper Martin told me. For the last twenty years of his life Belden lived in Paris, where he died in 1989 at the age of seventy-nine, at the time of the Tiananmen Square massacre. He was a great drinker, gambler and lover of women who supported his habits, in this country and in Europe, by driving taxis. In the early 1970s, he followed Edgar Snow's advice, and returned to China on his own steam. Reporters in the Nixon party found him at the airport in February 1972 when they arrived in Beijing. Belden was in a sorry state, however. He didn't even have a winter overcoat, according to Martin.[8] Disillusioned with Mao's China, he was recovering from a host of ailments and working on a book about Lin Piao. In the end, he told Till Durdin that he regretted all the years he had spent on China.[9] He was a literary man, a war writer without a war, who never again found his voice.

Graham Peck was another China Hand whose career came to a dead end after his book *Two Kinds of Time* was published in 1950. This was the book he had begun in Peiping, in between bouts of Pure Discourse with Barbara Stephens. It is a compendious account of wartime

China, which my father helped him edit in 1949 in Cambridge, Massachusetts. It reads like two books, a personal account, and an analysis of U.S. policy in wartime China. It is illustrated by Peck's pen-and-ink drawings, and it is informed by his witty, descriptive prose throughout. *Two Kinds of Time* has become a standard reference work of the period in university courses on Kuomintang China. Yet, to quote Teddy White, "It was done the dog's dirt."[10] Nobody wanted to read about China in 1950. Peck retired to Pomfret, Vermont, where he lived out the rest of his life. He did write a third book about China. This was *China: The Remembered Life,* the as-told-to autobiography of Paul Frillmann, the Flying Tiger chaplain and OSS man in China. Like Peck's two earlier books, it is a witty, original read, and conveys the subtle essence of China that eludes most memoirists. It was published two months before Graham died of cancer at the age of fifty-six.

Time has washed away most of the sorrow and bitterness of those years. In 1985, the Chinese made a remarkable gesture to recognize the journalists who had been snubbed after the Communist victory. They invited a number of the correspondents to revisit China. The old hands, accompanied by a few stand-ins, myself included, were treated to a three-week blue-ribbon junket, which included a long session at the Great Hall of the People with Deng Xiaoping, a reception at the Great Hall, meetings with top officials, and visits by chartered plane to Yan'an (Yenan), Xi'an (Sian), Chongqing (Chung King) and a cruise down the Yangtze River. China had changed out of all recognition. People like Pepper Martin, Tillman Durdin and Annalee Jacoby could no longer find the essence of the China they had known in most of these places. Still, they felt strong pangs of nostalgia, especially in Chongqing, where they had spent so much time. The trip was a gesture, finally, of thanks, and a way of healing some old wounds.

Such recognition has never been extended to the American China Hands in their own country. Perhaps in the end this is too much to expect. America celebrates victories. For the China Hands, the ultimate reward was to have been there in the first place. "It was like sitting on a volcano," Teddy White once said. "It had to be the adventure of a man's life."[11]

ACKNOWLEDGMENTS

I N A SENSE, work on this book began in my childhood, and continued throughout my early life, as I was exposed, continuously, to the stories of China Hands at various Chinese dinners in New York and San Francisco, wherever, in fact, I happened to be in the company of my father and his friends from his China years. In the late 1970s, my wife and I traveled to Hong Kong, and various other sites in Asia, where my father had lived and written, and, in the course of our travels, we met others who had ties to the China past. But it was not until I came upon a file cabinet containing my father's China files and letters, as well as other papers, that I began a serious exploration of that lost world of pre-1949 China.

My guide to this world was Dorothy Borg, historian of American-Chinese diplomatic relations, who worked out of a strategically placed office at the Columbia University East Asian Institute situated next to the entrance to the administrative wing, where she could see all who passed in and out of that essential complex devoted to East Asian studies. Dorothy was a great authority on twentieth-century China. She had involved herself in the issues of modern China and Western journalism back in the 1930s, when she first worked at the Institute for Pacific Relations, in New York. Dorothy systematically educated many of the country's top scholars in the field, as a friend and mentor. As a writer, and a nonacademic one at that, I owe a great debt to her for her counsel and her friendship.

Harrison E. Salisbury provided yet another source of encouragement. He had known my father, admired his work, and held him in the highest esteem as a reporter and writer. He urged me to look deeply into my father's life and times in China. Harrison, who was one of the great foreign correspondents of this century, was a counselor and friend to innumerable younger writers and journalists. He was always immediately accessible for consultation and conversation when he wasn't traveling somewhere, and he had an exhilarating way of making me feel that I really had something of value to contribute to the world in this particular project.

Harrison had always regretted that the war had never taken him to China as a correspondent. His area of greatest expertise was the former Soviet Union, where he was the *New York Times* correspondent in the last years of Stalin. His intimate knowledge of the ways of the Kremlin and

Communist Party machinations in the Soviet Union equipped him to grasp the basics of the Chinese Communist Party game, and he became a latter-day authority on Communist China, but he believed that the earlier China Hands, my father among them, were an elect tribe. Edgar Snow, indeed, was one of his heroes. Before Harrison died, he placed Snow in his personal Pantheon, and for posterity he chose, as a journalist, to place himself in the tradition, not of the great twentieth-century American experts on Soviet Russia, but of Edgar Snow and other romantic realists, as he called them, who reported from China in the 1930s and 1940s. He felt that these journalists represented the values he as a newspaper correspondent had always tried to personify.

Many others besides these two friends gave me their time and assistance. Sadly, some have died in the last few years and I sorely regret that I can't thank them now for all they did on my behalf. I would nevertheless like to include their names among those living, China Hands and others, who were so generous in different ways. They include Richard Aldrich, Joseph W. Alsop, A. Doak Barnett, Keyes Beech, Linda Benson, Elizabeth Bird, John Bowers, Bu Jin, Josephine Burke, Robert Burton, Julia Child, Mariann Clubb, O. Edmund Clubb, Sylvia Crane, Gerald Curtis, Hugh Deane, M. A. DeMott, Dr. E. Gray Dimond, Robert Drummond, F. Tillman Durdin, Peggy Durdin, Peter Elliston, Israel Epstein, Annalee Jacoby Fadiman, J. K. Fairbank, Wilma Fairbank, Robert Farnsworth, F. McCracken Fisher, Louise Frillmann, Rhonda Glazier, Prof. A. Tom Grunfeld, Emily Hahn, Han Suyin, Nancy Hearst, Nancy Hector, John Hersey, Alger Hiss, John Hlavicek, Pegge Hlavicek, Joyce Hoffman, Edwin P. Hoyt, Richard Hughes, Katherine Hutton, Arnold Isaacs, E. J. Kahn, Jr., Arthur Knodel, Irene Kuhn, Martha Labell, Betty Lee, Hank Lieberman, Prof. Roderick MacFarquhar, Janice R. MacKinnon, Stephen R. MacKinnon, Mary Marshall, Lee Martin, Robert P. Martin, William McGuire, Ellen Milligan, Harriet Mills, Carl Mydans, Shelley Mydans, Prof. Andrew Nathan, Margaret Padnoy, Jean Pool, Phil Potter, John W. Powell, Sylvia Powell, Caroline Preston, Elizabeth Purcell, John Purcell, Eric Purdon, Professor Lucian Pye, Christopher T. Rand, Mrs. Samson Raphaelson, Albert Ravenholt, Sidney Rittenberg, Frank Robertson, Mordechai Rozanski, Ruan Ming, Linda Salter, Martha Sandlin, Doreen Schoyer, Julian Schuman, John S. Service, William Shawn, Jim Silberman, Carol Lew Simons, Leslie Smith, William E. Smith, Helen Foster Snow, A. T. Steele, David Stowe, Prof. Lawrence Sullivan, Mary Sullivan, Yungmei Tang, John Taylor, Bernard Thomas, James C. Thomson, Jr., Nancy Bernkopf Tucker, Samuel Vaughan, Frederick Wakeman, Jr., Prof. Alan Wald, Wang Fanxi, Prof. Martin Wilbur, Dr. Ira Wilson, Prof. Brantley Womack and Ye Dezhuang.

I was very fortunate, also, as I began my researches into twentieth-century China, to have been invited with a group of journalists who had covered preliberation China on a trip, called the China Revisited Program, sponsored by *China Daily* and the All-China Journalists Association, which took us to Beijing, Yan'an, Xi'an, Chongqing, Wuhan, Nanjing and Shanghai, in 1985. Thus, in the company of veterans, I was privileged to visit haunts that many had not seen in forty years.

This trip also gave me the gift of my friendship with Viola Robinson Isaacs, the widow of Harold Isaacs, who was a giant among China Hands. Viola subsequently invited me to the house she had shared for many years with Harold in Newton, Massachusetts, where, in his old basement office, she reread, out loud, for the first time, the letters he had written to her from China in his youth, in 1931. This was an invaluable, and very moving, original source of history.

For this book is built on letters, written from China by the China Hands, and preserved either in archives or private collections, and on oral recollections of participants. Through access provided in a generous spirit by the family of Theodore H. White and the Harvard University Archives, I was able to use the primary source material of Teddy White's voluminous correspondence. The Hoover Institution at Stanford University made much material available to me. Marilyn Burlingame at the Edgar Snow Memorial Library in Kansas City, Missouri, helped me sort through Edgar Snow's letters and provided invaluable assistance. To the Department of Oral History and the Rare Books Division, both located in Butler Library, at Columbia University, I owe a large debt of gratitude. I am fortunate, also, to have benefited from the kindness of Alexander Buchman, who sent me the Moscow correspondence of Rayna Prohme, which forms part of the Grace Simons Archive.

Lawrence Sullivan, Nancy Hearst, Nicholas Clifford and Robert Elegant read the manuscript of *China Hands;* each, in the order listed, provided invaluable editorial insights and rescued me from at least some, if by no means all, of my factual inaccuracies and misstatements and to them each I extend my warm thanks.

To two others I also want to express a special note of thanks: Dominick Anfuso, my editor, has been steadfast and continually supportive over the long haul. My literary agent, Wendy Weil, is a guardian angel, one of those rare beings who make it possible to be a writer at all in these times.

To Melford Yuan I am indebted for his beautiful translation of the inscription on the headstone of Barbara Stephens's grave in Nanjing.

My wife, Bliss, has been a mainstay to me throughout the writing of this book. She also contributed her superb editorial skill and insight to the final, painstaking job of line editing this book. This was a gift for which no thanks are adequate.

Frank MacShane, the distinguished literary biographer, deserves my final and most heartfelt expression of gratitude. He told me to write this particular book. He encouraged me, advised me and bolstered my spirits at all times with laughter and good cheer, and without him it would not have been written.

Appendix

AMERICAN JOURNALISTS WHO COVERED CHINA: 1905–1949

Abbot, Willis John	*Christian Science Monitor*
Abend, Hallett	*New York Times*
Alexanderson, George	*New York Times*
Alley, Norman	Hearst
Atkinson, Brooks	*New York Times*
Ayers, William	*Shanghai Post*
Babb, Glenn	Associated Press
Baldwin, Hanson	*New York Times*
Barnett, A. Doak	*Chicago Daily News*
Beech, Keyes	*Chicago Daily News*
Belden, Jack	United Press, *Time*
Bennett, Milly	*People's Tribune*
Berrigan, Darrell	*New York Post,* United Press
Bess, Demaree	*Christian Science Monitor*
Bisson, T. A.	*Far Eastern Survey*
Booker, Edna Lee	*China Press*
Borg, Dorothy	*Far Eastern Survey*
Bryant, Bob	International News Pictures
Buchman, Alexander	Photojournalist, freelance
Burke, James	Freelance
Burton, Robert	Freelance
Burton, Wilbur	*Shanghai Courier*
Butts, James	*Chicago Daily News*
Chamberlin, W. H.	*Christian Science Monitor*
Chao, Thomas	Reuters
Clark, Grover	*Peking Leader*
Close, Upton	*China Press*
Clurman, Robert	United Press
Cooper, H.	Associated Press
Crow, Carl	*China Press*
Dailey, Charles	*Chicago Tribune*
Deane, Hugh	*Christian Science Monitor*
Dowling, John	*Chicago Sun*
Drake, Waldo	*Los Angeles Times*
Dunbar, Maygene	*Time* and *Life*
Durdin, F. Tillman	*The New York Times*
Durdin, Peggy	*New York Times, The Nation*

Ebener, Charlotte	International News Service
Egan, Martin	Associated Press
Ekins, H. R.	United Press
Epstein, Israel	United Press, *Allied Labor News*
Farnsworth, Clyde	Associated Press
Fisher, F. McC.	United Press
Fisher, William	*China Press*
Forman, Harrison	*New York Times,* London *Times*
Fox, Charles James	*North China Star*
Gayn, Mark	*China Press, Washington Post*
Gibbons, Floyd	International News Service
Gilbert, Rodney	*New York Herald Tribune*
Gilman, LaSelle	*Shanghai Post*
Goette, John	International News Service
Gould, Randall	United Press
Graham, Betty	Reuters, United Press, Associated Press, Havas
Gray, Paul	*Time* and *Life*
Griffin, Mirriam	*China Press*
Gruin, Frederick	*Time* and *Life*
Hahn, Emily	*The New Yorker*
Hammond, James	*China Press*
Hampson, Fred	Associated Press
Hansen, Haldore	Associated Press
Harding, Gardner	*Christian Science Monitor*
Harris, Morris	Associated Press
Hauser, Ernest O.	*Reader's Digest*
Hedges, Frank	Public Ledger Syndicate
Hersey, John	*Life*
Howe, J. P.	Associated Press
Hoyt, Edwin P.	United Press
Hull, Peggy	*New York Daily News*
Hunter, Edward	International News Service
Isaacs, Harold R.	*China Forum, Newsweek*
Jacoby, Annalee	*Time*
Jacoby, Melville	*San Francisco Chronicle, Time*
Jaffe, Philip	*Amerasia*
James, Weldon	United Press
Jessup, Al	*Business Week*
Keen, Victor	*New York Herald Tribune*
Kemp, Don	International News Service
King, D. K.	United Press
Kuhn, Irene	*China Press*
Lacks, George	*China Press*
Landman, Amos	Overseas News Agency
Landman, Lynn	Overseas News Agency
Lattimore, Owen	*Pacific Affairs*
Leaf, Earl	United Press

Lewis, Herbert	*Shanghai Press*
Lieberman, Henry	*New York Times*
Logan, Walter	United Press
Lyon, Jean	Freelance
Marshall, James	*Collier's*
Marshall, Ray	United Press
Martin, Lee	*Newsweek*
Martin, Robert Pepper	United Press, *New York Post*
Mayell, Eric	Fox Movietone
McCormick, Frederick	Associated Press
McDaniel, Yates	Associated Press
McDougall, William	United Press
McGrady, Patrick	*China Press*
Menken, Arthur	Paramount News
Milks, Harold	Associated Press
Millard, Thomas F.	*New York Herald, New York Times*
Mills, James	Associated Press
Misselwitz, Henry F.	*New York Times*
Moorad, George	*Shanghai Times*
Moore, Frederick	Associated Press, *New York Times*
Moosa, Spencer	Associated Press
Morin, Relman	*Shanghai Post,* Associated Press
Morris, John	United Press
Murphy, Charles	*Time*
Mydans, Carl	*Life*
Mydans, Shelley	*Life*
Ohl, J. Kingsley	*New York Herald*
Opper, Frederick	*Shanghai Post*
Parker, Pegge	*New York Daily News*
Patchin, Philip	*New York Sun, China Press*
Pearson, Earl	*Newsweek*
Peffer, Nathaniel	*China Press*
Potter, Philip	*Baltimore Sun*
Powell, J. B.	*China Weekly Review, Chicago Tribune*
Powell, J. W.	*China Weekly Review*
Prohme, Rayna	*Peking People's Tribune*
Prohme, William	Nationalist News Service
Purcell, John	*Life*
Rand, Christopher	*New York Herald Tribune*
Ravenholt, Albert	United Press
Ravenholt, Marjorie	*Time*
Rea, George Bronson	*Far Eastern Review*
Reid, Gilbert	*China Press*
Robinson, James	Freelance
Rich, Stanley	United Press
Robertson, Douglas	*New York Times*
Roderick, John	Associated Press
Rosholt, Malcolm	*China Press*

Rounds, Frank	*World Report*
Rowan, Roy	*Time*
Rundle, Walter	United Press
Schuman, Julian	*China Weekly Review*
Selle, Earle	*China Press*
Sevareid, Eric	CBS
Shanahan, Father Cormac	*Catholic Monthly, The Sign*
Shaplen, Robert	*Newsweek*
Sheean, Vincent	North American News Alliance
Silk, George	*Time* and *Life*
Smedley, Agnes	*The Nation, Frankfurter Zeitung*
Smith, C. Stephenson	Associated Press
Smothers, Frank	*Chicago Daily News*
Snow, Edgar Parks	*London Daily Herald*
Sokolsky, George	*Philadelphia Ledger, Far Eastern Review*
Sommers, Martin	United Press
Soong, Norman	*New York Times*
Starr, Donald	*Chicago Tribune*
Stead, Ronald	*Christian Science Monitor*
Steele, A. T.	*New York Herald Tribune*
Stephens, Barbara	Agence France Presse, *Life*
Stewart, James	*Time,* Associated Press
Stowe, Leland	*Chicago Daily News*
Strong, Anna Louise	Newspaper Syndicate
Sullivan, Mary	*China Weekly Review*
Sullivan, Walter	*New York Times*
Sweetland, Reginald	*Chicago Daily News*
Taylor, Floyd	*New York World Telegram*
Tighe, Dixie	*Time* and *Life*
Topping, Seymour	Associated Press
Utley, Freda	*London News Chronicle*
Vandivert, William	*Life*
Vaughn, Miles	United Press
Vincent, Irene	Freelance
von Wiegand, Karl	Hearst
Votaw, Maurice	*Baltimore Sun*
Webb, C. Herbert	*China Press*
Wedekind, A.	International News Service
Weller, George	*Chicago Daily News*
Welles, Benjamin	*New York Times*
Whiffen, Walter	Associated Press
White, James	Associated Press
White, Theodore H.	*Time* and *Life*
Wilson, Julian	Associated Press
Wong, Newsreel	*News of the Day*
Wyant, Toby	Associated Press

Notes

Key to Abbreviations

CR	Christopher Rand	CRP	Christopher Rand papers
ES	Edgar Snow	ESP	Edgar Snow papers
HFS	Helen Foster Snow		
HI	Harold Isaacs	HRIP	Harold R. Isaacs papers
RP	Rayna Prohme	GSGP	Grace Simons Glass papers
THW	Theodore H. White	THWP	Theodore H. White papers

INTRODUCTION

The epigraph of *China Hands,* attributed to Harold Nicolson, appears as a footnote in Cyril Connolly, Chapter 13, "The Poppies," *Enemies of Promise and Other Essays: An Autobiography of Ideas* (Garden City: Anchor, 1960).

1. I am indebted for much of what I know about Thomas Millard and his career to Mordechai Rozanski and his groundbreaking work on the whole subject of American journalism in China, "American Journalists in Chinese-American Relations, 1900–1923" (Ph.D. diss., Columbia University, 1974).

CROWN OF FIRE

1. Milly Bennett, *On Her Own,* edited and annotated by A. Tom Grunfeld (Armonk, N.Y.: M. E. Sharpe, 1993), p. 49.
2. Dorothy Day, *The Long Loneliness* (New York: Harper & Row, 1981).
3. William D. Miller, *Dorothy Day: A Biography* (New York: Harper & Row, 1982).
4. Bennett, *On Her Own,* p. 50.
5. A. Tom Grunfeld, "Friends of the Revolution: America's Supporters of China's Communists, 1925–1939" (Ph.D diss., New York University).
6. Rayna Raphaelson, "We Meet at Sea," *American Review,* May 1924, p. 290.
7. Prohme was accompanied by Mrs. Milman Parry when he went to see Rayna off on her first voyage to China. Mrs. Parry, whose husband was a distinguished classics scholar at the University of California at Berkeley, gave an account of the send-off to Professor Arthur Knodel, who very kindly passed it on to me in a telephone conversation in the autumn of 1990.
8. Bennett, *On Her Own,* p. 53.

9. Professor Arthur Knodel to author, autumn 1990.
10. "Rayna: Letters from the Chinese Revolution," unpublished manuscript, edited and annotated by Professor Arthur Knodel.
11. Rayna Prohme [hereinafter RP], letter, "Dear Raph," June 6, 1925, Samson Raphaelson papers, Butler Library, Columbia University. Also, Bennett, *On Her Own*, pp. 49–50.
12. RP, letter, "Dear Raph," July 6, 1925, Samson Raphaelson papers. "The household seemed a mad place and all the people ogres," Rayna wrote Raphaelson from Tokyo after she had visited her family in Chicago. "I don't see how people can keep on living so, with life so discordant. Really, I think my family is a ghastly crew taken as a unit. Individually some of them would be all right, I think. Rudovic and Max Pinner, whom I saw in Chicago, are right, I think, when they say that they have never seen so much good stuff so misdirected as in father. But how misdirected! He has disowned me, by the way. We probably will never communicate again."
13. Knodel, "Rayna: Letters from the Chinese Revolution," p. 20.
14. RP, letter, "Beanie Darling," 10/26/27, Grace Simons Glass papers [hereinafter GSGP].
15. After the formation of the Red Army of the USSR Leon Trotsky considered it both necessary and useful to retain officers and soldiers who had served under the czar and had remained loyal to the motherland. These recruits to the Red Army were not, however, considered politically reliable. In the structure of the new army, therefore, Trotsky instituted a political department, the task of which was to educate White Russian recruits to the political goals of the Revolution. This structural innovation was duplicated in the military organization of the Nationalist armies in Canton. A political department, staffed by Chinese Communists and Russian advisers, was also built into the new military academy at Whampoa, and provided one means by which the Chinese Communists could assert their influence within the system.
16. Lenin's calculated subversion of the Chinese democracy movement had been surreptitious and swift. Gregory Voitinsky, head of the Far Eastern Bureau of the Comintern at Irkutsk, had arrived without fanfare in Peking in March 1920, accompanied by his wife, several secretaries and a Chinese interpreter. He had made contact at Peking University with student radicals and met with Li Ta-chao, who sent him on to Shanghai with an introduction to Ch'en Tu-hsiu, dean of College of Letters at Peking University, and editor of the journal *New Youth*. By the time he left China at the end of the year, Voitinsky had seeded the ground for a Chinese Communist movement. He'd traveled to Fukien, Kwangtung and the Yangtze River Valley, where he'd initiated Marxist study groups. He'd also visited Dr. Sun in November, in Shanghai, and begun to explore the possibility of setting up a United Front with the Kuomintang. The Chinese Communist Party was founded in Shanghai in July 1921. Ch'en Tu-hsiu was elected general secretary. By now, Dr. Sun was back in southern China, trying to launch a Northern Expedition from Kweilin, when he was visited by J. F. M. Sneevliet, a Dutch Comintern agent, who had recently organized a Communist movement in the Dutch East Indies, and was in China to carry on the work that Voitinsky had begun. He had just supervised the founding of the CCP in Shanghai. Now he and Dr. Sun discussed the importance of forming a United Front between the brand-new

CCP and the Kuomintang. A year later, this had become a real possibility. Dr. Sun by then had been chased once again out of Canton by Ch'en Chiung-ming, the on-again, off-again governor of Kwangtung Province. He and his wife, Soong Ching-ling, had barely escaped with their lives aboard a gunboat, the *Yung-feng,* and were back in Shanghai. Sneevliet meanwhile had gone to Moscow, where he made a strong argument for backing the Kuomintang, based on what he'd seen of the Kuomintang workers' movement in Kwangtung. In Shanghai, meanwhile, Dr. Sun paved the way for a United Front, urged on by some of his closest lieutenants, radicals like the American-born and bred Liao Chung-k'ai, and Tai Chi-t'ao. Dr. Sun reorganized the Kuomintang, and admitted leaders of the Chinese Communist Party into its ranks. Sneevliet had pressured the Chinese Communists to work with the Kuomintang, and now Ch'en Tu-hsiu agreed to serve on the committee Dr. Sun appointed to reorganize his party. The final deal was struck in January 1923. Forces loyal to Dr. Sun had chased Ch'en Chiung-ming out of Canton and the Nationalist leader was about to return for a third time to set up a government there. On the eve of his departure, Dr. Sun met in his house on the Rue Molière in the French Concession in Shanghai with Dr. Adolph Joffe, a high-ranking Soviet negotiator. After a flurry of meetings, the two men had issued a joint statement. Dr. Sun declared that Communism could never work in China. Dr. Joffe confirmed that he agreed with Dr. Sun, and further stated that national unification was China's most urgent priority. And he promised Dr. Sun that he could count on Soviet support for this endeavor. Thus began a period of intense cooperation between the Chinese Communist Party and the Kuomintang. It was a partnership that both Chinese parties approached with great reservations. Only after bitter debate, and under pressure from Sneevliet, did the membership of the CCP in 1923 agree to concentrate its efforts on the Nationalist revolutionary movement and to recognize the Kuomintang as the leader of this movement. Although the Comintern required the Communists to subordinate themselves to the Kuomintang, the Chinese Communists used their influence to try to control the KMT and turn it to their own radical purposes. This was foreseen by right-wing members of the KMT who were opposed to the union. Dr. Sun went ahead with it anyway, but he absolutely refused to merge the KMT with the CCP. Although he permitted members of the CCP to join the KMT individually, he strictly forbade members of his party to join the CCP. It was a forced alliance fated to break into conflict; yet it was also an arrangement that enabled Dr. Sun to create, at last, a powerful revolutionary vehicle.

17. For a more detailed discussion of Chang Tso-lin, see Howard L. Boorman, ed., *Biographical Dictionary of Republican China,* Vol. I (New York: Columbia University Press, 1967), p. 115.
18. Grunfeld, "Friends of the Revolution"; Knodel, "Rayna: Letters from the Chinese Revolution," pp. 25–26; Bennett, *On Her Own,* p. 84. Customarily the Chinese authorities seal a building by pasting a piece of paper between the door and the door frame of a building and then affixing an official seal on the paper, according to a friend of the author's from Peking, whose own quarters were sealed during the Cultural Revolution.
19. Miles W. Vaughn, *Covering the Far East* (New York: Covici Friede, 1936), pp. 160–61.

20. Ibid., p. 111.
21. A discussion of how Stalin gained control of the party at the Twelfth Party Congress, convened in Moscow on April 17, 1923, while Lenin lay incapacitated by strokes, may be found in Ruth Fischer, *Stalin and German Communism: A Study in the Origins of the State Party* (Cambridge: Harvard University Press, 1948), Chapter 11, "Struggle for Succession in the Russian Party," pp. 232–51.
22. Dan N. Jacobs, *Borodin: Stalin's Man in China* (Cambridge: Harvard University Press, 1981), pp. 193–211.
23. For a lucid and comprehensive discussion of the Stalin-Trotsky debate and the role of the Kremlin power struggle on the Great Chinese Revolution of 1925–1927, see Harold Isaacs, *The Tragedy of the Chinese Revolution,* first revised edition, Chapter 3, "World Crisis: The Russian Impact" (Stanford: Stanford University Press, 1951).
24. C. Martin Wilbur, "The Nationalist Revolution: From Canton to Nanking, 1923–1928," *The Cambridge History of China,* Vol. 12, *Republican China, 1912–1949,* Part I, Denis Twitchett and John K. Fairbank, general editors (Cambridge: Cambridge University Press, 1983), pp. 527–697, provides an authoritative and detailed account of the Northern Expedition and the events immediately following.
25. This story has been rendered by André Malraux in *Man's Fate,* and Harold Isaacs has also provided a gripping historical accounting in *The Tragedy of the Chinese Revolution.*
26. Bennett, *On Her Own,* p. 225.
27. Jacobs, *Borodin: Stalin's Man in China,* provides a very thorough account of the life and times of Borodin. Jacobs suggests that Borodin may have borrowed his pseudonym from an agricultural specialist named Professor N. Borodin. It's Milly Bennett's assertion, however, that he took the name in honor of the composer. "So enamored was he of the music of the Petersburg physician and composer A.P. Borodin that when he came to take a revolutionary pseudonym, he once told me, he chose Borodin." (*On Her Own,* p. 222.)
28. Bennett, *On Her Own,* p. 223.
29. Ibid., p. 226.
30. Randall Gould, *China in the Sun* (Garden City: Doubleday, 1946), p. 69.
31. Bennett, *On Her Own,* p. 214.
32. Ibid., p. 198.
33. Ibid., p. 194.
34. Ibid., p. 182.
35. Ibid., p. 226.
36. Ibid.
37. Ibid., p. 213.
38. John Hohenberg, *Foreign Correspondence: The Great Reporters and Their Times* (New York: Columbia University Press, 1964), pp. 274–76.
39. Vincent Sheean, *Personal History* (New York: Random House, 1934), pp. 117–18.
40. Ibid., p. 223.
41. Ibid., p. 226.
42. Ibid., p. 221.
43. Ibid.
44. Ibid.

45. Ibid., p. 243.
46. Ibid., p. 232.
47. Ibid., p. 282.
48. Israel Epstein, *Woman in World History: Life and Times of Soong Ching Ling (Mme. Sun Yat-sen)* (Beijing: New World Press, 1993), p. 208.
49. Bennett, *On Her Own,* p. 229.
50. Sheean, *Personal History,* p. 233.
51. Ibid., p. 234.
52. Ibid., p. 235.
53. Ibid., p. 234.
54. Ibid., p. 235.
55. Ibid.
56. Bennett, *On Her Own,* p. 198.
57. Ibid., p. 199.
58. Sheean, *Personal History,* pp. 249–50.
59. Ibid., p. 250.
60. Ibid., p. 248.
61. Ibid., pp. 248–49.
62. Ibid., p. 246.
63. Bennett, *On Her Own,* p. 200.
64. Ibid., p. 201.
65. Ibid., p. 200.
66. Ibid., p. 201.
67. Anna Louise Strong, *China's Millions* (New York: Coward-McCann, 1928), pp. 38–39.
68. Bennett, *On Her Own,* p. 233.
69. Ibid., p. 236.
70. Ibid., p. 235.
71. Sheean, *Personal History,* p. 141.
72. Bennett, *On Her Own,* p. 234.
73. Ibid.
74. Ibid.
75. Ibid., p. 236.
76. Ibid., p. 237.
77. Ibid.
78. Ibid.
79. Ibid., p. 238.
80. Ibid.
81. Ibid.
82. Strong, *China's Millions.*
83. Tracy B. Strong and Helene Keyssar, *Right in Her Soul: The Life of Anna Louise Strong* (New York: Random House, 1983), pp. 69, 96; Jacobs, *Borodin: Stalin's Man in China,* pp. 29–39.
84. Strong and Keyssar, *Right in Her Soul,* p. 112.
85. Ilona Ralf Sues, *Shark's Fins and Millet* (Boston: Little, Brown, 1944), p. 188.
86. Bennett, *On Her Own,* p. 260.
87. Ibid., p. 261: "Maybe it was right then and there that I learned that the people who make a business out of saving the world make damn poor neighbors," Milly wrote of Miss Strong, who had moved into the Lutheran Mission House, one floor above the Prohmes. (Eleven years later,

Anna Louise Strong, in the very same city, once again drew attention upward to herself as she stomped about in an overhead room. As reported by Sues, in *Shark's Fins and Millet.*)

88. Bennett, *On Her Own,* p. 263.
89. Isaacs, *The Tragedy of the Chinese Revolution,* pp. 245, 246.
90. Quoted in *The Cambridge History of China,* p. 657.
91. Isaacs, *The Tragedy of the Chinese Revolution,* p. 269.
92. Quoted in Ibid.
93. Bennett, *On Her Own,* p. 295.
94. Fanny Borodin, UPI dispatch, 7/30/27, Randall Gould Papers, Hoover Institution, Stanford University. Mrs. Borodin often put herself to sleep at night during her incarceration by imagining that she was back in Rivonia Park, in Chicago, lying on a hillock, listening to a performance of the Chicago Symphony Orchestra. Rayna later described Fanny as a "Powder Pidgeon, all puffed up and strutting" (RP, letter, "Dear Billium," 11/2/27, GSGP). Fanny was unquestionably important to Borodin. She was his helpmeet throughout most of the Chinese Revolution. Of Fanny, Rayna also wrote, in the above-quoted letter, "She pretends to greater usefulness which I doubt that she has. But her role is a particularly necessary one for a man like B.—he's so much at sixes and sevens about his own life. Tragically so, really."
95. Sheean, *Personal History,* p. 258.
96. Bennett, *On Her Own,* pp. 275–77.
97. Sheean, *Personal History,* p. 267.
98. "Madame Sun's Withdrawal," *The Nation,* 9/21/27.
99. Ibid.
100. Firsthand accounts of this extraordinary journey may be found in Strong, *China's Millions,* and Percy Chen, *China Called Me: My Life Inside the Chinese Revolution* (Boston: Little, Brown, 1979). Percy Chen, along with his brother, Jack, both sons of Eugene Chen, accompanied Strong, Borodin and some of his advisers on a motor caravan across northwest China and the Gobi Desert into Russia on their inland flight out of China. "It was apparent to me that Anna Louise had a crush on Borodin," Chen wrote (p. 137). This became clear to Chen at Lin-t'ung, a hot springs resort outside Sian, when he chanced upon the high adviser and Strong. "Borodin was reclining on a chaise longue, and at his feet Anna Louise Strong was sitting on a stool. She was singing," he wrote. "She had him where she wanted him." The song was "While Shepherds Watched Their Sheep by Night." Borodin, dozing after a soak in the warm curative waters, woke up, "fixed her with a glare," Chen wrote, "and said fiercely, 'For God's sake, woman, sing the "Internationale." ' Strong burst into tears and departed. Spotting Chen, Borodin smiled weakly. 'Did I hurt her? I did not mean to,' he said." (pp. 138–39).
101. Excerpt, 7/31/27, from a brief, typewritten diary kept during this period by Rayna Prohme, GSGP. Until now it has been generally assumed that Rayna accompanied Madame Sun on her downriver trip to Shanghai. This impression has been reinforced by the account given by Milly Bennett in *On Her Own.* Bennett claims to have seen Rayna off on the boat with Madame Sun. Rayna's explicit diary entry for the period does not bear this out. In her detailed memoranda, Rayna makes it clear that she stayed behind after Madame Sun departed, helped her husband hand over the

People's Tribune to its new managers and accompanied her husband to a dinner with Bishop Logan Roots before herself departing by boat for Shanghai two weeks after Madame Sun's surreptitious escape. Rayna also describes encountering, en route, Madame Sun's brother T. V. Soong, who, along with his wife, his in-laws and Tommy Tong, boarded the boat at Kiukiang. "They—and I—were not pleased to be boat-mates," Rayna wrote. "T.V. and his wife stayed in their cabin almost the entire time. He did not introduce me to his wife, although there was opportunity, and in fact did not speak to me at all except to nod once and to ask me just as we were docking in Shanghai where I was stopping. I had told Tommy I was going to a hotel. I told T.V. I would see Burton first thing." (A reference to Wilbur Burton, most probably; Burton, friend and colleague of Milly Bennett, later married Rayna's sister Grace.) Rayna then wrote, "I was met at the dock by Cook, the C.I.D. man who trails people. Took a taxi and drve [sic] out to Mrs. Sun's—not directly, because the taxi-man didn't know where the place was. Reached there about 7:30. She expected me and seemed glad to see me. Her nerves were in a badly shattered state. She told me something of her difficulties, people bothering her, detectives watching at either side of the house, asking questions of her house-boys. She was not going out at all." This firsthand account by Rayna of her trip to Shanghai and her arrival there suggests that not only did she travel alone to Shanghai, but that Madame Sun had already been in that city for some time when Rayna arrived. The diary also sheds light on Madame Sun's initial reluctance to flee China for Russia. Rayna's diary continues: "I told her Chen's suggested plans and she said she could not consider going direct to Russia, because of the interpretation that would be put on it by people in China. She spoke also of worry about funds and the amount that would be needed if she went by way of America. No decision that night—or until Chen himself came down several days later. Finally, as a result of what arguments I do not know, she decided to go direct to Russia, but unofficially: he going in his ca acity [sic] of foreign minister—to what I di [sic] not know."

102. Ibid.
103. Ibid.
104. Sheean, *Personal History,* p. 275.
105. Ibid.
106. Ibid., pp. 272–73. Sheean also relates how Fanny Borodin was tried and acquitted in Peking by a judge. After the judgment, Fanny and the judge both fled Chang Tso-lin's wrath—the judge to Japan, Fanny to Moscow via Japan and Vladivostok (pp. 277–78). Once Fanny had made her escape, Borodin felt free to leave China, as he had been commanded to do by Feng Yu-hsiang, the formerly pro-Communist warlord who joined forces in June 1927 with Chiang Kai-shek.
107. Ibid., p. 276.
108. Bennett, *On Her Own,* p. 308.
109. Ibid.
110. RP, diary excerpt, undated, GSGP.
111. RP, letter, "Beanie Darling," 8/25/27, GSGP.
112. Ibid.
113. RP, letter, "Beanie Darling," 8/30/27, GSGP.
114. Ibid.

115. RP, letter, "Beanie Darling," 9/6/27, GSGP.
116. Ibid.
117. RP, letter, "Beanie, darling, darling," 9/7/27, GSGP.
118. Ibid.
119. Ibid.
120. Ibid.
121. Ibid.
122. RP, letter, "Beanie Darling," 9/12/27, GSGP.
123. Ibid.: "The head man, Oumanski, told me the other day that the idea is for a man, preferably an American and they like your work, to be a sort of travelling correspondent, going to the place where the news is hottest."
124. Ibid.
125. RP, letter, "Billium," 9/16/27, GSGP.
126. RP, letter, "Beanie Darling," 9/25/27, GSGP.
127. RP, letter, "Beanie Darling," 10/7/27, GSGP.
128. RP, letter, "Beanie Darling," 10/7/27, GSGP.
129. RP, letter, "Billium," 9/16/27, GSGP.
130. Sheean, *Personal History*, p. 282: "It was by this time eight o'clock in the evening, and I had not much hope of finding anybody in an office, but I found a droshky and went to the Metropole. There, just as I reached the top of the marble steps and was about to ask the hall porter for information, I saw Rayna Prohme coming towards me. For six weeks I had imagined her dead, torn into pieces by a mob, broken and sunk in the mud of the Yangtze-Kiang or buried obscurely, after days of torture, in some dreary and forgotten Chinese field. These morbid fancies had alternated with others in which I imagined meeting her again, but it had never been wholly credible to me that I might find her, alive and well, by the mere effort of going to Moscow. And yet here she was, coming swiftly across the hall, hands stretched out, her eyes alight beneath the conflagration of her hair." Sheean wrote his version six or seven years after the event, as far as I know. Although he may have reconstructed it from notes, it nevertheless differs from the version recorded less than twenty-four hours after their meeting by Rayna, who wrote: "There is much more to tell of many things, including bumping into Herbie Elliston and having some very pleasant time with him before he dashed away to Berlin, and so to London the next day, and last night having Jimmy Sheean, who was trying to reach Chen by phone, reach me by mistake, and going down to meet him in the lobby of the hotel to find him pipped to the gills with vodka, embarrassingly enthusiastic about seeing me (you remember his affectionate streak (when he is tight) to the point of telling a translator from TASS who was dictating some articles to me in my room all about his devotion." (letter, "Billium," 9/16/27, GSGP.) Herbie Elliston (Herbert Berridge Elliston) was a British correspondent from Yorkshire who went out to China as a young man. He became the *Manchester Guardian* Washington correspondent, and subsequently a Pulitzer Prize winning editor of the *Washington Post*.
131. RP, letter, "Billium," 9/16/27, GSGP.
132. Sheean, *Personal History*, p. 292.
133. RP, letter, "Beanie Darling," 9/21/27, GSGP.
134. RP, letter, "Beanie," 9/22/27, GSGP.
135. Ibid.

136. RP, letter, "Beanie Darling," 9/21/27, GSGP.
137. Ibid.
138. Ibid.
139. RP, letter, "Dear Beanie," 10/18–19/27, GSGP.
140. Ibid.
141. Ibid.
142. RP, letter, "Beanie Darling," 10/26/27, GSGP.
143. RP, letter, "Beanie Darling," 10/21/27, GSGP.
144. RP, letter, "Billium," 11/2/27, GSGP.
145. RP, letter, "Beanie Darling," 10/26/27, GSGP.
146. Ibid.
147. RP, letter, "Beanie Darling," 10/26/27, GSGP.
148. RP, letter, "Beanie Darling," 10/30/27, GSGP: Opera was bountiful on this strangely festive eve of Russia's forty-year-long dark night of the soul: besides *Carmen,* there were performances during Rayna's short stay in Moscow of *Czar Feodor, Twelfth Night,* and *Romeo and Juliet* among others.
149. RP, letter, "Billium Darling," 10/8/27, GSGP.
150. Ibid.
151. Ibid.
152. Ibid.
153. Harrison E. Salisbury to author, July 1988. See also Salisbury's memoir, *A Time of Change: A Reporter's Tale of Our Time* (New York: Harper & Row, 1980), pp. 200–201: "My romantic image of them [Anna Louise Strong and Borodin] and many others whom I would come to know—or know about—was drawn from the pages of Vincent Sheean's *Personal History,* which I had gulped down (like tens of thousands of Americans) when it appeared in 1934." Among those Salisbury read about of course were Rayna and Bill Prohme, whom Salisbury writes was "later to die in some mysterious underground way in Manila." Salisbury was certain that Prohme worked for the Comintern in Manila, although despite Rayna's efforts to secure a job for Bill with TASS, there's no evidence to my knowledge that supports this theory. Actually, Prohme was not in Manila very long. He did not, as Salisbury thought, die there, nor did he die mysteriously—see my final endnote for this chapter.
154. Salisbury in his memoir reflects the power of Sheean's mythmaking talents when he writes that Sheean "fell hopelessly in love" with Rayna.
155. Sheean, *Personal History,* pp. 295–305.
156. Ibid., p. 309.
157. Ibid., p. 305.
158. Ibid., p. 309.
159. Ibid.
160. Ibid.
161. Ibid., p. 310.
162. Ibid., p. 314.
163. Ibid.
164. Ibid.
165. RP, letter, "Beanie Darling," 11/9/27, GSGP.
166. Ibid.
167. Ibid.
168. Ibid.

169. Ibid.
170. Ibid.
171. Ibid.
172. Ibid.
173. Sheean, *Personal History*, p. 315.
174. Ibid., pp. 315–16.
175. Ibid.
176. Ibid.
177. Ibid., p. 307.
178. Ibid., p. 317.
179. Ibid., p. 318.
180. Ibid.
181. Ibid., p. 320.
182. Ibid.
183. Later, a distinguished professor of international affairs at Harvard University.
184. Epstein, *Woman in World History*, p. 208.
185. Sheean, *Personal History*, p. 321.
186. Ibid., p. 322.
187. Ibid.
188. Knodel, "Rayna: Letters from the Chinese Revolution."
189. Sheean, *Personal History*, p. 323.
190. Ibid.
191. William Prohme, "Rayna Simons Prohme: A Report on the Last Months of Her Life," mimeographed bulletin, p. 11, GSGP.
192. Sheean, *Personal History*, p. 323.
193. Ibid., p. 324.
194. Ibid.
195. Jacobs, *Borodin: Stalin's Man in China*, pp. 303–4.
196. Sheean, *Personal History*, p. 325.
197. Ibid.
198. Ibid., p. 326.
199. Ibid.
200. William Prohme, "Rayna Simons Prohme," p. 15.
201. Ibid., p. 16.
202. Sheean, *Personal History*, p. 326.

Note: In much of the latter part of this story I have relied on letters written in the autumn of 1927 by Rayna Prohme from Moscow to William Prohme, who was in Shanghai and then in Manila. Many of these letters did not even reach Prohme until after Rayna died, and indeed followed him halfway around the world, to Paris. Prohme, suffering from tuberculosis, killed himself in Hawaii on November 21, 1935, on the eighth anniversary of Rayna's death. Six months earlier, on June 6, 1935, Prohme dispatched these last letters to him from Rayna to her sister Grace with the following note:

"Dear Gracie, I'm having all my papers, letters, pictures etc burned. I want to be 'sunk without a trace' when I crack. But these final letters of Rayna's, on that final separation, you should have, I thought, so I send them. Also the few pages of a diary she started but did not carry on. The letters, if read all at once, give the terrifying picture of her awful (in the real sense) state of mind during those last weeks. It is all too tragic. Re-reading them caused again to rise the hatred I felt for Chen, for it was he who was responsible for the 'plan' to keep me behind in Shanghai as reporter to him and Mrs. S. and as disseminator of their statements (in Moscow) to the Chinese press. You will see hints in Rayna's letters that in the long debate we had as to whether we would accept the plan, even on a 2-month understanding, I had expressed a lack of trust in Chen's sincerity. The fact is I distrusted him in advance. And Rayna distractedly writes, 'but I can't distrust people.' When she wrote that, she had reluctantly come to see my advance judgement had been right. There is infinite tragedy in that letter which tells of her encounter with him in the hotel corridor. It can make me furious even at this distance, in time. I'm damned glad I never encountered him, all the while I lived two floors below him in the Met. Hotel. He never looked me up. I can hardly believe he thought I would look *him* up. But Jack, his son, (of whom Rayna writes so glowingly) did. A grand boy. ('She was the only one who talked to me about my drawing, and took my work seriously,' he told me, with tears in his eyes.) His political cartoons appear regularly in *Moscow News* and other places. The only place Sheean's book offends me personally is in his failure to make any word of explanation of why I remained behind in China and later was in Manila. And he knew; Rayna must have told him; ALS knew it and wrote it in letters to your mother and others. But he gives the impression almost (not quite) that I was somehow afraid to venture into Russia and even to remain in China. It is, to me, highly offensive and so easily open to real misunderstanding. So I was glad to find Rayna's own references to the matter. The other stuff is that report I sent out and which you did not see. And the translation of the autopsy report.

"I made a will the other day. I have a paragraph adding that my ashes be sent to your mother to be placed in same crypt with those of Rayna. It just occurs to me this perhaps could not be done except at some expense. In that case I'll just have them dumped here. Could you find out? How are you being addressed? Is my addressing on this envelope incorrect? love—Bill"

Prophet in a Foreign Land

1. Ira Wilson, "Harold Isaacs: Scratches on His Mind, 1930–1934" (term paper, Harvard College, 1976).
2. Ibid.
3. Viola Isaacs to author, March 1989.
4. A journey he'd begun to plan as a child: years later, a poem Isaacs composed at the age of eight about going around the world and ending up in China was discovered in his father's wallet when he died. Ibid.
5. Ibid.
6. Ibid.
7. Margaret Elizabeth Mais, "The Evolution of Bias: An Interpreter of China, Harold R. Isaacs" (honors thesis, Harvard College, 1970).
8. Harold Isaacs [hereinafter HI], letters, 2/31–3/31, Harold R. Isaacs papers, Massachusetts Institute of Technology [hereinafter HRIP].
9. An expression that seems to have originated with George Sokolsky, an American journalist who covered China for over a decade and was briefly employed by the Kuomintang before he left China for good in 1931.
10. HI, *Re-encounters in China: Notes of a Journey in a Time Capsule* (Armonk, N.Y. and London: M. E. Sharpe, 1985), p. 8.

11. Quoted in Janice R. Mackinnon and Stephen R. MacKinnon, *Agnes Smedley: The Life and Times of an American Radical* (Berkeley: University of California Press, 1988), p. 149.

12. Agnes Smedley, *Battle Hymn of China* (New York: Alfred A. Knopf, 1943), pp. 11–22.

13. Ibid., pp. 31–69.

14. MacKinnon and MacKinnon, *Agnes Smedley*, p. 144. Ch'en, known as the father of social science in China, had lived a long life, and is one of very few Communist intellectuals to weather Mao Tse-tung's various inquisitions, including the Cultural Revolution, relatively unscathed (although he was imprisoned for a period of fourteen months at that time). He survived, he told Harold Isaacs in 1980, by never taking on an important job after the Communists came to power, even though, in 1951, Chou En-lai invited him to be his deputy minister of foreign affairs (see HI, *Re-encounters in China*, pp. 122–23).

15. Smedley, *Battle Hymn of China*, p. 64.

16. MacKinnon and MacKinnon, *Agnes Smedley*, p. 142.

17. Quoted in Robert P. Newman, *Owen Lattimore and the "Loss" of China* (Berkeley: University of California Press, 1992), p. 23.

18. Quoted in MacKinnon and MacKinnon, *Agnes Smedley*, p. 144.

19. Smedley, *Battle Hymn of China*, p. 93.

20. Ibid.

21. Ibid., pp. 74, 75.

22. Ibid.

23. MacKinnon and MacKinnon, *Agnes Smedley*, pp. 147–49. Sorge informed the Russians that Japan was not going to extend its China front beyond Manchuria into Russia, which had been Stalin's fear. Once Sorge had put this particular fear to rest, Stalin felt free to move his armies in the East to Russia's western front, to fight the Germans.

24. Smedley, *Battle Hymn of China*, p. 75.

25. Ibid.

26. Ibid.

27. Frank Glass to Alan Wald, 4/5/83 (tape).

28. HI, letter, "hlo cheeild," 5/16/31, HRIP.

29. HI, letter, "well, hell's broken loose in china again yungelfritz," 5/4/31, HRIP.

30. HI, letter, "bravo, bravo, bravo," 5/21/31, HRIP.

31. Ibid.

32. HI, letter, "today you are much nearer the farther side of the 'lantic," 6/5/31, HRIP.

33. Frank Glass to Alan Wald, 4/5/83 (tape).

34. Ibid.

35. HI, letter, "today you are," 6/15/31, HRIP.

36. Frank Glass to Alan Wald, 4/5/83 (tape).

37. HI, notes, 6/13/31, HRIP.

38. HI, *Re-encounters in China*, p. 29.

39. HI, notes, 6/16/31, HRIP.

40. Ibid.

41. O. Edmund Clubb, *20th Century China* (New York: Columbia University Press, 1964), p. 191.

42. Ibid., p. 194.

43. HI, notes, 6/18/31, HRIP.
44. Ibid.
45. Ibid., 6/21/31.
46. Ibid.
47. Ibid., 6/22/31.
48. Ibid.
49. Ibid., 6/27/31.
50. Ibid.
51. Ibid.
52. Ibid.
53. Ibid.
54. HI, letter, "hullo viola cheeild," 7/24/31, HRIP.
55. Ibid.
56. Ibid.
57. Ibid.
58. Ibid.
59. Ibid. Clearly those sessions back at the Palace Hotel with Agnes Smedley had finally sunk in. Smedley had accused Isaacs of "fence sitting." This was a phrase much used in those days by radicals. It seems to have hit its mark. In Hankow, Rayna Prohme had hurled this very accusation at Vincent Sheean with at least momentary success, as Sheean reports in *Personal History,* p. 233.
60. HI, letter, "hullo again sweetheart," 7/29/31, HRIP.
61. HI, letter, "back at long last," 8/26/31, HRIP.
62. Ibid.
63. Ibid.
64. HI, letter, "hullo sweetheart," 9/19/31, HRIP.
65. Ibid.
66. HI, letter, "hullo cheeild," 10/24/31, HRIP.
67. HI, letter, "hullo sweetheart," 9/1/31, HRIP.
68. HI, letter, "at long last a letter," 9/8/31, HRIP.
69. HI, letter, "hullo cheeild," 10/21/31, HRIP.
70. HI, letter, "today i received your lengthy, exhaustive (and exhausting) tome anent a series of generalities involved in our present situation," 11/4/31, HRIP.
71. HI, letter, "hullo cheeild," 12/23/31, HRIP.
72. See John Israel, *Student Nationalism in China, 1927–1937* (Stanford: Stanford University Press, 1966).
73. HI, letter, "Hullo," 1/3/32, HRIP.
74. Viola Isaacs to author, spring 1992.
75. Far Eastern Press Correspondence, File 9, 1/3/32, HRIP.
76. HI, letter, "dear child," 1/9/32, HRIP.
77. Ibid.
78. Frederick S. Litten, "The Noulens Affair," *The China Quarterly* (Spring 1994) provides the most recent and detailed scholarship to date on the Noulens case, and I am indebted to Nicholas Clifford for bringing this article to my attention.
79. Edgar Snow, *Journey to the Beginning* (New York: Random House, 1972), p. 100.
80. HI, letter, "HULLO . . . fambly . . . ," 2/3/32, HRIP.
81. HI, letter, "hullo cheeild," 3/17/32, HRIP.

82. HI, letter, "Hullo fambly . . . ," 2/3/32, HRIP.
83. Ibid.
84. Ibid.
85. HI, letter, "hullo cheeild," 2/14/32, HRIP.
86. HI, letter, "hullo viola sweetheart," 2/6/32, HRIP.
87. "Commission Flips Coin for Routes," *The China Forum*, 4/23/32, p. 2.
88. *The China Forum*, Shanghai, January 1932–January 1934, Vol. 1, No. 1–Vol. 3, No. 4 (40 issues), Harold R. Isaacs, editor and publisher, reprinted by the Center for Chinese Research Materials, Association of Research Libraries, Washington, D.C., 1976.
89. HI, *Re-encounters in China*, p. 26.
90. Observer, "The Great Game of Chinese Politics," *The China Forum*, 1/30/32, p. 6.
91. Ibid., 4/23/32, p. 6.
92. HI, letter, "hullo sweetheart," 9/1/31, HRIP.
93. Viola Isaacs to author, spring 1992.
94. HI, letter, "hullo cheeild," 4/26/32, HRIP.
95. "Five Years of Kuomintang Reaction," *The China Forum*, Vol. 1, Nos. 11, 12, 13 (May 1932), p. 3.
96. HI, letter to Viola, 5/32, HRIP.
97. Ibid.
98. "Forum Injures Christian Sensibilities; Invited to Change Its Location," *The China Forum*, Vol. 1, No. 19, 6/25/32.
99. HI, letter to Viola, 7/32, HRIP.
100. "Gag *The China Forum*," *The China Forum*, 7/23/32, p. 6.
101. "State Department Threatens *Forum*," *The China Forum*, 7/30/32, p. 1.
102. Ibid.
103. Ibid.
104. "American Warned of Trial by China," *New York Times*, 7/29/32.
105. Ibid.
106. Ibid.
107. Ibid.
108. HI, letter to family, 8/6/32, HRIP.
109. Ibid.
110. HI, letter, "goooooood moorororororninngnnngg sweet cheeild!," 4/18/32, HRIP.
111. Viola Isaacs to author, September 1991.
112. Ibid., March 1989.
113. Ibid., September 1991.
114. Ibid.
115. HI, *Re-encounters in China*, pp. 18–19.
116. "the tass man's a sonofabitch" Isaacs had earlier written to Viola (letter, "hullo cheeild," 4/26/32, HRIP).
117. HI, *Re-encounters in China*, pp. 18–19.
118. Arnold Isaacs and Viola Isaacs to author, 7/13/94.
119. HI, *Re-encounters in China*, pp. 31–32.
120. Robert Isaacs, letter, "Dear Sam Gertie," 2/15/34, HRIP.
121. Ibid.
122. Ibid.
123. Ibid.
124. Viola Isaacs to author, July 1994.

125. "I never did know just where she was located in the Communist apparatus but I certainly did get to know that she was well in from its fringes," Isaacs notes in *Re-encounters* (p. 28). "Besides whatever she wrote for the *Frankfurter Zeitung*, her principal outlets were in the extensive international publishing and propaganda network headed by Willi Munzenberg," whom Isaacs calls "a mobilizer" of "sympathizers" for the Soviet cause. Helen Foster Snow to author, July 1989.

126. Viola Isaacs to author, September 1991.

127. Ibid., March 1989.

128. HI, *Re-encounters in China*, p. 66.

129. Viola Isaacs to author, September 1992; HI, *Re-encounters in China*, p. 66.

130. Viola Isaacs to author, September 1992.

131. Wang, Fan-hsi, *Memoirs of a Chinese Revolutionary*, translated and with an introduction by Gregor Benton (New York: Columbia University Press, 1991), pp. 127–29.

132. HI, *Re-encounters in China*, pp. 31–32.

133. Viola Isaacs to author, May 1993.

134. HI, *Re-encounters in China*, pp. 35–36.

135. Ibid.

136. "League of Left Writers Takes Up Reuter's Gage," *The China Forum*, 1/13/32.

137. HI, *The Tragedy of the Chinese Revolution*.

138. In 1937, the Noulenses found their way to Shanghai, where Madame Sun looked after them, and eventually they made it back to Russia where they lived out their lives into the 1960s.

139. Viola Isaacs to author, March 1989.

140. Quoted in HI, *The Tragedy of the Chinese Revolution*, p. 162.

141. Quoted in Ibid., p. 351, n. 12.

142. Quoted in Ibid.

143. Viola Isaacs to author, May 1992.

144. Ibid.

145. Ibid.

146. Ibid.

147. Ibid.

148. Ibid.

149. Ibid.

YIN AND YANG

1. Helen Foster Snow, Oral History, Oral History Dept., Columbia University, letter, "Dear Mr. Snow," 9/27/33.

2. Helen Foster Snow [hereinafter HFS], *My China Years* (New York: William Morrow, 1984), p. 127. Helen Foster Snow's work on China in the 1930s and 1940s was published under her pseudonym, Nym Wales. For her China memoir, *My China Years,* she has used Helen Foster Snow. She is also occasionally referred to by her husband and others by her nickname, Peg.

3. Ibid.

4. Ibid., p. 128.

5. Ibid.

6. HFS to author, March 1990.
7. HFS, *My China Years*, p. 87.
8. Ibid.
9. Ibid., p. 185.
10. Edgar Snow [hereinafter ES], *Journey to the Beginning*, p. 119.
11. Ibid.
12. Graham Peck, *Through China's Wall* (Boston: Houghton Mifflin, 1940), p. 26.
13. O. Edmund Clubb to author, February 1983.
14. Peck, *Through China's Wall*, pp. 26, 27. This was 1936. "The only foreigners who seemed to be insensible to the languors of Peking," wrote Peck, "were the Japanese. All during the first months of my stay in the city, they were swarming down upon it in active hordes, putting up a great show of activity, perhaps already aware of the necessity of getting Peking before Peking got them." (Ibid.)
15. HFS, *My China Years*, pp. 100–106.
16. Ibid., p. 132.
17. James Bertram, "Capes of China Slide Away," manuscript, p. 153.
18. HFS, "Self-Portrait: For Whom It May Concern," Nym Wales Collection, Hoover Institution, Stanford University, p. 6.
19. Viola Isaacs to author, November 1994.
20. ES, letter, "Dearest Father," 2/15/30, Edgar Snow Papers [hereinafter ESP], Edgar Snow Memorial Library, University of Missouri-Kansas City, Kansas City, Missouri.
21. ES, *Journey to the Beginning*, pp. 123–24.
22. Ibid., p. 124.
23. Ibid.
24. Ibid., p. 125.
25. Ibid.
26. Ibid., p. 126.
27. HFS, *My China Years*, pp. 122–23.
28. Ibid., p. 132.
29. Ibid., p. 201.
30. ES, letter, "Dearest Sis," 1/17/34, ESP.
31. Ibid.
32. A. T. Steele to author, November 1990.
33. Ibid.
34. Han Suyin, *A Mortal Flower* (London: Granada, 1972, 1978), p. 232.
35. ES, *Journey to the Beginning*, p. 130.
36. HFS, *My China Years*, pp. 135–40.
37. ES, *Journey to the Beginning*, p. 133.
38. Richard Walsh, letter, "Dear Ed," 5/20/35, ESP. Snow was not unaware of this. When Walsh, of the publishing house John Day, sent the Snows a letter rejecting their first manuscript of *Living China*, Edgar Snow jotted in the margin of the letter, "He's probably buying Isaacs!"
39. ES, *Journey to the Beginning*, p. 133.
40. Ibid., p. 136.
41. Ibid., p. 137.
42. Ibid.
43. HFS, *My China Years*, p. 141.
44. Clubb, *20th Century China*, pp. 203–4; ES, *Journey to the Beginning*, p. 139.

45. ES, *Journey to the Beginning,* p. 140.

46. HFS, *My China Years,* p. 141.

47. Ibid., p. 156.

48. ES, *Journey to the Beginning,* p. 140.

49. Ibid.

50. Ibid.

51. Ibid.

52. Ibid., p. 141.

53. Ibid.

54. Ibid.

55. Ibid., p. 142.

56. Ibid., p. 139.

57. HFS, *My China Years,* pp. 100–161.

58. Ibid.

59. Ibid.

60. ES, *Journey to the Beginning,* p. 142.

61. John Maxwell Hamilton, *Edgar Snow: A Biography* (Bloomington: Indiana University Press, 1988), p. 14.

62. ES, *Journey to the Beginning,* p. 142.

63. Ibid., p. 143.

64. Ibid.

65. Ibid.

66. HFS, *My China Years,* p. 163.

67. Ibid.

68. ES, *Journey to the Beginning,* p. 143.

69. Ibid., p. 144.

70. Ibid.

71. Israel, *Student Nationalism in China,* p. 129.

72. Victor Keen, "Canton Student Defiance Brings Tokyo Gunboat," *New York Herald Tribune,* 12/13/35.

73. Ibid.

74. Keen, "5000 Chinese Riot Against Japan's Rule, Police Fell 60." *New York Herald Tribune,* 12/17/35.

75. ES, *Journey to the Beginning,* p. 143.

76. Ibid.

77. Ibid.

78. Israel, *Student Nationalism in China,* pp. 137–38.

79. ES, *Journey to the Beginning,* p. 145.

80. See Shanghai Municipal Police reports of the period, 1932–1937.

81. A lecture at the Foreign YMCA on October 31, 1933, by Mr. G. J. Yorke (Shanghai Municipal Police Report No. D 5409, 11/7/33) is a good example of the kind of sketchy, somewhat inaccurate, but hard-won, information available on the Kiangsi Chinese Soviet Republic. Yorke originally obtained information about the Communists as a member of a party inspecting dikes on the Yangtze, in discussion with engineers who had worked in Communist territory repairing dikes. The following year, Yorke accompanied the London *Times* special correspondent, Peter Fleming, on a trip to Kiangsi, Hunan and Kwangtung. This was a solid effort at investigative reporting, and Yorke returned to Kiangsi later as a special correspondent for Reuters. But he makes what John Maxwell Hamilton calls "the usual quota of mistakes," (Hamilton, *Edgar Snow,* p. 63), as-

serting, for example, that Mao Tse-tung studied at "Lenin University, Moscow."

82. Dick Wilson, *The Long March 1935: The Epic of Chinese Communism's Survival* (New York: Viking, 1971), p. 53; F. F. Liu, *A Military History of Modern China, 1924–1949* (Princeton: Princeton University Press, 1956), p. 98; Stuart Schram, *Mao Tse-tung* (New York: Penguin, 1977), p. 175.

83. Owen Lattimore, *China Memoirs: Chiang Kai-shek and the War Against Japan,* compiled by Fujiko Isono (Tokyo: University of Tokyo Press, 1990), p. 129.

84. Ibid., pp. 129–30.

85. ES, *Red Star Over China* (New York: Random House, 1944).

86. ES, *Journey to the Beginning,* p. 152.

87. Mariann Clubb to author, October 1989.

88. Ibid.

89. Ibid.

90. ES, *Journey to the Beginning,* p. 147.

91. Ibid., p. 152.

92. Wang, as the first ambassador to the United Nations from the People's Republic of China, became known to the world as Huang Hua (his Communist *nom de guerre,* which, translated, means "yellow flower").

93. HFS, *My China Years,* p. 164.

94. Ibid.

95. Ibid., p. 349.

96. Hamilton, *Edgar Snow,* p. 64.

97. ES, *My China Years,* p. 180.

98. ES, letter, "Dear Mr. MacBride," 6/1/36, ESP.

99. ES, *My China Years,* p. 181.

100. Quoted in Hamilton, *Edgar Snow,* p. 64.

101. Harrison Salisbury, "China Reporting, Red Star to Long-March," in *Voices of China: The Interplay of Politics and Journalism,* edited by Chin-Chuan Lee (New York: Guilford Press, 1990), p. 219.

102. Hamilton, *Edgar Snow,* p. 68.

103. Ibid., p. 70.

104. ES, *Red Star Over China,* p. 33.

105. Helen Foster Snow to author, June 1989.

106. Ibid.

107. ES, *Red Star Over China,* p. 70.

108. Hamilton, *Edgar Snow,* p. 88.

109. ES, *Journey to the Beginning,* p. 167: "He was not the only politburo member with a wife—women were extremely scarce in that camp—but the only one I noticed whose wife seemed completely under her husband's spell and domination."

110. Smedley, *Battle Hymn of China,* p. 169.

111. This is a subject of some speculation in academic circles. Ruan Ming, author of *Deng Xiaoping: Chronicle of an Empire* (Boulder: Westview 1994), and a Mao scholar, takes exception to certain current notions that Mao was someone who later in life was incapable of forming friendships. He was, rather, according to Ruan Ming, a man of feeling who formed strong, if not necessarily lasting friendships. The traditional system of Chinese leadership, Ruan believes, was what prevented Mao from forming bonds of friendship with people in the Chinese Communist Party.

Ruan stresses, nevertheless, that Mao was a dangerous person to have as a friend because he was ruled by his feelings. This drawback became fatally apparent during the Cultural Revolution to those men who had presumed to believe that their friendship with Mao was dependable.

112. ES, *Red Star Over China*, p. 123.

113. Ibid.

114. Stuart Schram to author, May 1993; Snow, for instance, is used as a reference by Arif Dirlik in *The Origins of Chinese Communism* (New York: Oxford University Press, 1989), p. 45.

115. Dirlik, *The Origins of Chinese Communism*, pp. 178–80.

116. Snow, at Chou's request, withheld from publication in *Red Star* material on this and other matters, although he later included the omitted material in *Random Notes on Red China, 1936–1945* (Cambridge: Harvard University Press, 1957), p. 60. This volume contains notes Snow made from interviews with Chou En-lai in Yenan (see Snow's Diary, Book 13, ESP) but which Snow, at Chou's request, refrained from using in *Red Star*. Some of Chou's comments on Chiang Kai-shek were quite scathing, and he didn't want to publicly offend Chiang, with whom at the time he was negotiating a United Front agreement. However, some of Chou's remarks, including one concerning the Kiangsi debacle, cast doubt on his own judgment, and he well may not have wanted to see these in print, either. In any case, Chou clearly had misgivings about his interviews with Snow. "Chou En-lai was irked that you published the interview with him stating the information about radio stations," Helen Snow wrote her husband, from Yenan, on June 23, 1936, "and that the R [Reds] had discovered all Nanking codes etc. He said this was meant to be secret, and he didn't personally give it to you that he remembers anyway. He is afraid you are going to publish names of commanders and forces he gave you confidentially, so be careful about this." Nym Wales, *My Yenan Notebooks* (Madison, Conn., 1961). According to John Maxwell Hamilton, Snow's biographer, Snow was himself angered by Chou's subsequent request to remove passages from his book based on his interviews with Chou, some of which may have been held informally, since, in Pao An, the two lived side-by-side. Snow acceded to Chou's request nevertheless.

117. ES, *Red Star Over China*, p. 196.

118. ES, Diary, Book 17, 9/18/36, ESP.

119. Lattimore, *China Memoirs*, p. 155.

120. ES, Diary, Book 17, 8/27/36, ESP.

121. ES, *Red Star Over China*, p. 371.

122. ES, Diary, Book 17, 9/9/36, ESP.

123. Ibid., 8/26/36.

124. Ibid., 8/30/36.

125. ES, *Red Star Over China*, p. 400.

126. Ibid., pp. 400–401.

127. Ibid.

128. Ibid., p. 427.

129. Ibid., p. 429.

130. HFS to author, March 1990.

131. Ibid.

132. Two little points about this are worth remarking upon solely in passing: Yang Kwei Fei, the concubine of the emperor, and celebrated in literature

and song as the most beautiful woman in Chinese history, who met her end famously by strangulation during the An Lu-shan rebellion, is celebrated for having bathed in these very hot springs, and so Chiang Kai-shek is forever joined in legend with that earlier visitor; and "Chieh-shih," or "Kai-shek," means "between two stones," which very nicely sums up Chiang Kai-shek's particular dilemma at Tiger Rock. It might almost be said that Chiang, when captured, was between a rock and a hard place.

133. ES, *Random Notes on Red China*, pp. 1–5; see also Schram, *Mao Tse-tung*, p. 199.

134. HFS, *My China Years*, p. 202. Hamilton makes the additional point that by transcribing Mao's story, Snow could duck responsibility for any errors committed to him by Mao, yet maintain his integrity as a reporter. "The reader was warned he was getting a subjective view." Hamilton, *Edgar Snow*, p. 89.

135. HFS, *My China Years*, p. 234.

136. Along with others, who also suffered from these cataclysmic upheavals.

137. MacKinnon and MacKinnon, *Agnes Smedley*, pp. 170–72.

138. Hatem was the medical emissary who accompanied Edgar Snow into Red territory. He was among the first of several doctors Smedley sponsored on behalf of the Reds, who urgently needed whatever medical aid—supplies, personnel—they could get; Hatem, born in Buffalo, spent half a century with the Communists, helping them eradicate leprosy and venereal disease, and on his death in 1988 was eulogized for his medical accomplishments on behalf of the Chinese. Hatem went to Shanghai originally to treat venereal disease there in the early 1930s, but, he later told Edgar Snow, "I didn't spend my old man's money learning to become a V.D. quack for a gangster society. Maybe these people up north are interested in putting an end to the whole business. I want to see what they're like." Walter Sullivan, "George Hatem Is Dead At 78; Leader in Public Health in China," *New York Times*, 10/6/88.

139. Smedley had arrived in China the same year as Edgar Snow, and they were old friends from their early *China Weekly Review* days. There is reason to believe that they might even have had a brief affair.

140. MacKinnon and MacKinnon, *Agnes Smedley*, p. 173.

141. Ibid., p. 175.

142. Ibid., pp. 177–78.

143. Ibid., p. 187.

144. Ibid.

145. HFS to author, June 1989.

146. Ibid.

147. Ibid.

148. Ibid.

149. Smedley, *Battle Hymn of China*, p. 168.

150. Ibid., p. 170.

151. MacKinnon and MacKinnon, *Agnes Smedley*, p. 90. My account of the Lily Wu episode is drawn from the excerpt used by the MacKinnons, which was reported (in Japanese) by Edgar Snow as recounted to him by Smedley.

152. Ibid.

153. HFS, *My Yenan Notebooks*.

154. HFS, *My China Years*, p. 274.

155. Ibid., p. 261.
156. Ibid., p. 262.
157. Ibid. Braun, by then, was even more paranoid than Smedley. Long having overstayed his welcome, this strange bird, whom Edgar Snow described as one of the ugliest men he had ever laid eyes on, lived in virtual isolation, sick with dysentery. "I am maximum anti-social," he told Helen Snow (HFS to author, June 1989). He even suspected her, and Snow, of being secret agents, sent to spy on him by the government of the United States.
158. HFS to author, June 1989.
159. Ibid.
160. Note on letter, 7/26/37, Helen Snow papers, Hoover Institution, Stanford University.
161. HFS, *My China Years,* p. 282.
162. Ibid., p. 283.
163. Wilma Fairbank to author, October 1993.
164. Peck, *Through China's Wall,* pp. 336–37.
165. ES, *Journey to the Beginning,* p. 188.
166. Ibid., p. 189. Although Madame Chou later denied that she had ever disguised herself as a servant to a foreigner, James Bertram writes, "The fact was that she did travel with us, on the assumption that Ed or I would claim her as our personal *amah,* if she ran into any trouble on the railway platform at Tientsin, or on the wharf at Tangku." She wore, he notes, "white tunic, black trousers, and blue cloth shoes; she carried his parcels for the journey, keeping always a little to the rear." ("Capes of China Slide Away," p. 198.) Another witness was John S. Service, who that day happened to be on the Peiping-Tientsin train: "The train was crowded beyond belief and took some 14 hours to make the normal two-hour run to Tientsin—sidetracked most of the time while Japanese troop trains from Manchuria streamed past us rushing to the China front." Eventually Service discovered that Snow was on board. "Having at least a slight acquaintance with the Snows' domestic menage," Service recalled, "I was a bit surprised at an *amah* that he was carefully keeping under his eye. Under his breath he muttered vaguely that she was someone who would be in serious trouble if discovered by the Japanese. It was not until seven years later in Yenan that I recognized Teng Ying-ch'ao, the wife of Chou En-lai. Ed, of course, knew full well that he too would be in serious trouble if the Japanese had discovered her." John S. Service, "Edgar Snow: Some Personal Reminiscences," reprinted from *The China Quarterly,* No. 50, April-June 1972 (Berkeley, California: Center for Chinese Studies, University of California), p. 213.
167. HFS, *My China Years,* p. 185.
168. Ibid., p. 299.
169. A. T. Steele to author, 11/25/90.
170. Tillman Durdin, "Nanking Butchery Marked Its Fall," *New York Times,* 12/18/37.
171. ES, letter, "Dear Dad," 1/16/38, ESP.
172. Ibid.
173. HFS, *My China Years,* p. 301.
174. Ibid., p. 304 (quoted by HFS from a 1982 speech given by Rewi Alley at a service held in Peiping to commemorate Edgar Snow on the tenth anniversary of his death).

175. Ibid.
176. Hamilton, *Edgar Snow,* pp. 85–86.
177. Christopher Isherwood and W. H. Auden, *Journey to a War* (New York: Random House, 1939), p. 49.
178. Ibid.
179. ES, letter, "Dear J.B.," 8/28/38, ESP.
180. HFS, *My China Years,* p. 323.
181. ES, Diary excerpt, "Midway, Jan. 13th," ESP.

TEDDY

1. Robert P. Martin to author, winter 1990.
2. Theodore H. White, "Chongqing Transformed," *The New York Times,* 2/10/85, travel section, p. 15.
3. Emily Hahn, letter, "I shall try to send this airmail," 12/19/39, Emily Hahn papers, University of Minnesota.
4. Lattimore, *China Memoirs,* p. 101.
5. Theodore H. White [hereinafter THW], *In Search of History: A Personal Adventure* (New York: Harper & Row, 1978), p. 53: "Both Charlie Duhig and John Fairbank thought I was not really and truly of the stuff of scholarship. Without being specific, both implied that I had the manners, lust and ego of someone who might be a journalist. Fairbank had known Edgar Snow in China; and he thought I should try to do what Snow was doing."
6. Carl Mydans to author, October 1988.
7. THW, *In Search of History,* p. 52.
8. Ibid., pp. 76, 77; Hollington K. Tong, *Dateline: China* (New York: Rockport, 1950), p. 101.
9. THW, *In Search of History,* pp. 76, 77.
10. A. T. Steele to author, 11/23/90.
11. Robert P. Martin to author, April 1985.
12. Hugh Deane to author, spring 1989.
13. Emily Hahn to author, January 1989.
14. Annalee Jacoby Fadiman to author, April 1990.
15. Ibid.
16. Hugh Deane to author, spring 1989.
17. THW, *In Search of History,* p. 81.
18. Ibid., p. 84.
19. THW, letter, "I wonder whether I've done a fairly honest job of it," 10/40, T. H. White papers, Pusey Library, Harvard University [hereinafter THWP].
20. THW, letter, "As for," 5/12/44, THWP.
21. Annalee Jacoby, letter, "Belden's having a tough time," 8/20/44, THWP.
22. THW, letter, "This week concurrently," 6/9/39, THWP.
23. W. A. Swanberg, *Luce and His Empire* (New York: Scribner, 1972), p. 149.
24. Ibid., p. 152.
25. THW, letter, "Here is a secret," 4/17/40, THWP. I owe the battleship reference to Viola Isaacs, who told me that in 1928, when he went to work for the *Times,* Isaacs was admonished by an editor there, "the color of the *New York Times* is battleship gray."

26. THW, *In Search of History,* p. 85.
27. Shelley Mydans to author, October 1988.
28. THW, *In Search of History,* p. 94.
29. Hugh Deane to author, spring 1989.
30. James C. Thomson, Jr. to author, 3/14/89.
31. Robert P. Martin to author, 11/13/88.
32. THW, letter, "Re the trip north," 1/11/40, THWP.
33. THW, *In Search of History,* p. 103.
34. Robert P. Martin to author, winter 1990.
35. John Stewart Service to author, July 1989.
36. Ibid.
37. And just missed getting blown up, along with the Durdins, with whom he was staying; Peggy Durdin had with some difficulty managed to persuade her guest to accompany her and her husband, Till, to a bomb shelter during a Japanese air attack during which the Durdins' house was razed; when they returned after the bombing raid, however, the mantelpiece and chimney still stood, along with a bottle of gin and a pair of Snow's underpants. (See Stephen R. MacKinnon and Oris Friesen, eds., *China Reporting* (Berkeley: University of California Press, 1987), pp. 51–52.
38. Robert P. Martin to author, winter 1990.
39. John Paton Davies, Jr., *Dragon by the Tail: American, British, Japanese and Russian Encounters with China and One Another* (New York: W.W. Norton, 1972), p. 163.
40. Joseph W. Alsop, with Adam Platt, *I've Seen the Best of It* (New York: W. W. Norton, 1992), p. 161.
41. Emily Hahn, *China to Me: A Partial Autobiography* (Philadelphia: Blakiston, 1944), p. 124; and p. 171: " 'Tita' Clark Kerr is much more like a doll, with golden curls and tiny perfect features."
42. THW, *Time* dispatch, 3/15/40, THWP.
43. Tillman Durdin to author, July 1989.
44. Christopher Isherwood, *Christopher and His Kind* (New York: Farrar, Straus Giroux, 1976), p. 308.
45. THW, *In Search of History,* p. 76: "Yardley was excessively kind to me," Teddy wrote of yet another older friend, "as were so many older men in Chiang Kai-shek's Chungking."
46. Annalee Jacoby Fadiman to author, April 1990.
47. THW, *Time* dispatch, 3/15/40, THWP.
48. THW, letter, "Re the trip north," 1/11/40, THWP.
49. Ibid.
50. Emily Hahn, letter, "I shall try to send this airmail," 12/19/39, Emily Hahn papers.
51. THW, *In Search of History,* p. 103.
52. John Stewart Service to author, July 1989.
53. Carl Mydans to author, October 1988.
54. THW, letter, "Re Mel:," 8/24/40, THWP.
55. Graham Peck, *Two Kinds of Time* (Boston: Houghton Mifflin, 1940), p. 58.
56. Ibid.
57. Hahn, *China to Me,* p. 169.
58. M. A. Demott to author, May 1983.
59. Robert P. Martin to author, winter 1990.
60. THW, letter, "My technique is this," 12/7/40, THWP.

61. Ibid.
62. Ibid.
63. Robert P. Martin to author, winter 1990.
64. THW, *In Search of History,* p. 105.
65. Robert P. Martin to author, winter 1990.
66. THW, letter, "I think he was wearing slippers," 8/3/42, THWP.
67. THW, *In Search of History,* p. 110.
68. Lattimore, *China Memoirs,* p. 127.
69. Jean Pool to author, July 1993.
70. Carl Mydans to author, October 1988.
71. Annalee Jacoby Fadiman to author, April 1990.
72. Ibid.
73. Carl Mydans to author, October 1988.
74. Shelley Mydans to author, October 1988.
75. Carl Mydans to author, October 1988.
76. Ibid.
77. Swanberg, *Luce and His Empire,* p. 146.
78. Ibid.
79. THW, *In Search of History,* p. 104.
80. Carl Mydans to author, October 1988.
81. Tong, *Dateline: China,* p. 137.
82. Carl Mydans to author, October 1988.
83. F. Tillman Durdin to author, July 1989.
84. Carl Mydans to author, October 1988.
85. THW, *In Search of History,* p. 128.
86. Annalee Jacoby Fadiman to author, April 1990.
87. Ibid.
88. Ibid., April 1985.
89. Hugh Deane to author, spring 1989.
90. Annalee Jacoby Fadiman to author, April 1990.
91. Ibid.
92. Carl Mydans to author, October 1988.
93. Annalee Jacoby Fadiman to author, April 1990.
94. Ibid.
95. Ibid.
96. Ibid.
97. Ibid.
98. Ibid.
99. Ibid.
100. Ibid.
101. Ibid.
102. Quoted in Robert T. Elson, *The World of Time Inc: The Intimate History of a Publishing Enterprise* (New York: Atheneum, 1968–1986), pp. 4–5.
103. THW, *In Search of History,* p. 130.
104. Carl Mydans to author, October 1988, and, again, autumn 1991. Annalee Jacoby Fadiman gives a somewhat less gory version of the accident, in which the second P-40 crashed into General George's plane and killed everyone in his party. Mydans obtained his version from someone who witnessed the accident.
105. Annalee Jacoby Fadiman to author, April 1990.

106. THW, letter, "The month of May also saw me struggling with two other problems," 6/14/42, THWP.
107. Ibid.
108. Ibid.
109. THW, letter, "One of these days I hope I can wring a yes out of her," September 1944, THWP.
110. Joseph W. Alsop to author, July 1982.
111. THW, expense itemization, 9/13/42–12/1/42, THWP.
112. THW, letter, "Jack Belden is now off to Cairo," 12/2/42, THWP.
113. Ibid.
114. THW, expense itemization, 9/13/42–12/1/42, THWP.
115. Robert P. Martin to author, winter 1990.
116. Ibid.
117. THW, letter, "Now that was interesting," 11/8/42, THWP.
118. The term "courtesy general" is used by Graham Peck to describe General Hurley in *Two Kinds of Time*.
119. Elson, *The World of Time Inc.*, p. 73.
120. THW, letter, "Dear Dave, I haven't written you now since December 3," 5/14/43, THWP.
121. Ibid.
122. Ibid.
123. Quoted in Elson, *The World of Time Inc.*, pp. 120–21.
124. THW, letter, "Last spring we wrote a column on Ambassador Gauss," 1/12/43, THWP.
125. THW, letter to Robert P. Martin, 11/1/43, THWP.
126. Memo to THW from Henry Luce, 4/3/44, THWP.
127. THW, letter, "Thank you ever so much for the very kind things you said about the article," THW to Henry R. Luce, April 1944.
128. David Hulburd, letter, "The dark age in our history of Australia," 8/24/42, THWP.
129. THW, letter, "Dear Dave, I haven't written you now since December 3," 4/15/43, THWP.
130. Ibid.
131. THW, letter, "Jack is now a big shot," 5/3/43, THWP.
132. THW, letter, "Personally, too," April 1944, THWP.
133. THW, letter, "The news you gave me caused me to gulp," May 1944, THWP.
134. THW, "Life Looks at China," *Life,* May 1, 1944.
135. Ibid.
136. "The Hump," *Life,* 9/11/44.
137. Lattimore, *China Memoirs,* p. 100.
138. Herbert Feis, *The China Tangle* (Princeton: Princeton University Press, 1953), pp. 140–41.
139. Eric Sevareid, *Not So Wild a Dream* (New York: Alfred A. Knopf, 1947), p. 327.
140. Lattimore, *China Memoirs,* p. 185.
141. John Paton Davies Interview, "China in Revolution," PBS documentary, September 27, 1989. However, the ultimate geopolitical reason for striking up a relationship with the Reds has found supporters now among those adamantly opposed to the idea at the time. In his reminiscences,

Joseph Alsop, Chennault's champion, suggested that to have had relations with Mao, to have established and fostered them, might have prevented subsequent grief. For one thing, this argument advances that if the United States had established diplomatic relations with Mao's China, the Korean War might have been averted. Without a U.S. embargo brought about by China's involvement in Korea, Mao might not have sought the chilly embrace of the USSR. He would not necessarily have become quite such a Stalinist, one who presided over a monolithic, authoritarian regime that plundered the peasants and regimented Chinese society for the purpose of building an industrialized state, one dependent, moreover, on a heavy armaments industry.

142. MacKinnon and Friesen, *China Reporting*.
143. Tillman Durdin to author, July 1989. See Dai Qing, *Wang Shiwei and "Wild Lilies," Rectification and Purges in the Chinese Communist Party 1942–1944,* edited by David F. Apter and Timothy Cheek, translated by Nancy Liu and Lawrence R. Sullivan (N.Y.: M. E. Sharpe, 1994).
144. HI, letter, "hello darling," 7/31/44, HRIP.
145. HI, letter, No. 3, "hello darling," 7/31/44, HRIP.
146. Annalee Jacoby Fadiman to author, April 1990.
147. HI, letter, No. 3, "hello darling," 8/3/44, HRIP.
148. HI, notes, 9/10/44, HRIP. Soong Ching-ling still loved a good, juicy chat, however. "She's full of feline bitterness about AS [Agnes Smedley], apparently," Isaacs wrote. "Gleefully passed on gossip about how AS has reportedly changed. 'You know she hardly had any hair. I understand she's now wearing a wig. (She is very close to the bishop, bishop root, or is it hall?')"
149. HI, letter, No. 24, "hello darling," 10/7/44, HRIP.
150. Ibid.
151. HI, letter, No. 31, "hello sweetheart," 10/30/44, HRIP.
152. HI, letter, No. 34, "hello sweetheart," 11/2/44, HRIP.
153. HI, letter, No. 3, "hello darling," 8/3/44, HRIP.
154. Viola Isaacs to author, September 1991.
155. HI, letter, No. 15, "hello darling," 9/10/44, HRIP.
156. Ibid.
157. Ibid.
158. Dean Acheson, *Present at the Creation: My Years in the State Department* (New York: W.W. Norton, 1969), p. 133.
159. Alsop, *I've Seen the Best of It,* p. 237.
160. Joseph W. Alsop to author, July 1982.
161. Quoted in Barbara Tuchman, *Stilwell and the American Experience in China, 1911–1945* (New York: Bantam, 1980), p. 629.
162. It seems that Stilwell's chief objective in this exchange was to insult Chiang Kai-shek and cause him to lose face. The last verse of a poem he wrote for his wife on the matter puts it succinctly:

> *I know I've still to suffer*
> *And run a weary race,*
> *But oh! the blessed pleasure!*
> *I've wrecked the peanut's face.*

163. General Joseph W. Stilwell, *The Stilwell Papers,* edited by Theodore H. White (New York: William Sloane, 1948). This is the version tidied up by

Teddy White. Stilwell's official record made that night in Chungking reads, according to John Paton Davies, "The harpoon hit him in the solar plexus, but, although he turned green, he never batted an eye. He just turned to me and said: 'I understand' . . . got out promptly and came home." (*Dragon by the Tail*, p. 331.)

164. Davies, *Dragon by the Tail*, p. 355.
165. Alsop, *I've Seen the Best of It*, p. 255.
166. THW, *In Search of History*, p. 174.
167. HI, letter, No. 53, 12/20/44, HRIP.
168. White, *In Search of History*, p. 176.
169. ES, *Journey to the Beginning*, p. 383.
170. THW, *In Search of History*, p. 209.
171. Ibid.
172. HI, notes, 9/9/44, HRIP.
173. HI, letter, No. 15, "hello darling," 9/10/44, HRIP.
174. HI, letter, No. 31, "hello sweetheart," 10/30/44, HRIP.
175. Ibid.
176. Ibid.
177. Brooks Atkinson, "Long Schism Seen in Stilwell Shift, Stilwell Recall Bares Rift." *New York Times*, 10/31/44.
178. THW to author, March 1982.
179. HI, letter, "I have just returned from one of the most bizarre sessions I have ever had with a public man," 10/24/44, HRIP.
180. Ibid.
181. HI, letter, "Dear Chet," 2/7/45, HRIP.
182. Ibid.
183. HI, letter, No. 78, 2/11/45, HRIP.
184. Ibid.
185. Ibid.
186. Davies had gone up to Yenan on a mission for the U.S. Army to investigate a peace proposal the OSS had composed. Hence, he was not in Yenan as Hurley's subordinate. Indeed, Hurley hadn't even known of Davies's departure. Since, at the time, Davies was under U.S. Army command, he did not inform Hurley that he was going. When the ever-informed, ever-suspicious T. V. Soong, who hated Davies, asked Hurley why Davies had gone to Yenan, Hurley denied that he had. As Teddy White put it in a memo to David Hulburd on May 23, 1945, "When Hurley checked he found John actually had gone, he hit the ceiling and claimed that John was undermining his negotiations." When Hurley later purged his staff of China Hands, according to White, "he has claimed that he removed John Davies and Jack Service because 'they were leaking to Teddy White.'" White also maintained, in his memo to Hulburd, that Hurley "got rid of John Davies to cover" the blunder he'd made when he'd denied to T. V. Soong that Davies had gone to Yenan, which had been a major loss of face for Hurley. But Davies did try to call Hurley before he left for Yenan, and when he couldn't reach him—he was told that Hurley was away for the weekend—he sent him a note. This note is interesting because it suggests that although Hurley's arrival in Yenan seemed unplanned and unexpected, a visit to Yenan by Hurley was in fact in the works. THW memo to Hulburd, 5/23/45, THWP; Davies, *Dragon by the Tail*, p. 344.
187. Davies, *Dragon by the Tail*, p. 366.

188. Feis, *The China Tangle*, p. 216.
189. THW, *In Search of History*, p. 201. Although not everyone agreed that Hurley was senile. As Joseph Alsop put it, "Hurley was a shit, but he was not stupid." Joseph W. Alsop to author, July 1982.
190. MacKinnon and Frieson, *China Reporting*, pp. 141–44.
191. THW, *In Search of History*, p. 211.
192. Ibid.
193. HI, letter, No. 78, "did it I actually did it," 2/11/45, HRIP.
194. This was not their last effort to reach an agreement. In 1946, the American negotiator, General George C. Marshall, obtained a cease-fire agreement from both sides. That, however, was after the civil war had begun.
195. THW, *In Search of History*, p. 211.
196. Annalee Jacoby, letter, "All day I've been trying to decide whether to go to Nanking for the surrender or not," 8/1/45, THWP.
197. Annalee Jacoby Fadiman to author, April 1990.
198. Ibid.
199. Christopher Rand [hereinafter CR], letter, "Dear Graham," 3/11/46, Christopher Rand papers, Boston University [hereinafter CRP].
200. Annalee Jacoby Fadiman to author, April 1990.
201. THW, letter, "Dear Annalee," 4/3/46, THWP.
202. CR, Chungking diary, 8/20/43, CRP.
203. THW, letter, "Let's see now," 12/25/46, THWP.
204. THW, letter, "Dear Harry," 6/26/46, THWP.
205. THW, *In Search of History*, p. 247.
206. John Hersey, "Henry Luce's China Dream," *The New Republic*, 5/2/83.

ALIVE IN OUR HEARTS

1. M. A. DeMott to author, May 1983.
2. CR to author, July 1968.
3. Keyes Beech to author, July 1982.
4. M. A. DeMott to author, May 1983.
5. Robert P. Martin to author, November 1988.
6. John Hersey to author, February 1982.
7. Photographs, Graham Peck archive, Boston University.
8. THW to author, March 1982.
9. Robert Payne to author, May 1981.
10. Emily Hahn to author, May 1981.
11. Joseph W. Alsop to author, July 1982.
12. M. A. DeMott to author, May 1983.
13. CR unpublished recollections, CRP.
14. John Hersey to author, February 1982.
15. "Life Goes on a Date in Chungking," *Life*, 11/5/45.
16. Edwin P. Hoyt to author, spring 1989.
17. Peck, *Two Kinds of Time*, p. 60.
18. Ibid.
19. Holmes Welch, *Taoism: The Parting of the Way*, revised edition (Boston: Beacon Press, 1965), pp. 124–26.
20. *China Handbook, 1937–1945,* compiled by the Chinese Ministry of Infor-

mation, third revised edition (New York: Macmillan, 1947), p. 14. The version quoted by Graham Peck in *Two Kinds of Time* is from an earlier edition and reads, "Excessive drinking, nihilistic behavior, and the ridiculing of all the peoples of the earth."

21. Lattimore, *China Memoirs,* pp. 206–7.
22. Barbara Stephens, letter, "Dear Chris," 11/26/45, CRP.
23. CR, letter, "Barbara," 12/20/45, CRP.
24. Leonard Mosely, *Marshall: Hero for Our Times* (New York: Hearst Books, 1982), p. 367.
25. CR, letter, "Barbara," 2/27/46, CRP.
26. CR, letter, "Dearest Madget," 7/13/46, CRP.
27. Keyes Beech to author, July 1982.
28. Ibid.
29. Elizabeth Purcell to author, spring 1989.
30. A. T. Steele to author, September 1982.
31. CR, letter, "Barbara," 2/27/46, CRP.
32. Stephens, letter, "Dear Chris," 1/15/46, CRP.
33. Stephens, letter, "Dear Chris," 4/6/46, CRP.
34. Ibid. Barbara also wrote: "Peking is a very pleasant and comfortable city to live in and also a very rotten one. Every foreigner was a collaborator and they are impossible to talk to or even be in the same room with. They spend most of their time telling you how the guy across the room is a Fascist and how they really suffered with the Japs—the only way apparently to get rid of them when they were bothering you was to invite them in for a cup of tea and some small talk. They are all the same. And they are all most popular with the high marine and army officers who think they are breaking into old Peking society—at the price of a plane ride here and there, px supplies, and concomitantly, the indulgence of the Kuomintang and municipal authorities who might have liked to use their fancy houses for their own nefarious purposes. Some of the marines here are talking already [sic] of how cooperative the Japs are and how they are really so grateful for the small favors done them by the Marine Corps—'They won't forget we've helped them, but these damn stubborn Chinese.' It is very sickening and discouraging."
35. A. T. Steele to author, September 1982.
36. Edwin P. Hoyt to author, spring 1989.
37. Louise Frillmann to author, spring 1982.
38. John Hersey to author, February 1982.
39. Robert Drummond to author, June 1979.
40. CR, "Letter from Peiping," typescript, undated, CRP.
41. Steven I. Levine, *Anvil of Victory: The Communist Revolution in Manchuria, 1945–1948* (New York: Columbia University Press, 1987), pp. 81–82.
42. Robert P. Martin to author, 11/12/88.
43. CR, letter, "Barbara," 8/28/46, CRP.
44. Was she also on a retainer from the EDS, an offshoot at the time of the OSS and a precursor to the CIA? It's possible, according to Edwin P. Hoyt, who speculated about this in a letter he wrote to me in the spring of 1989. Yet it also seems unlikely that she would have considered any promise to report on her findings to the U.S. embassy, or any U.S. agency, a vital part of her trip. Certainly she never mentioned any such

connection to Paxton, the U.S. consul in Tihwa, nor, in the subsequent cable traffic, does any such clandestine project receive the slightest mention.

45. CR, letter, 8/28/46, CRP.
46. CR, letter, "Barbara," 9/11/46, CRP.
47. Ibid.
48. Stephens, letter, 12/24/46, CRP.
49. Stephens, letter, "Dear Chris," 1/18/46, CRP.
50. Ibid.
51. Ibid.
52. Stephens, letter, "Dear Chris," 2/24/47, CRP.
53. Stephens, letter, "Dear Chris," 1/18/47, CRP.
54. Ibid.
55. Graham Peck, letter, "Dear Chris," 4/8/47, CRP.
56. Stephens, letter, "Dear Chris," 3/3/47, CRP.
57. CR, letter, "Graham," 12/2/47, CRP.
58. United States Consul Report, Peiping, 1/6/47, U.S. Military Archives, Suitland, Maryland.
59. CR, letter, "Barbara," 5/20/47, CRP.
60. Ibid.
61. CR, "China Retarded in Recovery by Shipping Lack," *New York Herald Tribune,* 9/18/46.
62. CR, "Reporting in the Far East," in *Reporting the News,* edited by Louis Lyons (Cambridge: Belknap Press of Harvard University Press, 1965), p. 310.
63. CR, "Chinese Reds Keep Foothold in Kwangtung," *New York Herald Tribune,* 11/3/46.
64. Keyes Beech to author, July 1982.
65. CR, "Chinese Reds Keep Foothold in Kwangtung," By traveling to Yenan with the returning Communists, Dad was able to observe that the Reds were preparing to evacuate Yenan, an important development.
66. CR, "Chinese Troops Slay 5,000 in Formosa Strife," *New York Herald Tribune,* 3/24/47.
67. A. T. Steele to author, 11/12/90.
68. Christopher T. Rand to author, fall 1982.
69. Stephens, letter, "Dear Chris," 7/25/47, CRP.
70. Ibid.
71. India Office records, London File: L/P&S/12/2360, Internal Situation; British Consul Eric Shipton, Letter No. 737-H/5/L-47, 5/1/47.
72. U.S. Military Archives, Suitland, Maryland, File 891, Press Correspondents—Stephens, B, John Hall Paxton, Dispatch No. 24, American Consulate, Tihwa, 8/20/47, Subject: Disappearance of Chinese Airforce plane on which Miss Barbara Stephens was a passenger.
73. CR, letter, "Dear Chris," 7/25/47, CRP.
74. Paxton, Dispatch No. 24.
75. Ibid.
76. U.S. Military Archives, Suitland, Maryland, File 891, Press Correspondents—Stephens, B. Telegram #326, 8/1/47, from Paxton in Tihwa to American Embassy, Nanking.
77. Telegram No. 327, 8/2/47, Paxton to Embassy, Nanking.
78. Telegram No. 329, 8/4/47, Paxton to Embassy, Nanking.

79. Telegram No. 331, 8/6/47, 2 p.m., Paxton to Embassy, Nanking.
80. Telegram No. 978, 8/8/47, United States Secretary of State Gen. George C. Marshall, Washington, to Embassy, Nanking.
81. John F. Melby, *The Mandate of Heaven* (Toronto: University of Toronto Press, 1968), p. 229.
82. Paxton, Dispatch No. 24.
83. Ibid.
84. John F. Melby to author, November 1982.
85. CR, letter, "Barbara," 7/28/47, CRP.
86. Ibid.
87. CR, *A Nostalgia for Camels* (Boston: Little, Brown, 1957), p. 23.
88. CR, letter, "Dear Mrs. Stephens," 9/12/47, CRP.
89. CR, letter, "Graham," 12/2/47, CRP.
90. Ibid.
91. Ibid.
92. CR, letter, "Darling Madget," 7/13/46, CRP.
93. CR, letter, "Darling Madget," 11/5/46, CRP.
94. M. A. DeMott to author, May 1983.
95. Robert Burton to author, June 1979.
96. M. A. DeMott to author, May 1983.
97. Ibid.
98. Ibid.
99. Ibid.
100. Ibid.
101. U.S. Military Archives, Suitland, Maryland, File 891, Press Correspondents—Stephens, B. *Third Person Note*. From: Ministry of Foreign Affairs to: American Embassy, October 13, 1947, No. Mei—36/21734.
102. Ibid., Memorandum OMA 373.5. Attention: Mr. Raymond P. Ludden. Subject: Identification and return of bodies of Barbara Stephens and Brian Sorensen to Nanking, 10/17/47.
103. M. A. DeMott to author, May 1983.
104. Ibid.
105. Robert Drummond, an American businessman who had lived among the journalists in Peiping, saw it in terms of Camembert; Leslie Smith, a British correspondent who had also been in Peiping at the time, likened it to Stilton. The two gentlemen shared a capacious apartment in Dina House, in Hong Kong, where my wife and I visited them in June 1979.
106. Robert Drummond to author, June 1979.
107. Mary Sullivan to author, winter 1994.
108. CR, letter, "Dear Mrs. Stephens," 11/23/47, CRP.
109. O. Edmund Clubb to author, 1983.
110. Quoted by Mrs. M. E. Stephens from a letter written to her by Barbara Stephens, 7/24/47, in a letter to CR, "Dear Chris," 9/25/47, CRP.

AFTERWORD

1. A. E. Steele, letter, "Dear Chris," 11/10/47, CRP.
2. Quoted in Laughlin Currie's obituary, *New York Times,* December 1993.
3. Hamilton, *Edgar Snow,* p. 187.
4. Viola Isaacs to author, March 1989.

5. Jack Belden, letter, "Ed," November 1962, Belden papers, Hoover Institution.
6. Jack Belden, letter, "Dear Cass," 1950, Belden papers.
7. Robert P. Martin to author, 11/12/88.
8. Ibid.
9. Tillman Durdin to author, July 1989.
10. THW to author, March 1982.
11. Ibid.

Bibliography

Abend, Hallett. *My Life in China, 1926–1941*. New York: Harcourt Brace, 1943.

Acheson, Dean. *Present at the Creation: My Years in the State Department*. New York: W. W. Norton, 1969.

Alsop, Joseph W., with Adam Platt. *I've Seen the Best of It*. New York: W. W. Norton, 1992.

Band, Claire, and William Band. *Two Years with the Chinese Communists*. New Haven: Yale University Press, 1948.

Barber, Noel. *The Fall of Shanghai*. New York: Coward, McCann & Geoghegan, 1979.

Barnes, Joseph, ed. *Empire in the East*. Garden City: Doubleday, Doran, 1934.

Barnett, A. Doak. *China on the Eve of Communist Takeover*. New York: Frederick A. Praeger, 1963.

Barnett, Robert W. *Economic Shanghai: Hostage to Politics, 1937–1941*. New York: Institute of Pacific Relations, 1941.

Belden, Jack. *China Shakes the World*. New York: Harper, 1949.

———. *Retreat with Stilwell*. New York: Alfred A. Knopf, 1943.

———. *Still Time to Die*. New York: Da Capo, 1975.

Bennett, Milly. *On Her Own*. Edited and annotated by A. Tom Grunfeld. Armonk, N.Y.: M. E. Sharpe, 1993.

Bertram, James M. *First Act in China*. New York: Viking, 1938.

Bland, J. O. P. *Houseboat Days in China*. New York: Doubleday, Page, 1919.

Blofeld, John. *City of Lingering Splendor*. Boston: Shambhala, 1989.

Bodde, Derk. *Peking Diary*. New York: Schuman, 1950.

Booker, Edna Lee. *News Is My Job*. New York: Macmillan, 1940.

Boorman, Howard L., ed. *Biographical Dictionary of Republican China*. Vols. 1–5. New York: Columbia University Press, 1967–79.

Borg, Dorothy. *American Policy and the Chinese Revolution, 1925–1928*. New York: American Institute of Pacific Relations and Macmillan, 1947.

———. *The United States and the Far Eastern Crisis of 1933–1938*. Cambridge: Harvard University Press, 1964.

Borg, Dorothy, and Waldo Heinrichs, eds. *Uncertain Years: Chinese-American Relations, 1947–1950*. New York: Columbia University Press, 1980.

Bosse, Malcolm. *The Warlord*. New York: Simon & Schuster, 1983.

Bredon, Juliet. *Peking*. Hong Kong: Oxford University Press, 1982.

Bridge, Ann. *The Ginger Griffin*. Boston: Little, Brown, 1934.

———. *Peking Picnic*. Boston: Little, Brown, 1932.

Buck, Pearl. *The Exile*. New York: Triangle, 1936.

———. *The Good Earth*. New York: Grosset & Dunlap, 1931.

Burke, James. *My Father in China*. New York: Farrar & Rinehart, 1942.

Cameron, Meribeth E. *The Reform Movement in China, 1898–1912*. Stanford: Stanford University Press, 1931.

Carl, Katharine A. *With the Empress Dowager of China*. New York: Century, 1906.

Carlson, Evans Fordyce. *Twin Stars of China*. New York: Dodd, Mead, 1940.

Cartier-Bresson, Henri. *China*. New York: Bantam, 1964.

Chambers, Whittaker. *Witness*. New York: Random House, 1952.

Chang, H. H. *Chiang Kai-shek: Asia's Man of Destiny*. Garden City: Doubleday, Doran, 1944.

Chapman, H. Owen. *The Chinese Revolution, 1926–27*. London: Constable, 1928.

Chen, Han-seng. *Landlord and Peasant in China*. New York: International Publishers, 1936.

Chen, Jerome. *Mao and the Chinese Revolution*. London: Oxford University Press, 1965.

Chen, Percy. *China Called Me*. Boston: Little, Brown, 1979.

Chien, Tuan-sheng. *The Government and Politics of China*. Cambridge: Harvard University Press, 1950.

Chinese Ministry of Information. *China Handbook, 1937–1945*. Third revised edition. New York: Macmillan, 1947.

Christopher, James William. *Conflict in the Far East: American Diplomacy in China from 1928–1933*. Leiden: E. J. Brill, 1950.

Clifford, Nicholas R. *Spoilt Children of Empire: Westerners in Shanghai and the Chinese Revolution of the 1920s*. Hanover, N.H.: Middlebury College Press, 1991.

Clubb, O. Edmund. *20th Century China*. New York: Columbia University Press, 1964.

———. *The Witness and I*. New York: Columbia University Press, 1974.

Cohen, Warren I. *The Chinese Connection*. New York: Columbia University Press, 1978.

Collis, Maurice. *Foreign Mud*. New York: Alfred A. Knopf, 1947.

Cressy-Marcks, Violet. *Journey into China*. London: Hodder & Stoughton, 1940.

Crockett, Albert Stevens. *When James Gordon Bennett Was Caliph of Baghdad*. New York: Funk and Wagnalls, 1926.

Crow, Carl. *The Chinese Are Like That*. Cleveland and New York: World, 1943.

———. *Four Hundred Million Customers*. New York: Harper & Brothers, 1937.

Davies, John Paton. *Dragon by the Tail: American, British, Japanese and Russian Encounters with China and One Another*. New York: W. W. Norton, 1972.

Day, Dorothy. *The Long Loneliness*. San Francisco: Harper & Row, 1981.

Deakin, F. W., and G. R. Storry. *The Case of Richard Sorge*. New York: Harper & Row, 1966.

Ding Ling. *Miss Sophie's Diary*. Beijing: Panda Books, 1985.

Dirlik, Arif. *The Origins of Chinese Communism*. New York: Oxford University Press, 1989.

Dulles, Foster Rhea. *China and America*. Port Washington, N.Y.: Kennikat Press, 1967.

Duranty, Walter. *I Write As I Please*. New York: Simon & Schuster, 1935.

Eastman, Lloyd E. *Seeds of Destruction: Nationalist China in War and Revolution, 1937–1949*. Stanford: Stanford University Press, 1984.

Ekins, H. R., and Theon Wright. *China Fights for Her Life*. New York and London: Whittlesey House, 1938.

Elson, Robert T. *The World of Time Inc: The Intimate History of a Publishing Enterprise*. New York: Atheneum, 1968–1986.

Esherick, Joseph, ed. *Lost Chance in China: The World War II Despatches of John S. Service*. New York: Random House, 1974.

Epstein, Israel. *The Unfinished Revolution in China*. Boston: Little, Brown, 1947.

———. *Woman in World History: Life and Times of Soong Ching Ling (Mme. Sun Yatsen)*. Beijing: New World Press, 1993.

Fairbank, John K. *Chinabound*. New York: Harper & Row, 1982.

———. *The Great Chinese Revolution, 1800–1985*. New York: Harper & Row, 1986.

———. *The United States and China*. Cambridge: Harvard University Press, 1948.

Fairbank, John K., ed. *The Cambridge History of China*, Vol. 12, *Republican China, 1912–1949*. Part I. Cambridge: Cambridge University Press, 1983.

Feis, Herbert. *The China Tangle*. Princeton: Princeton University Press, 1953.

Field, Frederick V. *American Participation in the Chinese Consortiums*. Chicago: University of Chicago Press, 1931.

Finney, Charles G. *The Old China Hands*. Garden City: Doubleday, 1961.

Fischer, Ruth. *Stalin and German Communism*. Cambridge: Harvard University Press, 1948.

Fitzgerald, C. P. *China: A Short Cultural History*. London: Cresset Press, 1935.

———. *Revolution in China*. New York: Praeger, 1952.

Fleming, Peter. *The Siege at Peking*. New York: Harper, 1959.

———. *One's Company: A Journey to China*. New York: Scribner's, 1934.

Foreign Relations of the United States. Volumes covering the 1930s and 1940s. Washington, D. C.: U.S. Government Printing Office.

Forman, Harrison. *Report from Red China*. New York: Henry Holt, 1945.

Franck, Harry A. *Roving Through Southern China*. New York and London: Century, 1925.

Frillmann, Paul, and Graham Peck. *China: The Remembered Life*. Boston: Houghton Mifflin, 1968.

Gaddis, John Lewis. *The United States and the Origins of the Cold War, 1941–1947*. New York: Columbia University Press, 1972.

Gayn, Mark J. *Journey from the East: An Autobiography*. New York: Alfred A. Knopf, 1944.

Gellhorn, Martha. *The Face of War*. New York: Atlantic Monthly Press, 1988.

Gerhardi, William. *The Polyglots*. New York: Duffield, 1925.

Gilbert, Rodney. *What's Wrong with China*. London: John Murray, 1926.

Gillin, Donald G. *Warlord*. Princeton: Princeton University Press, 1967.

Gould, Randall. *China in the Sun*. Garden City: Doubleday, 1946.

Granet, Marcel. *Chinese Civilization*. London: Kegan, Paul, Trench, Trubner; and New York: Alfred A. Knopf, 1930.

Grunfeld, A. Tom. "Friends of the Revolution: America's Supporters of China's Communists, 1925–1939." Ph.D. diss., New York University, 1985.

Hahn, Emily. *China Only Yesterday, 1850–1950: A Century of Change*. Garden City: Doubleday, 1963.

———. *China To Me: A Partial Autobiography*. Philadelphia: Blakiston, 1944.

———. *The Soong Sisters*. Garden City: Doubleday, Doran, 1942.

Halliburton, Richard. *The Royal Road to Romance*. Garden City: Garden City Publishing, 1925.

Hamilton, John Maxwell. *Edgar Snow: A Biography*. Bloomington: Indiana University Press, 1988.

Han, Suyin. *Destination Chungking*. Boston: Little, Brown, 1942.

———. *A Many-Splendored Thing*. Boston: Little, Brown, 1952.

———. *A Mortal Flower*. London: Granada, 1972, 1978.

——— *Birdless Summer*. London: Granada, 1972.

——— *My House Has Two Doors*. London: Granada, 1982.

——— *Phoenix Harvest*. London: Granada, 1982.

——— *The Crippled Tree*. London: Granada, 1982.

Herd, Harold. *The March of Journalism*. London: Allen & Unwin, 1952.

Hersey, John. *The Call*. New York: Alfred A. Knopf, 1985.

Hinton, Harold, ed. *The People's Republic of China: A Handbook*. Boulder, Colo.: Westview Press, 1979.

Hiss, Alger. *Recollections of a Life*. New York: Henry Holt, 1988.

Hobart, Alice Tisdale. *Oil for the Lamps of China*. Indianapolis: Bobbs-Merrill, 1933.

Hohenberg, John. *Foreign Correspondence: The Great Reporters and Their Times*. New York: Columbia University Press, 1964.

Hsiao, Ch'ien. *Traveller Without A Map*. Translated by Jeffrey C. Kinkley. London: Hutchinson, 1990.

Hsieh, Chiao-min. *Atlas of China*. New York: McGraw-Hill, 1973.

Hsu, Francis L. K. *Americans and Chinese*. London: Cresset Press, 1955.

Hughes, Richard. *Foreign Devil*. London: Century, 1984.

Hunt, Michael H. *The Making of a Special Relationship: The United States and China to 1914*. New York: Columbia University Press, 1983.

Iriye, Akira. *The Cold War in Asia: A Historical Introduction*. Englewood Cliffs, N.J.: Prentice-Hall, 1974.

Isaacs, Harold R. *Images of Asia*. Published originally as *Scratches on Our Minds*. New York: Capricorn, 1962.

———. *No Peace for Asia*. New York: Macmillan, 1947.

———. *Re-encounters in China: Notes of a Journey in a Time Capsule*. Armonk, N.Y.: M. E. Sharpe, 1985.

———. *Straw Sandals: Chinese Stories, 1918–1933*. Cambridge: The MIT Press, 1974.

———. *The Tragedy of the Chinese Revolution*. Revised edition. Stanford: Stanford University Press, 1951.

Isherwood, Christopher. *Christopher and His Kind*. New York: Farrar, Straus & Giroux, 1976.

Isherwood, Christopher, and W. H. Auden. *Journey to a War*. New York: Random House, 1939.

Israel, John. *Student Nationalism in China, 1927–1937*. Stanford: Stanford University Press, 1966.

Jackson, Stanley. *The Sassoons*. London: Heinemann, 1968.

Jacobs, Dan N. *Borodin, Stalin's Man in China*. Cambridge: Harvard University Press, 1981.

Jansen, Marius B. *Japan and China from War to Peace, 1894–1972*. Chicago: Rand McNally College Publishing, 1975.

Kahn, E. J., Jr. *The China Hands*. New York: Viking, 1975.

Karaka, D. F. *Chungking Diary*. Bombay: Thacker, 1945.

Kasanin, Marc. *China in the Twenties.* Translated from the Russian by Hilda Kasanin. Moscow: Central Department of Oriental Literature, 1973.

Kates, George N. *The Years That Were Fat.* Cambridge: The MIT Press, 1967.

Kempton, Murray. *Part of Our Time: Some Ruins and Monuments of the Thirties.* New York: Simon & Schuster, 1955.

Kennan, George F. *Russia and the West Under Lenin and Stalin.* Boston: Little, Brown, 1961.

Keon, Michael. *The Tiger in Summer.* New York: Harper, 1953.

Kidd, David. *Peking Story.* New York: Clarkson N. Potter, 1988.

Landman, Lynn, and Amos Landman. *Profile of Red China.* New York: Simon & Schuster, 1951.

Latourette, Kenneth Scott. *A History of Christian Missions in China.* New York: Macmillan, 1929.

Lattimore, Owen. *China Memoirs: Chiang Kai-shek and the War Against Japan.* Compiled by Fujiko Isono. Tokyo: University of Tokyo Press, 1990.

———. *Pivot of Asia.* Boston: Little, Brown, 1950.

Lee, Chin-chuan, ed. *Voices of China: The Interplay of Politics and Journalism.* New York: Guilford Press, 1990.

Lerner, Warren. *Karl Radek: The Last Internationalist.* Stanford: Stanford University Press, 1970.

Levenson, Joseph R. *Confucian China and Its Modern Fate: A Trilogy.* Berkeley: University of California Press, 1968.

Levine, Steven I. *Anvil of Victory: The Communist Revolution in Manchuria, 1945–1948.* New York: Columbia University Press, 1987.

Liebling, A. J. *The Press.* New York: Pantheon, 1981.

Lifton, Robert Jay. *Revolutionary Immortality.* New York: Random House, 1968.

———. *Thought Reform and the Psychology of Totalism.* New York: W. W. Norton, 1961.

Lindbergh, Anne Morrow. *North to the Orient.* New York: Harcourt, Brace, 1935.

Liu, F. F. *A Military History of Modern China, 1924–1949.* Princeton: Princeton University Press, 1956.

Lubow, Arthur. *The Reporter Who Would Be King: A Biography of Richard Harding Davis.* New York: Scribner, 1992.

Lyons, Louis M. *Reporting the News.* Cambridge: Belknap Press of Harvard University Press, 1965.

MacKinnon, Janice R., and Stephen R. MacKinnon. *Agnes Smedley: The Life and Times of an American Radical.* Berkeley: University of California Press, 1988.

MacKinnon, Stephen R., and Oris Friesen. *China Reporting.* Berkeley: University of California Press, 1987.

Malraux, André. *The Conquerers.* Translated by Stephen Becker. New York: Grove Press, 1977.

———. *Man's Fate.* Translated by Haakon Chevalier. New York: Random House, 1961.

Manchester, William. *American Caesar: Douglas MacArthur, 1880–1964.* Boston: Little, Brown, 1978.

Mao Tse-tung. *Selected Military Writings.* Peking: Foreign Languages Press, 1963.

———. *Selected Works.* Vols. 1–4. Peking: Foreign Languages Press, 1961–1965.

Martin, Edwin W. *Divided Counsel*. Lexington: University Press of Kentucky, 1986.

May, Gary. *China Scapegoat*. Washington, D.C.: New Republic Books, 1979.

McCormick, Thomas J. *China Market*. Chicago: Quadrangle, 1967.

Melby, John F. *The Mandate of Heaven*. Toronto: University of Toronto Press, 1968.

Menon, K. P. S. *Delhi-Chungking*. Bombay: Oxford University Press, 1947.

Millard, Thomas F. *America and the Far Eastern Question*. New York: Moffat, Yard, 1909.

Miller, William D. *Dorothy Day: A Biography*. New York: Harper & Row, 1982.

Misselwitz, Henry Francis. *The Dragon Stirs*. New York: Harbinger House, 1941.

Morin, Relman. *East Wind Rising*. New York: Alfred A. Knopf, 1960.

Mosely, Leonard. *Marshall: Hero for Our Times*. New York: Hearst Books, 1982.

Mosher, Steven. *China Misperceived*. New York: Basic Books, 1990.

Mydans, Carl. *More Than Meets the Eye*. New York: Harper, 1959.

Nathan, Andrew J. *Peking Politics, 1918–1923*. Berkeley: University of California Press, 1976.

Newman, Robert P. *Owen Lattimore and the "Loss" of China*. Berkeley: University of California Press, 1992.

Paddock, Paul. *China Diary*. Ames: Iowa State University Press, 1977.

Payne, Robert. *Forever China*. New York: Dodd, Mead, 1945.

Peck, Graham. *Through China's Wall*. Boston: Houghton Mifflin, 1940.

———. *Two Kinds of Time*. Boston: Houghton Mifflin, 1950.

Peffer, Nathaniel. *The Far East*. Ann Arbor: University of Michigan Press, 1958.

Pott, F. L. Hawks. *The Emergency in China*. New York: Missionary Education Movement of the United States and Canada, 1913.

Pruitt, Ida. *A Daughter of Han*. Stanford: Stanford University Press, 1967.

Rand, Christopher. *Hongkong: The Island Between*. New York: Alfred A. Knopf, 1952.

———. *Mountains and Water*. New York: Oxford University Press, 1965.

———. *A Nostalgia for Camels*. Boston: Little, Brown, 1957.

Reed, John. *Ten Days That Shook the World*. New York: Random House, 1935.

Remer, C. F. *A Study of Chinese Boycotts*. Baltimore: Johns Hopkins Press, 1932.

Rolsholt, Malcom. *Press Corps of Old Shanghai*. Rosholt, Wisc.: Rosholt House, 1994.

Roy, M. N. *Revolution and Counter-Revolution in China*. Calcutta: Renaissance Publishers, 1946.

Rozanski, Mordechai. "American Journalists in Chinese-American Relations, 1900–1923." Ph.D. diss., Columbia University, 1974.

Salisbury, Harrison E. *The Long March: The Untold Story*. New York: Harper & Row, 1985.

———. *The New Emperors*. Boston: Little, Brown, 1992.

Schaller, Michael. *The U.S. Crusade in China, 1938–1945*. New York: Columbia University Press, 1979.

Schiffrin, Harold Z. *Sun Yat-sen and the Origins of the Chinese Revolution*. Berkeley: University of California Press, 1968.

Schoyer, Preston. *The Foreigners*. New York: Dodd, Mead, 1942.

Schram, Stuart. *Mao Tse-tung*. New York: Penguin, 1977.

Schuman, Julian. *Assignment China*. New York: Whittier Books, 1956.

Schwartz, Benjamin I. *Chinese Communism and the Rise of Mao*. Cambridge: Harvard University Press, 1951.

Seagrave, Sterling. *The Soong Dynasty*. New York: Harper & Row, 1985.

Selden, Mark. *The Yenan Way in Revolutionary China*. Cambridge: Harvard University Press, 1971.

Sergeant, Harriet. *Shanghai*. New York: Crown, 1990.

Sevareid, Eric. *Not So Wild a Dream*. New York: Alfred A. Knopf, 1946.

Selz, Lucile. *Peking Journal*. New York: Vantage Press, 1978.

Shaplen, Robert A. *A Corner of the World*. New York: Alfred A. Knopf, 1949.

Sheean, Vincent. *Between the Thunder and the Sun*. New York: Garden City Publishing, 1944.

———. *Personal History*. New York: Random House, 1934.

Shewmaker, Kenneth E. *Americans and Chinese Communists, 1927–1945: A Persuading Encounter*. Ithaca, N.Y.: Cornell University Press, 1971.

Smedley, Agnes. *Battle Hymn of China*. New York: Alfred A. Knopf, 1943.

———. *Daughter of Earth*. New York: Feminist Press of the City University of New York, 1987.

———. *The Great Road*. New York: Monthly Review Press, 1956.

———. *Portraits of Chinese Women in Revolution*. New York: Feminist Press, 1976.

Smith, Arthur H. *Chinese Characteristics*. New York: Fleming H. Revell, 1894.

Snow, Edgar. *Far Eastern Front*. New York: Harrison Smith & Robert Haas, 1933.

———. *Journey to the Beginning*. New York: Random House, 1972.

———. *Random Notes on Red China, 1936–1945*. Cambridge: Harvard University, 1957.

———. *Red Star Over China*. New York: Random House, 1944.

———. *Scorched Earth*. Books One and Two. London: Left Book Club Edition, Victor Gollancz, 1941.

Snow, Helen Foster (Nym Wales). *Inside Red China*. New York: Doubleday, Doran, 1939.

———. *My China Years: A Memoir*. New York: William Morrow, 1984.

———. *My Yenan Notebooks*. Madison, Conn., 1972.

Spence, Jonathan D. *Emperor of China: Self Portrait of K'ang Hsi*. New York: Alfred A. Knopf, 1974.

———. *The Gate of Heavenly Peace*. New York: Viking, 1981.

———. *To Change China: Western Advisers in China, 1620–1960*. New York: Penguin, 1980.

Steel, Ronald. *Walter Lippmann and the American Century*. Boston: Little, Brown, 1980.

Steele, A. T. *The American People and China*. New York: McGraw-Hill, 1966.

Stilwell, General Joseph W. *The Stilwell Papers*. Edited by Theodore H. White. New York: William Sloane, 1948.

Strong, Anna Louise. *China's Millions*. New York: Coward McCann, 1928.

Strong, Tracy B., and Helene Keyssar. *Right in Her Soul: The Life of Anna Louise Strong*. New York: Random House, 1983.

Sues, Ilona Ralf. *Shark's Fins and Millet*. Boston: Little, Brown, 1944.

Sun Yat-sen. *San Min Chu I: The Three Principles of the People.* Shanghai: China Committee, Institute of Pacific Relations, 1927.

Swanberg, W. A. *Luce and His Empire.* New York: Scribner, 1972.

T'ang, Leang-li. *The Inner History of the Chinese Revolution.* London: George Routledge & Sons, 1930.

Taylor, George E. *The Struggle for North China.* New York: Institute of Pacific Relations, 1940.

Terrill, Ross. *The White-Boned Demon.* New York: Simon & Schuster, 1984.

Thomas, John N. *The Institute of Pacific Relations.* Seattle: University of Washington Press, 1974.

Thomson, James C., Jr. *While China Faced West.* Cambridge: Harvard University Press, 1969.

Thomson, James C., Jr., Peter W. Stanley, and John Curtis Perry. *Sentimental Imperialists.* New York: Harper & Row, 1981.

Tong, Hollington. *Dateline China.* New York: Rockport, 1950.

Trevor-Roper, Hugh. *Hermit of Peking.* New York: Penguin, 1978.

Trotsky, Leon. *Problems of the Chinese Revolution.* Ann Arbor: University of Michigan Press, 1967.

Tuchman, Barbara. *Stilwell and the American Experience in China, 1911–1945.* New York: Bantam, 1980.

Tucker, Nancy Bernkopf. *Patterns in the Dust.* New York: Columbia University Press, 1983.

Varg, Paul A. *The Making of a Myth.* East Lansing: Michigan State University Press, 1968.

Vaughn, Miles W. *Covering the Far East.* New York: Covici Friede, 1936.

Vladimirov, Peter. *The Vladimirov Diaries.* Garden City: Doubleday, 1975.

United States Relations with China. Washington, D.C.: U.S. Government Printing Office, 1949.

Wakeman, Frederick, Jr. *Strangers at the Gate: Social Disorder in South China, 1839–1861.* Berkeley: University of California Press, 1966.

Waln, Nora. *The House of Exile.* Boston: Little, Brown, 1933.

Wang, Fan-hsi. *Memoirs of a Chinese Revolutionary.* Translated by Gregor Benton. New York: Columbia University Press, 1991.

Welch, Holmes. *Taoism: The Parting of the Way.* Boston: Beacon Press, 1965.

White, Theodore H. *In Search of History: A Personal Adventure.* New York: Harper & Row, 1978.

———. *The Mountain Road.* New York: William Sloane, 1958.

White, Theodore, and Annalee Jacoby. *Thunder Out of China.* New York: William Sloane, 1946.

Whiting, Allen S. *Soviet Policies in China, 1917–1924.* New York: Columbia University Press, 1953.

Whiting, Allen S., and General Sheng Shih-ts'ai. *Sinkiang: Pawn or Pivot?* East Lansing: Michigan State University Press, 1958.

Wilbur, C. Martin. *Sun Yat-sen: Frustrated Patriot.* New York: Columbia University Press, 1976.

Wilbur, C. Martin, and Julie Lien-ying How. *Documents on Communism, Nationalism and Soviet Advisers in China, 1918–1927.* New York: Columbia University Press, 1956.

Willoughby, Maj. Gen. Charles H. *Shanghai Conspiracy.* New York: E. P. Dutton, 1952.

Wilson, Dick. *The Long March 1935: The Epic of Chinese Communism's Survival.* New York: Viking, 1971.

Winnington, Alan. *Tibet: Record of a Journey.* New York: International Publishers, 1957.

Wolfe, Bertram D. *Three Who Made a Revolution.* New York: Dial Press, 1948.

Index